Politics in Eastern Europe

Politics in Eastern Europe

Ivan Volgyes

University of Nebraska at Lincoln

The Dorsey Press
Chicago, Illinois   60604

Cover Art: Prague with the Moldau River in the middle of the 19th century (Courtesy of The Bettmann Archive 136 East 57th Street, New York, NY 10022, Plaza 8-0362)

This book contains selected portions of earlier articles, from which I quote with the publishers' permission: "A Conceptual Framework for the Study of Political Socialization in Eastern Europe," *Journal of Political and Military Sociology* (Fall, 1973), pp. 261–277; "Politics, Ideology and Culture: The STP's of Life in Communist Eastern Europe," *The Social Science Journal* (October, 1976), pp. 93–102; "The Warsaw Treaty Organization in the 1980s: Can Internal Differences Be Managed?" in *The 1980s: Decade of Confrontation?* (Washington, D.C.: National Defense University Press, 1981), pp. 189–218

ISBN 0-256-03144-4
Library of Congress Catalog Card No. 85-73807

Printed in the United States of America
 3 4 5 6 7 8 9 0 ML 3 2 1 0 9 8 7

For Gabrielle and Elizabeth

Foreword

■ The idea of writing a textbook on the politics of Eastern Europe arose out of necessity; having taught several courses on this topic for the last quarter of a century, I have always had to grapple with finding a suitable text. In the beginning of my career as a professor of political science, it seemed a bit easier to make the necessary choices: Zbigniew Brzezinski's, Ghita Ionescu's and Gordon Skilling's volumes were fine tools from which the students of the region's politics could glean a great deal of information and obtain exciting and new ideas. Later, as the field of political science became more scientific, and as many of our colleagues became interested in searching for more modern approaches, one could no longer find general texts on Eastern Europe. There were—as there have always been—excellent texts on the politics of separate nations; on special events, such as the various revolutions or reforms in Eastern Europe; and there have always been also the ever-present edited works on the politics of the region; but for undergraduate students, they have not answered the need for a comprehensive textbook.

I began the preparation for writing this textbook in 1980, just as Solidarity emerged as a major force in Poland, and ended the work the day the murderers of Father Jerzy Popieluszko received their prison sentences from the Polish authorities. Thus, the manuscript is undoubtedly characterized by alternating hopes and despair, as the history of the region has been throughout the past centuries. Symbolically, the latest crisis of Communism in Eastern Europe forms both the background and one of the major focuses of this volume.

In defining the region of Eastern Europe, I have tried to use an eclectic delineation. Generally, I refer to the postwar region of Eastern Europe as being composed of those states of Europe that have been ruled by Communist governments since the 1940s and are not incorporated parts of the USSR. Thus this study concentrates on Albania, Bulgaria, Czechoslovakia, East Germany, Hungary, Poland, Romania, and Yugoslavia, even though neither Albania nor Yugoslavia is today formally a member of the Soviet bloc.

My aim throughout has been to provide students with a readable and comprehensible text in comparative politics. I have used a cross-national, topical pattern of analysis rather than a study of individual countries. I forsook the prevailing political science jargon wherever possible for the sake of clarity, and gave up using micropolitical, quantitative, and behavioral models and approaches in order to speak more directly to all interested students, including those who are not yet specialists.

This book also contains selected portions of earlier articles that I quote freely. The original articles from which some of the material was taken appeared in various publications. They have, of course, been updated and altered.

In the end, of course, this volume is intended for the student as a guide to the politics of a region that has always been dynamic, volatile, and fascinating. In providing an informative and, I hope, interesting account of the politics of these states, I was guided by a desire to remain objective in my analysis, but that does not mean that the volume is value-free. I consider the Communist systems that have existed in these states since the end of World War II, by and large, to have placed the individual citizen subordinate to the perceived needs of the state. As in all such systems, this has meant that the citizen has been treated as a subject. Thus, from my own scale of values, while I tried to be objective in the evaluation of the positive accomplishments of the Communist states of the region, I could not help interjecting a bias toward the intrinsic value of the individual and a desire and hope to see the emergence of pluralism and democracy in the development of these states. Though I know the prospects of attaining these goals are bleak, I still applaud every effort in these states that is aimed at giving a greater role, importance, and dignity to the individual citizen.

ACKNOWLEDGMENTS

The cartoons and line drawings that appear in this book are taken from a number of journals and newspapers that were published in Poland, Hungary, and Czechoslovakia during the various years of revolutions, liberalizations, and renewals. They are the signs of the inherent spirit of freedom in the people of the region in opposition to the exercise of Communist power. But they also show a different reality as well; the cartoonists of liberalization and freedom, when operating under restrictions imposed by the regime, also serve their masters. The cartoons from Czechoslovakia were all drawn in 1967–1969. They first came to my attention in Otto Ulc's excellent study, *Politics in Czechoslovakia* (San Francisco: Freeman, 1974). The Polish and Hungarian cartoons appeared in issues of *Polytika* and *Ludas Matyi*, respectively.

Several persons have assisted me greatly by reading and commenting on selected portions of the manuscript. Professors Charles Gati, Trond Gilberg, Joseph Held, Paul Marer, Gyorgy Ranki, George Schopflin, and Samuel L. Sharp were especially helpful; their timely and welcome critiques were all greatly appreciated and of great value to me. My thanks to all of them for taking the time and trouble to help with the preparation of this volume. I greatly appreciate the efforts of John Sturman, who edited my manuscript so very conscientiously. Thanks are also due to Laura Holmgren and Susan Swartz for typing and getting this book ready for publication.

Camden, New Jersey
August, 1985

Ivan Volgyes

Contents

PART II

THE STRUCTURE OF POWER

PART III
THE ISSUES OF POLITICS

PART IV

POLITICAL VALUES IN COMMUNIST EASTERN EUROPE

PART V
FOREIGN POLICY AND THE FUTURE OF EASTERN EUROPE

LIST OF ILLUSTRATIONS

Figures

Tables

Contents

THE PEOPLE, THE LAND, AND THE HISTORY OF EASTERN EUROPE

CHAPTER 1

The People of Eastern Europe

■ Throughout its history, Eastern Europe has been characterized by ethnic, cultural, economic, political and social diversities. Perhaps no other region of the world possesses so many different ethnic or national groups as this part of Europe, which stretches roughly from the western borders of the Soviet Union to the eastern boundaries of West Germany, Austria, and Italy. A bewildering variety of people populates the region, and for Western students the mere task of differentiating one group from another may pose problems.

The first problem is the fact that in Eastern Europe the idea of "people" is not synonymous with the idea of "nation." It is easy for students of Western history to state that the French live in France, the Spaniards in Spain, and the Norwegians in Norway. But in Eastern Europe the situation is much more complex. For example, the large multiethnic empires of the past—Hungary, Austria, Prussia, and Russia, for instance—each contained many different ethnic groups. Thus Slovaks and Magyars lived in the Hungarian state for some 900 years; Czechs and Germans lived in the Austrian state; and Germans and Poles and other Slavic peoples lived within the borders of Russia. Even today different peoples, or national groups, live together in Yugoslavia. Hence we must maintain a distinction between the terms "people" and "nation" when discussing Eastern Europe.

Second, the link between language and people—which today passes widely as an automatic identification of the allegiance of people to a "national" cause—is a poor guide to the history of Eastern Europe.

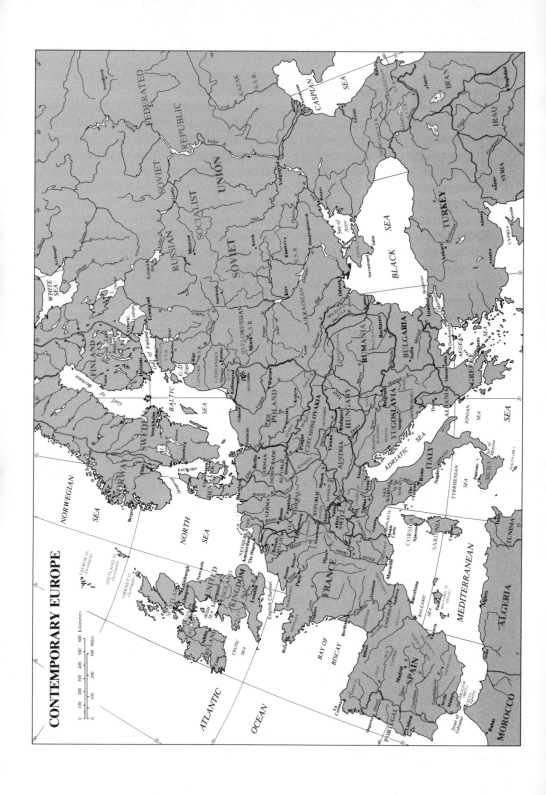

CONTEMPORARY EUROPE

There are many reasons for this fact, and the following seem to be the most significant:

1. Although linguistic differentiation was pronounced among the various peoples of the region until states developed in the Middle Ages, it was then impeded among various groups by assimilationist pressures forced on these groups from above and promoted by some of the group members themselves. For instance, Slovaks lost their distinctive speech vis-à-vis Czechs, some urbanized Hungarians could hardly speak the Magyar language, and many Slavic people came to claim German as their mother tongue. Perhaps only in Poland has the identification of the language with the "nation" remained strong, even when the Polish state has ceased to exist.

2. Much of Eastern Europe has always been ruled by foreign kings and princes. A king from the Neapolitan branch of the Anjou dynasty placed on the throne of Poland or Hungary was not likely to speak the language of the people over whom he ruled; his court usually had its own language—French, German, or even Russian. Moreover, the Roman Catholic Church, by insisting on Latin as the language of church communication until this century, maintained its universal character, but the "national" characters of the parts of Eastern Europe where Catholicism has been dominant have been stunted. However, we should note that the Catholic Church, especially the Franciscan order, sometimes championed the use of the vernacular. While it did so to distinguish the "sacred" from the "profane," in promoting such a separation it occasionally became an originator or a supporter of native literary revivals.

3. In Eastern Europe, except in a few regions, until the second half of the nineteenth century, each social class had its own language. The court and most of the clergy spoke and wrote Latin, French, or German, and common people, mostly peasants or serfs, spoke their own language, the vernacular tongue. The peasants were looked down on by the ruling classes, who did not regard them as a part of the "historic nation." The peasants spoke a language that the elite often found incomprehensible and even contemptible.

The Reformation—specifically in the Czech lands, Germany, Austria, Transylvania, and even Poland—pushed, to some extent, for the establishment of national churches and the revitalization of national languages. Similarly, the Orthodox Church, which has always been nation-centered, also assisted in the identification of the people with their national languages. But the greatest boost to the importance of language as "ethnic" identification was provided by the nationalism that swept Eastern Europe in the nineteenth century. Under its impact, the cultural function of the language—the pride in one's language as a part of the pride in one's "nation"—increased greatly. This movement was led by linguistic reformers throughout the nineteenth century, but especially toward its close. New dictionaries appeared in most of the region's languages, and a new pride emerged in being a Slovak or a Magyar, a Croat or a Romanian, and in speaking one's "national" language. Although the resulting "nationalism" could—and sometimes did—lead to chauvinism and to the hatreds we can still identify in the region today, linguistic nationalism has done much to re-establish the ties between the people and their native tongues. Today, indeed, one's "nationality" in Eastern Europe is determined by the mother tongue one claims in the census—a far cry from attitudes that most people in the region possessed a century or so ago.

A third area of confusion regarding Eastern Europe lies in the Western custom of identifying a people with a state—a legal entity that presumably acts in the people's interest. The state in Eastern Europe, as will be made clear in the historical segment of this volume in Chapters 2 and 3, is an entity superimposed by various forces of history on every people of the region. States have come and gone, but the people have survived. For example, the Polish and Hungarian states disappeared from the map several times, sometimes for centuries of foreign rule, but no one ever doubted that a Polish people or a Magyar people continued to exist. State boundaries changed arbitrarily, and the new borders encompassed people—as the old ones had as well—without regard to their nationality. Thus not only Magyars but Slovaks and Czechs, Germans, Croats and Slovenes, Serbians, Greeks, and Bulgars lived at one time under Hungarian rule. After World War I, when independent states were created in the region, there was not a single state that did not have relatively large ethnic minority populations, and as before, these minorities were not allowed to choose in which of the new states they could live. Today, the only Eastern European states without large ethnic minorities are Poland, Hungary, Albania, and East Germany; all the others are largely multinational in character.

The diversity of Eastern Europe's religious heritage compounds the problem of attempting to distinguish between "people" and "nation." In recent history, there has been no religious uniformity in the region. The Catholic, Orthodox, and Protestant churches have fought one another as well as combating Islam and Judaism. While it is true that there is some correlation between religion and ethnic background in the region—for example, the Poles are largely Catholic, the Romanians Orthodox—the states of Eastern Europe have always included large religious minorities whose nationality was not always the best guide to their religion; large numbers of both Magyar Protestants and Catholics lived in Czechoslovakia between the world wars, for instance. Even today, the only really religiously homogeneous state in the region is Poland, where 95 percent of the people are Catholic.

Finally, Eastern Europe is an ethnic cauldron. There are no racially

The Poles' attachment to Roman Catholicism has remained very strong for one thousand years. Here, in rural Poland, household religious symbols are common and comforting tokens of the church. (Jean Pierre Laffont/Sygma)

or even ethnically pure groups anywhere in the region. Occupations by invading armies and the intermingling of peoples has obliterated traces of "racial" purity. For example, the Magyars of the first half of the twentieth century who claimed Hungarian racial purity were hard put to prove their theory; the high cheekbones of the Magyars are as likely to be the result of the Turkish or Tartar rape of young Hungarian women as they are of "ethnic" traces of an uncertain past.

Consequently, as we proceed to identify the people of the region, we must recall that the typologies and ethnic backgrounds of the people of the region are "ideal types" only; they exist as abstractions, as philosophical and organizational concepts, and all claims to their supposed "racial purity" should be regarded only with suspicion.

THE PEOPLE: ETHNICITY

The Slavs

The people of Eastern Europe are generally identified racially as Indo-Europeans, although Mongol influences are also clearly observable. The majority of the Indo-Europeans of the region, probably about

Ethnic Groupings and Regions of Eastern Europe

two-thirds of the entire population, are of Slavic origin. The Slavs, whose original homeland was somewhere around the Vistula and Dnieper Rivers, occupied much of the area and became the dominant group in Eastern Europe between the fifth and seventh centuries A.D. The Slavs can be divided into three major groupings: the Eastern, Western, and Southern Slavs.

The Eastern Slavs are made up mostly of Great Russians,

Ukrainians, White Russians, and Ruthenians. Most of these people today live in the Soviet Union, which we shall not discuss directly in this volume. The Ruthenians, however—not a separate ethnic group but people of a mixed Ukrainian and Great Russian origin—are now scattered throughout Romania, the USSR, and Czechoslovakia.

The Western Slavs reside mostly in the northern tier of the region. They comprise three major subgroups, the Poles, the Czechs, and the Slovaks, although smaller groups such as the Wends, Sorbs, and Kaszubs also fall into this category. The Poles and the Czechs for centuries had their own states, but both sooner or later were conquered by greater powers; the Slovaks, until they attained co-ruler status in the new state of Czechoslovakia in 1918, never had a major domain of their own, even if some Slovak historians claimed otherwise.

Linguistically, Polish and Czech are distinctly separate tongues, although grammatically and morphologically they have much in common. Czech and Slovak are more closely related; their vocabularies and syntaxes are mutually comprehensible to speakers of either language. All of the West Slavic languages are written in the Latin alphabet; the cultural and religious influences of Western Christianity remain very strong.

The Southern Slavs present a greater variety than their Western counterparts. Their history, including 500 years of Turkish domination, Habsburg rule, and so on, has resulted in more ethnic diversity than in the north, but their characters are fiercely individualistic.

Ethnically the Southern Slavs can be subdivided into Serbs, Croats, Slovenes, Macedonians, Montenegrins, and Bulgars. The Bulgarians' name is actually a misnomer. In the seventh century, the Southern Slavs who settled present-day Bulgaria were overrun by the Bulgars, a Turkic people who established an empire of their own. However, within a couple of hundred years, as so frequently occurred in the region, the Bulgars were assimilated by the South Slavic tribes, and today only their name survives. The Bulgarian language was influenced by that of nearby Constantinople; the Byzantine monks Sts. Cyril and Methodius, who laid the groundwork for converting the "heathen" Bulgarians to the Orthodox religion in the ninth century, also laid the foundation of the Cyrillic alphabet in which Bulgarian, Serbian, and Russian are written today. In fact, the Bulgarian language remains strongly influenced by, and has affinities to, Russian.

The Serbs, Macedonians, and Montenegrins who today occupy the southern and eastern parts of Yugoslavia, form a second group of Southern Slavs. They share a common history, including centuries of existence under Ottoman Turkish occupation, and most Serbs, Macedonians, and Montenegrins are also Eastern Orthodox, like the Bulgarians. Their languages are all written in the Cyrillic alphabet, but they and their many dialects are not always mutually comprehensible.

The other two Southern Slavic groups, the Croats and the Slovenes, have followed a somewhat divergent course. Affected strongly by their geographical proximity to Italy and by their centuries-long occupation first by the Hungarian and later by the Habsburg empires, the Croatian and Slovene languages are written in the Latin alphabet, even though, in spoken form, the Croatian and Serbian languages are quite similar. Moreover, both Croatians and Slovenes are nearly exclusively Roman Catholic and thus, in terms of religion, have very little in common with the other Southern Slavs.

"Racially" the Slavs today are as diverse as people of any origin can be. Round faces, blonde hair, blue eyes, and light skin are slightly more common in the north than in the south, where darker, "Mediterranian" faces, hair, and eyes can be more often seen. Most Greeks and Italians resemble some burly Bulgarians more closely than those Bulgarians resemble Czechs and Poles to the north. Similarly, the Poles look more like Germans or Swedes, though of different ethnic stock, than they do the South Slavic Macedonians. The variety, because of the historical commingling, is endless and striking.

Non-Slavic Groups

Interspersed with the various Slavic groups of the region are non-Slavic peoples who have occupied the region nearly as long as the Slavs. The three major non-Slavic groups are the Romanians, the Magyars (or Hungarians), and the Germans; three smaller but also significant groups—the Albanians, the Gypsies, and the Jews—are scattered throughout the region. The Romanians, or Rumanians, as they were referred to until the mid-1960s, claim as their ancestors the Dacians, and Romans who were distant relatives of the Thracians of Greece. In reality, modern Romanians are a rather heterogeneous mixture; many are descendants of a nomadic tribe called the Vlachs. Their language is based on Romance (Latin) roots—though it has mixed with Slavic tongues and indigenous and long-lost languages such as that of the Gepids of the fifth century A.D.—and it is now written in the Latin alphabet. Romanian historians have boasted that their people are also the descendants of the Romans, who once occupied a part of present-day Romania. However, in reality, that occupation, which lasted only 163 years and was limited to thinly populated military outposts, was too superficial to leave substantial traces. The Romanian people, who generally adhere to the Eastern Orthodox religion, have a richly diverse culture.

The Magyars are descended from invaders who arrived in the Carpathian basin at the end of the ninth century. Composed of various tribes of mixed Ural-Altaic, Turkic, and Bulgarian origin, the Magyars threatened most of Western Europe's strongholds of power for nearly a century. Then, in the eleventh century, they adopted the Latin alphabet and were converted to Roman Catholicism. They established an empire that dominated the region and drove a wedge through the Danube basin, separating the Western and Southern Slavs. Perhaps because their language was different from those of the Slavs, the Magyars developed in partial cultural isolation from them. Even today the Magyar language remains a symbol of Hungarian nationalism, but the difficulty of learning it has prompted speakers of other languages to call Magyar not a language but a national tragedy. The Magyar language is also spoken by the Szeklers (székelys) and csángós, who reside in present-day Romania and are regarded as ethnic Magyars living outside of Hungarian boundaries, and by Magyars residing in Czechoslovakia, Yugoslavia, and Austria.

Groups of Germans migrated first into present-day Poland and the mountains of Bohemia, but after the eleventh century, German settlements emerged in other areas—specifically the Baltic coast of Poland and the mountains of Transylvania, Slovakia, and Hungary. The Germans' urban orientation, their industriousness, and their involvement in mining, commerce, and manufacturing made them, until the end of World War II, an extremely important part of Eastern Europe's cultural, economic, and political life. Their expulsion from the region—due to the shift of Poland's borders to the west and to the forced expatriation resulting from Germany's responsibility for World War II—is a sad chapter in the history of the region.

The Albanians, who claim a Thraco-Illyrian cultural heritage, have their own state, but one-third of this small nation lives in neighboring Yugoslavia. Their language contains a small number of ancient Illyrian words, in addition to words taken from medieval Greek, Latin, Italian, and Serbian; it has been written with Latin letters since the end of the nineteenth century. Most Albanians have converted to Islam, but about 20 percent remain nominally Eastern Orthodox, and about 10 percent claim some allegiance to the Roman Catholic Church.

The Gypsies of Eastern Europe trace their origin to India and not to ancient Egypt, as was once commonly thought. Social outcasts in the Byzantine Empire, where they lived for centuries, this tightly knit, nomadic people spread into Eastern Europe by the fifteenth century. Wherever they traveled they adapted their ancient tongue by incorporating into it elements from the local language, but they quietly resisted any attempt at conversion to Christianity, and in some of the closed communities where they still survive they continue to practice their ancient rituals. They are known for their colorful customs as well as for some traits—nomadic wanderings, thievery, crime, begging—that are hardly welcome in modern societies.

Finally, the Jews of Eastern Europe began to arrive in large numbers in the fifteenth and sixteenth centuries due to the brutal anti-Semitism then practiced in Western Europe and England. A large number of Jews were forced to live in eastern Poland and western Russia, in the so-called Pale of Settlement; they were excluded from the towns and barred from owning land. In the eighteenth century more tolerant attitudes slowly allowed the Jews of Europe to be incorporated into community life, and they formed the base of the region's budding bourgeoisie, especially in cities and in the Muslim Ottoman-controlled regions, where religious tolerance was the greatest. The Jews became especially well assimilated in Hungary, in Czechoslovakia and in the Balkans; they were less well assimilated in Poland. As a

Table 1.1 Minority Populations in Eastern Europe

	Total population (millions)	Total minorities	Make-up of minorities	Size of minorities
Albania	2.86	70,000	Greeks	35,000
			Kutuzo-Vlachs	35,000
Bulgaria	9.11	980,000	Turks	750,000
			Macedonians	200,000
			Armenians	30,000
Czechoslovakia	15.37	750,000	Hungarians	500,000
			Germans	100,000
			Poles	70,000
			Ruthenians	80,000
East Germany	16.86	30,000	Sorbs	30,000
Hungary	10.71	460,000	Germans	205,000
			Slovaks	120,000
			Southern Slavs	110,000
			Romanians	25,000
Poland	36.23	650,000	Ukrainians	200,000
			Byelorussians	200,000
			Russians	150,000
			Slovaks	25,000
			Lithuanians	25,000
			Germans	50,000
Romania	22.64	2,300,000	Hungarians	2,000,000
			Germans	100,000
			Ukrainians	60,000
			Southern Slavs	50,000
			Russians	40,000
			Others	50,000
Yugoslavia	22.65	2,400,000	Albanians	1,500,000
			Hungarians	500,000
			Slovaks	80,000
			Romanians	70,000
			Turks	200,000
			Others	50,000

result of the Holocaust during World War II, most of the Jews in Poland, Czechoslovakia, Germany, and Hungary were annihilated, and many of the remaining Jews sought to emigrate from the region.

Eastern Europe today is a far cry from the Eastern Europe of the pre–World War I years, when multinational empires were dominant in the region. As Table 1.1 indicates, Poland, East Germany, and Hungary have become almost ethnically homogeneous, with very few minority residents. But Czechoslovakia, Romania, Bulgaria, and Yugoslavia still have a large number of ethnically and linguistically different peoples residing within their boundaries. Yugoslavia, the most clearly multiethnic state in Eastern Europe, encompasses, in addition to five major South Slavic ethnic groups (Serbs, Croats, Slovenes, Montenegrins, and Macedonians), as well as some seventeen non–South Slavic groups, such as Albanians, Magyars, Turks, Czechs, Slovaks, Russians, Gypsies, Italians, Romanians, Vlachs, Poles, Germans, and Ruthenians.

The problems of discrimination against and hatred of ethnic groups other than one's own remain serious in the region. Although discrimination has always existed in the region, it has raged largely unabated since the latter part of the nineteenth century. Discrimination against Jews persists in Poland, despite the fact that there were only about 5,000 Jews living there at the beginning of the 1980s, and in Romania discrimination against Hungarians and Germans borders on cultural genocide. But there are fine examples of coexistence as well. In spite of tremendous antagonisms between Croats and Serbs, which resulted in atrocities during World War II, postwar Yugoslavia stands out as a multiethnic state *par excellence* with a generally fine record in interethnic relations (although its record was marred by the 1981 riots among the Albanians in the southern part of the country).

Ethnic hatreds, the discriminatory treatment of nationalities, and longstanding territorial disputes have also impaired relations among the new Communist states, despite their alleged commitment to the "socialist community of nations." Hungary's conflicts with both Romania and Czechoslovakia over the treatment of Magyars residing in those countries have poisoned their relations; and Bulgarian-Yugoslavian disputes over Macedonia have often reached vituperative levels. For the ordinary citizen, national identity remains a strong and quite exclusive category. It is a sad fact that national hatreds remain and are evident in the region today.

The Geographical Setting

■ As we indicated in the introduction, our definition of Eastern Europe is arbitrary and can even be viewed as capricious. It certainly influences readers to view the area in political terms, as a group of states currently ruled by Communist, Soviet-type systems. But geographers have not been much more successful than historians or political analysts in delineating the area as a distinct region. In defining Eastern Europe, they have applied many criteria, some of which are useful, some of which are perhaps less relevant.

First, to define the region as "Eastern" Europe places importance on the adjective "Eastern," as distinct from "Western." The problems with this definition, however, are:

1. There is no clear geographical division between Eastern and Western Europe; for centuries, East Germany and Bohemia clearly were regarded as part of Western Europe, and Prague, now in Czechoslovakia, was as distinctly "Western" as Vienna.
2. Nor are there any clearly delineated eastern boundaries of the region; parts of Russia are certainly as "European" as most of the region under discussion. For instance, Leningrad is just as much a European city as Belgrade, and Moscow looks more European than does Sarajevo, Yugoslavia, or Bucharest, Romania.
3. East versus West as an organizing concept does not recognize the major differentiation that exists in the region between southern, or Mediterranean, cultures and northern, or more mainstream European, cultures. Indeed, the differences between "European" and "Balkan" cultures and behavior are so marked that to classify them together as "Eastern European" is simply counterproductive.

Another attempt to define the region geographically involves the organizing concept of the "eastern marchland," an area where a culture distinct from both Western European and Asiatic cultures exists. This explanation is superficially valid; after all, the culture that exists in this region certainly *is* distinctive. The problem, however, is that this mode of reasoning treats the region as a unified cultural area; in reality, nothing could be farther from the truth. The "marchland" encompasses regions that were occupied—and culturally influenced—by the Ottoman Turks for 500 years and those that were not, and the Orthodox-Catholic religious and cultural cleavages that split the region are far greater than Protestant-Catholic differences in Western Europe.

Another common way of looking at Eastern Europe is to treat the region as a "shatter zone," in which the boundaries of states have always been broken up by one power or another. Historically, this region has always been subject to the influences and control of great powers; frontiers have been established through political decisions in which the native people of the region have seldom been consulted. However, Eastern Europe has been regarded in geopolitical terms as a pivotal area and the key to world domination. As Sir Halford Mackinder, one of the world's great geopolitical thinkers, said in 1904: "Whoever controls Eastern Europe controls the Heartland of Europe . . . and thus controls the world." While it is true that most of the continent's great imperial powers—the Ottomans, the Germans, the Habsburgs, the French, and the Russians—have attempted to control Eastern Europe, it is by no means certain, however, that they did so for geopolitical reasons. But the simple fact remains that the greatest empires of Europe have always maintained, or striven for, control of this geographically indefinable region.

For our purposes, it would accomplish little to engage in debate about the "natural" or "geographical" limits of the region. So, for the sake of convenience, we shall define Eastern Europe as the area of Europe currently under Communist rule, including the eight states of Albania, Bulgaria, Czechoslovakia, the German Democratic Republic (East Germany), Hungary, Poland, Romania, and Yugoslavia. And we shall consider East Germany as having become a part of the region only since the end of World War II in 1945. Using the term Eastern Europe rather eclectically, no attempt will be made to strive for uniform or rigid guidelines in the treatment of the region.

TOPOGRAPHY

Eastern Europe lies between the Baltic Sea and Greece and Turkey, at the narrow "waist" of Europe; it stretches only 800 miles from north to south at its narrowest point. In the east it extends to the

Black Sea and the Soviet Union. In the west it borders on West Germany, Austria, Italy, and the Adriatic Sea. Only those boundaries that face the seas of Europe, however, can be regarded as natural borders; all the others have been defined by politics, not by any natural geographical barriers.

It is important to note that Eastern Europe has relatively few natural harbors and less than 1,500 miles of coastline; the whole area has less coastline than France. This means that most of the region has always had to rely for its overseas trade on major ports that lay outside its own territory and were controlled by other powers. Such ports as Trieste (formerly in Austria-Hungary and now in Italy), Salonika, in Greece, Istanbul, in Turkey, and Hamburg, in West Germany, have been crucial to the region; without access to them, Eastern Europe would be faced with major transportation and communication problems.

The region is not large in terms of world geography; its area is only some 500,000 square miles—about as much territory as covered by the seven Great Plains states of the United States; the two Dakotas, Minnesota, Nebraska, Kansas, Iowa, and Missouri. It is, however, a densely populated region. While the Great Plains states have a population of only 20 million, Eastern Europe has more than 120 million people. Table 2.1 indicates the size and population of the various countries.

No single state in Eastern Europe is an easily identifiable geographical unit. Indeed, the land forms of one state melt imperceptibly into those of another; only barbed wires, mine fields, or some more pleasant barriers indicate borderlines. But if one looks at the map of Eastern Europe, some geographical formations become evident. In the north, Poland and East Germany appear as a series of flatlands and fairly low, rolling hills; the southern parts of these states and parts of Czechoslovakia are more mountainous. One finger of the Alpine chain juts

Table 2.1   Areas and Populations of the Eastern European States (1983)

	Area (sq. miles)	Population (millions)
Albania	10,600	2.86
Bulgaria	42,800	9.11
Czechoslovakia	49,900	15.37
East Germany	41,500	16.86
Hungary	35,900	10.71
Poland	120,400	36.23
Romania	91,700	22.64
Yugoslavia	99,300	22.65

Eastern Europe

into Czechoslovakia, enfolds Hungary's plains and gentle hills, and turns south through Romania into Bulgaria; another dominates western Yugoslavia and thrusts its way into Bulgaria. The Alps in Eastern Europe are divided into several mountain ranges. Those of Poland and Czechoslovakia are called the Carpathian Mountains; those of Romania, the Transylvanian Mountains; and those extending through Bulgaria

south of the Danube, the Balkan Mountains. The branch of the Carpathians that extends to Yugoslavia through Italy is referred to as the
Dinaric Mountains, and these rugged, enormous mountains, which rise
along the warm Adriatic coastline, are especially breathtakingly beautiful.

The flat and gently rolling terrain that encompasses most of Poland
and East Germany is called the Northern European Plain. Lakes, rivers,
marshes, and plateaus dot this still largely agricultural area. The Central
European and Pannonian Plains extend from southern Slovakia to
northern Yugoslavia; this is a rich, fertile agricultural area, as is the
Wallachian Plain, which extends from the Carpathians in southern
Romania to the northern Balkans of Bulgaria.

The term "Balkans" generally refers to the southern parts of Romania, and to Bulgaria, Yugoslavia, and Albania. One point must be clarified here, however. Occasionally, references are made to the "Balkan
mentality" or "Balkan-style politics." Such terms do not allude specifically to the geographical Balkan region, but rather to the area that
was longest under Turkish occupation and has thus adopted many
traits that are clearly different from Western European political, social,
and cultural norms. Such practices as the *bakshish*—the ever-present
tip or bribe—as well as certain specific types of political rule and political corruption are all part of the "Balkan style." The use of this term
implies that the so-called Balkan states—Yugoslavia, Bulgaria, Albania,
and Romania—belong wholly to the Balkans geographically as well
as politically. However, one certainly cannot regard Slovenia in Yugoslavia or Transylvania in Romania, for instance, as being the part of
the Balkans in a geographical or even a political sense; great caution,
indeed, should be observed with the use of the term "Balkan."

CORE AREAS

Although it is difficult to identify any Eastern European state with
a distinctive topography, each of the states has certain historical-territo-
rial "core areas" that identify the territory with the state's history.
Just as the United States could not be imagined without the New England–New York–Northern Virginia axis, one cannot imagine a Czechoslovakia without Prague and the Moldau (Vltava) River or Yugoslavia
without Belgrade. Such core areas essentially represent the heart of
a nation's territorial and historical identity.

Poland's core area centers around the great Vistula River, which
rises in the Carpathian Mountains and winds its way to the Baltic
Sea. The first Polish kingdom was founded near the Odra and Warta
rivers and then expanded to the rolling plains that flank the Vistula

Wenceslas Square was developed and laid out in 1348, during the Golden Age of Prague. (UPI Photo)

and its tributaries, including the sites of the capitals of Poland, Warsaw and the ancient city of Cracow.

East Germany's core area is the *mark,* or frontier province, of Brandenburg, established as a military defensive outpost under the Holy Roman Empire. The capital of the province was later moved to Berlin, which—as the capital of Prussia and then as the capital of united Germany—became the transportation capital of central Europe. At the center of a neat network of canals that link the flatlands of East Germany, the city of Berlin remains a symbol for the unification of Germany, and while West Berlin is no longer the capital of West Germany, it remains a strong rallying point for that nation for historical as well as political reasons.

The Bohemian basin is the center and core area of Bohemia-Moravia, the hilly, historic Czech homeland. Its proximity to the Moldau and the Elbe rivers and to the communication routes to Vienna and many major German cities made Prague an ideal center of commerce and communication. Prague has historically been the center of Czech culture from the fifteenth century onward to the present day. Of all the cities in the region, only Budapest can match Prague's lovely location and charming atmosphere.

Hungarian history is closely connected with three major regions that can be regarded as core areas: Transdanubia, the Plain of Hungary, and Transylvania. Hilly Transdanubia was the site of Hungary's first capital in the tenth century, not far from long, thin Lake Balaton, the largest lake in Eastern Europe. The remarkably fertile Great Plain, stretching between the Danube and Tisza rivers, boasts abundant harvests of golden wheat and rye. The Transylvania Mountains, extending from the wastelands *(pusztas)* east of the Tisza river and rising to rugged peaks, enclose a civilization that has remained ethnically Hungarian, even when Hungary was partitioned. Although today Transylvania belongs to Romania, Hungarian culture is still ferociously preserved among the ethnic Magyars who live there. The Danube and Tisza rivers, and the city of Budapest, which sprawls along both banks of the Danube, are symbols of these core areas of Hungary, which boasts one of the longest continuous histories in the region.

The core areas of Romania include the former principality of Wallachia, with its rolling flatlands and fertile fields, and a mountainous region called Moldavia, dotted with beautifully painted monasteries that are the repositories of Orthodox Romanian culture. When the state of Romania was created in the nineteenth century, its capital, Bucharest, was chosen because of its location, south of the Carpathians and near both Wallachia and Moldavia. Following the disintegration of the Austro-Hungarian Empire in 1918, the Treaty of Trianon, based on the secret 1916 "understanding" between France and England, awarded Transylvania to Romania, and the infusion of ethnic Romanians into that region has made Transylvania a third core area of the state.

Bulgaria, a Balkan state that was occupied for five centuries by the Ottoman Turks, has several core areas. Some areas—for instance, Preslav and Trnovo, between the Danube River and the Balkan Mountains—were ancient historical sites. Others, such as Rila, with its magnificent monastery, are located in steep valleys within craggy mountains; these became core regions because of their significance as rallying points for Bulgarian culture during the centuries of Ottoman rule. The city of Sofia, located on Bulgaria's central plateau, became the capital only in the nineteenth century, due to its easy accessibility from all parts of the country.

The historic areas of Yugoslavia, which lay in the Kosovo basin, in the south of the ancient Serbian kingdom, were destroyed by Ottoman rule. In many ways, however, Belgrade, the Yugoslav capital, located at the confluence of the Sava and Danube rivers, has supplanted the ancient cores. But the core area of Yugoslavia as a whole has to be considered more broadly than those of other states of the region, since it is a truly multinational state. Indeed, for the Croatians and Dalmatians who live along the Adriatic coast, the coastline and Zagreb, the historical capital of Croatia, are just as strong rallying points as Belgrade is for the Serbs.

In mountainous, tiny Albania the two rival tribal groups—the Ghegs in the north and the Tosks in the south—both consider Tirana, the capital, which is located between them, the only attraction zone of the state. Albanians believe that their country has a "historic" right to include the nearly 1.5 million Albanians who now reside in the Kosovo, in southern Yugoslavia; hence, at least some Albanians consider the Kosovo as a core area as well.

The capital of each state thus lies in one of that state's core areas, but the core areas are generally far larger than the capital and its surroundings. It is important to emphasize, however, that Eastern Europeans would be hard put to identify the core of the region as a whole; for every nation, the importance of the region, not unnaturally, lies in its own cores, its own historic and emotional ties.

CLIMATE

The diversity of the region is also manifest in its climate. Poland, East Germany, and Czechoslovakia have cool, humid summers, while Hungary, Romania, and northern Yugoslavia all have warm, humid, continental summers; only in southern Bulgaria, Dalmatia, and Albania is the presence of the warm, dry Mediterranean climate clearly evident. The winters, except in the areas with a Mediterranean climate, are uniformly cold; the rivers freeze, the snows are heavy and frequent, and, especially on the flat plains, bitter winds rip through the fields with bone-chilling ferocity. The growing season is longest in Hungary (an average of 180 days) and shortest in Czechoslovakia (130 days), but a great deal of variation characterizes the region in this regard as well.

NATURAL RESOURCES

Eastern Europe is far from poor in resources. Agriculture remains one of the important resources of the region, especially in Hungary, Bulgaria, and Yugoslavia; there is a wide variety of production patterns, ranging from domination by small, private producers in Poland and Yugoslavia to near total collectivization elsewhere. Poland, in spite of its high percentage of cropland (52 percent of its total area) and its emphasis on private production, has been forced to become the region's major importer of agricultural produce, while Hungary, where only 15 percent of the people are engaged full-time in agriculture, typically on collectivized farms, has become the major exporter of agricultural goods.

Other resources are also abundant in the region, though the distribution of these assets is far from equitable. In the area of vital fossil fuels, East Germany is a major producer of lignite, while Poland and Czechoslovakia and East Germany are major producers of bituminous coal; all other states in the region must import this scarce commodity. As far as oil is concerned, the situation is more unfavorable; every state in the region (including oil-producing Romania, which in 1981 supplied about 30 percent of its own oil needs) must import most of its oil. A great deal of this oil comes through major pipelines from the USSR, but the region has also had to import significant quantities from other sources. The rise in the price of oil, both from the USSR and from the OPEC countries, during the 1970s forced the Eastern European states to cut spending on economic growth simply in order to maintain existing conditions.

The potential for hydroelectric power is great in the region, especially in the south, but it is still relatively untapped. The most important installations are in Bulgaria, Romania, and Yugoslavia, although a large dam on the Danube above Budapest is expected to be built to harness the power of Europe's longest river. Electric power production is highest in East Germany, Poland, and Czechoslovakia and lowest in Albania, Bulgaria, and Hungary.

Among mineral resources, ferrous ores are most abundant in Bohemia, Yugoslavia, and southern Poland; nonferrous ores are more widely available throughout the region. Both types of ores are essential indicators of the health of any modern economy; if a nation must import raw materials (whose prices rise ever so steeply in today's scarce world market), it must use cheap labor or up-to-date technology to produce goods that are competitive in the international market in order to pay for these resources. Although labor costs were relatively inexpensive in Eastern Europe until the mid-1970s, labor scarcity and inefficiency have slowly forced Eastern European decision makers to attempt to make much-needed technological improvements; however, their successes in this field have not been markedly great.

Very few mineral resources of the region are in high international demand, although potash in East Germany, sulfur and rock salt in southern Poland, kaolin and rock salt in Czechoslovakia, and bauxite in Hungary are all important to their respective national economies. Lumber is abundant in all of these states, except Hungary. But food processing and food production, whether based on state-owned facilities or derived from the private secondary economy, remain the most important indicators of economic health in the region. Wherever one finds abundant food, one also finds a relatively contented population;

where food is in short supply, discontent with a regime that promised paradise but delivered an economic purgatory is going to run high.

SETTLEMENT PATTERNS

Prior to World War II, most of the countries of Eastern Europe were agrarian states, and most of the people were peasants who worked in agriculture, living in rural areas. Although cities have existed in Eastern Europe since earliest times, urban, as well as industrial, development in the region lagged behind that of Western Europe. Cities such as Cracow, Prague, or Budapest, which usually contained a royal residence and housing for the court and the church hierarchy, were often located on hills, in defensible positions overlooking fertile fields. Table 2.2 compares the urban versus rural populations before World War II and at the end of the 1970s. The table suggests that urbanization has been the most observable form of modernization in the region.

The modern Eastern European city generally belongs to one of two types. The first one grew up around a historic kernel, or town center, that grew continuously, if sporadically, as the nation's fortunes waxed and waned. With the recent burst of industrialization, new modern housing developments, dwarfing the old cities, have grown up around the old town center; today, these consist of ugly, grey, cement prefabricated dwellings of eight–ten stories, built according to Soviet

Table 2.2   Urban and Rural Populations, 1938–1977

Country	Year	Urban (percent)	Rural (percent)
Bulgaria	1934	21.4	78.6
	1975	33.6	66.4
Czechoslovakia	1930	47.4	52.6
	1975	66.7	33.3
Hungary	1941	34.8	65.2
	1976	50.4	49.6
Romania	1930	21.4	78.6
	1977	47.8	52.2
Yugoslavia	1931	12.2	87.8
	1971	38.6	61.4
Poland	1931	17.0	83.0
	1975	42.7	57.3
Albania	1938	6.9	93.1
	1965	22.1	77.9
East Germany	1939	43.4	56.6
	1975	46.5	53.5

housing industry specifications. Shoddily constructed, these units of inconveniently small apartments now ring old towns and former small villages.

The second type of urban center is referred to as the "socialist town," and there are far fewer of these towns than those that grew from a historic kernel. Developed near new concentrations of industry, usually on the site of small, leveled villages, these places—such as Duna-pentele in Hungary, Nowa Huta in Poland, Victoria in Romania, and Havirov in Czechoslovakia—are "planned settlements," where everything is built from scratch. Roads, restaurants, parks, theaters, and shops, as well as housing units and workplaces, are all in accordance with a master plan; thankfully, time occasionally humanizes them to accommodate their residents.

In Eastern Europe, as well as elsewhere on the continent, the proximity of nature remains very strong, and the people's desire to be out in the woods or on the lakes and rivers continues to run high. The natural landscape, outside the busy cities with their grime, soot, and pollution from industrial, residential, and automotive sources, is greatly prized. Even in places where people have come to engage entirely in urban-industrialized labor, small garden plots dot the land. City dwellers, after working long hours in industry, grow food, flowers, or vegetables for themselves and their families—and occasionally for profit—during the summer. In these small plots, in the gardens and away from the omnipresent power of the state, people still feel that they can be free and independent; the very presence of these countless gardens attests to the fact that people everywhere—and especially in Eastern Europe—cherish even a small amount of freedom and independence.

The History of Eastern Europe: A Troubled Heritage

■ As we have indicated, states and tribes, informal groups and religious orders, nations and empires have commingled throughout the history of Eastern Europe. Yet for analytical purposes we must divide this history into somewhat arbitrary periods in order to view the development of the region more clearly. Therefore this chapter shall deal with: (1) the settlement and tribal period, (2) the establishment of "native" states, (3) the creation of multiethnic dynastic empires, (4) the nation-states, while Chapter 4 will be devoted to the post–World War II experiences of the region.

SETTLEMENT, TRIBES, AND ANCIENT EMPIRES

The lands stretching from the Baltic to the Adriatic and the Black Seas were rather sparsely populated in ancient times. In 500 B.C. only a few nomadic shepherds and some marauding tribes occupied the vast area which was viewed by those who traversed it as hostile and largely uninhabitable. There were no settled, populated areas or city-states or cities, as there were in the Middle East, at this time. The first empire to have any impact on the region was that of Alexander the Great, with its Hellenistic civilization. It claimed the eastern territories of Eastern Europe as its own, but its influence was minimal in areas other than the Balkans.

The Balkans

Alexander, as well as his successors, sought his fortunes in Asia to a far greater extent than in Europe; thus only a very few of his outposts were built on the Adriatic side of the Balkan Peninsula. Although his empire was to make an imprint on the culture of Macedonia, its effects on the settlement of the Balkan region—let alone on areas north of the Rhodope Mountains, which separate Greece from Bulgaria—was to be minimal.

After it conquered Greece in 146 B.C., the emerging Roman Empire began to make its power felt in Eastern Europe. The Romans conquered the pleasant Dalmatian coast first—one must admit that they certainly had a taste for fine living. Then, pushing northward, they slowly occupied the Danube basin and reached a site just north of present-day Budapest. There they established their strongest outpost, Aquincum. Aquincum, whose residents enjoyed running hot and cold water, amphitheaters, and a large forum, has been excavated and now stands as a testament to the genius and expansive power of the Roman Empire.

In Eastern Europe, the Romans first did what they knew how to do best. They built military outposts, roads, and settlements, and they established vast communication networks that linked the region to Rome. Through a system of mirror-relayed messages in the second century, one could transmit a message from central Hungary to Rome faster than one can send a telegram today! Paved stone and brick roads connected far-flung provinces of the empire; they ran from Savaria (Szombathely) in Pannonia (Transdanubia) and Tergeste (Trieste) in the southwestern part of the region to Salonika and Constantinople in the east. These roads even today form the major basis of Eastern Europe's network of communications, and in some places they are still visible—and usable!—even 2,000 years later.

Conquering more land and building more roads, the Romans occupied the Carpathian Mountain passes, and between 100 and 270 A.D. they annexed the region known as Dacia, in what is now Romania. By 275, however, the Romans decided that it was not worth sending legion after legion to control this area; they withdrew their forces. Their power waned along with the break-up of the Roman Empire. When, under Diocletian, the empire was subdivided along a line running roughly from what is now Belgrade, Yugoslavia, south to the Bay of Kotor, the fact that two distinct civilizations would diverge and evolve could scarcely have been known. And yet this thin strand drawn on a primitive map was to separate—with some modifications, of course—Western and Balkan cultures and influences. The East, influenced by and ruled from Constantinople, and the West, influenced by and ruled from Rome, were to remain apart throughout much of their history. Even the emergence of the multinational state of Yugoslavia or Eastern Europe's "common faith" in Communism has not completely obliterated this historical separation.

As Diocletian's empire began to crumble, the Romans slowly relinquished control of the area that lay north of the Danube. Goths and Gepids, wandering Germanic tribes, pushed their way into the western part of the empire, followed by nomadic Slavic and Turkic tribes, such as the Avars, the Huns, and Pechenegs, the Serbs, the Bulgars, and the Magyars, all contributing to the destruction of Rome as the seat of the Roman Empire by the sixth–seventh century. But in the Balkan Peninsula the Byzantine Empire was to survive, with some fluctuations in size and fortunes, until 1453, when Constantinople fell to the Turks.

The Slavic invasions of the eighth century placed the first pressure points on the Byzantine Empire. In the Balkans, the Bulgars created a primitive principality, which lasted until the eleventh century and interposed itself between the northern region of the Byzantine Empire and Constantinople itself. In addition, the independent kingdom of Serbia, as well as some small city-states and principalities commercially linked with Venice, were established between the Balkan mountains and on the Dalmatian coast, while in the mountains of Albania, budding "principalities" occupied the mountain passes and strangled intraempire communications. The rising power of the Ottoman Turks in the east further crippled the power of the once-great empire; by the beginning of the thirteenth century, Constantinople ruled a region encompassing little more than present-day European Turkey and Dobruja in southeastern Romania.

The enduring nature of Byzantine influences however, cannot be disregarded. The empire's zeal in promoting the Eastern Orthodox faith throughout its domains, through complex and well-organized missions, and its architecture have had a lasting imprint on the entire Balkan Peninsula. Orthodoxy was adopted from Romania in the north to Albania in the south. In addition, the Cyrillic alphabet and its Greek-oriented caligraphy continue to characterize the civilization of the vast majority of the people of the Balkans.

North of the Danube

In the eighth and ninth centuries, north of the Danube, Slavs spread into the region pushed along by the great population expansion known as the "migration of peoples." Nomadic empires, such as that of the Avars, rose briefly and fell, to disappear forever. The Slavic state of Great Moravia—centered in, according to some scholars, the regions of Bratislava and Pannonia—was established in the ninth century, and its citizens converted to Eastern Christianity. But due to the slowly intensifying rivalry between Rome and Constantinople, it soon became a region of struggle between Orthodoxy and Roman Catholicism; the population soon accepted the latter, and the invading Magyar tribes made communication between Constantinople and Moravia physically nearly impossible. The demise of Great Moravia occurred much later; the character of that state, however, and its orientation toward Western Europe, became clear as it accepted its dissociation from Constantinople and adopted Roman Catholicism.

A second major state was established by the Magyars. The Magyar tribes invaded central Europe in 896. Until the middle of the tenth century, the Magyars wrought havoc on Europe; their marauding armies burned the cities of the Byzantine Empire and the towns of the German principalities in order to expand their influence. Only in 955, when the Holy Roman emperor finally defeated the Magyars in the West did they decide to settle down. Occupying the Carpathian basin, with all other populations in that region at their mercy, the Magyars were to establish one of the most important states in Europe.

Farther north, the Poles began to settle the region of the Warta and Vistula rivers in the ninth century. Slowly expanding their influence to the north, west, and east, their numbers increased. They accepted Catholicism, and in the region they informally still call *Wielkopolska*, or Great Poland, they established their first kingdom, which was to be the core of modern Poland.

Although other smaller Slavic and non-Slavic states exercised some rather brief rule in the region—such as the Croats' kingdom and the Avars' empire—the three states of Great Moravia (later Bohemia-Moravia), Hungary, and Poland, were to remain the most important kingdoms in the region until the great multinational empires replaced them in the fourteenth–sixteenth centuries.

THE FIRST CHRISTIAN STATES OF EASTERN EUROPE

Bohemia-Moravia

The Czech state, the kingdom of Bohemia-Moravia, grew slowly. Arising out of Great Moravia, this state was an amalgam of many tribes, peoples, and cultures. Originally, two families, the Premysl in western Bohemia and the Slavnici in the east, vied for power; when the Slavnicis were wiped out in the tenth century, the Premysl family aspired to and received undisputed "royal" authority. Although indisputably Czech in character, the culture and history of Bohemia were intertwined with those of the surrounding German principalities and of the Holy Roman Empire and after the Premysls died out, the Bohemian throne was often occupied by German princes and dynasties.

Prague, especially for the 200 years beginning with the rule of Charles IV in the fourteenth century, was one of the great capitals of Europe. Such foremost astronomers as Johannes Kepler and Tycho Brahe frequented the court in Hradcany Castle. Alchemists were drawn to the city to participate in the first major state-organized research and development program in Eastern Europe. Charles IV established the world-famous Charles University in 1348, began construction of the great St. Vitus's Cathedral, and built the imposing granite and marble bridges across the Vltava River.

Bohemia's power declined during the fifteenth century when it was wracked by civil war and the first wave of the Protestant Reformation. In 1415 Jan Hus, the leader of the Reformation in Bohemia, was burned at the stake. His execution sparked one of the great cataclysmic civil wars the region was to know only too well. The war raged until 1431, and afterward Bohemia's slow drift toward domination by the Habsburg dynasty could not be halted. Finally, in 1620, after the disastrous Battle of White Mountain, in which the Catholic Habsburg armies defeated the largely Protestant Czech forces, Bohemia ceased to exist as an independent state. Its native aristocracy was destroyed, and the country was incorporated into the Habsburg domains and disappeared from the political map of Europe for three centuries.

Poland

Poland's history is equally complex and just as tragic. Poland became a Christian state in 966, when King Mieszko accepted the crown from the pope. Although a unified Poland existed throughout the tenth and eleventh centuries, it was not until the reign of Boleslaw III, in the second decade of the twelfth century, that the country became a powerful voice in the determination of the affairs of Europe. Though invaded and occupied several times by Tatars and Teutonic knights, Poland continued to flourish and when in 1386 it united with Lithuania and the Lithuanian Jagiello dynasty acceded to the Polish throne, it became the largest power in the region. The Jagiello University was founded in Cracow, trade centers developed, the court was expanded, and Warsaw became the capital of Poland; during this "Golden Age," the fifteenth century, Poland was one of Europe's great centers of culture, civilization, and power.

But feuding among the ruling aristocracy and conflicts with other states weakened Poland, and during the seventeenth and eighteenth centuries the country's power diminished, while that of its two great neighbors, Prussia to the west and Russia to the east, increased. It was a drift that could not be stopped. In 1772 Prussia and Russia annexed significant portions of Polish territory in the First Partition of Poland. Poland then tried to re-create its former greatness by

The statue of Adam Mickiewicz (1798–1855), perhaps the greatest Polish poet, stands in front of the ancient Cloth Hall in Cracow. Mickiewicz's poetry is imbued with love for his nation, and even today, it remains a rallying point for nationalists against the socialist internationalism of the Polish government. (AP/Wide World Photos)

reforming the obsolete workings of its government. But in 1793 in a Second Partition, Poland was completely wiped off the map. Even though the Poles, under the brilliant general Tadeusz Kosciuszko, fought valiantly against the partition, the dream of Polish independence was brutally crushed by the invading Prussian and Russian armies. The Third Partition, now including the Austrians, in 1795, was the end of Poland as a political entity, as a state. But Poland as an ideal to which the Polish people owed their allegiance survived until the state was resurrected in 1918.

Hungary

Hungary's history is also replete with victories and defeats, unity and strife, greatness and subjugation. The Hungarian state was established by St. Istvan at the beginning of the eleventh century, and its early history was based on aristocratic rule and external expansion. This state controlled the Carpathian basin and therefore many nationalities, including the Slovaks and other Slavic peoples of the region. In the twelfth century the Hungarians incorporated the small, independent kingdom of Croatia. By then, Szekelys (or *szeklers*), ethnically related to the Magyars, were well established in the border towns of Transylvania to secure Hungary's eastern frontiers. Although destroyed by the brief but ferocious invasion by the Asiatic Tatars in 1241, the Hungarian state was quickly rebuilt and extended its rule to the Dalmatian coast in the south and parts of Serbia and historical Bulgaria in the southeast. Under Lajos the Great, a Hungarian king from France's Anjou dynasty, they even participated in the Western dynastic wars of the fourteenth century and laid claim to the kingdom of Naples. In addition, one of Lajos's daughters had married King Wladyslaw Jagiello of Poland, and Hungary thus had ties born in northern and southern Eastern Europe.

The arrival of the Ottoman Turks in Europe and their determined advance westward and northward, however, ended all further Hungarian efforts to expand in the southeast. In fact, Hungary was soon enmeshed in wars of defense against the onslaught of the Ottoman armies. For a while these wars—under the leadership of Janos Hunyadi, a Transylvanian nobleman, and his son Matyas Corvinus, a great king of Hungary during the Renaissance—were successful. But internal strife and the peasant revolt of 1514, led by György Dózsa, so weakened the state that in 1526, in the Battle of Mohacs, the armies of Hungary were defeated by the Turks. King Lajos II died on the battlefield, and Hungary—and the great Renaissance culture that existed in Matyas's court—disappeared in a few decades. The Plain of Hungary and the southern half of Transdanubia were occupied by the Ottomans, the rest of Transdanubia and northern Hungary by the Austrian Habsburgs. Hungary as an entity—much like Bohemia and Poland before—vanished from the map. Only in Transylvania, under Ottoman *suzerainty*, and to a lesser extent in the western areas under Austrian control, did Hungarian life and Magyar culture survive. Politically, the great multiethnic empires would now occupy Eastern Europe for centuries to come.

THE MULTIETHNIC EMPIRES

The dynastic, multiethnic empires that made the greatest inroads into Eastern Europe emerged at different times, and their contributions to the development of the region were unequal. The Ottomans were present in Eastern Europe the longest: they occupied Hungary for 150 years, but they controlled the Balkans for nearly 500 years. The Habsburg Empire was dominant in Hungary, Bohemia, and southern Poland for three centuries, the longest (in Bohemia), and for a little more than a "mere" century (in Poland). The Russians occupied

Europe 1815–1914

EUROPE 1815–1914

——— National boundaries, 1914

------- Boundaries of the Congress of
Vienna, 1815, where different

0   100   200 MILES

Poland "only" for little more than a century, and—except possibly in eastern Romania—played no real occupation role in the rest of Eastern Europe.

The Ottoman Empire

Ottoman forces appeared in the Balkans in the fourteenth century, and their encroachment on Eastern Europe was gradual; their rule in the Balkans lasted for five hundred years. At the height of their power, they twice besieged Vienna, in 1541 and in 1683, but were defeated by combined Christian armies. Wherever the Ottomans went, they established their rule according to certain standards; some of these were derived from their Muslim faith as written in the Koran, and others came from their Eastern culture.

Ottoman rule was grounded in several institutions. The first of these was the *devshirme*, a system of child tribute. Once a year, the officials of the sultan appeared in the Christian villages and took the strongest and most able boys between the ages of five and twelve to be raised in Constantinople to become *Janissaries*—professional soldiers, cruel and efficient, who were forbidden to marry and who were expected to live only for the sake of warring on the sultan's behalf. The *devshirme* was ended only toward the end of the sixteenth century.

A second key institution was the *millet* system. The Ottoman empire was not subdivided along simple territorial lines. Rather, the administration was organized into *millets*, or religious districts, each of which was responsible for the affairs of a single religion. Thus within the same territory there could have been a Muslim, an Orthodox, a Catholic, an Armenian Christian, and/or a Jewish *millet*; there was little or no commingling of these religious groups. In practice, this meant that nationality had little significance to the Ottomans as far as administration was concerned. For example, the Catholics of Hungary and the Catholics of the Dalmatian coast were governed by the same *millet*.

The effect of dividing the population into *millets* did not result in forced conversions as some had feared, for the Ottomans never really attempted to convert their non-Muslim subjects. Naturally, they were happy if someone did convert, but this decision was regarded as a personal choice. As long as the non-Muslims paid their taxes—which were collected rather strictly—the Turks sent no missionaries bent on forcible conversion.

A third Ottoman institution was the empire's bureaucracy, which reflected its way of life. Betraying their Middle Eastern origin, the Ottomans believed in the relativity of all things, the negotiation of all prices and tributes, and the ever-present possibility of compromise.

The system of rule that they developed was based on continuous bargaining, nepotism, "back-door" solutions, *bakshish,* and a recognized, clearly delineated corruption that somehow was the quasi-legal lifeblood of the empire.

The Ottomans in Eastern Europe, however, were relatively few in number, and their power was based on the simple conquest of large areas, rather than on maintaining continuous and strict imposition of a specific political culture. They did establish garrisons and had armies at the ready to squash any force considered potentially dangerous. The Turks who settled in the garrisons—the soldiers, the administrators, the judges, the bureaucrats—mingled easily with the native commercial classes and the slowly growing urban bourgeoisie. As the Ottoman Empire dwindled in size and power throughout the centuries, many of the Turks were assimilated into the local population and helped to make the region a true melting pot.

There were many reasons for the demise of the Ottoman Empire. The sultans, who originally created the *Janissaries* as a sort of Praetorian Guard and army of Islam, now feared them—and with good reason. Many a sultan came to an untimely death at the *Janissaries'* hands as they began to put their own interests over those of the empire. Furthermore, the merciless terror the Ottomans sometimes practiced drove whole populations from fertile fields into the mountains, which were frequently havens for occupied populations. The Great Plain of Hungary became depopulated, and the Magyars fled to the Slovak and Transylvanian uplands. The mountainous parts of Montenegro became near-independent states under the effective leadership of princes and religious leaders, and the cost of occupying them became too high for the Ottomans to pay.

However, most significantly, the nineteenth century ushered in a new and strong nationalism, and the Balkan peoples under Turkish control felt the exhilaration of these first national liberation movements. Patriotic ideals sparked by the French Revolution and carried eastward by Napoleon's troops began to penetrate the Balkans, and the Ottoman Empire, buffeted by the rising power of both Russia and the Habsburg Empire—on its eastern and northern frontiers, respectively—became known as the "sick man of Europe." By the second half of the nineteenth century, the Ottoman Empire in Europe began to fall apart.

The Habsburg Empire

The Habsburgs were a baronial family who, through successful intermarriages and dynastic control, assumed a dominant role in Europe. They had kings and emperors on many thrones of Europe, from Spain to Austria; princes, bishops, and Holy Roman emperors also came from this distinguished line. But in Western Europe in the sixteenth century, the Habsburgs' power and influence began to be thwarted by two developments: the rise of Protestantism and the emergence of France as a great power. These events limited the extent to which Catholic Austria could become the center of an all-powerful domain. The Habsburgs grudgingly recognized this by signing the Peace of Westphalia in 1648 with Louis XIV of France, Christina, Queen of Sweden, and Holy Roman Emperor Ferdinand II.

In the East, however, the Habsburgs' power was clearly ascendant when its fortunes were ebbing in the West. After the defeat of the Ottomans at Vienna in 1683, the Habsburgs began to encroach deliberately and slowly on the Turkish realm; in 1686 they conquered Buda and pushed the Ottomans south of the Danube within thirty years. They began to recolonize the depopulated areas of Hungary. The new settlers were not Magyars, however, but mostly Germans and Serbs; this process manifested itself both in urbanization and in the rise of a German-speaking peasantry. The independent-minded Magyars, and some non-Magyars, whose loyalty to Austria was gravely doubted, were excluded from ruling their own realm. The Habsburgs attempted to revive hundreds of small settlements that existed in the fifteenth century on the Great Plain of Hungary, but there was no longer a native Hungarian population to rule over. The depopulation under the Turks had been so complete that in most of these towns the new settlers could find only boars, wolves, and screeching wild birds.

The Czech lands gave the Habsburgs another opportunity to expand. Though they had intermittently ruled Bohemia since 1526, the Habsburgs were challenged by the Czech aristocracy and the Protestants, eventually resulting in the disastrous Thirty Years' War. By 1620, though, the Habsburgs had triumphed. Religious heterodoxy and the Czech aristocracy were both wiped out, and the Austrian landowners and those who willingly served them reigned in Bohemia for 300 years.

Only one piece of territory resisted Habsburg rule: Transylvania. Situated in the remnants of historic Hungary, the Transylvanians, though they lived under Ottoman and Habsburg domination in the sixteenth and seventeenth centuries, managed to retain their Hungarian culture, practice religious toleration, recognize equality among the various nationalities residing there—though not the equality of the Romanians—and elevated Magyar culture and national pride to perhaps new heights. Fighting a continuous rear-guard battle against both the Ottomans and the encroaching Habsburgs, the Transylvanian Magyar princes were constantly squeezed "among two infidels," their "blood freely shed for the sake of a single homeland," as a Hungarian folk song puts it. Their struggle for independence against the Habsburgs became especially strong after the Turks were expelled by the Austrian armies from Buda; the first national revolt for freedom and independence was fought primarily against the Habsburgs in 1703–1711. Led by Ferenc Rakoczi II, this rebellion ended in defeat, and Rakoczi was forced into exile in the Ottoman Empire, abandoned by such allies as France, which lost interest in Hungary's freedom. This pattern was to persist throughout Magyar history. Although, under the treaty of 1711, the Austrians granted the Hungarian aristocracy some lower-level power by allowing them to control the non-German and non-Magyar ethnic groups, the Magyars still did not rule over their own destiny. In fact, the tax records now available to us indicate that more tax was collected by the Austrians in the first decade of their rule in Hungary than had been taken by the Muslims during their entire 150-year reign.

But the French Revolution and the subsequent reign of Napoleon belatedly brought about rebellion, nearly revolution, aimed at bringing independence and principles of democracy to most areas under Habsburg control. The Magyars began first to undertake a revival of their national language and literature—an attempt to glorify the Magyar nation and its culture. This pattern was soon followed by the Serbs, Croats, and Romanians. The agitation for reform in Hungary that had been initiated by leaders such as Counts Miklos Wesselenyi and Istvan Szechenyi introduced modern ideas of liberalism to the public. This prepared the ground for parliamentary efforts to move Hungary toward independence and freedom. When the moderates failed, the more radical revolution of March 15, 1848, became inevitable. Fueled by the antimonarchist riots and rebellions in France, Germany, and even Austria, the Magyars, led by Lajos Kossuth, attempted to secure a free, constitutional Hungary. When the Habsburgs retaliated with force, the Magyars fought back, and the Austrians had to retreat. Only the armies of Russia, along with Austrian and Croatian assistance, could still the revolt. In 1849 the Magyars surrendered, Kossuth and his supporters fled into exile, and Hungary was ruled by dictatorial coercion for nearly two decades.

In 1867 Austria and Hungary officially ended their long-standing hostility in the famous *Ausgleich,* or "compromise." Under the *Ausgleich,* the emperor of Austria, Franz Josef II, also became officially recognized as the king of Hungary and was crowned with the crown of St. Istvan. But Hungary became a politically separate entity, a kingdom in a personal union with Habsburg, Austria, a ruler over its own realm. From 1867 to 1918, we thus speak of the Austro-Hungarian Empire. Tragically, though, the map of Hungary was drawn with complete disregard for ethnicity: autonomous Hungary now ruled over

Slovaks, Romanians, Croats, Slovenes, and Serbs in territories whose dreams of independence were just as strong as those of the Magyars. The Magyars, who had suffered political repression at the hands of the Ottomans and the Habsburgs for centuries, became the oppressors themselves. Such rule was doomed from the beginning, and in 1918 the Austro-Hungarian Empire fell apart and the Hungarian state shrank.

Russia

Russia, the land of the Eastern Slavs, had begun to extend its dominion westward in the seventeenth century. Although the Russians, the Ukrainians, and the Byelorussians are all Slavs, a great cultural gulf separated them from their Slavic Polish neighbors to the west. That gulf was visible during the intermittent wars in which Poles had occupied large sections of Russia as late as the seventeenth century, as well as during the Russian push toward the West that started in the eighteenth century. Although some Russians embraced and propagated the ideas of pan-Slavism in the late nineteenth century—for example, the unity and commonality of interests of all Slavic peoples—Russia was really more interested in expanding its powers as an empire and as the "Third Rome," the seat of "all true faith"—specifically that of Orthodox Christianity and later Communism.

Poland's eastern, southern, and northern neighbors sought to destroy Poland, and Russia used this fact to its advantage. Between 1655 and 1667, in a combined assault with the Swedes and the Ottomans, Russia occupied all the territories that Poland controlled east of the Dnieper River. During the eighteenth century it nibbled away at Poland's independence, together with Prussia and the Habsburg Empire. As we discussed earlier, in the Third Partition, in 1795, Poland as a state completely disappeared from the political map of Europe. Although Napoleon created the Grand Duchy of Warsaw in 1810 as an independent Polish entity, the Congress of Vienna of 1815 returned power over Poland to the three previous partitioning empires.

Throughout the nineteenth century Russian power increased in Europe, and Russian attention turned toward territories held by the Ottoman Empire to the south. As the Ottoman state grew weaker, Russia stepped into the resultant power vacuum. In 1812 Russian forces occupied Bessarabia and began to press southward into the Balkans; a half-century later Russia, together with the Austro-Hungarian Empire, became the dominant force that shaped the emerging new nation-states in the Balkan region.

THE RISE OF THE NATION-STATES: 1875–1918

Russian Intervention, The Balkan Wars, and World War I

The forces of nationalism contributed to the establishment of Hungary as an independent state within the Habsburg Empire without outside intervention. Elsewhere in Eastern Europe, however, nationalism was assisted and encouraged by Russia. As the Russians saw it, their strategic interests compelled them to encroach on the power of Turkey, the "sick man of Europe," and the best way to accomplish this end was to fan the fires of nationalism among the Balkan peoples. The first Balkan states, based on ethnic nationality, were created under Russia's active supervision and through its able maneuvering.

Balkan dreams of statehood were always present, and only force was able to keep the people of the Balkans under the Ottoman yoke. A Serbian uprising in 1804, led by Karageorge, a Serbian pig dealer, signaled the national aspirations of his people, and while this revolt did not lead to the creation of a free Serbian state, the Turks did have to grant Serbia autonomy in internal affairs by 1830. In 1858 the two Romanian principalities—Moldavia and Wallachia—merged, much against Turkish wishes, to form what would become the core of modern Romania. And in 1875 nationalistic revolts against Turkish rule broke out in Bosnia, Herzegovina, and Bulgaria. Turkey's brutal and savage oppression of these rebellions prompted Russia—supported by the "civilized" Western powers—to come to the aid of the revolutionaries, and the Russian army defeated the Turkish forces south of the Danube. But in dictating the terms of the Treaty of San Stefano, Russia was motivated by its own interests; the treaty created a large, independent Bulgarian state, and it indirectly laid the foundations of Bulgaria's allegiance to Russia.

Russia's role in this affair signaled to the West that Russia's power might need to be curtailed. Consequently, in the Treaty of Berlin three years later, Bosnia and Herzegovina came under the control of Austria-Hungary, not Russia, and Austrian garrisons occupied the Adriatic coastline as far south as Kotor. Serbia became free, though not totally independent, and Bulgaria's claim to the greatest empire of its history was substantially reduced. But this was an uneasy compromise, and it lasted only until 1908. During this period, every single national group attempted to seize more and more territory from the Turks—and from each other. Although Romania, Serbia, Montenegro, Bulgaria, and Greece combined forces in the First Balkan War against the Turks in 1912–1913, they turned on each other once the Turks were defeated. The Treaty of London (1913), which ended this conflict, established the Albanian state, although even the explicit provisions contained in the treaty failed to prevent the outbreak of the Second Balkan War (1913–1914). In this disastrous and fratricidal war, which broke out over the assassination of the Habsburg Archduke Franz Ferdinand by a Serbian student in Sarajevo, Serbia, the map of Europe assumed the form it kept through World War I. Called the "war to end all wars," World War I crushed the great multinational empires: Germany, Austria-Hungary, and Russia were all reduced in size and power. In their place arose the smaller nations that exist in Eastern Europe today.

The Paris "Peace" Settlements, 1919–1920

In the Paris settlements of 1919–1920, the boundaries of Eastern Europe were supposedly redrawn to recognize territorial and ethnic realities. But the nationalities had commingled, and ethnic "islands" existed everywhere. Furthermore, when the "peacemakers" gathered in Paris in 1919, the treaties that emerged from their deliberations reflected the three thoughts that were uppermost in their minds: (1) punishment of the former oppressors, the Central Powers, and reward of the faithful Allies (including the newly emerging nations that had fought against the Central Powers); (2) the threat of Bolshevism, against which the Western Allies felt they had to be on guard; and (3) the need to reach a "settlement," regardless of the actual complexities the Allied negotiators faced.

The "oppressors"—Germany, Austria-Hungary, and Russia—were held responsible for the long disappearance from the map of states such as Poland and Bohemia; they now had to pay the price. The reward of the Allies was equally simple: Poles, Czechs, Serbs, and Romanians had all fought against the Central Powers; new states had to be created for them at the expense of their former oppressors. But the threat of Bolshevism added a totally new dimension to the deliberations, and in 1919 this threat seemed strong to the "peacemakers."

The simple fact was that after the Bolsheviks won power in Russia in October 1917, they immediately pulled out of the war against the Central Powers. The Western Allies considered this act as the betrayal of Western principles. Moreover, due to the uses and misuses of Communist ideology and to the prediction that Communism would inevitably triumph over "imperialism" and "capitalism," the Western nations saw the spread of Communism as a danger to their very existence.

There were plenty of reasons for the West to fear the Communists. Several uprisings, in fact, had occurred at the end of the war or shortly afterward in Berlin, Bavaria, Austria and Hungary, and all of these revolts were financed by Russian money and benefited from Russian

The Peace Settlement, 1919–1923

EUROPE AFTER WORLD WAR I

Lost by Germany
Lost by Austria-Hungary
Lost by Bulgaria
Lost by Russia

0   100   200   300   400 MILES

Communist advice and, in some cases, assistance. In 1919 the Hungarian Soviet Republic became the first Communist state outside Russia. Led by Bela Kun, this short-lived regime—it existed for 133 days— emerged largely as a result of the Allies' excessive territorial demands against Hungary's first and only truly democratic government; it seemed to prove to the Allies that Communism had to be contained and confirmed that the Magyars had to be punished. The final peace treaty included that punishment.

The "just" Treaty of Paris created irreconcilable conflicts among the various ethnic groups of Eastern Europe. Though East Prussia and the city of Danzig (Gdansk) remained German, the Polish Corridor, a narrow strip of land giving Poland access to the sea, effectively cut them off from Germany proper. Though Silesia, where a large number of Germans lived, was awarded to the new Polish state, a plebiscite there rejected incorporation into Poland. Poland responded by sending in its armies and forcibly seizing Silesian territories, and the Allies did nothing to enforce the principles of self-determination for which they had allegedly gone to war. In the east, Poland—after a seesaw battle that saw Polish troops in Kiev and Russian troops on the Vistula River—gained sovereignty over 4 million Ukrainians and other non-Polish nationalities. In the south, a conflict with the Czechs over the city of Teschen resulted in a miniwar and ended in its forcible incorporation by the Poles.

The new Czechoslovak state was as territory-hungry as its northern neighbor. Czechoslovakia included a very large German population—close to 3 million—and 750,000 Magyars in ethnic islands in the Sudetenland and in Slovakia, respectively. Czechoslovakia's territorial appetites were sated primarily by the weakness of its neighbors, Germany and Hungary, and Adolf Hitler's tragic seizure of the Sudetanland in 1938 clearly was a result of the ill-advised provisions of the Paris peace treaties of 1919–1920.

Hungary was punished most harshly by the Paris Peace Conference: two-thirds of its territory and 60 percent of its population were taken from it. The reasons were manifold. Unlike the Czechs, Hungarians had a poor press in the West; they were regarded as oppressors of "free" peoples, and, to some extent, the Hungary of 1867–1918 did indeed fit the bill. Furthermore, Austria-Hungary had fought on the side of the Central Powers in World War I, and it was thus viewed to have fought against the "high principles" represented by the Western democracies. Finally, Hungary had dared turn to Bolshevism in 1919, while the Allies were firmly committed to opposing such a dangerous movement.

The terms of the Paris peace treaties affecting Hungary were indeed drastic: most of Hungary's historical, commercial, and urban centers, except Budapest, were given to other states. Bratislava, Kosice, Cluj, Oradea Mare, Timisoara, Arad, Novi Sad, and Osijek—ethnically largely Hungarian towns whose strongest commercial ties were to Budapest—overnight became Czechoslovak, Romanian, or Yugoslav cities. Even Austria was given the historically, though not ethnically, Hungarian territory of the Burgenland. Thus in 1920, some 30 percent of the roughly 10 million Magyars lived outside of Hungary's new borders, in territories whose majority national groups now oppressed the Magyars at least as cruelly as the Hungarian state had treated its minorities before World War I.

Bulgaria, like Hungary, had fought with the vanquished Central Powers, and the neighbors of this mountainous state were also determined to punish it for its choice of comrades-in-arms. Eastern Thrace, Bulgaria's access to the Aegean Sea, was given to Greece, and four "disputed provinces" on its western borders had to be ceded to Yugoslavia.

The new Yugoslav state—originally called the Kingdom of Serbs, Croats, and Slovenes—was immediately confronted by grave territorial and ethnic problems. As we discussed in Chapter 2, the differences between the Serbs on the one hand and the Croats and Slovenes on the other are great: the Serbians are Orthodox and use the Cyrillic alphabet, while the Croats and Slovenes are Catholic and use the Latin alphabet; the Serbians were long associated with Turkey, the Croats and Slovenes with Austria-Hungary; and so on. But this basic rift was further compounded by the presence of some 50,000–100,000 Slovenes in Austria, the constant conflict with Bulgaria over Macedonia, and Yugoslavia's incorporation of more than a quarter of a million Albanians. Most serious of all, however, was Yugoslavia's conflict with Italy over the Adriatic coast, the Istrian peninsula, and the city of Fiume. Although Fiume (Rijeka in Serbo-Croatian) was scheduled to become a free city, much like Danzig in the north, Gabriele d'Annunzio reconquered it for Italy in 1919, and it was fully incorporated into that state in 1924.

To the Romanians, however, the war was a godsend. Though they started on the losing side and were forced to surrender in 1916, they switched sides and became partners of the victorious Allies at the very end of the war. The Paris peace gave them twice the territory possessed before the war: Transylvania and Bukovina were now deemed to be parts of Romania. Along with these territories, though, Romania also inherited large numbers of "minorities"—Hungarians, Germans, Jews, Ukrainians, Poles, Turks, Tatars, Bulgars, Ruthenians, and Gypsies— who now all became regarded as second-class citizens of Romania.

THE INTERWAR YEARS: 1918–1939

The new states of Eastern Europe had to deal with a number of important problems, and solving these was necessary to their very existence. Politically, they had to delineate and institute structures and styles of government. Economically, they had to hope for self-sufficient and self-contained economic development. Socially, they had to adapt to the new political and social structure that emerged after the dislocations of World War I. And in foreign policy, they had to choose roads that would guarantee their independence and survival as powers in the region.

Economically, the first and most important problems that all these states faced were those of land reform of the land-tenure system. Except for the Czech lands and parts of Silesia, Eastern Europe was characterized by vast numbers of peasants and an underdeveloped urban-industrial sector. Although some industrialization and urbanization did take place between 1870 and 1914, the region still had a higher percentage of peasants than Western Europe. Not even the vast emigration from the area to America between 1860 and World War I was able to alleviate the overpopulation of the rural sphere significantly.

In areas controlled by Hungary and Poland, this problem was complicated by the fact that serfdom, which had been dismantled in the fifteenth-seventeenth centuries, was reintroduced in the so-called Second Serfdom of the nineteenth century. Binding the peasants to lands owned by a re-emergent aristocracy created labor-repressive and labor-intensive systems, hindered the development of opportunities for the peasants to become landowners themselves, and concentrated the larger estates in the hands of a small elite. The political order in these two states was based on an aristocracy that was proud to wear its full plumage and to act as the guardian of the "historic" nation, but that really saw no necessity to create a society in which peasants would become farmers and subjects would become citizens. For example, after World War I, in Hungary a minimal land reform affected merely 6 percent of the arable land; out of some 5 million peasants, only 250,000 received land; less than 1 percent of the population still owned 43.1 percent of all land.

The Polish post-World War I land reform was not much better; only 10 percent of Poland's arable lands were subdivided. The largest landowners suffered very little, since only 25 percent of their lands were expropriated and 20 percent of the land was still in their hands. The number of estates made available for allocation could not keep pace with the rising number of landless peasants, and peasant families had no choice but to divide their small farms into ever smaller and smaller strip-holdings as their families grew. Rural unemployment and overpopulation thus combined with the lack of land and opportunity to fuel the peasants' discontent in these two states.

A radically different situation existed in the other states of Eastern Europe. In these states, large estates had existed only in areas formerly owned or occupied by Austrian, Hungarian, or Russian landlords; the Turks had not favored large estates but small parcels of land. And when these states achieved their final boundaries, most of the large landowners fled to Austria or Hungary, leaving their large estates lock, stock, and barrel to the new state. In such states as Romania, therefore, land reform basically involved subdividing these estates to create a largely uniform system of small or medium-sized peasant holdings.

In Yugoslavia, too, the regent confiscated all estates—most of them in the north—with 50 hectares of land or more and redistributed them among some 650,000 peasant families, out of nearly 12 million peasants. An even more significant land reform alloted 45 percent of all expropriated land to 1.4 million peasant families, making the independent peasant the dominant type of agrarian producer. In Bulgaria, where the small-plot economy was already preponderant, all estates of more than 30–50 hectares—an additional 6 percent of the total arable area—were subdivided.

And in Czechoslovakia, unlike in the other Eastern European states, there was a solid industrial base and thus a proportionally smaller peasantry; hence land hunger was considerably less evident than it was elsewhere in the region. There were large estates throughout the country, but those in Bohemia and Moravia were strikingly different from those in Slovakia. In the west (Bohemia-Moravia), the large farms were modern and industrialized; in the east (Slovakia), which had been formerly occupied by Hungary, the traditional labor-intensive estates were held mostly by Hungarian and Austrian owners, most of whom returned to their homelands after World War I. The Czech government originally sought to expropriate all estates larger than 150–250 hectares, but that desire remained largely unrealized; only 300,000 hectares had been redistributed by 1931, and most of this subdivision occurred in Slovakia. In fact, Czechoslovakia—like Poland and Hungary—remained a country of large estates throughout the interwar period: 40 percent of all arable land was in the hands of landowners with estates larger than 500 hectares. There was an important difference, however: the large Czech estates were modern commercial farming ventures, by and large, while those of Poland and Hungary were not.

Every country in Eastern Europe faced major financial hardships immediately after the war, and financial stability came slowly and painfully. Skyrocketing inflation made most of the region's currencies weak, sometimes even worthless. Only after new foreign trade agreements were made among these states, and between them and the West, were their currencies stabilized. By 1922 the general recovery of the world economy also came to their assistance and slow economic growth was noted everywhere. In fact, the region which, until 1918, had been characterized by economic cooperation and the interlinking of all trade became fragmented by economic self-sufficiency and reliance on one's own resources, restrictive trade policies, and high tariffs and customs duties. Radical protectionism, however, was no solution to the problem that was caused by the lack of regional cooperation. Annual growth rates averaged 3–4 percent before the war; they hovered at 1–1.5 percent in the 1920s. Stagnation was especially heavy in the railroad, communications, and housing industries and in the development of

Table 3.1   Percentage Distribution of National Incomes by Economic Sectors, 1920 and 1938

	Agriculture		Industry		Other	
	1920	1938	1920	1938	1920	1938
Bulgaria	71.4	63.3	5.6	18.3	23.0	18.4
Czechoslovakia	33.0	23.2	50.8	53.2	16.2	23.6
Hungary	41.8	36.5	29.8	35.7	28.4	27.8
Poland*	—	39.0	—	32.2	—	28.8
Romania	60.2	53.2	24.2	28.4	15.6	18.4
Yugoslavia	58.0	53.6	20.9	22.1	21.1	24.3

* Data not available for 1920.

agrarian technology. Of the region's agrarian population of about 60 million, 25 percent remained unemployed and agrarian exports dropped to 20–25 percent of pre–World War I levels.

Only in one area—namely, industrial development—was there noticeable growth. But even this growth was hampered by a lack of capital for much of the era (1924–1929) and then by the severe effects of the worldwide depression of in the 1930s. Most significantly, Eastern Europe continued to lag behind the rest of the continent in the development of heavy machine industry.

All in all, the interwar era was one of dismal economic performance for the entire area. Rural unemployment and underemployment remained enormous; hunger and poverty, undermechanization and labor-intensive production blighted the region. The peasants frequently had no draft animals, and they tilled the land for only minimal market production. The nonagrarian population also increased, but there was no corresponding decline in the agrarian population; the rural population before World War II was still more than 50 percent in Hungary and 80 percent in Romania.

Most significantly, as can be seen in Table 3.1, the industrial-agricultural ratio of contribution to the national incomes of these states was little altered during the interwar era. Unlike Western Europe, where the contribution of industry to the national income ranged between 60 and 70 percent, in Eastern Europe, only in Czechoslovakia (specifically Bohemia) was the figure above 50 percent; elsewhere in the region agriculture remained the most important contributor to national wealth. These states, in spite of the interwar industrialization drives, remained largely agrarian, rural states, underdeveloped, with low per capita incomes and widespread poverty. Such were the economic legacies inherited by the Communists after they assumed power at the end of World War II.

Society and Change

Eastern Europe's economic problems in the interwar period were compounded by societal developments and ills that few of the new states were able to cope with. The region, as we have seen, had only just evolved from semifeudal or aristocratic structures into national states, and in the make-up of society all the ills that stemmed from such slow development were present—and in most cases were only exacerbated by emerging industrialization and urbanization.

The social structure of Czechoslovakia was the most modern, with industrial and urban populations; there was a well-developed bourgeoisie, confronted by a strong urban proletariat; there was also a relatively satisfied landed peasantry. The importance of the urban, entrepreneurial strata overshadowed the influence of the landed and "hereditary" aristocracy, much of which had been destroyed after 1620. It was true that Slovakian society resembled that of Hungary or Poland more than it did Bohemia's, but overall the Czechoslovak social structure was still closer to the Western type than that of any other Eastern European country.

Poland and Hungary were radically different. In both states the peasants still comprised the majority of the population, but the growth of industry brought about a numerical and qualitative strengthening of the working class, the industrial proletariat. And in these two states the influence of the large landowners and of the aristocracy remained exceedingly strong. Parading in somewhat comic sixteenth-century garments, the aristocracy, the *szlachta* (the petty nobility), and the gentry were anachronisms in the modern world. Though they no longer had sole control over the destiny of their countries, they still shared that destiny with the bourgeoisie, the large capitalists. In Hungary, for instance, about fifty families owned and operated the banks and nearly all of the manufacturing industries. And in both Poland and Hungary the Jews exerted an undeniable influence over industry, commerce, and banking, and some of the urban professions such as law, medicine, and journalism. Radical and vicious anti-Semitism was commonplace in both states—and government-supported during much of the era— but it primarily affected the lower-class Jews, who were far more numerous; the large capitalist Jewish families remained largely untouched by it. Restrictive legislation and the "Christianization" of things Jewish in both states only slowly reduced the power of these families and replaced them with non-Jews. Of course, Hitler and World War II finished this job.

The increasing importance of other social classes in Poland and Hungary was one of the major indicators of change in the region. On the one hand, the development of the intelligentsia in both countries, the growing populations of urban areas, the rising employment in the trades, commerce, the service sector, and industry were all extensive in the interwar years. On the other hand, there continued to exist extreme rural poverty. Whole peasant families shared one pair of boots, and children went barefoot, sometimes freezing and starving to death. Rural unemployment and lack of land had forced much of the peasantry to seek urban employment as live-in maids—*de rigueur* for every middle-class urban family—or unskilled industrial labor. Viable peasant estates of 10–50 hectares in both countries provided a living for only a quarter of the rural population. Landless peasants, for all practical purposes were still bound to the rural sphere and poverty; with the tightening of Eastern European immigration to America in the 1920s, they had nowhere to go.

The industrial proletariat, in spite of urban growth, remained weak in these two countries in the interwar era. In Hungary it encompassed less than 600,000 people, or one-tenth of the work force. More unskilled and semiskilled—and hence female—employees were hired by the emerging industries than skilled workers who have traditionally been the backbone of rapid industrialization. The permanent unemployment of large numbers of urban dwellers—living in hovels or in cheap, state-built complexes without running water or indoor toilets—became a constant factor in the life of the cities. In Poland the situation was much the same: before the war, the number of industrial workers barely exceeded a million; the number of so-called organized or class-conscious skilled workers—second- and third-generation working-class men—was astonishingly small when compared to those in Western Europe. Even these skilled workers, however, were employed in only a very few sectors of industry and used very low technology.

A different type of development characterized the Balkans—with some variations among countries, of course—though in some respects Romania resembled the Hungarian model more closely. In these states a Turkish legacy of cultural and economic development meant a slower growth of the middle class and the almost total absence of a native aristocracy. In Romania, as in other Balkan states, the middle class mostly consisted of ethnic minorities—Hungarians or Germans—at the end of World War I. In this region the bases of social mobility became education and employment in the government. Rich peasants, merchants, and successful entrepreneurs mingled with the members of this new state bureaucracy to form an urban-oriented middle class. The vast majority of the population, though, remained peasants, with farms that ranged from 3 to 50 hectares in area. These small-scale farms were not geared toward market-oriented production; they were barely adequate, in terms of size and level of mechanization, to maintain the owners and their families. Consequently, as the agrarian population grew, and as no more lands became available, agrarian unemployment grew even more widespread and its consequences were even

more tragic than was the case in Poland and Hungary; 33–50 percent
of the agrarian population in the Balkans was largely unemployed.
They suffered serious health problems—especially malnutrition, tuber-
culosis, and sicknesses caused by primitive sanitary facilities—and more
than 50 percent were illiterate.

Urbanization was very slow throughout the Balkans in the interwar
years. In Yugoslavia, urban-industrial workers accounted for perhaps,
one-tenth of the population in 1930, and in Bulgaria perhaps for only
2 percent. Even in Romania, which made the greatest progress during
this period, the industrial proletariat accounted only for about 500,000
people; in 1939, nearly 80 percent of the Romanian population were
still employed in agriculture—the same percentage as in 1910.

As a result of all these factors, the social legacy inherited by the
Communists of the region was complex. They began ruling over an
economically underdeveloped and socially backward area peopled
mostly by peasants, and their attempt to transform this society was
to cause them as many problems as their attempted transformation
of the existing economic systems.

Political Problems: Domestic and External Influences

After long periods of oppressive foreign rule, the infant states of
Eastern Europe were certainly not prepared to introduce Western-
style political systems. Despite the expectations of an often naive
American leadership that there would be democratic institutions and
processes in Eastern Europe, the region remained characterized by
dictatorships, restricted suffrage, and a superficial "parliamentarism"
that frequently masked the reality of a narrow base of power and
wealth.

Czechoslovakia was the only exception during the interwar years;
it alone had a system of Western-style democracy. Even there, the
political system that emerged under the leadership of Thomas Garigue
Masaryk and Edward Benes did not fully satisfy the Slovaks, who
wanted their own administrative system, parliament, and courts; they
received, at best, local autonomy in a federal state. Thus, coupled with
its other minority problems, which we shall discuss below, and the
rising power of Germany, Czechoslovakia lived in the shadow of impending doom of disintegration by Slovak demands from within.

The Czechoslovak constitution limited the power of the presidency, emphasized the influence of parliament over political affairs,
and allowed full political participation for all parties—even the Communist party. The principle of proportional representation created a
real, not merely a formal, possibility for the exercise of electoral power
by various strata of the population. Executive power was exercised

by a coalition government. Until its formal dismemberment in 1939, Czechoslovakia was indeed the shining light of democracy in the region.

Poland also became a parliamentary republic after World War I. Based on the extraordinary personality and charisma of Marshal Jozef Pilsudski, who led Poland's forces against the Central Powers, and the strong popularity of the prominent politician Roman Dmowski, a precarious parliamentary balance existed. The supporters of both leaders were strongly anti-Semitic, nationalistic, and conservative, and they believed in the maintenance of the entrenched values of the *szlachta* and the middle and upper classes. A constitution was adopted in 1921 that was closely modeled on France's and that emphasized, according to historic Polish traditions, the power of the Sejm (parliament) and restricted the power of the presidency. Pilsudski, who had secured the victory against the Russians in the "Miracle on the Vistula"—when Polish troops destroyed the badly overextended Bolshevik armies—thought that his work was done and retired from politics.

But Pilsudski became increasingly restless at his country home; Poland's new democracy was, as he saw it, beginning to undercut the security of the state and the importance of the military. In May 1926 he led a march on Warsaw, his army captured the capital, and he seized control of the government. He forced the president and the prime minister to hand over the reins of power, which he controlled until his death in May 1935. His rule as defense minister and often as prime minister was disguised in constitutional terms, and he appointed a personal puppet to occupy the presidency. His rule served the interests of the upper classes and the military, and the formal trappings of Polish democracy were essentially merely cosmetic.

Between Pilsudski's death and the joint Nazi-Soviet dismemberment of Poland in 1939, power passed into the hands of Pilsudski's military inner circle, composed of Jozef Beck, Walery Slawek, and Adam Koc, who wielded nearly total power. Although locally there remained ample room for relatively unfettered political participation for most opposition parties, on the national scene the "colonels" decided all important questions. Their inability to govern, their internecine rivalry, and their unwillingness to evaluate the diminished strength of their state vis-à-vis the rising power of Germany and the USSR ultimately contributed to Poland's Fourth Partition between Hitler's Germany and Stalin's Soviet Union in 1939.

The interwar situation in Hungary similarly depended on the power of national leaders who had emerged out of the chaos of World War I. A national uprising in October 1918, under the strong influence of Count Mihaly Karolyi, established a republic separate from Austria and tried to introduce democratic policies—including the redistribution of the large estates, a truly democratic nationality policy based on equality before the law, and freedom of expression for millions of previoulsy dispossessed people. But faced with intractable territorial demands by France and her wartime allies and particularly by Hungary's newly independent, territory-hungry neighbors, whose troops already were fighting alongside the victorious Allies, Karolyi resigned in disgust in March 1919 and handed power over to the Communists, who led the Hungarian Soviet Republic for 133 days. When the Communist leader, Bela Kun, also failed to harness the forces of nationalism and was faced with superior forces everywhere, the Hungarian army melted away, and the Romanians occupied Hungary without any major opposition. But the Allies did not wish to see Hungary completely disappear from the map, and they ordered the Romanians to withdraw. Soon a right-wing, anti-Communist, and strongly anti-Semitic government, led by Admiral Miklos Horthy, came to power. He was named regent for life on March 1, 1920, supposedly to rule until the return of the Habsburg king. However, when Charles IV, the last king of Hungary and emperor of Austria, dispossessed of his thrones in 1919, attempted to seize power in 1922, his forces were rapidly defeated by the regent's loyal troops.

Horthy ruled a country whose problems were impossible to overcome swiftly: it was deprived of huge chunks of territory; Magyar populations now lived as oppressed minorities in neighboring states; the traditional markets for Hungary's economy were cut off; and its society was just turning onto the road to broad-based national development. Thus Hungary was hardly in the position to pull itself up by its own bootstraps. It had a formal, liberal, and constitutional order— guaranteeing an elected parliament and the right to vote—but after 1922 suffrage was greatly curtailed in the countryside, and the peasants were forced to vote by open ballot. Only in the cities were elections still by secret ballot. Here, too, however, true opposition parties could not operate freely. For example, the Social Democratic party, the traditional voice for workers' rights, made an agreement with Count Istvan Bethlen, the prime minister of Hungary between 1921 and 1931. In return for being allowed to participate in political life, the Social Democratic party agreed not to organize the rural laborers and to cease the largely formalistic organization efforts among the peasants and state employees. And, needless to say, the Communist party, the party of the disastrous 133 days, was totally outlawed and savagely prosecuted.

Following Bethlen's resignation in 1931, more authoritarian and openly Fascist tendencies became clearly visible under the leadership of Gyula Gombos. Hungary drifted toward Fascism, and the power of the Arrow-Cross party, a blatantly anti-Semitic, pro-German, chauvinistic splinter group grew alarmingly. Although a law enacted in May 1939 allowed the extension of the secret ballot to the rural villages and brought into power a new government led by Count Pal Teleki, an internationally recognized scholar and probably one of Hungary's most pro-Western and anti-German statesmen, forty-three Nazis were legally elected to Hungary's parliament that year. Pressed primarily by foreign policy considerations (see below), Hungary allied itself with Germany. Teleki committed suicide, and Hungary's doom was sealed.

Romania's internal policies were rather similar to those of Hungary, but the context of those policies was different. Emerging from the war as a victorious power, its territory was now twice that of its pre-1914 limits and encompassed nationalities that were as opposed to Romanian rule as the Romanians had formerly been to Hungarian rule. The formal basis of rule was explicitly laid down in the constitution of 1923; under King Ferdinand and Prime Minister Ionel Bratianu the country's "royal parliamentarism" was based on universal suffrage and the participation of opposition parties. Until 1927–1928, when both Ferdinand and Bratianu died, the relatively liberal rule of the Romanian elite was stable; even if it was oppressive toward the non-Romanian minorities, it was certainly not exceptionally brutal.

After Bratianu's death, the opposition parties formed a new government under Juliu Maniu, and, since he stood for a Romanian version of populism, he concentrated on, though did not solve, the country's agrarian problems. However, the domestic situation became worse as the royal authority became confused. Ferdinand was succeeded by his grandson Michael, who was still a minor; Ferdinand had exiled his son Carol before he died. In 1930, however, Carol returned home and forced Michael's abdication, establishing his own royal dictatorship that lasted ten years. Cabinet crises, power plays, internecine rivalry, anti-Semitism and the emergence of a Fascist and pro-German movement called the Iron Guard marked these years, and parliamentarism slowly deteriorated. Even the minimal bases of democracy disappeared. Although Carol tried to maintain personal power by ordering the murder of the leaders of the Iron Guard in 1938, that party's influence continued unabated. The assassination of prime ministers and politicians became the rule in Romania.

When Hitler's Vienna Award of 1940 returned to Hungary those parts of Transylvania that were populated largely by ethnic Hungarians, Carol finally recognized his folly. He handed power over to General Ion Antonescu, returned the crown to his son, and fled the country. Under Antonescu, the Iron Guard went on a rampage, murdering former opponents on the right and the left, brutally slaying Jews, and pressing for Romanian entry into World War II on the side of the Nazis. The power of the Iron Guards became severely limited again in early 1941, but by June 1941 the Romanian army became part of the German war machine on the Eastern front.

The history of Yugoslavia was different from that of these other states. This South Slav state was formally forged from the Kingdom of Serbs, Croats, and Slovenes in 1929. It was founded on the basic unity of the South Slavic people—e.g., Serbs, Croats, and Slovenes—but that unity was not a reality. The majority Serbs were distanced from their minority South Slavic brethren not only by religion and written alphabet, but also by the difference between peoples of Eastern and Western cultural orientation. The Serbs' desire for centralization, an attempt to keep alive the nucleus of the earlier Serbian kingdom, was actively and continuously opposed by the Croats and Slovenes, who advocated the decentralization and self-government that they had enjoyed even under Hungarian and Austrian rule. Only the common social origin of the large peasant majority bound the kingdom together. The first constitution, issued in 1921 under King Alexander, came out strongly in favor of centralism; the Croats opposed it from the very beginning. The centralist forces were led by the Serb Nikola Pasic, while the opposition was led by the Croat Stepan Radic. Radic was shot—as was characteristic of Balkan politics—while speaking to parliament in 1928, and the country seemed to be on the verge of civil war. In response to these chaotic conditions, King Alexander established his own dictatorship in January 1929. From then on, Yugoslavia was subdivided into geographical, rather than ethnic, regions, each supervised by a governor appointed by the king.

The new constitution of 1931 seemed to return some semblance of democracy to the country, though the power of the opposition was severely curtailed. But the assassination of King Alexander in Marseilles, France, in 1934 once again pushed the country toward anarchy. The king's brother, Prince Paul, became regent until the king's young son, Peter II, would be old enough to take the throne. The antagonism between the government and the opposition continued unabated until the elections of August 1939, which the opposition won. As a result, the first steps toward decentralization were taken, and Croatia became a semiautonomous province of Yugoslavia. The right to secret ballot and the freedom of political activities were restored, and it seemed that ethnic peace was finally assured.

But this peace was short-lived. In March 1941 Prince Paul acceded to German demands for an access to the Adriatic Sea, and the Serbs revolted against the decision which they viewed as an attempt to dismember the state. King Peter II assumed full power, hoping to keep the country intact. But Hitler had different plans. On April 6, 1941, Germany destroyed Belgrade from the air. The Nazis invaded the country, set up a semi-Fascist regime in Croatia and divided up the rest of the country among Italy, Hungary, Germany, and Bulgaria. The state of Yugoslavia disappeared from the map until the end of World War II.

Bulgaria also compiled a rather mixed record during the interwar era. This state, was reduced in size and importance after World War I. King Boris III then attempted to incorporate democratic elements into monarchical rule. With the able assistance of the leader of the majority party, Alexander Stambolisky, democratic government became a matter of practice, even though the new system seemed to serve more the interests of the huge peasant class than the small urban classes. However, radical opposition to Stambolisky's policies resulted in his assassination in 1923, and anarchy and terror then reigned until 1934, when Prime Minister Kimon Georgiev and Colonel Damian Velchev took power and established a dictatorship. Although the king attempted to limit the arbitrary use of force, Bulgarian politics were so solidly based on the dictatorial curbing of nearly all opposition that he failed; any organized opposition to the government was regarded as "extremist" by the power elite. In foreign policy Bulgaria, though it had considerable pro-German sympathies and assisted in the dismemberment of Yugoslavia, also had sympathies toward the USSR, whose predecessor, imperial Russia, had been instrumental in the creation of the Bulgarian state. Although allied with Germany during the war, Bulgaria never declared war on the USSR.

Finally, Albania was granted independence in 1913, but it was not until 1920 that the decisive influence of Ahmet Bey Zogu was first felt. Zogu served first as a minister of the Interior, then as prime minister, and in 1924, after a two-year stint in exile, he became president. Convinced that the largely illiterate Albanians were not ready to accept democracy—and because he was hungry for power—he declared himself King Zog I in 1928. Zog was instrumental in an effort to modernize Albania. In the 1930s he launched a drive that included attempts to develop the cities, educate the population, and establish a modern code of law. Although Italian influence remained strong and there was a not totally unwanted Italian interference in Albania's affairs, Zog rejected the offer of a customs union with Italy and even closed the country's Italian schools. In 1938 Zog married the daughter of a Hungarian aristocrat, and, when an heir was born, he seemed to be on the way to establishing a dynasty. In 1939, however, Albania fell victim to the aggression of the Fascist powers, as Italy, assisted by Germany, destroyed its short-lived independence.

Anti-Semitism and Ethnic Hostilities

Throughout the interwar era, all of the states of Eastern Europe except Czechoslovakia, experienced dictatorship supported by the aristocracy, the gentry, the rich capitalists, the state bureaucracy, the military, the intelligentsia, and the middle class. All of these countries also faced major problems, among which the most outstanding were economic and social disintegration. This was caused largely by the destruction of international markets, which had been integrated under the old empires, and was exacerbated by the Great Depression. Compounded by the inability of the rulers to undertake major social reforms or to create opportunities for the unemployed masses, this situation spelled disaster. In these multiethnic, developing states, two elements were always present, though to a varied extent: virulent anti-Semitism and ethnic hostilities. Although the former was not a serious problem in the Balkans, except Romania, the latter was a menace everywhere in Eastern Europe.

The Jews of Eastern Europe were, by and large, divided into two distinct communities; one could be called "rural" and the other "urban," although "national" and "assimilationist," "uneducated" and "educated," "poor" and "rich" are other labels that have been applied to them. The rural, unassimilated Jews—chiefly in Poland, Romania, and the Balkans—lived in small hamlets and did not participate in the political life of their respective nations. More orthodox than their urban brethren, they generally had few "cosmopolitan" aspirations, except to send their sons to school to become members of the professional or merchant classes.

On the other hand—specifically in Poland, Bohemia, Hungary, and Romania—there existed strong urban Jewish communities, associated with finance, capital, the intelligentsia, and the professions. These Jews were viewed as a threat by the nationalist groups who came to power in the post-World War I states. Anxious to increase their own power and influence, the newcomers to the political scene, including the petty gentry and the landless aristocracy, could hope to improve their existence most easily by forcing the urban Jews out of the important roles they held. Anti-Semitism here was thus prompted by even baser motivations than usual and could easily receive the support of most "Christian" populations accustomed to a history of virulent, demagogic anti-Semitism.

The fear of Bolshevism—and the fact that many Bolshevik leaders were explicitly linked to their Jewish religious origins (Karl Radek, Lev Trotsky, and Bela Kun, to name just a few)—also led to Jew-baiting. Movements hiding under the guise of romantic and rural nationalism railed against "Jewish capitalism" and "plutocratic Jewish Bolshevism"; these movements were all basically similar to German Fascism and imitated the Fascist style that was so clearly incorporated into Hitler's reign. In Poland, Silesia, Slovakia, Hungary, Romania, and Croatia, the seeds of full-blown anti-Semitism found fertile ground. Small but well-organized and well-financed groups of thugs impelled their governments to tilt toward the Nazi cause or to surrender as German power grew. One cannot disregard the link between the domestic and foreign policies of the Eastern European states in this respect.

The problem of ethnic minorities also had both domestic and foreign causes and implications. The presence of large ethnic minority populations had become a major concern after World War I. For example, the presence of large German ethnic populations in Poland and Czechoslovakia gave Hitler an excuse to intervene in those states. He fomented discontent in both countries and ultimately used the ethnic Germans to bring down Czechoslovakia in 1938 and to weaken Poland a year later. A large percentage of Magyars lived beyond Hungary's borders, but there was also an important German minority inside the country. Hitler here used the-carrot-and-stick approach: Hungary could recover its ethnically Magyar populations if it sided with Germany as the latter expanded eastward; conversely, Hitler's support for German ethnic and Fascist claims for power sharing in Hungary would be withdrawn only if Hungary in effect joined Hitler's alliance. The Vienna Awards, which returned to Hungary some of its former territories in exchange for the Hungarian-German alliance against Russia, was the price Hungary had to pay; the cost was enormous. For Romania, which lost Transylvania in this bargain, the Vienna Awards were made somewhat sweeter by Hitler's promise to return Bessarabia to Romania after the defeat of the USSR. After Hitler's dismemberment of Yugoslavia, "independent" Croatia was ruled by Ante Pavelic, a local Fascist quisling. Thus both the ascendant power of Germany and the relations among the various states in the region sealed the future of Eastern Europe.

World War II

Eastern Europe was a power vacuum. The destruction of the three major powers in the region—Austria-Hungary, Germany, and Tsarist Russia—in 1917–1919 made it possible for new states to come into being. Pressed by circumstances, Poland, Czechoslovakia, Romania, Yugoslavia, and Albania all desired to maintain the status quo and wanted to hold on to the territories gained after World War I at all costs. Not surprisingly, then, these states tried at different times to forge common foreign policies; the Czechoslovak-Romanian-Yugoslav alliance known as the Little Entente was one example. But this alliance's only common concerns were maintaining the status quo and opposing Hungary. It did not defend its members against either Germany or Soviet Russia. Since little Hungary alone did not really represent a threat to the status quo, the Little Entente was a preposterous alliance, especially because the only large state that could have really provided power to the alliance, Poland, never joined. Furthermore, Romania's main enemy among the would-be great powers was Russia; Czechoslovakia's was Germany. But neither Eastern European state considered the other's enemy as its own and would not defend its ally against threats from that enemy.

On the other hand, Hungary and Bulgaria can be considered to have been truly revanchist, or determined to reclaim lost territories, during these years. Hungary did try to break out of its isolation from its neighbors by flirting with both Italy and Britain, but the only power that could possibly help it to recover Magyar lands was Germany. In this respect, the inevitable inheritance of the peace treaties of 1919–1920 was a German-Hungarian-Bulgarian alliance. The rising importance of Germany, especially after 1933, when Hitler assumed rule, and the success of Fascism in Italy, combined with the West's inertia and its underestimation of Germany's hunger for power, were bound to be disastrous for states that had come to exist as a result of the Paris peace treaties.

After Germany's *Anschluss* (Union) with Austria in 1938, the first impact of the intensified Nazi power in the region was felt in Czechoslovakia; Hitler demanded the dismemberment of this state. There had been a Czechoslovak-French-Soviet treaty, but Romania and Poland refused permission for Soviet troops to be trans-shipped to Czechoslovakia (the Soviet Union had no common borders with Czechoslovakia). At any rate, the issue was academic, since the Soviets were bound only by a conditional treaty, meaning that they were obligated to assist the Czechoslovaks solely if the French were to aid them as well, and France was in no mood to do this. In March 1939 Czechoslovakia was carved up. Bohemia and Moravia were incorporated into Germany, while the Germans created a puppet regime in Slovakia under the leadership of a local Fascist, Monsignor Jozef Tiso.

The Nazi-Soviet Nonaggression Pact of August 23, 1939, between Germany and the USSR was an act of perfidy, clear and simple. But it could also have been expected. Drawn together by a common interest in devouring Poland, the two powers effected the Fourth Partition. Attacking Poland from the west on September 1, 1939, Hitler's troops swept their way to Warsaw, destroying everything in sight; the onslaught of Soviet troops from the east on September 17, 1939, sealed the fate of the unhappy country. A few Polish leaders fled and established a government-in-exile first in France and later in England. Several thousand Polish officers fleeing eastward were captured by or surrendered to the Soviets in combat; a few years later thousands of these men were killed by Soviet forces in the Katyn Forest in eastern Poland. Poland as a state disappeared again. Its western portion became a part of the German Reich; its eastern regions were incorporated into the USSR; and a General Government of German Occupation ruled over a restive, brutalized population. Although partisan resistance continued throughout the war, the Polish state was occupied by both sides. The Nazi-Soviet pact lasted less than two years: on June 22, 1941, Hitler's army invaded the USSR.

Hitler's power was also felt in the Balkans. Convinced that the Balkans had to be "pacified" before he could attack Russia, Hitler claimed to be appalled at the "gall" of the independent-minded King Peter II and his Yugoslav countrymen who refused to join the Tripartite Agreement between Italy, Germany, and Hungary. German forces thus struck Belgrade on April 6, 1941, and invaded Yugoslavia from Hungary, Romania, and Bulgaria simultaneously. By August 29, 1941, they established a puppet regime in Croatia, but the puppet had no authority as far as the Yugoslavians were concerned. Loyal either to their king, in exile in London, his representative, General Mihajlovic and his Serbian "Chetniks" on the one hand, or to the Communist Josip Broz (Tito) on the other, many Serbs fought an underground partisan battle against the Germans—and against each other—that was to last throughout the war. However, most Croatians and many Slovenes actively supported the Germans against the Serbs.

The Eastern Europe of 1941–1944 was quite dissimilar to the Eastern Europe of the interwar years. Czechoslovakia, Poland, and Yugoslavia had been partitioned, dismantled, and destroyed, and two new states, Slovakia and Croatia, led by pro-Fascist puppets, appeared on the map. Romania lost territory to Hungary, Hungary gained some of the territories taken away from it in the Paris peace treaties of 1919, and both of these states were now led by largely pro-German, proto-Fascist governments and sided with Germany against the Allies; they both actively assisted Hitler's army in its war against the USSR. Bulgaria, having gained some territory through German assistance and design, was also a faithful ally of Germany, but—as we noted above—because of its historic ties with Russia, it refused to declare war on the USSR.

It would be impossible in this chapter to describe the tragedies of World War II. For most people the events of those six years, now a couple of generations in the past, remain incomprehensible. The war losses everywhere were enormous, cities and countrysides were devastated, great capitals such as Warsaw and Budapest lay in rubble. Suffice it to say that though the burdens of the war were not felt evenly by all of the Eastern European states, the Nazi occupation and the terror and destruction it caused could never be forgotten. Hitler's allies in the region—Hungary, Romania, and Bulgaria, until the latter two pulled out of the war in 1944—initially were far freer than the occupied territories. However, since these states were all ruled by pro-German elements, Germany's "requests" of these states—whether to increase trade, step up war production, or exterminate "undesirables"—were generally granted. In effect, therefore, all of Eastern Europe was in the German sphere of interest.

It is difficult, if not impossible, to talk with even a modicum of objectivity about the treatment of the Jews in Hitler's realm. The extermination of 6 million people in and out of concentration camps located

Table 3.2   Wartime Losses of Jewish Populations

	Estimated Jewish population pre–1940	Estimated Jewish population annihilated	
		Number	Percent
Bulgaria	64,000	14,000	22
Czechoslovakia	180,000	155,000	86
Hungary	650,000	450,000	70
Poland	3,300,000	3,000,000	90
Romania	600,000	300,000	50
Yugoslavia	43,000	26,000	60

mostly in Poland, is a nightmare that cannot be compared to any event in human history. Although it is true that Hitler's policies of extermination were also aimed at Gypsies and some other "undesirables"—including Slavs, partisans, and Communists—not all those who were placed in concentration camps were scheduled for systematic extermination in gas chambers and through every conceivable means—only the Jews were. Table 3.2 indicates the enormity of Hitler's war against the Jews.

The differences in the percentage of Jews exterminated in different countries seem to lie in the attitude of each population toward Jews and in each government's policies, if there was a government to conduct policies. In Poland and Bohemia, occupied outright by the Germans, the policies of "native" politicians hardly mattered. Although the widespread anti-Semitism exhibited by the largely Catholic population of these states contributed to—and, in the case of Poland, even assisted in—German "successes," German policy itself offers much of the explanation. In the puppet states of Slovakia and Croatia, also predominantly Catholic, Father Tiso and Ante Pavelic both ably and willingly helped Hitler to round up Jews and send them to extermination camps. Most Croatian Jews perished, while most other Yugoslav Jews survived—and were even protected by the local population and resistance movements. The extermination of Hungarian Jews was pressed by the Germans, but Regent Horthy refused to buckle under until 1944, when the rural Jews of Hungary began to be shipped to Auschwitz and other camps. The Jews who lived in the ghetto of Budapest survived relatively intact as a group until Horthy was replaced by the Fascist Arrow Cross leader Ferenc Szalasi on October 15, 1944 after an abortive and belated attempt by Horthy to pull out of the war and switch to the Allies' side. In the remaining two months more Hungarian Jews from Budapest were deported and killed than during the entire previous war period.

The murder of the Romanian Jews under the Iron Guard was also vicious and brutal, but, interestingly, most of the Jews who were exterminated in Romania came from non-Romanian nationalities; the Hungarian and Bessarabian German Jews suffered far more than did the Wallachian-Moldavian Jews. Moreover, much of the extermination of the Romanian Jews took place not from shipping them to German concentration camps, but by cruelly "relocating" them in eastern Romania and in areas of Russia occupied by Romanian troops. And Bulgaria, unlike Hungary after 1944 or Slovakia, refused to deliver its Jews to Hitler for extermination; except for those Jews in Bulgarian-occupied Yugoslavia—who were systematically exterminated—more than three-fourths of the Bulgarian Jews also survived the war.

It seems curious that in spite of the brutality of Hitler's occupation policies in the region, resistance movements and activities emerged rather slowly and unevenly. Resistance movements were strong in Poland and Yugoslavia, creditable in Bulgaria, and weak or nonexistent in the remaining states. (There were isolated acts of terrorism against German officials in Prague and Budapest, and during the last days of the war there was a Slovak uprising against the retreating German armies.)

Although Poland was subdued jointly by Germany and the USSR in September 1939, Polish resistance to occupation continued throughout the war. At first, the resistance consisted of strictly local efforts, although the resistance fighters maintained radio contact with the government-in-exile in London. The Polish resistance could not, of course, count on help from the Russians: Hitler's Soviet allies during the twenty-two-month existence of the Nazi-Soviet Nonaggression Pact, did everything they could to exterminate members of the Polish underground or to take them to the USSR as prisoners. About 500,000–1 million Poles perished at the hands of the Soviet occupation forces during these terrible months, even in those regions of eastern Poland where the "Slavic brethren" were clearly in control.

The situation changed rapidly after the German occupation of parts of the USSR. A mere three weeks after the outbreak of hostilities, an agreement between the USSR and the Polish government-in-exile extended mutual recognition to each other and declared the territorial provisions contained in the Secret Addendum to the 1939 Nazi-Soviet pact null and void, although the Soviet government never gave up its earlier territorial demands on Poland. The Soviet government now allowed a Polish army to form on Soviet territory. But the USSR did not place all of its eggs in one basket. Indeed, while the Germans were heading toward Moscow, Stalin had already ordered the creation of a pro-Soviet, Communist-led Union of Polish Patriots. Although Stalin also allowed the formation of a pro-Allied Polish army—one that was led by General Wladyslaw Anders and served bravely in Italy and the Near East—Stalin trusted only the pro-Soviet Polish Communists. As a result of Stalin's suspicion of the "London Poles" and his understanding of how little Poland *really* mattered to the major powers fighting Hitler, after the uproar over the discovery of the Katyn massacre of Polish officers by Soviet troops, Stalin broke off relations with the government in London, refused to allow Allied aircraft to land in the USSR after they dropped supplies to the Polish partisan units, and prepared to unleash his own government on Poland as soon as Germany was defeated.

The darkest days of the Polish partisan movement against the Germans came in August 1944. Soviet troops were already on the eastern side of the Vistula. Warsaw—whose Jewish ghetto had just over a year before struggled defiantly for nearly a month against Hitler's best combat forces before being exterminated in bloody fighting—was quietly preparing for its greatest act of resistance against the Germans: the Warsaw uprising. Led by General Tadeusz Bor-Komorowski, the uprising began on August 1, 1944, lasted for sixty-three days, and was crushed with the greatest brutality Hitler's forces could amass. From the other side of the Vistula River the Soviet forces watched the struggle and did not help. From their point of view, the destruction of the non-Communist Polish partisans was a welcome event, as was the death of many Germans. At the end of the uprising, Warsaw stood empty and devastated. As the Germans began to leave, the Russians were poised and continued to push the Germans back further west. Poland was already lost, once again.

The partisan movement of Yugoslavia faced a different problem and yet one that was at least symbolically similar to that encountered by the Poles. As mentioned earlier, Yugoslav partisan movements were, from the very beginning, divided between the pro-Western Serbian Chetniks, led by General Mihajlovic and loyal to the Yugoslav government-in-exile in London, and the partisans of Josip Broz (Tito), a Serbo-Croat Communist who was trained in Moscow. The Western governments, however, also supported Tito, who, under joint Allied pressure, established a national front against the Germans. After the King dismissed Mihajlovic in 1944, Tito welcomed the king's representative, Ivan Subasic, into his new national council. The forces under Tito's command thus became recognized as the real government of Yugoslavia, and their truly heroic fight against German occupation justified their claim to legitimacy. As the war ended, however, it soon became clear that their solidly anti-German record also meant their total loyalty to Communism and dictatorship, which the Western Allies never really expected.

The extent of the resistance movements does not account for the destruction suffered by the various populations. Poland suffered the greatest destruction of any Eastern European state. Less than 10 percent of Warsaw's population survived the war and few of its buildings remained intact. Yugoslavia was the second most damaged state, though other states were also scarred. One of the hardest-hit countries in the region was Hungary, which—unlike Romania and Bulgaria in 1944 as Soviet troops stood nearby—was unable to switch sides on October 15, 1944. Ruled by native Fascists, it remained Hitler's last ally and therefore suffered from continuous devastation from the air by Allied bombers and from the ground by Soviet troops driving west. Budapest was badly damaged; its bridges, which tied the two halves of the city together, had been destroyed by the Germans and lay in the Danube. Poland, Hungary, and the war-ravaged cities of Yugoslavia showed scars that were to last into our own times.

But it was not merely the cities that suffered and not merely the fighting and bombing that caused the damage. The retreating German troops dismantled industries, carried away rail stock, and transported whatever they could to the West. Food was confiscated, and starvation prevailed everywhere as the German retreat intensified. Where the Germans failed, the "liberating" Soviet forces succeeded; every conceivable movable property now was transported east from "victors" and "vanquished" alike. As Soviet soldiers hoisted their flag on the Reichstag in Berlin, the war ended for Eastern Europe, but a new era of Soviet occupation began.

Eastern Europe Since 1945

■ By May 1945 the guns of World War II were finally stilled in Eastern Europe. Hitler was dead, Germany was occupied and defeated, but the lasting imprint of the war was visible everywhere in the region. The destruction was enormous. Great cities such as Warsaw had been reduced to rubble, empty of people and of hope. Bridges on the great rivers were blown up, and icy waters swirled around their shattered structures. Factories lay in ruin, fields were scorched and pockmarked by shells, bombs, and the furrows of trenches, hastily dug and even more quickly abandoned.

And there were the corpses. In the bitter winter of 1944–1945 they lay piled up like logs, frozen in the cold, on roadsides, in the courtyards of overcrowded hospitals, and in the fields, their stiff limbs helpless. Typhoid and other diseases would be inevitable if the bodies were left exposed, but the frozen ground resisted efforts to bury the dead. The land seemed to be saying; "No more. I have had enough."

There were refugees, too—people whose homes and apartments had been bombed out, families looking for families, children for parents. Mothers awaited every scarce train with pictures of babies, husbands, fathers, asking everyone, "Did you see this person?"

Above all there was confusion, about the past and the present as much as about the future. "Why did this happen to us?" people asked, and no one could answer. "What is our present?" "What can we do?" "How can we eat?" people asked, and no one seemed to know. "What will become of us?" "What have the great powers decided about us?" they asked, and there was silence and then a cacophony of answers, each different, each uncertain, each hesitant.

Amid all the doubts there was only one certainty: the Soviet Army was there, evident everywhere in the region. Like other empires before, the USSR came to Eastern Europe as a liberator—and stayed as an oppressor. The pattern of domination had been established earlier; however, the Soviets were a new type of ruler. To some extent Austrian rule was also backed by a degree of force that imposed a foreign culture and pattern of life on the region. But the new "liberators" brought with them a new form of government and radically different values and compelled their open and enthusiastic adoption everywhere their forces had been stationed. This form was a totalitarian dictatorship that attempted to control all aspects of life. Like zealot missionaries, the Russians insisted that theirs was the *only* true religion and that anyone who opposed it would be destroyed.

And yet, we must not totally ignore the claim that the Soviet Union liberated the area from the Germans and that the Soviet people paid a tremendous price in human life for that liberation. The USSR clearly was a liberator for Czechoslovakia, for the surviving Jews, and for the prisoners in the concentration camps.

But for other people in the region the claim of liberation was not so clearly delineated. For example, the Poles welcomed the fact that the Soviet army drove the Germans out, but they were embittered by the despicable role Stalin's army had played in failing to support the Warsaw uprising, as well as by the murder of Polish officers by the Soviet forces during the war in the Katyn Forest. Thus Poland found Russia's alleged liberation hypocritical, to say the least.

For the East Germans the claim of liberation from Hitler was just as spurious; after all, most Germans had supported Hitler once, and many did so to the bitter end. The indignities suffered by the East Germans in the Soviet zone of occupation did not endear the Russians to the German people, although the Nazi troops had been a brutal occupying force in the USSR as well. And while it is true that the Red Army liberated the German people from one of the most brutal dictatorships in history, their claim of liberation merely meant the replacement of one totalitarian rule with another.

In Hungary the situation was less ambivalent; the Hungarians had indeed been liberated from the brutal puppet regime of Ferenc Szalasi. However, the vast majority of Hungarians had earlier supported the Germans, since only Germany was willing to return to Hungary its "lost territories" and thus rectify the injustices contained in the Paris peace treaties ending World War I. Moreover, Hungarian forces had fought against the Soviet Union, and Hungary's entire Second Army perished at the Don River at the hands of Soviet forces. Finally, the brutality of the Soviet army as it cut through Hungary and expelled the German and Hungarian forces has been well documented. Given the fact that Hungary was Hitler's last ally, it could be claimed that the Soviet soldiers behaved as the occupying regime of any invading army would. But certainly the Red Army's behavior was far worse than that of the Romanians two and a half decades earlier.

The Romanians, until shortly before the end of the war, had also been allies of Hitler. But in August 1944, as Soviet troops neared Bucharest, the capital, a popular revolt overthrew the semi-Fascist regime, and Romania switched sides, pulling out of the war. For the Romanians, therefore, "liberation" meant something different again. They realized that they could not regain their territories Bessarabia and Dobruja, but they recognized that there at least existed the possibility of regaining Transylvania, taken away from Romania by Hitler's Vienna Awards. In joining the war on the side of the Allies—in spite of the notorious brutalities previously committed by Romanian troops in the USSR—Romania redeemed itself and became an "ally" on the side of its liberators almost overnight.

For Bulgaria, too, the cost of "liberation" was high. Bulgaria had been a staunch ally of Germany, except in the case of Russia, against whom it refused to declare war. But when the Russian armies approached and crossed the Danube, Stalin's government declared war on Bulgaria, despite Bulgaria's neutrality in the Nazi-Soviet conflict. On September 9, 1944, as the Soviet troops approached Sofia, the Bulgarian capital, the relatively liberal Bulgarian government was overthrown and replaced by a pro-Russian government that welcomed the Soviet forces with open arms. Joining the Red Army, the Bulgarian forces now became combatants against Germany, and they fought well into Austria before the end of the war. Thus Bulgaria did not need to be liberated from the Germans, nor occupied forcibly by the Russians; it was liberated only from a *Western*-oriented, semidemocratic regime.

Unlike these states, Yugoslavia's liberation was indeed accomplished primarily by its own partisan armies; Soviet forces participated in anti-German operations only in the north of the country. Moreover, Tito's Communist government was not assisted in coming to power by the presence of the Soviet army; Tito's forces had captured power all by themselves, in fact, with a significant amount of assistance from the West.

Finally, in Albania's liberation the USSR played no role at all. There, Italy's pre-war occupation of Albania was reinforced to some extent by the Germans, but as the fortunes of Italy and Germany waned toward the end of the war, most German and Italian soldiers were withdrawn from the country. By 1945 Albania had become free of Axis occupation and did not need Soviet liberation. That Albania became Communist was therefore due to the victory of Tito's Communist partisans and their contacts with an Albanian Communist named Enver Hoxha, rather than to assistance rendered by the Soviet army.

YALTA, POTSDAM, AND THE POSTWAR SETTLEMENTS: 1944–1948

Although the Atlantic Charter, signed by President Franklin D. Roosevelt and British Prime Minister Winston Churchill on August 14, 1941, had promised the people of Eastern Europe sovereign rights, including self-government for those "who had been forcibly deprived of them," the post-World War II governments of the area were not themselves sure of the future of their region. Some, including the Romanian, Bulgarian, Yugoslav, Czechoslovak, and Polish regimes, initially desired regional cooperation, but that option had to be discarded when the USSR expressed vigorous opposition to any regional alliance—such as a Balkan federation—that would involve a state neighboring the USSR. The most serious problems about the future arose in connection with Poland, and Polish-Soviet relations became the litmus test of Allied cooperation in the eyes of many observers; from the beginning the litmus paper turned the wrong color.

The murder of several thousand Polish officers in the Katyn Forest of eastern Poland in 1941 and Germany's charge that the Soviet Union committed the act focused attention on the chasm between Soviet territorial demands and Polish desires to hold on to prewar boundaries. Russia's inaction during and consequent responsibility for the failure of the Warsaw uprising hammered more nails into the coffin of Polish-Soviet cooperation. In the meantime, the fate of Poland had lost much of its real importance to the United States and Great Britain, who, of course, cared mostly about winning their global war against Germany and Japan, and the question of democracy in Poland seemed secondary. Although Churchill recognized that the USSR sought permanent control over Eastern Europe, the Allies continued to think in terms of appeasing the USSR with only *some* territorial changes.

But for Russia, minor changes were no longer enough. As soon as the Soviet army entered Lublin, the first Polish city they liberated from the Germans, a Polish Committee of National Liberation was established under Soviet tutelage. Under the leadership of the Soviet puppet Boleslaw Bierut, this committee, composed almost exclusively of Polish Communists, became the true Polish government, as far as the Soviets were concerned. Since the Soviet Union was adamant about this, the Western powers soon stopped trying to obtain Soviet cooperation with the Polish government-in-exile in London, and the Allied recognition of the Bierut government was more a question of time than of principle. The reality, of course, was that the eastern frontiers of Eastern Europe were being redrawn by the Red Army as it marched toward the west.

The Soviet designs on Eastern Europe were clearly stated for the first time at a meeting between Churchill and Stalin in Moscow in

Territorial Changes after World War II

TERRITORIAL CHANGES
AFTER WORLD WAR II

British zone
French zone
American zone
Soviet zone

Incorporated by Poland
Incorporated by the Soviet Union

Boundaries of areas
incorporated by other
states during or after
the war

0   100   200   MILES

NORTH SEA
DENMARK
SWEDEN
BALTIC SEA
NETHERLANDS
GERMANY
Berlin
Elbe
ODER
Danzig
Vistula
Warsaw
POLAND
Wrocław
Cracow
Lublin
LITHUANIAN
SOVIET
REPUBLIC
Kaunas
Vilna
S O V I E T   U N I O N
LUX.
FRANCE
SWITZERLAND
Prague
CZECHOSLOVAKIA
Bratislava
Vienna
AUSTRIA
Danube
HUNGARY
Zagreb
Belgrade
YUGOSLAVIA
Danube
SUB-CARPATHO
RUTHENIA
formerly Czechoslovak
Czernowitz
BESSARABIA and N. BUKOVINA
formerly Rumanian
Cluj
RUMANIA
Bucharest
Danube
BLACK SEA

October 1944. Although Churchill arrived with the intention of establishing spheres of political influence, he was not expressly empowered by the President of the United States to negotiate for their establishment on behalf of the United States. However, such niceties never really bothered either Churchill or Stalin. In quick negotiations the two leaders "divided" Europe, and the extent of Soviet "influence" over the Eastern European states was made explicit: the USSR would get 90 percent of Romania, 75 percent of Bulgaria and of Hungary; the British shared Yugoslavia with the Soviets 50–50. The fates of Poland and Czechoslovakia were not discussed in this context, but Churchill's accession to the recognition of Bierut and the "Lublin Poles" clearly implied Poland too would be in the Soviet sphere.

It is true that neither Churchill nor Roosevelt envisioned that these spheres of influence would become the basis for the Soviet occupation and total control of the region as Stalin had planned. Was this naiveté? Perhaps. But both Western leaders had great hopes for continued cooperation with the Soviets, and in this context some concessions were considered essential, and Roosevelt believed that the establishment of the United Nations would preclude any problems that would threaten peace. Thinking that Soviet cooperation was still vital to victory against Germany and Japan, Churchill and Roosevelt regarded the solutions arrived at in Moscow as perhaps creating only "minor" problem areas. And it was felt that the "Big Three" could arrive at better solutions at the upcoming meeting at Yalta, a Russian town on the Black Sea.

But the Yalta meeting of February 4–12, 1945, took place in an atmosphere of tension and fear. It was by then apparent that the USSR would not be content with mere "influence" over Eastern Europe; in fact, it was feared by many that Stalin would make the region an integral part of the USSR by incorporating the states as "Socialist Republics" in the Soviet empire. To this day we do not know why Stalin did not ever actually do this, but it is clear that he viewed "influence" as meaning his "right" to determine both the form of the government and the persons to place in power in the newly "liberated" countries. Moreover, the Western Allies believed they had little or no influence in the region; Soviet forces had already occupied most of the states in question, and the end of the war in Europe was less than three months away.

The Yalta meeting is regarded as a milestone in Eastern European history. But in reality it simply confirmed Soviet influence and territorial-strategic, as well as political, supremacy in the region. Although events have not worked out exactly as the USSR wished—as so often happens in life—the basic truth of the matter was that the USSR had the power by 1945 to enforce its own designs in Eastern Europe, and the Western leaders went to Yalta simply to codify, sign away, and agree or accede to Soviet wishes.

The USSR remained adamant in its territorial demands on Poland, but it was willing to allow some members of the Polish government-in-exile in London to join the Lublin government and promised "free and unfettered" elections. Of course, it was up to the USSR to name the date of such elections and, most important, to define what type of elections were "free and unfettered." When the democratic Polish leaders returned to Poland from London, many were immediately arrested and shipped to Moscow, and only a few, notably Stanislaw Mikolajczyk, were included in the Bierut government, mostly in unimportant positions. The West could do little but swallow hard and accept the fact of Soviet influence and Communist rule in Poland. At the Potsdam Conference in August 1945 Poland was given, in return for its concessions to the USSR in the east, all the German territory east of the Oder-Neisse line; these lands were to be "administered by the Polish state." The fact that Poland had already become part of the Soviet sphere had to be accepted by the West.

Nothing much could be settled at the Potsdam Conference about the question of a permanent peace treaty with Germany. Stalin did not push for the immediate dismemberment of Germany. He was content with having separate "zones of occupation" run by each of the Allies; the Western statesmen did not realize how permanent these zones would become. His agreement that each country's German reparations were to be extracted from the zone that it occupied meant that only the eastern part of Germany could be stripped by the Soviets.

By the end of the Potsdam meeting, the Communization—some called it, much later, satellization—of Eastern Europe was nearly complete. The states of Poland, Romania, Bulgaria, Yugoslavia, and Albania were to be replaced with republics led by Communists such as Boleslaw Bierut in Poland, Petru Groza in Romania, Georgi Dimitrov in Bulgaria, Josip Broz (Tito) in Yugoslavia, and Enver Hoxha in Albania. Only Hungary and Czechoslovakia remained relatively democratic for a couple of years.

One could ask why the USSR waited until 1947–1948 to impose Communism on Hungary and Czechoslovakia and why these two countries remained relative democracies in the midst of Communist-controlled neighbor states? Part of the answer lay in the strengths and weaknesses of the Communist movements in different parts of the area, and another lay in the international situation.

Support for the Communists was weak throughout the region; only in Czechoslovakia and—during a part of the interwar years—in Bulgaria and Yugoslavia, was the Communist party legal. The Communist International, established in Moscow in 1919 and used as the coordinating body of all Communist movements, was used by the Soviet leadership cynically and brutally to attain its own ends. Soviet policy, in fact, had little to offer the people of Eastern Europe. The supporters of domestic post–World War II Communist power in the region came from diverse backgrounds, but they generally tended to fall into one of the following categories:

1. *The industrial proletariat.* The appeal of Communism was strongest among those who were expected to be the "true" wielders of power under this system—the budding industrial proletariat. Among the proletariat, however, one could find significant syndicalist and Fascist support as well, and the Communists were viewed with suspicion by many a skilled worker, who recognized that the proletariat was not truly the ruling class in the USSR.

2. *Muscovite Communists.* Except in Yugoslavia, the leadership of the Eastern European Communist parties fell directly into the hands of Communist leaders who were officers in the Red Army or agents of the Soviet secret police, the dreaded NKVD. Although originally from the region of Eastern Europe, they became devoted Communists and most of them spent the interwar and war years in Moscow, isolated from the membership of their own party. Eager to please their Soviet masters, specifically Stalin, most of these Muscovites had little or no understanding of the actual conditions of the nation over which they were to rule and followed the Soviet example blindly. They survived the terrible purges of 1934–1938 in Moscow and were anxious to survive as the leaders of their own realm.

3. *"Native" Communists.* The "native" wing of the Eastern European Communist parties consisted generally of Communists who had fought the Germans in parts of their state actually under German control. These Communists welcomed the Soviet occupation or liberation. Many had been freed from German jails by the Red Army or led the partisan movement, as Tito had, and hoped to be at least equals of their Muscovite comrades who just returned home from the "land of socialism."

4. *Jews.* Many of the Jews who were liberated by the Soviet army or were saved just in time from the concentration camps and extermination by the armies of the USSR *and* decided to remain in Eastern Europe after World War II supported the Communist takeovers, expecting that "paradise on earth" could be established. Some idealistic—and naive—non-Jewish intellectuals and left-wing Socialists also hoped that the Communist experiment would end injustice and prejudice.

5. *Former Fascists.* Some former Fascists were recruited into the lower levels of the Communist party in order to increase the party's small membership. They frequently became members after being threatened with punishment for their Fascist involvement.

The strength of the Communist party varied from country to country at the end of the war. In Poland, Hungary, and Romania, where the Communist party was illegal before World War II, membership was minuscule. In Poland probably no more than 20,000–25,000 party members were registered, out of a population of some 25 million people. In Hungary, the party was even smaller: when the first democratic government was established in 1944, there were probably no more than 3,000 Communists out of a population of 10 million. In Romania Communist party membership at the time of the country's switch from the Axis to the Allied side in 1944 was estimated at no more than 1,000–2,000.

However, in Czechoslovakia, Bulgaria, and Yugoslavia a different pattern prevailed. For most of the interwar era, Czechoslovakia's Communist party was legal and its membership some 80,000 strong. It enjoyed equal political rights with other participants in the political arena. The Bulgarian Communist party was also relatively vigorous throughout much of the interwar period; even if it could not compete with the enormously powerful and popular Peasant party, its 30,000 membership was respectable by Eastern European standards. The Yugoslav party emerged largely from the victorious partisan movement and army led by Tito. The Serbs dominated this movement both before and during the war; Croatian nationalism attracted many Croats to the frail "independence" of Ante Pavelic's puppet state. At any rate, Yugoslov Communist party membership can best be estimated at 12,000 in 1941. Its numbers rose rapidly after Germany invaded Russia, as Tito moved toward nationalism and into active opposition to the Nazis. By the end of the war Tito's partisan army was estimated at anywhere between 200,000 and 750,000 people, of whom about 100,000 were Communists.

Although the Communist takeovers could not be considered popular acts, we must accept the fact that there was *some* genuine attraction to the theory—if not the practice—of the Soviet-type Communist political system. First, as far as *visible* proof was concerned, the Communist USSR had in fact won the war; a bankrupt political system, it was thought, could not have been so successful. Second, capitalism—except in Czechoslovakia—did not appear to have solved the problems of Eastern Europe in the interwar period. It certainly did not succeed in alleviating the poverty of the region, and many people were willing to try "something else," even Communism. Third, the Communists propagated a messianic myth of salvation and earthly paradise. Even intellectuals, who should have known better, fell for their "heaven on earth" promises without considering the USSR's record in handling its own problems. And finally, many Eastern Europeans expected that the Communism to be practiced in Eastern Europe would be different from the Russian variety. "After all," said one prominent Hungarian Communist, "we were more European than the Russians, and we certainly would not have the stupid Asiatic type of leadership that was so typical of Communist practice in the USSR." Needless to say, history was to prove such expectations totally wrong, especially during the early years of Communist power.

But even if some people were attracted to the ideals of Communism, the Communist regimes of Eastern Europe clearly came to power through the relentless pressure of the Red Army, exercised in conjunction with the security forces of the NKVD and its local subsidiary national organizations. Instituting land reform, subdividing large estates and thus liquidating the landed gentry, and nationalizing banks and large-scale industries, the Communists gained some popular support, especially among the urban poor, the impoverished peasants, and the disaffected middle classes and intelligentsia. Through reform as the carrot and the use of terror as the stick, the Communists, backed by the omnipresent NKVD and the Red Army, crushed all political opposition and assumed control over the political life in each country in the region.

The length of time during which the assumption of power took place varied. In Poland the arrest of members of the prewar government, who had returned from London to join the Lublin Poles, and their subsequent trial by the Russians, guaranteed complete control of the political spectrum by the USSR and its henchmen. Even though Stanislaw Mikolajczyk, the outspoken second deputy minister of agriculture and the leader of the strong Peasant party, tried valiantly during the ensuing two years to halt the process, near-total Communist control was established by the fall of 1945. In Romania, although the monarchy officially existed until 1947, real power was in the hands of the Communists by April 1945. In Bulgaria, through the coercive power of the Ministry of the Interior, the Communists systematically eliminated their "enemies" by early March 1945 and began a purge of the army. A year and a half later, Bulgaria was under total Communist control. In Yugoslavia the Communists had been the dominant force by the end of the war. In the first postwar elections held in November 1945, there was typically a single slate presented to the voters. And East Germany was under occupation by the Red Army.

In Czechoslovakia there had been some genuine support for the USSR, as well as some pro-Communist and pro-Russian sympathies among the population. The large and legal Communist party, the wartime excesses of Slovakia's Fascists, and the fact that the USSR did not participate in the dismantling of the Czechoslovak state in Munich in 1938 but had "offered" to come to its assistance, even though it had not actually done so—all of these factors assisted the transfer of power to Soviet-style Communism. In the first free postwar election, in 1946, the Communists won fully 38 percent of the vote. Klement Gottwald, the Communist Party leader, became the prime minister in a coalition government. Although the country was maintained as a genuinely democratic entity in 1945–1948, by 1947 Stalin began to urge the consolidation of all power in Communist hands. Hence in February 1948 the Communist Party provoked a governmental crisis that ended in a de facto political coup in which all non-Communists were expelled from the coalition. In June 1948 President Benes was forced to resign, and Jan Masaryk, his pro-Western foreign minister, died when he either jumped or was thrown out of the window of his office in Hradcany Castle. Czechoslovakia became a Communist state.

The assumption of power by the Communists followed a somewhat different path in Hungary. Hungarian hostility toward Russia—largely due to Russia's part in crushing the Hungarian revolution in 1848–1849 and to the dubious "liberation" of the country by brutal front-line Soviet Red Army troops—was obvious and could be expected by the leaders of the USSR. And Hungary's hostility toward Communism—resulting at least in part from Bela Kun's harsh policies during the Hungarian Soviet Republic of 1919—was clearly evident in the free elections of 1945. Contrary to Soviet expectations, the Communist party received only 17 percent of the vote, while the reform-populist Smallholders' party won 57 percent. But there was never any doubt that the USSR had already determined in 1945 that a Communist regime had to be established. Between 1946 and 1948 parliamentary maneuvering established a "leftist bloc," and the NKVD-supported secret police began to liquidate the "opponents of democracy." Yet, in spite of the terror used by the Soviet-dominated and supervised police, the "salami tactics" used to slice up the opposition forces, and illegal ballot-box stuffing, the Communist party gained little popular support. Even in 1947 the Communists polled only 22 percent of the vote.

By this time, though, Moscow was determined to move toward complete control. Following a September 1947 directive from Moscow, the Hungarian democratic opposition was destroyed, one slice at a time. A People's Front, made up of the leftist parties, assumed power in the name of all "progressive" forces, masking the reality of total Communist power. By mid-1948—contrary to the expectations of many Hungarian and Czech intellectuals that their two states could be bridges between the capitalist West and the Communist East for at least a couple of decades—all of Eastern Europe had slid behind the Iron Curtain. The policies of these states were now "coordinated" and dictated by the Communist Information Bureau, established in September 1947 and headquartered in Moscow. The capital of Russia became the place where all Eastern European policies were set for many years to come.

STALINISM: 1948–1953

During the years that followed, the Communist states established policies that were closely patterned on those of the "shining example of the guiding light of socialism," the USSR. The new regimes were called "people's democracies," in order to show the world that they were not yet ready to become "socialist" states. Ideologically, this was to be a transitory period between Western-style democracy and the Soviet type of rule.

By inferring that socialism had already been accomplished in the USSR and was just being built in Eastern Europe, Marxist-Leninist theory and practices soon hinged local developments to the "superior" role of the USSR, from which the guiding principles of all developments for the future had to be taken. Only in one country, Yugoslavia, would a nationally specific road to development be advocated—rather than the one dictated by the USSR. We shall say more about this case below.

The Communists established certain policies throughout the region: the institution of terror, forced collectivization, forced industrialization and urbanization, and the rapid development of armed forces— in short, all the policies practiced in the Soviet Union. Eastern Europeans were also required to praise all things Russian and to accord near-divine status to Stalin. Although terror began under Soviet direction, local thugs were readily available to do the bidding of their Communist masters. First, the Communists expelled all of their political opponents from positions of power and influence. Then members of "hostile" forces were dragged off to prisons, concentration camps, and appalling work camps. Many innocent families—judged to be opponents of the new regimes or merely remnants of the former ruling classes—were forced to leave the cities and work as hired hands in miserable villages, all in the name of "re-education" for the new glorious society—and in order to free their formerly elegant apartments for the new rulers of the land.

The Purges

By 1951 there were very few non-Communist opponents of the new order left against whom terror could be exercised, and, true to Soviet form, the Communists now turned on themselves. The "Muscovite" leaders, who had been trusted by the Soviets far more than the "natives" had, began mass purges of their parties. In country after country the "native" leaders—for example, Laszlo Rajk in Hungary, Wladyslaw Gomulka in Poland, Traicho Kostov in Bulgaria, or Rudolf

Slanski in Czechoslovakia, along with many others—were expelled
from their parties and then killed, including Rajk, Kostov, and Slanski.
Were these purges of 1948–1952 anti-Semitic, as some theorists suggest,
backed by the close connection many of these trials had to the clearly
anti-Semitic "Doctors' Plot" of 1952–1953 in the USSR? It is possible,
but in fact many of the Stalinist leaders, as well as those who were
purged, were Jewish. In the most extreme case, the very top leadership
of the Hungarian Communist party was composed only of Muscovite
Communists with Jewish backgrounds, a fact many Hungarians would
recall in 1956.

The purges went beyond the mere exorcism of higher party ranks.
Table 4.1 suggests their extent and shows that, on the average, at
least 25 percent of all party members were expelled. The purges were
most violent in Hungary and Czechoslovakia, the two countries that
were the most recent converts to Communism. The least violent
purges—with the fewest people murdered—occurred in Poland and
the Balkan states. It was as if the Czechoslovak and Hungarian Communist leaders wished to show to Moscow that they were "as good and
trustworthy," if not even better, Communists than their brethren in
the longer-established Communist states. The Hungarian Communist
leader, Matyas Rakosi, "affectionately" referred to by the population
as "Skin-Hair" because of his bald head, took great pains to identify
himself as the "best student of Comrade Stalin." Few would dispute
his claim.

Both a cause and an effect of the purges was the desire of the
Communist party to be supreme in every area of life. Trade unions,
other political parties, labor organizations, administrative bureaucracies, the army, the churches, and the police were purged of their
leadership in very quick succession. These institutions came under
the direct control of the Communist party and "articulation of indepen-

---

Table 4.1   Party Membership and Purges in Eastern Europe

	Party membership, 1945 (unless otherwise indicated)	Party membership before the purges, 1949–1950	Number purged
Bulgaria	25,000(Sept. 1944)	2,000,000	90,000
Czechoslovakia	712,776	2,311,066	550,000
East Germany	511,000(Feb. 1946)	1,750,000	300,000
Hungary	150,000	1,200,000	200,000
Poland	235,000	1,368,873	370,000
Romania	217,000	937,846	200,000
Yugoslavia	141,066	779,382	150,000

Recollecting Stalinism in Eastern Europe

"Middle Ages?"   "Of course, I remember them well!"

Dikobraz (Prague)

dent interest" was made impossible. The Communist party now ruled
the land under the effective dictatorship of a few Muscovite dictators.
Their only claim to control was that Moscow and the Red Army, the
NKVD, and the local secret police backed them unconditionally.

It is essential to note, however, that not only the Communist party
was purged in 1948–1953. A terror unprecedented in the history of
the region gripped entire nations. Rich peasants and barely subsisting
ones, skilled workers and unskilled, industrial laborers, intellectuals,
and students—all felt the wave of terror. Midnight knocks on bolted
doors and mass arrests, occurring both purposefully and randomly,
were the rule of the new Communist order. Former enemies and
former allies were treated alike. By the exercise of such random and
widespread terror they made opposition to the regime an impossibility;
by the use of ever-present informers, they collected information on
everyone. To a very large extent they succeeded in creating a society
in which betrayal and spying on friends and adversaries, family members and strangers alike had become accepted and indeed rewarded
forms of existence—and the *modus operandi* of most of the citizenry.
The sad legacy of those days can still be felt in Eastern Europe.

Collectivization

In addition to the use of terror, one of the first priorities of the
Communists after 1948 was the introduction of collectivization.
Throughout Eastern Europe, the Communists initially harnessed a

degree of popular peasant support by insisting on land reform. Everywhere in the region, but especially in Poland and Hungary, where
large and medium-sized estates were typical before the war, these
reforms were significant. Generally, all estates with more than 20–50
hectares of agricultural land were subdivided among the landless and
those who just had small plots. The results of these land reforms varied.
In Poland and Hungary they led to the division of lands into uneconom-
ical small farms. And even in these countries, as well as in all the
other states in the region, a large number of peasants still who had
little or no land and could not be assured of a decent existence.

Once Communist power was consolidated, widespread collectivization of agricultural activities began. Reasoning that the Soviet example
had to be followed, collectivization was launched everywhere in the
region in 1948–1949, and the process reached its height in 1950. The
Communist states used a variety of measures to coerce the peasants
into collective farms, including forced deliveries—really confiscations
of agricultural goods—heavy and punitive taxes on peasants who pre-
ferred to till their own lands, and police terror. Teams of urban "activists" and "socializers" roamed the countryside, agitating, bullying, and,
where possible, pitting the landless against the better-off peasants. Violence, police terror, beatings, the punishment of *kulaks*—people
branded as rich peasants—by banishment, arrest, or physical violence
were common in order to accomplish the task of collectivization.

It was obvious that such pressures were working; their success is
shown in Table 4.2 below. Although some collective farms were indeed
founded voluntarily by landless poor peasants or those who possessed
only a few acres, most peasants in the region, except the Bulgarians,
resisted the pressure for collectivization. They slaughtered their animals rather than taking them to the collectives, and they refused to
plant more than was absolutely necessary. Consequently, within a few
years food shortages were rife throughout Eastern Europe. Most significantly, the exploitation of the countryside resulted in the mass migration of the peasants and the accompanying rapid growth of urban

Table 4.2   Percent of Collectivized Arable Land

	1950	1953
Bulgaria	44%	62%
Czechoslovakia	25	48
East Germany	1	8
Hungary	19	37
Poland	12	17
Romania	12	21
Yugoslavia	18	24

centers. The peasants simply decided to become industrial workers rather than join the hated collectives and state farms. Thus forced collectivization indirectly contributed to the accomplishment of the third major goal of the regime—namely, industrialization and urbanization.

Industrialization and Urbanization

The Communist-induced process of industrialization always places great stress on the increasing of industrial growth rates, a process that is accomplished most easily by the continuous expansion of a cheap labor force. As long as there is an abundant and continuously expanding labor force available, Communist growth rates can register astounding increases. Cheap labor was readily available in the villages of Eastern Europe. All that these regimes had to do was harness the workers by making agrarian work unattractive and urban industrial labor seem like the "wave of the future." Exactly this kind of policy moved peasants en masse to enter the urban industrial labor force—some 400,000 in Bulgaria, 600,000 in Czechoslovakia, 750,000 in Hungary, nearly 2 million in Poland, 850,000 in Romania, and nearly 500,000 in Yugoslavia—in 1949–1953. Having lost their livelihood in the villages and answering the need to adapt to new living conditions and new occupations, these people were misplaced and were often unable to adjust quickly to urban life. They became people of a special kind—no longer peasants and not yet urban proletariat. As the Polish poet Adam Wazyk wrote in the 1950s, they were a people who

> With a storehouse of curses with a little feather pillow,
> a distrusting soul—wrenched from the bonds
> half-awake and half-mad,
> silent in words, singing snatches of songs—
> [were] suddenly thrust out of medieval darkness.
> A migrating mass . . . howling from boredom in December
> evenings. . . .

Whatever its social costs, the impact of the increase in labor activity on the industrial development of the Eastern European states was incalculable. In most countries industrial capacity and output doubled within only a few years. The industrialization effort was aimed to develop the heavy industry of the Communist states at a breakneck speed. The "commanding heights of industry" were emphasized, and the consumer and light industrial sectors received little or no attention. Terror was used here as well, and "labor discipline" was strictly enforced. A Stakhanovite movement, borrowed from the USSR, was implemented: people were forced to produce more and more, and their norms or quotas of work were increased continually. As a result, the early enthusiasm for creating modern industrial states out of economically backward nations evaporated under the heavy bonds of coercion by 1953–1954.

Some observers have stated that from the very beginning the Communist system was imposed on Eastern Europe without any popular support. But many intellectuals and members of the poorer segments of the population, both in the urban and the rural spheres, welcomed the modernization drive, especially at first. They were hoping to bring their countries and their lifestyles up to the level of industrialization and modernity that characterized many Western states, which were clearly ahead of the states of Eastern Europe by some fifty years. But that enthusiasm—and consequently support for the Communist cause—evaporated rapidly, as it became clear that the USSR was simply stripping these countries of their resources and exploiting them for its own purposes. It became obvious that only terror and coercion could ensure the collectivization and industrialization drives deemed essential by the party.

The reality of Communist rule lay in the creation of a new and exceedingly privileged elite backed by brutal secret police forces. The new elites, just like the old ones had done, lived in secluded neighborhoods, protected by barricades, armed guards, and police dogs—a "new class," as Yugoslav Communist Milovan Djilas called it. The Communist government's legitimacy—based on its claim to hold the "key to historic developments in their sole possession of the knowledge of Marxist ideology"—vanished as people everywhere realized that the sole basis of the regime's rule lay in its ability to use force and coercion. By the time Stalin died, on March 5, 1953, the ideological and economic bases of Communist rule were severely eroded, and riots, revolts, and revolutions began to be characteristic of social processes gone haywire.

The Break with Yugoslavia

We would be remiss if we failed to mention briefly the emergence of a different pattern of rule in the region—in Yugoslavia. Following the Communists' assumption of power in that country, a strongly centralized, Soviet-type system was established, and Tito embarked on a highly personalized rule based on the Stalinist model. In fact, Yugoslavia was, if possible, more Stalinist during the first few years of the postwar era than was the USSR itself. By 1948, however, Soviet meddling in Yugoslavia's internal affairs became so obvious that Tito and the Yugoslav leadership protested strongly to Moscow. Stalin paid no heed but decided to force Tito to accept the supremacy of the USSR. The dispute led to an open break with the USSR, but it also had more

far-reaching consequences. Slowly Yugoslavia altered its internal policies as well, moving closer to a market economy and to granting rights
of self-management to selected segments of society. While we shall
discuss this in more detail later in this chapter, suffice it to say that
in 1948–1953 Yugoslavia developed an alternative model of socialist
development and thereby posed a challenge to the USSR, which insisted that it practiced the only valid model of Communism.

THE THAW: 1953–1956

Stalin's death and the subsequent rise of Nikita Khrushchev to
power led to readjustments in Eastern Europe. The period of 1953–
1956 became known as the "Thaw" after Russian writer Ilya Ehrenburg's "liberalizing" novel of the same name was published in the
Soviet Union. Taking their cue from Khrushchev, the Eastern European politicians of this brief era also attempted to liberalize their regimes, to embark on a "new course," and to remove some elements
of the Stalinist legacy. The greatest and most significant changes initiated by the Communist parties were attempted in Hungary and Poland, and the least significant took place in Albania, Bulgaria, and Romania. Czechoslovakia and East Germany stood somewhere in the middle
of the spectrum, while Yugoslavia, continued on its separate course
of development in both the domestic and the external political spheres.

The first and most significant step that had to be taken was the
curbing of the power of the omnipresent secret police. Both in the
USSR and in Eastern Europe, this dreaded organization had become
the major tool of control not merely over a frightened and terrorized
population but over the Communist parties themselves. The secret
police did the bidding of the local dictators without question, killing
off their real or suspected "enemies" and jailing and torturing all potential opponents of the regime.

It was not enough to fear the dictator. The secret police also ensured that he was "loved" by the population, using all the available
tools of terror and socialization propaganda. The ubiquitous display
of posters of the "great, exalted leaders" reached heights that even
Hitler never practiced; the Soviet phrase "Stalin is the peace of the
world . . . the wisest of all men" was used in Eastern Europe in reference to his regional counterparts. In fact, when the "new course"
chipped away at the power of the secret police, it simultaneously reduced the power and prestige of these leaders. Eventually the process
led to the downfall of these personal idols in many of the Eastern
European states.

The economic mismanagement of the entire area also had to be
overcome. The years of forced industrialization and the miserable

treatment accorded to agriculture finally culminated in bread riots, dissatisfaction, and rapidly declining growth rates of the region's economies. A "new course" based on less intensive and more extensive methods of development, less on coercion and more on rewards, had to be initiated. Taking its cue from Georgi Malenkov, Stalin's first successor, who initiated the more liberal, consumer-oriented New Course in the USSR shortly after Stalin's death, the new Moscow power elite insisted that the Eastern European leadership once again follow the Soviet example. The major idea of the Soviet-initiated New Course was to offer economic concessions while at the same time maintaining political power in the hands of the party. Many of the regimes did in fact begin to adopt economic reforms and abandoned the previous pattern of forced heavy industrialization. In East Germany, Bulgaria, Romania, and Czechoslovakia the piecemeal introduction of economic reforms caused no great dislocations. Popular support of the respective regimes of these countries increased, while political control remained firmly in the hands of the leadership.

But the New Course resulted in major dislocations in Poland and Hungary. In Hungary Imre Nagy—originally a Muscovite Communist who had openly opposed rapid collectivization and advocated a "go-slow" approach in 1948–1949 and was then kept outside the immediate ruling elite of the party—was supported by Malenkov. He became prime minister in June 1953, when Matyas Rakosi, the "best disciple of Stalin," was severely reprimanded by the Soviet Politburo for being a too dreaded, all too faithful student of the late dictator's methods. Nagy introduced a series of reforms, abolishing forced collectivization and forced deliveries of impossible quantities of produce, easing the burden on the population as a whole, and starting to transfer industry to a more sound and more limited basis. He also attempted to "renew" the Communist party as an instrument of national unity, one that would fit the circumstances of Hungary and not merely replicate those of the USSR. While Nagy closely followed Malenkov's New Course, especially in limiting the power of the secret police and urging greater tolerance, his own power base was severely curbed by the continued presence and power of hard-line Muscovite Communists—such as Rakosi, Erno Gero, and Mihaly Farkas—in the Hungarian Politburo. Ultimately, by January 1955, Rakosi and his supporters counterattacked. They successfully excluded Nagy from the Politburo, and through scarcely disguised political maneuverings, returned to their disastrous Stalinist course. Heedless of Khrushchev's anti-Stalin speech in February 1956 and the resulting de-Stalinization in the USSR, Rakosi and his colleagues clung to power until they were swept away by an uprising of the entire Hungarian nation against Soviet-style Communism on October 23, 1956.

The revolt brought Imre Nagy back to power with a "national

De-Stalinization

Literarni noviny (Prague)

Communist" regime that moved rapidly toward greater democracy. As the power of the Communist party dissipated and was repudiated by the nation as a whole, the Soviet leadership decided to act; its control of its Hungarian satellite was becoming questionable. On November 4, 1956, an overwhelming Red Army force destroyed the first democratic, multiparty government Hungary had possessed since 1947 and put in power Janos Kadar, whom the Soviets considered to be a reliable supporter of theirs. Although Hungarian resistance, led by the working class, continued well into 1957, it was eventually eliminated by the KGB and Hungarian police units. National Communism and experimentation with a specifically national road to development ended with the death of some 2,000–4,000 Hungarians in the streets of Budapest. Truly the events of 1956 were a national tragedy.

The changes that were made in Poland were far more important than they were elsewhere in the region, though they lacked the drama of the Hungarian episode. Initially, Poland's New Course was to be limited to economic experimentation and liberalization, but, as in Hungary, it soon began to take on political overtones as well. And again the brutal methods of the secret police precipitated the effort to reestablish the rule of the party over the police. Soon Wladyslaw Gomulka, a "native" Communist who, like Nagy in Hungary, favored the end of collectivization, was released from years of house arrest. But unlike in Hungary, the party's internal machinery and top leadership continued to permit gradual relaxation throughout 1955, and the Muscovites slowly yielded power to the emerging, moderate "nativist" wing of the Polish party.

The Twentieth Congress of the Communist Party of the Soviet Union (CPSU) and Khrushchev's de-Stalinization speech in February 1956 gave further impetus for the rise of small, independent discussion clubs and organizations, which began to flourish. Since the power of the secret police had been seriously curbed, these clubs succeeded in promoting a national debate on the "renewal" of the party and on other issues important for the nation as a whole. The "Polish way of socialism"—as contrasted with Stalin's, or the Soviet, road—appeared to become an acceptable alternative, and Polish anti-Semitism, directed against such figures of the former Stalinist elite as Jakob Berman and Edward Ochab, helped to fan the fires of Polish nationalism. The Muscovite dictator Boleslaw Bierut died in March 1956; amnesty for political prisoners was then declared, and Berman was dismissed a few months later. The party leadership, nonetheless, was still in the hands of forces that seemed to favor Moscow over a national Communist leader.

In late June 1956 the workers of the city of Poznan went on strike, and after two days the military was ordered to fire on the strikers. The military itself refused to fire on them and a few even joined the strikers. Though the strike was put down by the use of the security forces, the Soviet leadership interpreted it as the beginning of a threat to the socialist system and pushed the Polish leaders to try to suppress such occurrences. The "separate roads to socialism" doctrine had limitations, the Soviet leaders warned, and "nationalism" (in fact, independence from the USSR) would not be tolerated. After much internal debate between the Polish "soft-" and "hard"-liners, a compromise promised further democratization. However, by July both sides supported the rehabilitation of Wladyslaw Gomulka as a trusted comrade and his inclusion in the ruling Politburo. But the leadership still seemed unable to do anything definitive. By early October 1956 the discontent over the continuing debate about Gomulka's future role, the visible presence of Soviet forces, and the power of the Soviet overlord, Marshal Rokossowsky, came to a head. The Soviet leaders—along with the Polish hard-liners—wanted a pro-Moscow coup after the Gomulka faction won control over the Politburo, but their efforts were thwarted; the Polish army remained loyal to Polish, not Soviet, command.

The Soviet Union ordered its troops to advance toward Warsaw on October 19, 1956, at the same time that a top-level delegation from the Soviet Politburo, including Khrushchev, arrived uninvited in Warsaw. There, however, the Soviet leaders encountered a relatively united Polish Politburo, which now included Gomulka, who was nominated against Soviet wishes as the first secretary of the Polish party. The Soviets realized that their armies would face a Polish army loyal to Polish nationalism and that Gomulka was the candidate of the entire nation and would thus be backed by the people. They also learned that Polish nationalism could be controlled by Gomulka *only* if there was no Soviet intervention. On October 22, 1956, Khrushchev gave in. On the eve of the Hungarian revolution that was crushed so fiercely a mere twelve days later, Poland succeeded in attaining a leadership that was both nationalist and Communist. This regime was both accepted by the people and supported by Khrushchev. It would give the lands back to the peasants, and it still vowed to follow Communist industrial policies. The new regime could thus establish cordial relations with the Catholic church but would remain Marxist in ideology. National communism would be accepted in Poland but would not provide an intolerable challenge to Moscow's authority.

EVOLUTION, REFORM, AND THE LIMITS OF CHANGE: SINCE 1956

The period that began with the suppression of the Hungarian revolution concluded in the imposition of martial law in Poland nearly twenty-five years later. It is a distinct period, in spite of the traumatic events of the Prague Spring of 1968 and the formation of the Solidarity movement in Poland. Although differences could be found in the evolution of each country, several trends existed simultaneously in all of these states. When the Soviet forces entered Budapest in 1956, they actually served notice to the satellite states about the limits of their external and internal freedom. This included Soviet determination not to permit any of the Communist states in the region to achieve independence or to flirt with Western-type, multiparty democracy. At the same time, when the Soviets refrained from invading Poland that year, they also indicated that they were willing to allow a certain amount of domestic freedom, provided that such freedom did not lead to the emergence of independent, non-Communist elements in political life. The Soviet invasion of Czechoslovakia in 1968 and the imposition of martial law in Poland in 1981 underscored these policies dramatically.

The region as a whole, adopted a unified policy toward collectivization, decided on in Moscow in late 1957 and implemented by every state except Poland between 1959 and 1961. Using less brutal tactics than before but pointing out the inevitability of collectivization to all those who opposed it—and using force, where necessary, against the rural population—the second collectivization drive was accomplished within two years, and 90–95 percent of all arable lands were taken over by the collectives. Aside from Yugoslavia, only Poland— due to its large number of farmers, the small size of their lots, the enormous resistance of the peasants and of Gomulka—escaped collectivization. However, Poland would pay a heavy price for the often unsound agrarian policies that accompanied Gomulka's rule.

In the other states, except Bulgaria, the newly collectivized peasantry tended to be far less productive than they had been before.
Sullen populations, inadequate capital, the underutilization of fertiliz-
ers, and low labor productivity rendered the situation similar to the
failed policies of central planning. Only many years later, when the
governments of the region began to offer incentives and poured capital
into agricultural production did the collectives begin to be successful.
The bases of the large-scale commercial type of farming, employing
production systems borrowed from the United States, brought the parcels under the cultivation of large, unified farms. Hungary and East
Germany were to lead the way; but these accomplishments did not
occur until the 1970s. Nevertheless, a "doctrinal" goal of the regimes—
bringing the peasants under party control—was certainly accomplished
by collectivization.

In the 1960s after a few years during which stagnation characterized the regional economies, the modernization and industrialization
processes were resumed relentlessly everywhere in Eastern Europe.
As relations with the West improved somewhat and as more and more
produce from Eastern Europe could be exported to the West, the
economic imperatives of balanced growth replaced the heavy-indus-
trial model of development practiced earlier. Debates concerning the
virtues of a strong, centralized, planned, economic system on the one
hand and a market-oriented, decentralized economy on the other
abounded throughout the last two decades. The choice, however, was
not dictated by Moscow but by the national leaderships; policies of
decentralization were followed in Hungary and Yugoslavia—and were
introduced in Czechoslovakia in 1967–1969 and in Poland in 1980–
1981. The centralized model was followed in the rest of the states.
Regardless of the model they chose, some states—notably Hungary
and East Germany—achieved major economic progress and created
relatively balanced economies with major modernization programs;
the other states were less successful. In fact, at times some of the
states—Czechoslovakia in 1962–1968 and Poland in 1981–1982, for
instance—failed to show any growth at all. In some of the states the
standard of living has visibly improved and the population of these
states have seemed generally satisfied with their economic lot. In other
states, such as Romania and Poland, food shortages have been commonplace and general dissatisfaction has become ubiquitous.

Everywhere in Eastern Europe the modernization process involved continued urbanization; ever-larger numbers of former peasants
moved to the cities and newly constructed towns. Throughout the
region agriculture, once the dominant sector of the economy, lost out
to industry. The service sector also began to expand. Social services, which were once considered the great achievement of the Communist regimes—free medical care, cheap food, cheap transportation,

pensions, and other benefits—became *expected* and, until the 1970s, were generally well provided. But toward the end of the 1970s—as the Eastern European states began to have to contend with the enormous increases in the costs of energy from both the West and the East, and as Western inflation began to affect the Communist economies seriously—it was precisely these social services that were the most severely curtailed; increasingly, citizens became responsible for their own welfare, and they turned to an intricate network of social relationships maintained outside of state channels.

But in spite of real economic progress in much of the region, the most significant question for politically minded persons, the question of freedom, left little to cheer about. The omnipresent terror so characteristic of the early 1950s had waned in most states, but it was still practiced in Romania and to some extent in Bulgaria, East Germany,

Nothing represents the imposed division between East and West better than the greatest monstrosity of the postwar years: the Berlin Wall. Erected in 1961 to prevent further escape to the West from East Berlin, with its minefields and automatic mow-down zones, the Wall is the starkest reminder of both the attractiveness of the West and the extent to which the Eastern European governments are willing to go to keep their citizens hemmed in under Communist rule. (UPI Photo)

Czechoslovakia after 1968, and Poland in the mid-1980s. And the Communist regimes still practiced a dictatorship backed by the force of the police. Only in Hungary and Yugoslavia, and in Poland before martial law was imposed in 1981, were economic freedoms coupled with limited freedom of expression and travel. But one aspect of political life remained constant everywhere: the supremacy of the Communist party as at least the "director" of political life could not be openly questioned or challenged. When such a challenge was posed by Czechoslovakia's attempt to create "socialism with a human face" or in the urge toward real democracy in Poland in 1980–1981, it was crushed ruthlessly.

In the international arena, there could be no question that two tendencies operated side by side. On the one hand, there was a tacit agreement between the Kremlin and the Eastern European leaders, according to which the latter could follow their own courses of domestic development. While the term "separate roads to development" never really meant a total freedom to decide all issues independently, and while the Soviet Union continued to insist on certain interventionary safeguards, the leaders of Eastern Europe were basically responsible for their own policies. They were even free to fail, provided they were willing to face the consequences for doing so.

On the other hand, there was a far stronger integration within two alliances—one economic, the other military—that were developed between the states of Eastern Europe and the USSR: COMECON (CMEA) and the Warsaw Treaty Organization. As the economies of these states grew more complex, as the price of natural resources rose, and as Western Europe formed its own highly protectionist Common Market, trade within COMECON placed increasing pressures on each state for economic integration. The Council for Mutual Economic Assistance (CMEA or COMECON) began as a response to the Common Market. In its early days, it was a centrally planned instrument in the hands of Moscow. It met strong resistance, specifically by the Romanians, and a notable lack of enthusiasm for a centralized, integrated economic organization was evident in Hungary as well. Yugoslavia, while trading extensively with COMECON, formally stayed outside of its orbit altogether. But the worldwide economic crisis spurred trade within the organization, as did the fact that ready markets could always be found within COMECON for those goods that did not meet the demands of the Western market.

Finally, the Soviet drive for superiority in conventional and nuclear power, as well as the enormous increase in armaments produced by Eastern Europe and the USSR in the 1970s, was responsible for moving the Warsaw Pact toward closer integration. Romania was unwilling to use its forces against other Eastern European states and in fact had even ceased to send troops to participate in Warsaw Pact exercises in the 1960s and 1970s, Albania withdrew from the pact; and Yugoslavia never joined it. Nevertheless, the alliance remained a formidable military system. Its troops were used internally only in Czechoslovakia in 1968, but the Eastern armies remained poised both defensively and offensively as instruments of the Soviet Union. Throughout the détente with the West in the 1970s, the states of Eastern Europe became far more accessible to and far more cooperative with the West than before. However, the very fact of Soviet control and/or occupation, as well as the region's unquestioning support of the Warsaw Pact as a military organization, continued to separate these states from the culture and civilization of Western Europe.

INTERNAL CHALLENGES TO COMMUNIST RULE

In the concluding two sections of this chapter we shall attempt to recount the types of challenges to the authority of the Communist leaderships that have arisen since they assumed power. In general, such challenges should be considered as challenges to the legitimacy or internal authority of specific regimes. But the questioning of Moscow's leadership and resentment of Soviet pressures on external politics are also part of this process; internal and external challenges are frequently intermingled. For instance, Yugoslavia began its opposition to Soviet authority because of the USSR's foreign policy toward the Communist parties of the region. However, the type of regime that evolved in Yugoslavia also became a challenge to the domestic policies of the USSR and its satellites. Similarly, the events that led to the Hungarian revolution of 1956 began as a challenge to the domestic authority of the Communist party but led inevitably to the questioning of the Soviet-Hungarian alliance and Hungary's attempted withdrawal from the Warsaw Pact. On the other hand, though, Romania's or Albania's challenge to the Soviet leadership in external affairs has not meant that any organized challenge to Communist rule has existed in these countries.

In Communist societies *any* challenge—economic, educational, social, or other—also represents a potential political challenge to the authority of the Communist party and its leadership. The peculiarity of politics in these states is the party's insistence that it has the only "correct" theory about the evolution of human events and that it thus can answer every question. After all, Communists claim that the knowledge of Marxism-Leninism enables their leaders—and often these leaders alone—to grasp the truth; thus anyone who challenges a leader's policies challenges not merely specific policies but the very foundations of power. The constant attribution of successes in every field of life

On the Development of Socialism, 1945–1980

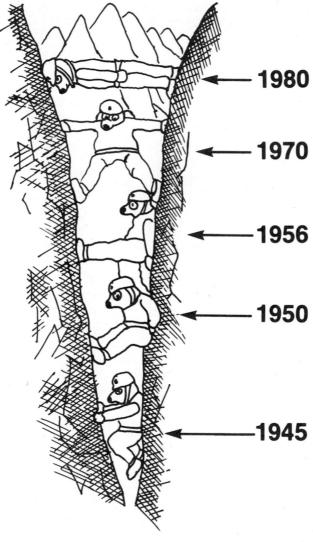

Polytika (Warsaw)

to the correctness of the Communist ideology and to the elite's correct interpretation of that ideology suggests, however, that the Communists may also be responsible for failures. Hence in Communist states one cannot blame, say, the Capital Transportation System for overcrowded or infrequent buses and streetcars, because any problems are inherently "caused" by the party and by the system, and every failure, however small, becomes a systemic failure. Economic or social demands, however minimal, inevitably become political demands and thus threaten the very bases of the regime. The leaders, if they wish to retain their position—and perhaps their lives—have to tread very cautiously between giving in to these demands, which could invite Soviet intervention, and resisting them, which could trigger a volatile response by an angry population.

East Berlin and Pilsen

The first open domestic challenges to the Communist system occurred in the cities of East Berlin and Pilsen, Czechoslovakia, in the summer of 1953. In both cases, the disturbances could be traced to poor economic decisions. In Czechoslovakia a currency reform wiped out a large part of the population's savings; in East Germany a 10 percent increase in the work quotas was instituted. The economic demands to rescind these "reforms" in both situations turned into political demands that the respective regimes ease their harsh policies. Demonstrations and strikes against the regimes' policies began spontaneously, led by workers, who were especially dissatisfied. In East Germany the leaders of the regime became so afraid that they began to discuss plans for evacuating the party elite to the USSR should the revolt spread beyond their control, and they called for assistance from the Red Army. This force obliged, firing on the strikers and crushing their revolt. In Pilsen the Czechoslovak security police viciously suppressed the riots on their own.

The Hungarian Revolution

As has been discussed earlier, the Hungarian crisis of 1956 provided another type of challenge to the party leadership. Originally the Hungarian population simply wished an end to Stalinist terror. Then the intellectuals sought a more democratic type of Communist rule, and the students and the workers desired a more humane form of government. The economic issues that forced the end of compulsory collectivization—mismanagement and accelerated industrialization—soon became intermingled with demands for democratic rights, the end of one-party rule, free trade unions, and, inevitably, an end to the exploitation of Hungary's resources by the USSR. There were demands for greater Hungarian autonomy, including demands for the withdrawal of Soviet troops from the country. The Rakosi-Gero regime refused to give in to these demands, and when the storm broke most of the leaders fled to the safety of the Soviet Union. The Red Army was again called in to put down a revolt.

The Prague Spring

In Czechoslovakia the tensions between outmoded doctrines and modern political-economic practices have led to the reform movement we now call the "Prague Spring" of 1968. The background of this movement lay in the fact that after the mid-1950s party rule in Czechoslovakia was characterized by dogmatic adherence to ideology, the result of which was a political-economic system that succeeded in producing less and less, until the Czech industrial base, once the most productive in the region, began to register, negative growth—that is, actual decline.

The Czechoslovak Communist party elite was sharply divided on the causes of and possible cures for this malaise. The hard-liners, led by First Secretary Antonin Novotny, held that nothing was really wrong with the traditional centralized model, while the reformers demanded an end to the bureaucratized, centralized system of government and production. When the hardliners and moderates began to implement— with the reluctant blessing of the party elite—the New Economic Model, on January 1, 1967, they hoped that this compromise measure between what was truly needed—a major reform—and what Novotny and his inner circle would buy would solve Czechoslovakia's economic problems.

"Thanks to the continuous development of socialism, we became a developing country."

Dikobraz (Prague)

The New Economic Model, however, offered too little and too late. The economists and the intelligentsia within the party hierarchy perceived that there could be no major progress without the removal of the entrenched Stalinist leadership. Aided by the unrest of the Slovaks—who for years had felt that their aspirations for autonomy within the Czechoslovak state were not being met—and by some astute and thoughtful members of the party leadership itself, these economists and intellectuals took the lead in criticizing the regime for its obvious failures. Coalescing slowly around a reform-minded Slovak Politburo member, Alexander Dubcek, the forces for reform began to gather ever-greater support from nearly every part of Czechoslovak society. By January 1968 Antonin Novotny, a consummate survivor, was no longer able to hold on to the reins of power—not with coercion, not with promises of reform, not even with the threat of possible Soviet intervention. And with his fall began the extraordinary reform experiment—the Prague Spring, an experiment in "socialism with a human face."

The Prague Spring had three basic aims: political liberalization of the Stalinist model, economic liberalization resulting in an efficient and decentralized economy, and the federalization of the national system, giving greater equality to the Slovak minority. At the heart of each of these reforms lay the goal of political liberalization, or the wish for greater freedom and pluralism to emerge within the restrictions of the Communist political system. Promoted by pressures from students, writers, and the economic elite, "socialism with a human face" resulted in the emergence of a system of rule that far more closely resembled the democracy of pre–World War II Czechoslovakia than the Stalinist bureaucracy characteristic of the post–1948 period. In such documents as the Writers' Union's resolution entitled *Two Thousand Words*, various segments of society demanded the restoration of the individual and societal rights that Stalinism had taken away. But the party's right to exercise power was not challenged; indeed, it was the reformist members of the party elite who championed the reforms. The press became autonomous and nearly completely free of outside constraints, the sanctity of freedom of expression and questioning was once again upheld, social scientists once again were allowed to research what they deemed to be important problems, and various groups began to emerge, representing a pluralization of society. Economic reforms began to be implemented, freeing the economy from centralized restrictions; planning began to be decentralized, managers' responsibility increased dramatically at the local level, and incentives began to be substituted for penalties as a means of ensuring that production would continue at a higher level. The Slovaks received full autonomy, a greater share of the economic and political allocations of power, their own separate Communist party, and their own separate legislative entity.

Not everyone was happy with the Prague Spring; both within and outside Czechoslovakia opposition to the reforms was evident. Within the country, the centralized mid-level state and party bureaucrats were displeased by the potential loss of their power. Joined by some of the top elite—specifically those who feared for the loss of their own political power and privileges or who were strong supporters of Soviet policy and the Soviet style of rule—these officials tried to sabotage the reforms, as they had done in Hungary in 1956. Nor were the industrial workers—specifically the unskilled laborers—entirely happy with the reform. After the abolition of the earlier forced Stalinist patterns of Stahkanovite production systems at the time of de-Stalinization, and having grown accustomed to little work and relatively equitable payment levels, they too felt threatened. And alienated from both the intelligentsia and the students, the workers generally remained apathetic or often even hostile to the reform leadership.

Moreover, by June 1968 the Soviet leadership began to be restive and grew suspicious of the Prague Spring. Egged on by hard-liners within the Soviet Politburo, who feared the potential consequences of the Czechoslovak liberalization on the USSR, the Politburo began to pressure the Czechoslovak reform leadership. Military maneuvers by members of the Soviet military alliance system, the Warsaw Pact, were held in and around Czechoslovakia, and several meetings between the party elites of the USSR and the Czechoslovak Communist party took place. But in spite of all assurances that Czechoslovakia was not anti-Soviet and that it intended to remain both Communist and a member of the Warsaw Pact, in the end Soviet mistrust of the Prague Spring resulted in the invasion of Czechslovakia by Russian, Hungarian, Bulgarian, and East German troops on August 21, 1968. Having received no orders from their minister of defense, the Czechoslovak army stayed in its barracks and did not fight back. Romania did not participate in and condemned the invasion, although Nicolae Ceausescu, the Romanian leader, was not at all happy about the "anti-Communist nature" of the Prague Spring.

Leonid I. Brezhnev, who replaced Khrushchev in 1965 as first secretary of the Communist party of the Soviet Union, reiterated long-standing Soviet policy: the USSR, he declared, reserved the right to intervene through any means in the policies of any Communist state if the Communist party elite in the USSR felt that "the interests of socialism were threatened." This policy has since become known as the Brezhnev Doctrine. Soviet forces kidnapped the members of the Czechoslovak Politburo, took them to Moscow, and coerced them to abandon, step by step, most of the reforms of the Prague Spring. Within two years every vestige of reform—with the sole exception of greater autonomy for Slovaks and Slovakia—was gone. Alexander Dubcek became a gardener, the reformers, by and large, emigrated or were forced into retirement, and a long winter of centralized party rule, under Gustav Husak, the Czech Communist party's new first secretary replaced the brief spring and summer of freedom.

Poland's Challenges

The many disturbances in Poland from 1954 to date present us with a different picture. The first tangible challenge to Communist power there occurred in Poznan in June 1956, followed in October of that year by the return to power, with Soviet consent, of Wladyslaw Gomulka, the popular "national Communist," and by the re-establishment of the Catholic Church as a major force. But the Soviet decision to allow Poland to have its own style of socialism had been won at the point of a bayonet; the threat of a major confrontation between the Soviet and the Polish armies brought it about. When the chips were down, the Soviet leaders chose to accept a "nationalist" Communist because they trusted him to keep Poland firmly in the Soviet camp—and also because they may well have sensed that, in reality, Gomulka would not be much of a domestic reformer.

After 1956 the Polish regime's initial zeal for reform was soon replaced by a return to rigid economic planning and by a manipulation of every facet of life by the party elite. As a result, Gomulka's initial popularity slowly vanished. His drive toward "stabilization" was in reality a policy of no major changes and resulted in the failure of the national economy; in 1968 his regime was rocked by protests against restrictive policies in the cultural sphere. Reviving a protest movement that had first surfaced in 1964, Polish intellectuals demanded greater cultural and artistic freedom. And even the arrest and expulsion of philosophers and writers from the Communist party failed to stem the tide, which culminated in angry sit-ins at the country's major universities. The police restored order by mass arrests, and the purge following the defeat of the intellectual opposition was based on Poland's traditional, despicable anti-Semitism. In a few months everyone with influence who was of Jewish origin—leaders, intellectuals, managers, and so on—was expelled or "encouraged to emigrate." Of Poland's 20,000 Jews who survived the Holocaust, less than 5,000 now remained. Spurred by the virulent anti-Semitism of highly nationalistic "patriotic" groups, such as the organization of former partisans led by General Mieczyslaw Moczar, the purges went unbated. Gomulka's authority, however, was weakened by factionalism and by the slow rise of Edward Gierek, the Silesian party chief.

The immediate crisis that led to Gomulka's downfall was economic in nature. Gomulka's plan for economic reform never really materialized and, on December 12, 1970, the government announced massive increases in the prices of food and fuel. Mass demonstrations followed. They had to be broken up by the use of army and police units, especially in Gdansk; hundreds were killed and wounded. Although Gomulka suffered a heart attack on December 19, 1970, his fate already had been sealed by these brutal acts; it was obvious to the Polish people that he had sanctioned the force his trusted lieutenants had used. Having lost support rapidly, he was replaced by Gierek, and once again a spirit of reform seemed to emerge.

Gierek's economic reform program of "renewal" took place at a time when Poland seemed to be on the verge of a major economic recovery. Taking advantage of the availability of "cheap" loans from the West as well as the beneficial atmosphere of Soviet-American détente, a new heavy industrialization program was started. Price increases were halted, social assistance was increased, and consumer goods became widely available. But Gierek's policies failed to solve Poland's fundamental problems—especially in the agrarian sector, where the state still paid the peasants lower prices for their products than it cost to produce them. Consequently, food production dwindled in the countryside, and in June 1976 food riots broke out all over the country. The Gierek regime ordered the police to fire on the workers who torched Communist party headquarters in several cities and realized that the army would also have to be called in. The army, however, was under the command of General Wojciech Jaruzelski, who is reputed to have issued his own statement: "Polish soldiers do not fire on Polish workers." In the end, price increases were rescinded as General Jaruzelski, among others, convinced the leadership of the futility of the course taken by the ruling party elite.

The most recent chapter in the history of Poland's challenges to party authority began in 1980, as it became clear that Gierek's policies were just as disastrous as those of his predecessors had been. His massive, rapid modernization policies, which involved enormous investments in heavy industry and huge foreign loans, were economic failures. Poland was unable to sustain its pattern of growth. The corruption at the highest levels of government was well known, and worker dissatisfaction and intellectual opposition to Gierek were widespread. However, once again, it was the near-doubling of meat prices by the government that dealt the death blow to Gierek's rule. New strikes began on July 1, 1980, and by the end of August the government had virtually no control over the people of Poland.

Most significantly, during the heady months of August 1980–December 1981, a genuine trade union—independent of the government and representing the interests of the workers rather than those of the party—was formed and eventually came to be identified with the name of its leader, Lech Walesa. Solidarity, as the union was called, was a true working-class movement that demanded greater economic and political rights for the workers of Poland. It soon became the real force in the country and pressed the government to put through all sorts of reforms. Eventually Gierek was removed from power. Democratic reforms hitherto impossible to bring about in postwar Eastern Europe—including the right to form free trade unions, relatively unfettered freedom of the press, assembly, and speech, and a liberal passport law—emerged.

The body that was hardest hit by the "spirit of the new Poland" was the Communist party. Although it promised to change its ways and adhere to the spirit of *odnowa* (renewal), it was torn between two major wings, the conservatives and liberals. The conservatives, the top- and middle-level bureaucrats who were fearful for their position, as they had been in Czechoslovakia in 1968 and Hungary in 1956, tried to sabotage the changes and eventually were relatively successful. The liberals although originally hopeful that a compromise would make possible a more humane and liberal Poland, began to be discouraged and bolted the party in ever-increasing numbers. By the time the military crackdown came on December 13, 1981, Solidarity claimed that 900,000 party members had given up their membership and that one-third to one-half of the Communist party members had joined Solidarity.

The party was forced on the defensive; it had to concede more and more. It had to recognize the workers' right to strike, their right to free Saturdays, the right to form independent trade unions by both workers and independent peasant, and the right of workers' councils in the factories to have a say in the hiring and firing of managers. The Communist party was adrift. Not willing to surrender its power or to implement a major reform program that would affect its very existence, the party simply became irrelevant. However, as Solidarity realized that the party was unwilling or unable to implement the oft-promised reforms, it, too, began to be more radical. And when it demanded to hold a referendum to determine Poland's form of government, General Jaruzelski—who had assumed the posts of prime minister, defense minister, and first secretary of the party—had an excuse to put an end to the Polish reforms. On December 13, 1981, using selected units of the army and the security forces, he organized a coup and installed a military junta. The pattern of Pilsuski's coup of 1926 was repeated. Claiming to have "saved" Poland from economic chaos, Soviet intervention, and the restoration of capitalism, the army imposed its will on the country. And yet, as it revoked newly granted freedoms and attempted to destroy Solidarity, by acting on its own, the army inadvertently also made the Communist party even less relevant. The martial law imposed on the population was well planned and relatively effectively enforced. The security forces broke resistance using their full military weight. At least 50 people were killed, many

Before the Jaruzelski Coup

"Your Majesty, the serfs have become haughty and boorish, they treat you like dirt . . . It is high time to bring in the dragon . . ."

Polytika (Warsaw)

more were injured, and about 50,000 were arrested and incarcerated. Yet another season of darkness descended on Poland.

No one can doubt that the real prime mover behind the crackdown was the Soviet leadership. In fact, Soviet troops stood ready to render "fraternal assistance" should it be needed. It is difficult to know whether Jaruzelski undertook the coup because he really believed that a Soviet intervention was imminent or whether he simply used threatened intervention as an excuse. In his and other observers' minds, the country was unquestionably near economic anarchy. The government, refusing to implement much-needed reforms, hoped that the anxious Poles would prefer dictatorship that delivered food to democracy and anarchy that did not. But to date the coup has failed to solve Poland's plight; though it has stopped the drift toward anarchy, it has yet to deliver food. It has merely exacerbated social and political tensions whose resolution is uncertain.

Hungary's New Economic Mechanism

Three divergent examples of domestic challenges to Communist authority need to be mentioned briefly: Hungary's New Economic Mechanism (NEM), the Romanian strikes, and Yugoslavia's internal reforms. Introduced in 1968 and continued in fits and starts since then, the NEM is an economic and social reform movement with far-reaching implications. The regime of Janos Kadar, brought to power after the revolt of 1956, was determined to avoid the policies that had led to the revolution. Though staunchly pro-Moscow in foreign policy, it attempted to liberalize internal life by introducing a novel approach in Communist politics—the process of depoliticization, allowing the people to remove politics from their daily lives. Slowly, beginning in the mid-1960s, most issues were permitted to be discussed on their own merit, and the Communist party only insisted on maintaining its control over the political—versus economic, social, and so on—affairs of the country. Consequently, with the zigs and zags that have always characterized Janos Kadar's policies of liberalization, under party rule a market mechanism was reintroduced, prices and wages were gradually adjusted in order to conform more closely to conditions in the world economy, profit motives and incentives were emphasized, private business was given freer rein, and a respect for the privacy of all activities marked Hungarian life in the 1970s. Hungarian Communism moved as far away from the Soviet and most other Eastern European models as the country's leaders thought possible. The NEM has challenged Communist authority. However, since it has not affected the political sphere, it has been generally overlooked by Moscow and has provided no pretext for Soviet military intervention in Hungarian affairs.

The Romanian Strikes

The Romanian strikes at first sight seemed to be mere economic dysfunctions. The facts are obvious: on four separate occasions, in 1977, 1980, 1981, and 1982, Romanian workers went on strike at several mines and oilfields. Twice they even seized officials who had come to "calm them"; they also insisted that Ceausescu himself come and "help" them. They demanded better allocation of food, meat in the stores, and simpler ways to solve local grievances. On all four occasions the regime has given in on the short run, but the situation has basically remained the same. The fact is that the tremendously high work quotas, the exploitation of the workers, and the ever-present scarcities in Romania stem from the systemic mismanagement of political, social, and economic life by Ceausescu and his highly personalized dictatorship;

only the instrument of terror keeps the state functioning. And thus, while sporadic challenges to the Ceausescu regime have yet to coalesce into a national movement, dissatisfaction is likely to cause its eventual collapse or profound alteration.

Yugoslavia

Yugoslavia developed its own independent policies, without regard to Moscow's model. Its internal evolution provided a clear challenge to the *type* of Communist rule advocated by Moscow. Yugoslav Communism, after a brief "Muscovite" period that lasted until the beginning of the 1950s, soon veered away from policies that typified Soviet rule elsewhere in the region—for example, collectivization, centralization, and police terror. Instead, the Yugoslav system is based on small individual peasant landholdings—largely without huge collective and state farms—and, in the factories, workers' councils that make all decisions affecting all aspects of daily work life, bringing some elements of popular democracy to the workplace. In practice, this is what Yugoslavia's so-called self-managing Communism is all about. While the Communist party retains national autonomy and remains the country's "leading social organization," the federal system grants equal rights to the various republics and ethnic groups that make up Yugoslavia. With the door open to the West, millions of Yugoslavs have been free to work in Western Europe. Police terror has generally been used against "nationalist" elements that have sought, for instance, independence for Croatia or the further diminution of the party's role in Yugoslav politics. While the Yugoslav example does not present a direct challenge to Soviet Communist power, the mere presence of the Yugoslav alternative nevertheless is a model that can be emulated by those who seek nation-specific types of Communist rule. For this reason, Yugoslavia continues to be regarded as a threat to the loyal leadership of the other Eastern European Communist states.

Ethnic Nationalism

Although ethnic nationalism has not been strong enough to provide a major challenge to Communist rule, its presence in Eastern Europe has been far from negligible. The three states where such tendencies have been exhibited are Czechoslovakia, Yugoslavia, and Romania. In Czechoslovakia the Slovaks always felt that they were treated as second-class citizens in a state traditionally dominated by Czechs, and even the postwar constitutional structure contained what the Slovaks felt was institutional discrimination. Stressing the need for greater autonomy and for differentiated investment to bring the level of production and standard of living in Slovakia up to those of Czech lands, the Slovak Communists, especially during the Prague Spring, gained tremendous momentum toward challenging the established Czech leadership. The liberal political and economic aspects of the Prague Spring, in spite of its close identification with Alexander Dubcek, a Slovak Communist, were not as popular in Slovakia as they were in the Czech lands, and the Slovak workers and party rank-and-file received the invading Soviet forces far more warmly than their Czech compatriots did. Naturally the Soviet Union exploited this distinction, and in the months following the occupation it installed a basically Slovak leadership that has ruled Czechoslovakia ever since. Under Soviet guidance, Slovakia became a somewhat more separate and equal partner in the state, with separate institutions and, frequently, different priorities. Through the Slovak leadership Czechoslovakia in effect experienced rule by an ethnic minority over a still dispirited Czech majority. And even if Slovak autonomy has received some setbacks since the early 1970s, the Slovaks feel as if they are more equal partners in Czechoslovakia than ever before.

Yugoslavia's problems with nationalism center in two distinct regions whose populations seek greater independence—Croatia-Dalmatia and the Albanian-dominated region of Kosovo. Croatian desires for decentralization and greater freedom, of course, go back to the interwar years, we discussed in Chapter 3. And in the 1970s, until a crackdown was ordered by the central government in Belgrade, the Croatian nationalist movement was probably supported by most Croatians. Convinced—correctly—that Croatia's resources were being used by Belgrade to subsidize the less developed areas of Yugoslavia, the Croatians wished to pursue their own independent policies, especially in economic matters. To some extent they were supported clandestinely by the Soviets, who would have welcomed the dismantling of Yugoslavia, and their efforts nearly succeeded. They were halted only through the determined action of the Communist-controlled police, which resulted in the arrest of thousands of Croatians in 1971–1974. In order to prevent further campaigns for Croatian independence, the government had to concede greater local freedoms to the constituent republics, and Yugoslavs today seem to accept this move.

Albanian dissatisfaction with presumed and real inequities also led to strikes and demonstrations in 1981. Only with a great deal of trouble was the Yugoslav regime able to control these disturbances. It was reported that several thousand people were injured during the three days of rioting. Once again, Belgrade had to grant greater local freedoms in hopes of appeasing the citizens of the region, and it had to back down on its attempt to centralize governmental authority. While these events did not directly challenge the Communist system as a whole, they challenged in a very significant way the *type* of Communist rule existing in the respective countries, and posed ethnic challenges that no regime could ignore.

Finally, the case of the Hungarian minority in Romania—and to a lesser extent in Czechoslovakia—is also instructive. Before 1965 Romania's roughly 2 million ethnic Magyars lived on a relatively equal basis with other citizens of the country. Since that year, however, Ceausescu's regime adopted a chauvinist-nationalist course against the USSR (which we shall discuss below) and to help garner popular support for such a "nationally based" rule, it began a deliberate campaign against the large Magyar minority—and to a lesser extent against the small German minority. A great deal of discrimination and hardship for these groups resulted. The brutal dictatorship of Ceausescu and his cronies and relatives made the cause of autonomy for these ethnic groups hopeless. Nonetheless, the existence of an oppressed and disgruntled minority, as well as the nationalism engendered by Ceausescu's anti-Soviet and anti-Magyar policies has created a specific challenge to the Communist party rule, allegedly based on the "equality of all men," so long a rallying cry of Communist ideology.

EXTERNAL CHALLENGES TO SOVIET LEADERSHIP

The external challenges to Moscow's leadership have differed from the challenges posed by the domestic evolution of these states. While the latter threatened the existence and type of Communist rule internally, the external challenges have all been aimed at reducing Moscow's central role in determining the affairs of Eastern Europe. While internal challenges could thus be regarded as attempts to achieve within-the-system changes in the domestic setting, the external challenges that took place have been aimed only at securing greater independence for the satellite states. And while the domestic changes have been more prevalent in the more northern states of Eastern Europe, the most successful external challenges to Moscow's leadership have come largely from the Balkan states—specifically Yugoslavia, Albania, and Romania. Bulgaria, however, has proved to be a rather quiescent ally of Moscow, and Bulgarian domestic developments have posed no real threats to the Communist regime.

The Communist assumption of power in Eastern Europe seemed to usher in an era of Soviet authority over the various states of the region, and Moscow seemed to be in complete control of the Communist movement as a whole. In order to "coordinate" the international

Communist movement, the Communist Information Bureau, or Cominform, was founded in 1947 to replace the Communist International that was dissolved in 1943. It was expected that—in addition to the bilateral treaties between the USSR and the "people's democracies" that guaranteed Soviet control—the Cominform would be able to regulate the policies of the region's Communist parties and thus render them subordinate to the Soviet party. But the rule of the USSR through the Cominform soon suffered a major setback. Led by the indomitably independent-minded Tito, Yugoslavia refused to come under Soviet supervision and control, and after 1948 it began to develop its own policies. The Yugoslav road to Communism thus challenged the very idea that all the states of the region had to follow the Soviet path of internal development. Yugoslavia's nonalignment also shattered the notion of a unified Communist orbit, the theory of a Communist commonwealth of nations under Soviet guidance. Although the Cominform was abolished under Khrushchev in 1955, the Soviet government failed to effect a lasting reconciliation with Yugoslavia. After January 1957 Yugoslavia continued on its "separate road to socialism" and went ahead with the process of "rivaling" the Soviet model of Communism.

In 1956 the USSR *theoretically* acceded to the right of the Eastern European states to independence and sovereignty and promised nonintervention in their domestic affairs; in the heady days of October 1956, in fact, the USSR even accorded legitimacy to the idea of national Communism in Poland and Hungary. But the brutal Soviet invasion of Hungary in the following month made a mockery of that promise, and Yugoslavia once again concluded that the Soviets desired only domination. The Yugoslav leaders recognized that if they indeed wished to pursue domestic policies deemed desirable for their own state, they should not be drawn back into the Communist commonwealth of nations. This conclusion has remained the firm basis of Yugoslavia's policy ever since, and the Yugoslav demand for recognition of the equal validity of the Soviet and Yugoslav models has never been met fully by the Kremlin. Although in the late 1970s the Soviet leadership conceded the theoretical point that the various Communist parties of the world are indeed able to follow different paths, they have always tried to dominate their neighbors and allies in Eastern Europe. In Yugoslavia these efforts have not met with success.

Other external challenges have also beset the Soviet Union; China, Albania, and Romania also challenged the Soviet position as the center of international Communism. In fact, the break with Yugoslavia was made more complete and permanent by the emerging Sino-Soviet conflict after 1959. Communist China felt that the USSR was not really anxious to help it to develop as a Communist state, and, comprehending that the USSR was not willing to risk a thermonuclear war for the sake of spreading the worldwide revolution, it began to drift away from Soviet influence. By 1961 the Chinese and the Soviets, at least doctrinally speaking, were at each other's throats. Taking advantage of its distance from the USSR, of Yugoslavia's hostility to the Soviet desire to control the Communist camp, and of its relatively isolated geographical position, Enver Hoxha's tiny Albania became the third Communist state to break with the USSR over the issue of Soviet domination. In fact, Albania opted to become China's first ally in Europe. Although this alliance terminated by the end of the 1970s, Albania has not drifted back into the Soviet camp.

The external challenge of Romania to Soviet leadership was also enhanced by the Sino-Soviet split, but its roots can be traced to an emergent nationalist form of Communist dictatorship, first under Gheorghe Gheorghiu-Dej, and later under his successor, Nicolae Ceausescu. Refusing to take sides in the conflict between China and the USSR—and thus indirectly repudiating Moscow—Ceausescu was especially angered by the Soviet invasion of Czechoslovakia in 1968 and by the announcement of what was euphemistically called the "Brezhnev Doctrine"—that is, the USSR's declaration that it had a right to intervene anywhere where the "forces of socialism" were being challenged. The threat to the Romanians and their leadership was made explicit by the continuous verbal attacks on Romania by the USSR after the Czechoslovak invasion. The Romanian leaders, however, refused to back down. While domestically the Ceausescu regime has been marked by a dictatorship of frightening severity, totalitarianism, demand for adulation, and centralization, in foreign affairs Romania's relative independence from the policies of the USSR has been clearly demonstrated. Thus, for instance, Romanian troops have not participated en masse in Warsaw Pact maneuvers and, since 1962, Romania has not allowed the troops of any other nation on its territory—not even for the purpose of joint exercises. And at the United Nations the Romanians supported the condemnation of the USSR for its entry into Afghanistan in 1980, although they cautiously voted only "present" when their vote was called for. In regards to the Middle East and China, the policies of the Romanians were also clearly at variance with those of the Soviet Union. The USSR consequently had to realize that the Romanians would not automatically support its moves—and in many cases would oppose them outright—in international affairs. Thus the Romanian challenge to Moscow's leadership also limited the USSR's total authority in the region.

Some specialists argue that the Soviet Union intervened in Hungary, Czechoslovakia, and indirectly in Poland because of the challenges that these regimes posed to Moscow's central authority in foreign affairs. It is also maintained that these regimes were crushed by superior military force when they sought to abandon the Soviet alliance system. In fact, in Hungary, Imre Nagy declared neutrality and withdrawal from the Warsaw Pact. That declaration, however, occurred on November 1, 1956, only *after* Soviet troops had begun to pour into the country and *after* the Soviet leaders had already decided to crush the Hungarian revolution with military might. In Czechoslovakia, though, no members of the leadership or the population advocated defection from the Communist camp or from the Warsaw Pact. And in Poland the Jaruzelski regime did not impose martial law on the beleaguered population because of the fear that the Polish people would become a hostile power in the hands of the imperialists to be used against the USSR. The fear of their defection from the Warsaw Pact was nil, as far as the Soviet leadership was concerned.

It seems that the most serious challenges to Communist authority and to Moscow's power have been met by the Communist regimes and by the Soviet rulers simply by resorting to brute force. Using the Red Army and state police units whenever the leaders were convinced that the Communist party was no longer in command, or when foreign policy considerations "made it necessary" to do so, the Soviet Union has tried to keep the region under its control. However, its record of successful bloodless power maintenance is at best mixed, and force has had to be used repeatedly to keep the Eastern European states in the Communist camp and under Moscow's control. The greatest failing of the USSR thus seems to be that during its roughly forty years of rule in the region, it still has not been able to instill in the people there a conviction that Communist rule is the "wave of the future" and that the Communist leaders are the legitimate choice of the population. As long as their rule must be backed by the continuous application of force, the regimes may remain stable, but periodic crises in the quest for a better life, for more freedom, greater democracy, and greater independence will persist.

PART II

THE STRUCTURE OF POWER

The Legitimating Ideology

■ The new states that were established when the Communists took power in Eastern Europe all called themselves "Communist" or "socialist," and, whatever name they used, they clearly considered their form of government to be closely identified with some aspects of Communist ideology. It is a moot point to argue that these states were in reality not Communist or that they were at an intermediate stage between "people's democracy" and actual Communism. For our purposes, what is most important is the self-identification of each of these regimes with Communist ideology, however each state interpreted that ideology in terms of its historical development or in accordance with whatever zigs and zags the politics of the moment dictated. Since these regimes were established, there has been a self-awareness among them of their common ideology, and the diversity of their political, social, and economic experiences merely served to emphasize this ideological commonality.

There has been a continuous debate among Western and Eastern students of Marxism as to whether one should refer to this ideology as Marxist, Marxist-Leninist, Stalinist, socialist, Communist, or something else. Eastern Europeans themselves are quite fond of relating the following sequence of riddles when discussing what Marxist ideology really is:

What is Marxism? One man chasing a black cat in a dark room.

What is Leninism? One man chasing a nonexistent black cat in a dark room.

What is Marxism-Leninism? One man chasing a nonexistent black cat in a dark room and claiming, "I've got it."

When viewed in this sense, ideology becomes something far different than the mere intellectual pursuit of truth through philosophical explanations of historical phenomena: it becomes the Communist leaders' claim that they have "it," the truth, the correct way to progress and development. Their corollary claim, that *only they* possess *the* truth, elevates ideology to what the Marxists would call *praxis*—that is, the transformation of society through their efforts to implement that ideology.

It is immaterial in this context that most people in Communist states would not be able to discuss the philosophy or the principles of Marxism-Leninism intelligently with Western specialists. In spite of protestations by Communist theoreticians to the contrary, ideology in Soviet-type systems does not create a society well versed in Marxist philosophy. In undertaking the ideological education of the Eastern Europeans, the best these regimes have been able to hope for has been to inculcate a few values that can be considered Marxist. These few values, to be discussed below, are all relayed to the population through key slogans that the regime uses to explain itself to its citizens.

The most significant role of ideology in Eastern Europe lies in its communicative nature: it is a primary vocabulary through which everything is expressed. The people of the region learn to read what the regime wishes to say in the regime's terms, and they also learn to read between the lines. Consider, for instance, the following story:

> The forces of socialism triumphed on Saturday when the USSR's 4×100 meter relay team scored a triumphant second place at the international meeting held in Kuala Lumpur with a Soviet record of 38.5 seconds. In contrast, the United States had to be content with reaching the next to last place.
> Question: How many participants were at the race, and who won?
> Answer: The United States won, the USSR came in second, and there were no other participants.

"Ideology" thus enables the regime, on the one hand, to transmit the desired messages, and it allows the population, on the other, to decode not only what "truth" they are supposed to grasp, but also what the truth actually is.

In addition, ideology in the Communist states serves to legitimize the rule of the party. Thus the party claims to hold the sole key to the future development of the state, because it knows from the Communist ideology what the only practicable way to success is. At the same time, the population is supposed to support the regime because it is expected (a) to believe that the Communist leadership really knows what it is doing; and (b) to recognize that Marxism or Communism as an ideology provides that only key to success. Following World War II in these two respects, the Communists initially had substantial popular support, but as such support evaporated, the Communist regimes have had to face crises of legitimacy, or the *crises of legitimating ideology,* in Eastern Europe.

These crises basically stem from the fact that Marxist ideology, before the Communists came to power in Russia and later in Eastern Europe, was "prescriptive," setting out a blueprint for what future Communist society was to be. When the Soviet regime came to power, however, reality compelled the Bolsheviks to alter many of Marx's original theories in order to maintain their power. At first, they tried to explain Marx away by maintaining that "Marx was not a Baedeker," in other words that Marx was not a complete tour guide for the future. However, later they brazenly falsified Marx, and by the mid-1920s it became clear that Marxist ideology had become a simply "descriptive" theory that would be used to justify any action the party deemed necessary to maintain power.

It was this usage that struck especially close to the innate cynicism of the people of Eastern Europe. At one moment they were expected to believe in, and strongly and openly endorse, Stalin as the wisest man, the greatest poet and philosopher, and the most beloved leader in history. A few historical minutes later he became the symbol of the "cult of personality," a ruthless murderer and dictator. The contradictions were so enormous that today no thinking individual can regard these ideological about-faces as anything but ongoing manipulations by the ruling group, which uses them cynically to maintain and justify its power and rationalize its current policies.

Can anyone at the top of the Soviet or the Eastern European elite, one may well ask, really continue to believe in the principles of Communism? We may never know, but it is clear that publicly these leaders always *act* as if they believe in the premises on which their actions are based. Certainly Ceausescu justifies his nepotistic and individualistic dictatorship in Marxist terms to the Romanian population. And Hungary's Kadar, who has followed a liberal domestic policy totally different from Ceausescu's autocratic reign, justifies his policies to his country in the same ideological terms. But it is essential to note that the decisions made by these men are generally *pragmatic* ones, intended to ensure maintenance of power and unaffected by ideological considerations. It is left up to the "ideologists" of the regime to justify these decisions in Marxist terms.

BASES OF COMMUNIST IDEOLOGY

Marx and Dialectical Materialism

However, some aspects of Communist ideology are all-pervasive; they are emphasized everywhere, at every turn, through the schools and the media. Some of these ideas will be examined briefly here. The first of these ideas relates to the very basis of the system: the idea of materialism. Borrowing from the German philosopher Ludwig Feuerbach (1804–1872), Marx postulated that "man is what man eats," meaning that a person's consciousness stems from his or her material, economic being. Enlarging on the materialism of Feuerbach, Communist leaders included in their ideology a crudely simplified theory of evolution including the denial of the existence of a deity; life, simply based on material processes, evolved without any intervention by God. Materialism, when coupled—again rather crudely—with Georg Hegel's theory of the dialectical interpretation of history, served as the basis of dialectical materialism—a theory that human history progresses in stages from primitive communism, through slave society, feudalism, and capitalism, to the final, blissful state of Communism. Although these stages represent various aspects of the class struggle, in the last phase of capitalism, according to Marx, the proletariat (the industrial working class) will be so impoverished by the merciless profit-taking of an ever-decreasing number of monopolists that a revolution will occur; the few remaining capitalists will be eliminated and only one class, the proletariat, will survive. They will own everything in common, everyone will be equal, the state—long an instrument of oppression in the hands of the ruling class—will wither away, and an international, brotherly society will come into being. But Marx and Engels posited two prerequisites for such an ideal state of being: an abundance of material goods and class consciousness among the proletariat. Only when these two preconditions were satisfied could the Marxist motto for Communism, "From each according to his ability, to each according to his needs," become a reality.

According to classical Marxism, abundance—the ability to satisfy everyone according to "his needs"—could, of course, be created only by the process of capitalism and its relentless exploitation of the proletariat. However, neither in Russia before 1917 nor in Eastern Europe before 1945 had there been full-blown capitalist systems that successfully produced abundance. Instead, Communist elites have continually attempted to "create" abundance, but they have never succeeded. Proletarian class consciousness has also had to be "created" by that special group of people, the Communists, who to Marx were not a political party, but committed educators of the people.

Lenin's Theories

However, to Lenin, who was far more pragmatic, the Communists were something else: a party of dedicated professional revolutionaries who were willing to give their lives to see Communism triumphant. Lenin, of course, had no desire to see a "bourgeois" democratic system survive, and he had no use for the kind of democracy that inspired real, democratic rights for the people. For Lenin, who based his own ideas on Russian realities under the repressive tsarist regime, the Communist party would be an instrument of change. He developed two major theories that have become the bases of rule in societies where Communist parties govern today: the theory of substitution and the theory of democratic centralism.

The founder of Bolshevik ideology was Vladimir Ilyich Lenin. By altering Marxist ideology from philosophical prescripts to a justification for the seizure of power, Lenin laid the groundwork for the practice of Communist dogma. (AP/Wide World Photos)

Substitution

Substitution theory held that the working class was the most advanced class of society. Therefore, its will had to be substituted for the will of society at large. But as the proletariat was still too amorphous and not sufficiently class-conscious, the will of its most advanced stratum, the Communists, had to be substituted for *its* general will. But to Lenin, the Communist party was still too big. Thus the will of the most advanced stratum of the party had to be substituted for the will of the party as a whole. Under Stalin the substitution theory reached its logical extension and became an expression of the will of the "maximum leader"—the Communist dictator, the first secretary of the party—and his closest colleagues, the true political elite in the Communist states. Under this system, the omniscient first secretary is supposed to know better and be wiser than everyone else, and therefore he is expected to "interpret" and "define" what the true interests of society are. In Communist states, the unquestionable authority of the dictator or party leader stems precisely from this aspect of "Communist substitutionism."

Democratic centralism

The theory of democratic centralism—a contradiction on terms in itself—was developed by Lenin to obtain and maintain complete control over the Communist party and, by extension, to give the party elite control over all elements of society. Briefly stated, democratic centralism is democratic because it is based on formal elections by the people and by majority rule. But it is also centralist, for mandatory nomination for office is made from the higher levels to the lower levels, and the narrow party elite is free to select those people who will be nominated to run the affairs of the party and the state. It is also centralist because the decisions made at the top and at the higher levels of the party are always binding on the lower levels, and the minority— once voted down—must unhesitatingly and willingly endorse the manipulated will of the majority. In practice, this democratic centralism maintains complete control by the party over all elements of public— and frequently even private—life in Communist states. Thus, there can be no real "interest groups" or independent organizations in these states: all *apparats,* or bureaucratic organizations having some well-defined function, are "transmission belts" of the party's wishes. There can be no independent labor unions, no independent writers or artists: all must serve the goals of society as defined by the party and ultimately by the leader in power. Ideally, therefore, the party rules society through obedient, centralized bureaucracies and enforces the implementation of policies by these "organisms" through the use of power and persuasion, terror when necessary and indoctrination when possible. Because of weakened, or nonexistent, independent institutional controls and the lack of societal autonomy, the party elite, even with limited effort, can muster enormous power to justify any and all policies.

Ideology versus Reality

As we noted in Chapter 4, however, Eastern Europeans have seen some positive features in Marxism, and most of these features still remain attractive to significant segments of the societies in the region. First, to many Eastern Europeans it seemed quite clear that the *Communist* USSR had won World War II in the region, and whether they privately supported or opposed the system as it later evolved, in the immediate postwar era the Soviet victory seemed to indicate the potential victory of Communist ideology as well. Second, Communism also was attractive because its ideology promised rapid development, rather than the largely unsuccessful gradualist approaches that characterized the interwar era in the region. In contrast to what seemed to be the obvious failures of "capitalism" in Eastern Europe between the world wars, the Communists promised the quick elimination of many problems. In a region of truly vast inequalities they promised a radical reduction in the differences among the various classes and segments of society; this would entail greater equality in opportunity, status, and wealth, as well as a higher standard of living than ever before. In a region where the means of production were owned by a very narrow stratum of society, they promised the end of exploitation of man by man by instituting the common ownership of the means of production. They promised to the working class that they would be the actual holders of power; except in Czechoslovakia, Eastern Europe had only a small industrial proletariat, and these people were truly dispossessed of power in the interwar era. The Communists further promised the opportunity for the powerless to rise to power, the opportunity for their children to belong to a new power elite; they promised land to the landless and wealth to the poor. Capitalizing on a long socialist tradition that had long sought the abolition of the ills of capitalism, the Communists depicted "socialism" or "Communism" as a panacea for all of these evils, and they pointed to the Marxist ideology as a guide to the successful development of Eastern Europe.

After the Communist takeovers in the region, ideological doctrines were advocated to varying extents of purity throughout the bloc, but the rigid principles set in motion by Lenin and Stalin were slowly eroded by the pragmatic necessities of state administration of developing or developed societies. And most of the promises of Communist rule were never fully kept. Egalitarianism was replaced by new social stratification, and exploitation of man by man was replaced by the exploitation of man by the state. The common ownership of the means of production did not give managerial function to the employees, except perhaps in Yugoslavia. The land—except in Poland and in Yugoslavia—was collectivized, and the peasants remained landless. But, most important, power was never ceded to the people. In fact, if any ideological stricture may be considered as central to Communist rule it is that of the permanence of party rule: this can never be openly challenged, as was amply proved in Hungary in 1956, in Poland in 1981, and elsewhere. Yet, there has been a waning of ideology as a "commitment"; ideological warfare has been trimmed of its shrill harshness. In an instructive statement two days before he declared martial law over Poland, a society that sought freedom from continuous and overwhelming Communist domination of every aspect of public life, General Wojciech Jaruzelski declared, "Thank goodness we don't live in medieval times, when people fought wars over ideas." He may have meant it, and he may not have viewed his brutal suppression of Solidarity as fighting a "war over ideas." In reality, though, he acted to preserve the domination of a small body of men over society as a whole. And if the declaration of martial law did *not* take place in defense of ideas, it then simply took place to ensure the maintenance of power. For whenever Communist power is challenged by rival ideas, the power considerations always win out, and ideology is simply used to describe, rationalize, or justify political choices made to defend the perpetuation of Communist party control.

Since the very inception of Communist rule, Communist ideology, even among the party membership, has always been used as a "ritual." The long passages from Marx or Lenin, or from such leaders as East German party First Secretary Erich Honecker, are recited with the same mindless abandon as passages in Christian churches are sometimes read from the Bible. One can find in both the Bible and in its Communist equivalent—the writings of Marx, Lenin, and others— something to justify any current theory. Similarly, Communist party meetings assume a catechistic, ritual form, complete with self-criticism, the primitive confessions of real or imagined sins, repetition of rites of passage, and authority invested in the leadership "from on high." The pictures of Marx, Engels, and Lenin and, depending on the country, Ceausescu, Tito, or other leaders, hang in the background. In its extreme form—as is currently the case in Albania or Romania—fawning, adulation, and medieval customs and medals signify recognition and praise of the leaders as the greatest interpreters of the truth; busts of the leaders cast in bronze or carved out of marble decorate desks, in the same way that pictures of saints in churches or in holy corners of houses bless their occupants. It is, of course, interesting to

Ideology and Reality

Polytika (Warsaw)

observe that in spite of these attempts to apply quasi-religious and symbolic representation to its leaders, the party still has yet to manage to garner as much appeal as the persecuted religions maintain.

Is ideology, therefore, "dead" in the Communist states of Eastern Europe, or is it simply irrelevant? Ideology as a guide to action certainly has had its ups and downs, but even today it cannot be ignored as a rationalizer and as a vocabulary; as such, it is not irrelevant. But to follow blindly what ancient German philosophers, dead Russian revolutionaries, or even current Soviet dictators have declared is certainly far less important than the leaders of the Eastern European states pretend it is.

THE STATE AND THE INDIVIDUAL

In our analysis of Communist ideology, the theoretical relationship between the state and society, on the one hand, and the question of social and personal autonomy, on the other, must be specifically stated. For students of Western political development it seems like a tautology to suggest that individualistic behavior, social change, and state power are not contradictory elements—that in democratic societies these elements are all applied to reach goals characterized more by commonalities than divergences. Buttressed by the historical development of Western societies—the limitations on absolute power that began with the Magna Carta, the freeing of the human spirit during the Renaissance, the liberation from oppressive state religions that grew out of the Reformation, the notion of free inquiry as represented by the Enlightenment—observers of the human condition in Western Europe, in the British Isles, and in the United States, tend to see the three components of the individual, society, and the state as a sort of unified trinity. They believe that the individual's supreme importance is supported by society and aided by the state. While such thinkers recognize that the state is sometimes necessary to fulfill some of the goals of individuality, they regard it as just one more—albeit very powerful—organ whose goal is to facilitate the total liberation of the individual from oppression and fear. Thus the excessive use of state power in the West is viewed as an aberration, and the process of enlarging the power of the state at the expense of the individual is regarded as running counter to the mainstream of Western history.

Students of Eastern European history, however, are presented with a far more complex pattern of historical development. While parts of the region have been affected by the same patterns of historical development that prevailed in the West, the area as a whole had developed certain "rhythms," social habits, and societal patterns that have been widely different from the Western model. One of the major differences is a societal authoritarianism, largely alien to the West, that has left its irrevocable mark on the region. Thus native societal authoritarian patterns of behavior and rule have been reinforced by Communist dogma, Marxist ideology, and socialist theory. Put into practice by dictatorial regimes under the guise of Communist party rule, autonomy and the sanctity of the individual and society were subordinated by "higher" social and political goals, as interpreted by basically antidemocratic regimes.

In the following pages we shall discuss: (1) the sources of native authoritarianism in Eastern Europe; (2) the authoritarian nature of Communist ideology; (3) the manner in which these patterns of thinking are socialized; and finally (4) the ways in which the dysfunctions resulting from the contradictions of democratic theory and dictatorial reality are resolved in the Eastern European political context. Viewed from these perspectives, perhaps, the relationships among the individual, society, and the state may be better examined than if we assume that Western development among these factors was simply replicated in Eastern Europe.

Native Authoritarianism in Eastern Europe

> K. now perceived clearly that he was supposed to seize the knife himself,
> as it traveled from hand to hand above him, and plunge it into his own
> breast. But he did not do so, he merely turned his head, which was
> still free to move, and gazed around him. He could not completely rise
> to the occasion, he could not relieve the officials of all their tasks; the
> responsibility for this last failure of his lay with him who had not left
> him the remnant of strength necessary for the deed.
>
> —Franz Kafka, *The Trial*

This chilling picture of K., who almost willingly submits to the
ultimate degradation of having to kill himself without knowing who
condemned him to death or why, describes the ritualism of submission,
unchallenged and nearly expected, and symbolizes the horrors of the
Eastern European political landscape. The Holocaust, the Stalinist
purges, the betrayals of neighbors—these are all patterns of behavior
that reflect the acceptance of hierarchical relationships and, above
all, the acceptance of native authoritarian rule. Contemporary Communist Eastern Europe has reasserted these patterns and re-emphasized
longstanding values of authoritarianism.

The native authoritarianism of Eastern European societies can be
seen in every major aspect of social intercourse today: the titles and
medals, the formalism and competitiveness, the power of the office-
holder, the corruption. The treatment meted out by a bureaucrat to
a petitioner, the "bossism" with which one is treated in an Eastern
European office, the deference shown to the "comrade director," the
client-patron relationships, the ever-present fear of "authority" are
all characteristics of these societies today. The states of the region
now operate as Communist systems, but the sources of their behavior
patterns are deeply embedded in historical processes and traditions.

For our purposes we shall look at four major historical sources of
authoritarian behavior: (1) the hierarchical traditions of Eastern European society; (2) the unquestioning acceptance of authority; (3) the
paternalism in the state, religion, and society; and (4) the unchallenged
nature of etatism.

Hierarchical traditions

The roots of Eastern European authoritarianism date back to the
early periods of the region's history. Generally, we may distinguish
two types of authoritarianism in Eastern Europe: native, personal, or
voluntary on the one hand, and imposed, or systemic on the other.
While it is true that one may make the same distinction for participants
of any system, the peculiarity of authoritarianism in Eastern Europe
lies in the fact that in this region, in just about every aspect of life,
the personal or voluntary tendencies toward authoritarianism have

been reinforced by the systemic factors. It seems almost as if the political systems in Eastern Europe—with very few short-lived exceptions—have been bent on cherishing authoritarian rule and encouraging the subjugation of individuals who live within the system. Unlike in Western Europe, authoritarian behavior has been *accepted* and *desired* as an ideal rather than as an aberration.

Perhaps no other source of native or personal authoritarianism has been as important as the traditional organization of Eastern European society. The historical hierarchies that characterize the region today have always been present and visible. *Every* institution—whether the courts, the aristocracies, the churches, the armies, or the landlords and the serfs had a hierarchical rather than an egalitarian nature.

Unquestioning acceptance of authority

Hence the involvement of people in their own affairs has been absent, as have such rights as participation in communal affairs—evident already in Western Europe, for instance, in the Hanseatic city states since the twelfth century. Instead, with the possible exception of the *zadrugas* (or small village communities) of the Balkans, Eastern Europeans have always been regarded as subjects who have to be "told" what the authorities expect the desired pattern of their behavior to be. The visible bearers of power have traditionally been regarded as bearers of "authority." A policeman in Poland, for instance, was *panie wladzo,* or Mr. Authority, and not a *representative* protector of the people charged by society to maintain order; he was the visible presence that represented the "authorities." Authority thus acquired legitimacy and was not to be questioned by the citizenry.

For Eastern Europeans, therefore, it is extremely difficult even to admit the notion that state authority and its practice are *not* always legitimate, that a representative of that state authority is not always "operationally legally justified" in what he is doing. For most Eastern Europeans, it would be unthinkable to ask to see a search warrant or an identification badge of an agent of the "authorities." It is simply accepted that people on the higher rungs of the legal-bureaucratic-administrative ladder have their "right" to undertake certain actions and that this "right" supersedes those of their subjects. The rights of the policeman to ask for identification papers are questioned as little as the right of just about anybody behind a desk to treat his "petitioners" with as much rudeness as he desires.

This native authoritarianism is so deep-seated that it need not be reinforced universally; random cruelty and terror serve as adequate reminders—and are also generally accepted in a passive manner. Furthermore, the dictator or autocrat tends to be regarded as an all-beneficent leader who, if only he knew of an injustice, would right it; in the West, in contrast, the citizenry is commonly believed to have the right to seek rightful redress for injustices done to them. For this reason, the cognition of the right to protest or revolt against unjust state authority, so prevalent in the thinking of *citizens* in the Western sense of the word rather than in those of *subjects,* is almost always absent in Eastern European thinking. Moral restraints at the individual level are expected to curb injustices stemming from the exercise of power, but institutional and legal restraints on the authorities are largely unexpected; *the right of authority and its legitimacy are rarely, if ever, challenged.*

Paternalism and the role of the church

At all levels of Eastern European society, familial relations have formed a basis of the accepted way of life, and specific "rights" have traditionally accrued to holders of familial authority. The pattern of accepting these rights as duly held was replicated from the small, singular familial tutelage to the greater "extended families," to the community and eventually to the "state" in whatever manifestations. They found representation in social structures and in legal arrangements, but most significantly in the accepted authoritarianism of the father or the father figure. Justified through both the Catholic and Orthodox churches—and priests, especially the Catholic "father"—these rights extended through institutional settings to sanctify the exercise of "paternal authority" in the interests of those under the father's control. Thus, elites have always been viewed, both by themselves and by the public at large, as always acting in the interests of the members of the "family." A young man's right to revolt against the "old ways" of his father—and hence the system—was therefore always negated in advance by the social contract of the father with other authorities; it was the paterfamilias who bore the responsibility for the actions of his family, who, in turn, was expected to obey his instructions. Although certain channels of disobedience were allowed—for example, joining the army or the priesthood—disobedience within the familial system met with strong social disapproval. The general lack of social mobility in the preindustrial states of Eastern Europe—largely intact until the twentieth century and, in many instances, even until the 1950s—retained and strengthened this pattern and contributed to the voluntary acceptance of authoritarian behavior throughout the region.

The Roman Catholic church and, to a lesser extent, the other churches of the region also contributed to the development of authoritarian patterns in Eastern Europe. Their contribution lay in part in the rigid hierarchy of the church and the unquestioned obedience of the lower clergy to their superiors—the priests to the bishops, and

so on—and the ultimate power of the pope's edicts. But their contribution was also evident in the merging of state and church interests
both in Catholic-dominated states as well as in states where the Orthodox church was dominant. The con-subordination of the church to
the king—as long as the latter accepted the Vicar of God as the guardian
of spiritual interests and gatherer of wealth needed for the propagation
of the faith—left a deep mark in society. While this situation, of course,
existed in the West as well, in Eastern Europe the "mix" of hierarchies
and church-state relations was vastly different in the latter region and
more beneficial to the state than in the West.

The church also contributed—whether unwittingly or in full knowledge is a matter of some debate among historians—to the development
of ingrained patterns of authoritarianism by imposing limitations on
individual and group autonomy. While in the West from the Renaissance through the Reformation and Enlightenment there has been a
continuous growth in the quest for the autonomy of the individual
and the small group, in Eastern Europe the church has always viewed
with suspicion groups and individuals that acted autonomously of
groups organized by church authorities. Autonomous groups or individual thinkers—whether Protestants, Orthodox Christians, Jews, or theists
existing outside the church—were viewed by the Catholic church as
potential heretics, and state authority was sought in crushing them.
And since in most of Eastern Europe the Catholic church has had a
far stronger hand in political rule determination than in most of Western Europe—witness, for instance, its continuing importance in the
politics of Poland—the limitations on the autonomy of the individual
and the small group tended to come as much from the church as
from the state. The fact that, in Hungary in the 1970s, the emergence
of local Catholic "basic communities" (small local groups acting independently of the church hierarchy) was viewed by the Catholic church
with greater alarm than by the Communist state is a vivid illustration
of this point. It should be noted, however, that in states where Orthodoxy predominated the same pattern also prevailed, though for different reasons. The unquestioning acceptance by the Orthodox church
of the temporal authority of the tsar or king in political matters also
discouraged local autonomy of the individual and the small group,
and the "Ceasaro-papist" religious doctrine regarded state power as
being legally exercised over the church.

Etatism

Etatism—a term that refers to a state's tight control over economic,
social, and political life at the expense of individual liberty—has been
far more prevalent in Eastern than in Western Europe. Etatism, like

the sources of native or voluntary authoritarianism discussed above, also attempts to control autonomous social developments. It suggests to the subjects that the state should be called on to redress inequities and grievances and that the subjects should thus eschew searching for "self-help" or the pursuit of individual rights. Etatism, in exchange for offering a balance of power more favorable to the citizenry as a whole, sanctifies the state as a benefactor and as a necessary force in the provision of values supposedly desired by all. The people of Eastern Europe have always accepted the state more readily than have Western Europeans; the quest for a balance among the individual, society, and the state has seldom, if ever, tilted toward either of the latter two. The state has historically been viewed as the "motor of progress" and the "grantor of rights." Society, with its anomic and unchallenged energies, was viewed as incapable of achieving as much development as that directed by the state; state-organized development was allegedly expected to serve "all who are worthy," rather than just a few.

The Authoritarianism of Communist Ideology

The emerging Communist ideology fit in very well with the "native authoritarianism" of the region during the post–World War II period; it was anti-individualistic and anti-autonomist by its very nature. Of course, as we mentioned earlier, it was not wholly an *imposed* ideology. But nonetheless, as far as the vast majority of the people were concerned, the system was imposed on them, and even those who initially were attracted to the ideals of Communism found out that they were not getting what they had bargained for.

In Communist systems the party plays an omnipotent and omniscient role. By the clever device of substitutionism (see pp. 112–115), Lenin made the party the "steam engine of history." By insisting on the theoretical supremacy—and hence in practice its monopoly—of Marxism-Leninism, Lenin endowed the party with omniscience. Since the party was allegedly the only organ to have interpreted history correctly, all those individuals and autonomous groups with other and varied ideals were relegated to the "dustbin of history."

Moreover, the party was not merely all-knowing, but also all-powerful and hence could not be rightfully opposed by any anomic or autonomous body. Since neither societal nor legal limitations of the party's power could be imposed, the party *had* to become the sole determiner of every value, the sole source of every decision, the sole organizer of society. The very concept of democratic centralism, which became the organizing principle of all Communist societies and states, rendered autonomous organizations useless—and potentially dangerous—and all such bodies became subordinated to the centralized decisions of the authoritarian party-state. Ultimately resulting in rule by the single "maximum leader," democratic centralism translated the party's fear of the individual and society and the fear of any aspect of autonomous behavior into policy. The behavior of every element of society from the fishermen's unions to local glee clubs had to be subordinated to the principle of democratic centralism; Communist ideological paranoia allowed not the slightest manifestation of autonomy.

This paranoia also extends to the party's distrust of spontaneity— that is, in every sense, a distrust of popular action. Every human act, according to Communist ideology, must be calculable and determinable; even if these calculations cannot be precise in every case, persons in positions of authority must at least be prepared to deal with every aspect of human behavior. This is not to say, however, that the *party's* behavior must be predictable. Quite the contrary, the nature of dictatorship is to be *unpredictable*. But since there cannot be any manifestation of societal or individual spontaneity, the party believes that even the results of its own unpredictability can be controlled and dealt with by the very limitation on the autonomy of action "permitted" to society.

Finally, the Communist system created a society, a social-political organization, that was totally output-oriented. In a sense, every policy was a "public policy" without regard to either the "input" or the "feedback loops." Communist states impose their will on people whom they regard as hostile, who do not know the "truth," who are not enlightened enough to understand why sacrifices are demanded of them. Therefore these people—whether they are peasants dazed by the terror used to confiscate their lands or industrial workers forced to work longer hours for lower pay than during the interwar era—cannot be trusted to provide any "correct" input. Nor can their thoughts and ideals, their feelings about policies, possibly be "enlightened enough" to be taken into consideration. The authoritarianism of the party and its output-orientation implicitly placed even further limitations on social and individual autonomy to those already existing in the region. In sum, then, the Marxist-Leninist ideology imposed on the people of Eastern Europe by a hostile system tended to reinforce the native roots of authoritarianism and further limited the development of societal and individual autonomy.

The Role of Socialization

It is worthwhile at this stage to inquire about the manner in which these patterns of authoritarian thought and behavior are perpetuated in Communist systems. For, indeed, the question "How long can these systems maintain their authoritarian hold over these people without the use of extensive terror?" is one that can logically be asked. The problem is that no system simply imposes values with the use of terror alone; while, unlike so many of our contemporary philosophers I do not believe that terror is the costliest way to maintain order, it is clear that terror *alone* is not sufficient to create internalized values; it can only force desired behavior.

The process of inducing desired behavior is called *value inculcation,* or *value socialization.* Authoritarian values in Eastern Europe have always been inculcated by the state's control of the socializing processes, by attempting to maintain a partial control over such socializing agencies as the family and the schools, and by a limited control over the socializing media. When the Communist regimes came to power they inherited a system where the primary processes of value inculcation were left relatively free. For, with the exception of the Fascist rule of the Arrow-Cross in Hungary, Eastern Europe before World War II and during the interwar era was characterized by a relative plurality of socialization processes and by relatively wide disagreements on the nature of values to be socialized. Although, as we emphasized above, there were some clearly definable native roots of authoritarianism, the processes of value socialization and value determination were still largely uncontrolled.

First and foremost, the Communist regimes attempted to bring these processes under their control. Unlike any system that existed in the region before, they attempted to maintain total control over both the content and the processes of socialization. Consequently the Communist party's immediate aim was to gain control over the socialization agencies, especially the schools and other secondary groups. But unlike any previous regime, the Communists also attempted to control the primary agencies, such as families and peer groups. Distrusting the family as a source of counterproductive value socialization, they tried to limit family autonomy by installing a network of informers, splintering society further and destroying even the inner sanctum of the most basic human social unit. Encouraging the betrayal of father by son, husband by wife, the regime atomized society and hoped for the total elimination of social autonomy. Controlling the media, the schools, the movies, the newspapers—in short, every source of information—to an extent never seen before was a matter of principle. Hence every manifestation of uncontrolled behavior, from self-publication *(samizdat)* to unauthorized meetings of writers' unions, became viewed as a direct effort to limit the rule of the party, to reinstate some social autonomy amid the authoritarianism sought by the hierarchical party. It should be noted that it was precisely in this area where the party was least able to enforce its constant will; malfunctions of the party's value socialization and hence the reassertion of autonomy over authoritarianism can be seen throughout the last forty years of Communist rule in Eastern Europe, especially in Poland in 1956, 1976, and 1981, in Hungary in 1956, and in Czechoslovakia during the Prague Spring.

It is virtually impossible for "social engineers" to create a society, either through terror or socialization, that will fit the prescription of desired dogmas or ideology perfectly. In fact, the patterns of behavior that come into being under such circumstances are not necessarily those desired by any regime. The link between socialization efforts and behavior is as tenuous as the link between values and behavior in any setting. One can coerce behavior; one cannot coerce the acceptance of values that run counter to deeply ingrained ones. However, the pre-existing native authoritarianism in Eastern European society, when reinforced by Communist authoritarian ideology (especially within the first couple of decades after the Communist takeover), seems to have created a system where, viewed from the outside, behavior and openly espoused values tended to coalesce.

This was, of course, understandable. Coming out of a war in which every country—even the "winners"—had suffered terrible losses, the people tended to look at the state exactly as the party wished them to: as the motor of progress, as the provider of material goods and welfare benefits unheard of under the previous regimes, as the beneficial and progressive center of all activities. Up to a point, the party could point with pride to its accomplishments in socioeconomic modernization, and it could insist that previous needs for "autonomy" had vanished as the centralized, if highly authoritarian state, fulfilled all desired ends.

All of these beneficial activities, however, disappeared as dysfunctions in the system became visible. It was easy to be "anticapitalist" or "statist" when the going was good, when signs of progress were tangible, when new towns and factories were built, when the stores were full of goods. It was easy to be a provider of these goods as long as the Communist state was able to reallocate apartments confiscated from the former "ruling classes" and distribute them to those not having had apartments before. It was easy to distribute "ownership" among "all." But the "supply" of what could be easily and freely given away sooner or later simply ran out.

As the failures of industrialization, of rigid, centralized, and faulty planning, of the forced adoption of the Soviet model became visible, the very authoritarianism of the system became a burden that it could simply not shake off. The party's claim to be the fount of knowledge and the only force that could unlock the keys to the future came crashing down with Khrushchev's de-Stalinization speech. The party's claim to be the provider of universal welfare crashed down with the hunger that resulted from the hasty and ill-conceived collectivization and industrialization plans and with the undeniable reality that the Westerners were faring better; the isolation enforced on Eastern Europe was not nearly as totally successful as the Communists hoped when they established the Iron Curtain across Europe.

But most significantly, Communist policies failed because the party's credibility was destroyed. Again, the main reason for this loss of credibility was the fact that there was simply no one else to blame for the failures. The party claimed to have total control, to be omniscient and omnipotent; if it failed, any shred of legitimacy was lost. At the same time, because it destroyed all autonomous organizations, because it had controlled all such organizations and insisted in the name of its ideology that it alone was responsible for everything, the party ran out of scapegoats to blame for evident failures. For a time it could—and did—blame "the cult of personality," the "mistaken applications of the concrete laws of scientific socialism," the "remnants of bourgeois mentality," "imperialist machinations," or whatever else it wished. But the fact is that in the view of the vast majority of the people of the region, the *party* was responsible for the mess it made.

Thus the very weakness of intermediary institutions, which had served the party exceedingly well during the take-over phase and which had reinforced the authoritarian behavior of the state and the members of the system, suddenly came back to haunt the party. There were no longer any autonomous intermediary organizations on which the party could count for support. Precisely because there were no such institutions, the people had little or no choice in moderating their behavior. In other words, as far as the Soviet and many members of Eastern European party elites were able to see, either the people accepted the party leadership in spite of all the problems or they revolted against it, and anyone who was not *with* the party was against it. The authoritarian patterns of Leninism thus forced the people of Eastern Europe either to revolt or to submit to unquestioned party rule. There was no middle ground on which reform movements could grow.

Some exceptions have emerged, to be sure. In Czechoslovakia the Communist party under Dubcek tried to combine the country's long-standing democratic traditions with that of limited party rule, but this experiment was stifled by the Soviet-led invasion in August 1968. Since 1965 Hungary has pursued an "alliance" policy to unite the isolated Communist party and the people; the "live and let live" motto of Kadarism is: "He who is not against us is with us." And for a while, in 1981, it seemed as if the Communist party of Poland would also be able to create a combination of democracy and party rule, autonomy and authority. But like the Prague Spring, this effort failed; only the Hungarian policy seems to have worked relatively successfully.

To thoughtful observers, the other side of the problem of autonomy and authority—the weakness of intermediary institutions—provides a clue to some of the failures of these regimes. The fact that there have never been strong traditions of autonomy in Eastern Europe as a whole also hurt the very groups that have tried to combine the traditional relationship between an authoritarian, ideological party and the needs of a free society. In Poland, for instance, Solidarity, the most promising autonomous movement of the working class, was weakened by such factors as the overwhelming role of Walesa and the strongly authoritarian nature of Solidarity vis-à-vis the state and party authorities. In Czechoslovakia the reform movement also relied on strongly hierarchical patterns, both in regard to the relationship of the party to society and to the internal power arrangements that were maintained within the party. And in Hungary, although the party has been trying to grant some elements of autonomy to individuals, there is a notable reluctance on the part of people to become involved in political activity—for example, the multicandidate elections for Parliament—outside of the rigidly authoritarian patterns set by the Communist party.

In the end, ideological authoritarianism in Eastern Europe remains a principal tool of the party as it seeks a bulwark for an increasingly bankrupt system. It tries to "modernize" Eastern European societies, without conceding the autonomy needed for such sociopolitical and economic modernization to take place. It tries to reward the authoritarian personality and the authoritarian system, claiming that these provide an elemental egalitarianism benefitting all. And it continues to claim the right to destroy or control all aspects of individual and societal autonomy. True progress, at least in the field of economic and social activity, is clearly impossible unless such autonomy is granted in at least the economic and social spheres. And the unwillingness to concede that autonomy is the Achilles heel of Soviet-type ideological systems as they struggle for continued modernization and development.

The Party and Its Functions

THE COMMUNIST PARTY IN EASTERN EUROPE

As students of Eastern European politics undoubtedly realize, all of the books written on this subject place heavy emphasis on the fact that the primary characteristic of the states of the region since the postwar era is that they have become "Communist." No one really takes this term to mean that these countries have reached the "blissful state of Communism." Rather, the word simply means that the Communist party in each state remains the most important component in all areas of political life, whether it is regarded as acting as an instrument of Moscow or as an entity of its own volition. It is not a question of whether the people of Eastern Europe wish for it to maintain this role; the superiority or hegemony of the party cannot be challenged. If such a challenge is posed, when the party either disappears or loses control—as, for example, in Hungary in 1956 or in Poland in 1981—native and/or Soviet tanks will render "assistance" and will restore the party to its dominant position.

The party is thus the most important of all structures, of all interest groups, of all mechanisms in Communist politics. It is simultaneously a formulator of policy for every nation in the region, the administrator and controller of the political process, and the monitor that oversees how the policies are carried out. In a planned society, the party takes on the responsibility for policy making, policy implementation, and policy evaluation in all areas of public life. It is the decision maker and the watchdog, the executive and the legislator, and the control mechanism that rules over the public and the private aspects of societal existence. It subordinates—theoretically as well as in practice—such other structures as the police and the army, the bureaucracy and the trade unions, the youth organizations and the intellectuals' associations. It attempts to, though it never really does, exercise "total" control over society. Though its power has been tempered somewhat by human nature, theoretically it reserves the right to be "totalitarian" at least over the implementation of policies that are deemed crucial to its political existence. Frequently the party has tried to bring reality closer to this theoretical premise.

But the Communist party is also a unique instrument in that it manipulates not only the input (recommendations for policy) and output (policy decisions) of the political process, but also what political scientists call the feedback loop of the policy process—the way the people react to, feel, support, or disobey certain policies. In Western democracies such support or opposition is freely expressed by public opinion or demonstrated opposition, often through the electoral process. But in Eastern Europe, the Communist party controls all these manifestations. Regardless of how people really feel about certain policies, the party may organize public marches and demonstrations, manufacture posters and placards, and compel factories to send a certain number of workers to carry those posters. Then the party focuses the official news media's attention on the "spontaneous demonstrations" to support, for instance, the "democratic struggle of the Nicaraguan people against American aggression" or to scream against "Zionist conspiracies." Its controlled press publishes wildly supportive letters from individuals "happy" to raise the existing quotas of production by 200 percent or to halve the meat rations. The party is everywhere, and it is, at least theoretically, omnipotent; armed with the "omniscience" that it and it alone allegedly possesses, the key to the future according to the (current interpretation) of Marxism-Leninism as proclaimed by the current leader, the party can do just about anything it desires.

The powerful role of the Communist party is enshrined in the constitutions of the Eastern European states. In these documents— whose phrasing is often based on the Soviet constitution—the party is generally referred to as "the vanguard organization of the working class and of all working masses in their endeavor to build the bases of socialism and the leading nucleus of all organizations of the working masses . . . social as well as state." In the Hungarian constitution the party is simply referred to as "the leading power of society"; in Poland the Polish United Workers' party is described as the "leading political force in the construction of socialism." And in East Germany's Constitution of 1968, Bulgaria's of 1971, and Yugoslavia's of 1974 "the leading roles of the working class" and its "Marxist-Leninist party" have been continually reaffirmed. Although these provisions were sometimes absent from earlier constitutional formulations, the very fact that the role of the party is now firmly embedded in the constitution of each of these states makes it very clear that the party lies at the core of political existence.

One could rightfully ask whether or not this implies that the Communist party is the sole "ruler" or "ruling party" in these states. After all, the origin of the word "party" comes from the French verb *partir*, which means "to divide,"—in other words, to divide the political spectrum. But according to Communist ideology, parties are expected to represent class interests in class societies; working-class parties in capitalist states supposedly express the interest of the working class, regardless how amorphous such interests may be, and "capitalistic" or "liberal" parties express the interests of the "bourgeoisie." In Communist states, where, theoretically, no classes are hostile to one another, the only parties that can exist are those that allegedly represent the workers' interests. Thus, at best there can be only two non-antagonistic parties—one for the workers, one for the peasants—and in most instances only one party is permitted to exist, one that combines the interests of the "working class" as a whole. This party is the Communist party.

THE NAME OF THE PARTY

Only in Bulgaria, Romania, Yugoslavia, and Czechoslovakia—and in the region of Slovakia—is the party actually named "Communist." Elsewhere the Communist party goes by various camouflaged names: the Albanian Labor party; the Socialist Unity party in East Germany; the Hungarian Socialist Workers' party; and the Polish United Workers' party. Is it because of "shyness" that these parties do not openly use the name "Communist," or is it because they are afraid that the population would not join the party if they knew that it was *really* the Communist party? Do they recall the joke about the blushing prostitute in the bordello, who when queried as to why she had not joined the party, replied: "My mother barely allowed me to work here. She certainly would not be willing to let me join the party"? Hardly. The reason for their hesitation to call the party by its rightful name lies in: (1) specific national developmental problems, such as the need to emphasize that the party contains, at least symbolically, all elements of the working class and represents all workers, not just the interests of the Communists; (2) an unwillingness to tie the party automatically to formulations that emanate from Moscow's authority; or (3) the particular desire in East Germany to emphasize the idea of "unity" in a divided state without implying that German unification would be acceptable to the East German elites only if it took place under "social-ist" circumstances. Suffice it to say that whatever their names, the Communist parties of the region do maintain control over the political life of their respective countries.

MULTIPARTY SYSTEMS AND THE NATIONAL FRONTS

Control, however, does not mean the total exclusion of all compet-ing political interests, at least on paper. Indeed, there are five non-Communist parties each in Czechoslovakia and East Germany, two such parties—the United Peasant party and the Democratic party—in Poland, and one—the Agrarian party—in Bulgaria. However, the key to their existence lies in the fact that they are viewed as "nonhos-tile," "nonoppositional" parties. They are there to represent the "nonantagonistic" interests of the socialist society and to prove that these states are truly "democratic" because there is more than one party in existence. In reality, all of these parties are under the thumb of the ruling Communist party, which controls the nomination of the leaders of these parties and of all the candidates who are expected to "run" for political office as representatives of these parties.

Czechoslovakia is unique in that there are two Communist parties instead of the customary one. The first party is the Communist party of Czechoslovakia; the second, the Communist party of Slovakia. The latter party is only a territorial subdivision of the Czechoslovak Com-munist party, and its existence is viewed as a concession to Slovak federalism; the current leaders of the state emphasize that the Commu-nist party of Czechoslovakia remains a "unitary" body. However, the very existence of the Slovak Communist party suggests deep divisions within Czechoslovakia's political system.

Everywhere in the region, even in states where non-Communist parties are permitted to exist, there is a catchall political organization, the National Front, or the People's Patriotic Front, that unites all these parties in their search for the "common good" of socialism. The Na-tional Front in each state allows some local initiatives concerning less than meaningful political matters and somewhat more meaningful non-political activities, and it coordinates the various mass organizations involved. Relegating various former non-Communist parties to such subsidiary, politically meaningless roles as played by the National Trade Union Council or the Women's Central Byciclist Organization, the non-Communist parties are regarded as "transmission belts" of the will of the Communist party leadership in the service of the "great goal." There cannot be any doubt, however, about the fact that the Communist party remains firmly in control of all the political, social, and economic processes.

National Front

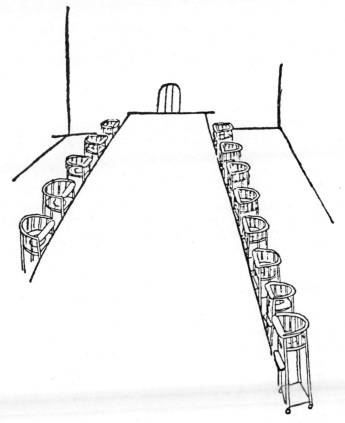

Literarni listy (Prague)

SIZE AND COMPOSITION OF THE PARTY

Recall that nearly everywhere in Eastern Europe the Communist parties were outlawed throughout much of the interwar era; only in Czechoslovakia was it legal. The illegal Communist parties that did exist in the region before World War II operated largely under the aegis of the Comintern and its Soviet-dictated policies, and they did not attract a mass following. They adopted the Russian Bolsheviks' organizational principles and structures. This made sense. The small local cells, where only a few members knew each other, enhanced the safety and the secrecy of the organization. The adopted aliases and the limited contact often helped to foil police round-ups and persecutions and served the tiny conspiratorial organization well while they were out of power. In the postwar era, however, the party became open and recognized. In most states the Communists competed for votes through elections that were sometimes free, sometimes rigged, sometimes a little bit of each.

Most of the parties were tiny at the end of the war, with their future leadership stationed in Moscow. These advanced slowly westward with the Red Army as it battled the Fascists. In the beginning, as the party became legal, it needed membership—and desperately. Expediency won out over principle, as would happen so often in the following years. The Communist party could, to be sure, attract those who were previously hidden supporters and sympathizers, as well as some of the left-wing socialists who were inclined to play at being revolutionaries or were mere opportunists. But even so, party membership remained small in the region, and there were relatively few organized industrial laborers who were a good source of recruitment. Moreover, the percentage of Fascists and former Nazis or Nazi sympathizers was quite high among the workers in several of the Eastern European states, and many Communists thus viewed the laborers as not exactly trustworthy. For some Communist party leaders, however, the mere fact that these people *were* Fascist meant that they could be "persuaded" to join the party in order to avoid an accounting for past deeds. In an interview, a former high official of one of the Communist parties in the region disclosed offhandedly that the Communist parties indeed consciously chose to recruit former Fascists, especially from the ranks of the working class. He said:

> Especially good material was provided to us by the workers who had for various reasons joined the Fascist cause. If they were ready to support the [Communist] party—as were all opportunists who thought that they saw the light and it was really Red—well, their sins would be forgiven, if not forgotten. If they refused to join, on the other hand, we could make sure that the whole strength of the law would be brought to bear on their heads—and we told them what the choices really were.

Thus the Communist parties grew rapidly in membership, as Table 6.1 illustrates. From minuscule bodies they very soon became mass parties, watered down in principles and representing a looser organization, at least for the time being.

As the parties assumed power, however, changes were again rapidly called for. Although the party became the ruling power practically overnight, it never dissociated itself from the Bolshevik organizational principles, continuing to organize itself in relatively small cells, shielded from the population by litany and double-talk. Its membership has undergone fluctuations as great as ever experienced in the history of political parties. Now purged, now dissolved, with frequent exchanges of party cards—and party members—the party nonetheless

Table 6.1   Changes in the Size of the Communist Parties of Eastern Europe as a Percentage of Population

	1945	1948	1956	1966	1976	
Albania	0.1	3.9	3.5	3.5	4.1	
Bulgaria	3.7	7.0	6.4	7.2	8.9	
Czechoslovakia	3.4	21.7	10.8	11.9	9.3	
	(1946)		(1957)			
East Germany	7.2	9.4	8.5	10.5	12.2	
Hungary	1.7	12.0	8.7	5.7	7.2	7.9 (1980)
			(1957)			
Poland	1.0	6.0	4.5	6.0	7.5	5.8 (1981)
			(1955)	(1967)		
Romania	1.6	5.7	3.4	9.0	11.8	
Yugoslavia	1.0	3.0	4.2	5.1	6.7	

has remained a tightly knit group of people who are bound by power cloaked in ideology. Comprising between 4 and 12 percent of the population of each state in the region—with a mean of about 7–8 percent—they are a small elite ruling over the vast majority. Although party membership alone does not necessarily guarantee success for any individual, in Communist states one must belong to the Communist party in order to succeed in the political sphere.

In terms of actual size, the Communist parties in the region have exhibited overall growth from 1948 to the present, although there was a temporary drop in all of the states except Yugoslavia in about 1956. During this period some parties purposefully narrowed their ranks. Others, such as the Hungarian and Polish parties, witnessed the abandonment of the party by many of the more "class-conscious" members. And nowhere has been the drop in party membership more dramatic than in Czechoslovakia, where the party, as elsewhere, changed from a mass organization into an exclusive club. However, before World War II the Czechoslovak Communist party had truly been a mass party, with great popular support both in membership and in voting preference. It should also be noted that during revolutionary upheavals, such as Hungary's in 1956 and Poland's in 1980–1981, Communist party membership has plummeted precipitously.

The Communist parties that today comprise the highest percentage of the population can be found in East Germany, Romania, Bulgaria, and Czechoslovakia. This is not very surprising, since these states are under the most rigid party control. Albania's low percentage—this state also has the most stable party membership in the region—is more attributable to the low level of development and to the large rural, nonindustrial population than to a benevolent rule by a liberal regime. In Yugoslavia, Hungary, and Poland, regarded as having the most

liberal regimes in the region, party membership is relatively low, between about 6 and 8 percent. In these states, party membership is
no longer the only avenue for economic advancement; other criteria
are necessary. And social and economic forces have pressed the party
to make major concessions to the population. In Poland, before martial
law was imposed on December 13, 1981, party membership dropped
by nearly 30 percent. This occurred in a highly polarized party whose
apparatchiks and leaders were unwilling to rescind the privileges and
power that came with holding of the reins of rule.

Is the Communist party really a party of workers and working
peasants? The evidence is often confusing and contradictory, and it
would be difficult to generalize on the subject. On the one hand, some
Communist leaders have spent a lifetime in government or party work
sitting at their desks and claiming to be "workers," lathe operators,
or simply "laboring people." Thus, a foreman or an engineer categorized as a worker, *originally may have been* a worker, or his *parents*
were once members of the working class. Many of the national statisti-
cal offices, moreover, deliberately overstate the percentage of manual
workers. On the other hand, they understate the numbers of the "working intelligentsia"—white-collared employees working for the state—
or the working peasantry in the party's ranks.

Consider if you will, the difficulty of judging one's "background"
for party membership on the basis of class. Application for party membership often came from people all claiming to be just typical workers.
For instance, this excerpt from a typical autobiography submitted for
party membership in Hungary in 1950, during the darkest era of Stalinism. Read it carefully, for it provides interesting clues to the mentality
of the times—and of the necessity of survival.

> I was born to simple people with a close attachment to the land. My
> father died a cruel death at the hand of a big landowner; my mother—
> with six children whom she had to support—had nowhere to go. We
> grew up in what some would regard as a hovel; while never lacking in
> love, we were forced to learn either a trade or continue to work the
> land.
>
> I chose a trade and was employed as a worker at a large factory
> until they drafted me for the Russian front. In spite of my attempts to
> resist our involvement in the war against the USSR, I was forced to
> march to war. Immediately, at the first opportunity, I and my fellow-
> soldiers chose freedom and surrendered to the victorious and glorious
> Red Army. Since my return to Hungary from the USSR, where I learned
> to love mother Russia and the great Soviet people, I have chosen to
> support the Communist party as the wave of the future. As a simple
> worker, all I ask is that the party consider my honest desires and accept
> me as a partner in our common task of building the glorious future of
> Communism.

One's heart is just about ready to open up to the lowly worker who was so eager to join the party, but one may read the autobiography slightly differently.

> My parents were not very smart, though they owned a huge area, 10,000 acres of land. My father died in a duel over a horse when killed by Count X and I lived on the estate in relative luxury with my mother, my six brothers and sisters. Some with greater wealth, of course, would think of our estate as a hovel and since mother insisted on education, we either had to become professionals, businessmen, or scholars. In fact, we all got very high-paying jobs, except for my oldest brother who continued to manage the estate. I became a lawyer but it did not matter, we were rich enough that we did not need my wages at the factory that employed me; during the war I joined as a first lieutenant in the war against the USSR. As the Hungarian army was defeated, I was captured by the Soviets. After three years in the prisoner-of-war camp in the USSR I returned to find that the only job a son of a former aristocrat could get would be to shovel manure at an industrial plant. Since I am tired of fighting the system and would like to work at a better job, I wish to join the party.

History does not tell us whether this individual received his party membership. What is essential for us to consider, though, is the fact that similar tactics were frequently used by applicants for party membership, and the party probably no longer knows who belonged to what class. We must simply note that the Communist leaders attempt to portray the party as a grouping of genuine workers and peasants. And whether it really is or not is relatively unimportant. What is important is that the ethos of wanting to be a party of the workers remains at the core of Communist party dogma. Communists—whose legitimacy of rule is largely based on the notion of "workers' power"— can hardly be expected to stand up one day and announce to the world, "Comrades, we are not really a workers' party anymore." But in order to cope with realities, these region's Communist parties have watered down the term "worker" and call everyone who "works" a "worker" in the "workers' paradise" of Eastern Europe.

Table 6.2 is an instructive reminder of the changes that have taken place in the "class" structure of these parties, regardless of the actual and rather exaggerated claims of the regimes to represent the workers' interests. When we examine the percentage of the workers in the party, two contradictory trends emerge. In some states, such as Albania, Bulgaria, East Germany, and Romania, the percentage of workers in the party has increased from 1948 to the present, although a temporary drop occurred in East Germany in 1966 and a decrease also can be noted in Romania from an all-time high of 51.1 percent in 1962 to 48.9 percent in 1974. A simple variable, such as the level of economic development of a state or the rigidity of the dictatorial policies of its

Table 6.2 Changes in the Class Structure of Eastern European Communist Parties, 1948–1976

		Workers	Peasants	White collar	Others	Unknown or unaccounted for
Albania	1948	20.1	66.5	3.7	9.0	—
	1961	29.7	26.8	41.9	1.6	—
	1976	37.5	29.0	—	—	33.5
Bulgaria	1948	26.5	44.7	16.3	12.5	—
	1962	37.2	32.1	23.6	7.2	—
	1971	40.0	26.1	28.2	—	5.7
Czechoslovakia	1947	45.7	7.9	16.4	4.5	25.5
	1962	36.0	6.6	33.7	23.6	—
	1968	30.8	5.2	6.2	—	58.2
East Germany	1947	48.1	9.4	22.0	20.5	—
	1966	45.6	6.4	28.4	19.6	—
	1976	56.1	5.2	20.0	—	—
Hungary	1951	40.5	11.7	26.3	—	21.6
	1962	39.6	8.7	39.0	17.7	—
	1980	35.6	8.1	47.2	8.1	—
Poland	1948	60.0	18.0	17.0	5.0	—
	1956	44.6	12.8	39.5	3.1	—
	1973	39.6	10.1	43.9	6.4	—
Romania	1955	42.6	22.0 (1960)	11.8	—	23.6
	1962	51.1	22.7	23.4	2.8	—
	1974	48.9	22.0	21.0	7.3 (1972)	—
Yugoslavia	1948	30.1	47.8	13.6	8.5	—
	1960	36.1	13.0	32.0	18.9	—
	1975	29.9	5.4	41.5	23.4	.8

party, probably will not suffice as an explanation. After all, Czechoslovakia is just as dictatorial as East Germany, and Yugoslavia is more underdeveloped than Czechoslovakia. Rather in these states we must seek
our explanation both in the alleged ideological "purity" of their respective regimes and in deliberate policies that favor the workers as the
power base vis-à-vis the "rest" of society.

A different trend is evident in Czechoslovakia, Hungary, Poland,
and Yugoslavia. In these countries the percentage of workers in their
respective parties has been decreasing. There seem to be two comple-
mentary reasons for this decrease. On the one hand, the labor pool
has been exhausted, and by the late 1970s the factories were adding
few new "workers." On the other hand, the regimes of these states
have been shrewd enough to realize that they need the intellectuals'
support far more than the workers'. After all, these leaders are vitally
interested in weathering the storm of international economic crises
that began in the latter half of the 1970s. Modernization requires the
allegiance of the intellectuals, and regardless of their original desires,
even the Polish authorities who imposed martial law in 1981 have
come to the conclusion that their "renewal" or modernization drive
will not succeed without the support of the intelligentsia.

It is important to note that the percentage of white-collar workers
has increased steadily in every party of the region since 1948, except
in East Germany and Czechoslovakia; in the latter, however, about
half of the large number of people "unaccounted for" are likely to
be otherwise classifiable as white-collar workers. In the most liberal
regimes at the time the data were taken—Hungary, Poland, and Yugoslavia—intellectuals accounted for a plurality, although in Albania we
are also witnessing similar trends, and these certainly cannot be explained by the "liberalism" of the Albanian regime. At the same time,
there seems to be a strong correlation between liberal socioeconomic
policies and the influence of intellectuals in the party of a given state.
We should also note the low and ever-decreasing percentage of the
peasants in the party throughout the region. In the Balkan states, where
the percentage of the peasants had been relatively high among the
population, the regimes, especially in Albania, Yugoslavia, and Bulgaria,
at first relied heavily on recruiting party members from the peasantry.
After all, there were only very few industrial workers and even fewer
intellectuals in these countries. But as these societies began to modernize—and as the peasants began to experience the horrors of collectivization in the 1950s—peasant membership in the party began to decline.
The trust of the peasants in the Communist leadership—even in Poland
and Yugoslavia, where collectivization has been rescinded—has never
returned, and the Communist parties even today regard the peasants
with suspicion, and vice versa. A story that is told widely in Eastern
Europe is illustrative. A peasant was beaten by the police for refusing

to join the collective, and his teeth were knocked out. Some time later his wife asks him why he is not having his teeth fixed. The peasant stops dead in his tracks and asks his wife, "For *them?*" While the story may be apocryphal, the distrust between the party and the peasants remains real. Only in Hungary has the regime been successful in easing this feeling, and even there peasants' participation in the symbolic aspects of party political life is still lower than their proportion in the population would suggest.

One more aspect of the composition of the party should be briefly discussed—namely, the percentage of women among the membership. For those who believe that Communism is going to provide equality between men and women, the Eastern European experience has been very disappointing. Women's membership in the party ranges between 25 percent in Romania and 28.3 percent in Hungary. Thus only one out of every three or four party members is a woman. Moreover, women's membership at the highest levels of power, as Table 6.3 depicts it, is even more minimal. Eastern European society and politics are still male-oriented, placing the burdens of compulsory work, housekeeping, and sometimes even forcible sex on women, leaving little time for them to participate meaningfully in the affairs of state.

As mentioned above, party membership does not automatically bestow power and prestige, benefits and privileges, on all members equally. In fact, few tangible benefits accrue to the lowly party member who has achieved no distinction or who does not aspire to or strive for higher office. Such people merely attend party meetings, take part in the everyday work of the party, carry posters and signs at "public demonstrations," and sometimes try to convince their fellow citizens of the "correctness" of the party's policies. While the party elite shop in special stores, commute to work in chauffeur-driven cars, and live

Table 6.3   Representation of Women in Eastern European Politburos, 1976

	Number of posts in Politburo	Number of women in Politburo
Albania	14	1
Bulgaria	14	1
Czechoslovakia	11	—
Slovakia	11	1
East Germany	19	—
Hungary	13	1
Poland	14	1 (1981)
Romania		
Permanent Bureau	15	1
Executive Committee	26	4
Yugoslavia	22	1

in huge houses or apartments leased to them at practically no cost, the average party member generally receives only those benefits that ordinary citizens are entitled to, but he or she is forced to bear the extra burden and work that stem from being a party member. Nonetheless, party membership is an absolute requirement in the allocation of political power, and in this sense, party membership opens up an opportunity for success not available to ordinary mortals.

THE ORGANIZATIONAL PRINCIPLES OF THE PARTY

Eastern European Communist parties follow the Soviet-Bolshevik model and have adopted a special principle of organization that allows them to duplicate and control even all nonparty bodies. This principle,

Entrance for non-Party people.

Literarni listy (Prague)

frequently referred to as "democratic centralism" (see Chapter 5), originated from early Bolshevik practice, developed when conspiratorial secrecy was necessary and Lenin had an insatiable appetite for disciplined revolutionaries who would be willing to obey unquestioningly the decisions made by the leadership.

In reality the principle of democratic centralism that guides each and every party in Eastern Europe is a relatively complex organizational tool that does contain both democratic and centralist elements. The democratic components of the system are easily identified. First, the organization of the party is democratic, because elections and votes are determined by majority rule. There is a strict adherence—in principle at least—to the idea of majority rights, though the rights of the minority are not protected against majority rule. Thus the minority must abide by the decisions of the majority, and they usually do. In practice, if the majority wins on a particular issue, a second vote is usually taken and even the minority now votes in favor of the resolution. It is at least partially for this reason that the votes that are recorded are always "unanimous." Second, there is—theoretically—free debate on every issue within the various organs of the party until all views are expressed. Questions are supposed to be voiced freely and the debates extended. However, this provision becomes, at best, a pedantic exercise, and the questions asked are rarely, if ever, about real issues. In illustrating this principle in operation, Eastern Europeans frequently tell the following story of the "free debate" at a party meeting. The party secretary has been trying in vain to engage the members in a debate. Finally, in exasperation, the proverbial Jew, Kohn, gets up and says, "Comrade Party Secretary, I have only three questions: (1) where is the sugar from our stores? (2) where is the meat? and (3) where is the bread?" The Secretary nods and says, "Comrade Kohn, I'll give you the answer at the next party meeting." At the next party meeting once again free debate and questions are encouraged but once again there are no takers. Finally, after much prompting, the second proverbial Jew, Gruen, gets up and says: "Comrade Party Secretary, I have only one question: where is Kohn?"

This apocryphal story emphasizes the point that free debate is never free of consequence, and any serious questioning of the leadership is dangerous. "Democracy" functions within formal bounds set by the party authorities, who are the only ones allowed to question the course of events. Before a decision is taken in the party, there must be full agreement among the party members, who are given only the facts the leadership chooses to give them and who are expected to endorse in "free debate" the decisions taken by the higher-level party authorities. As the Czechoslovak bon mot went after the ouster of Dubcek by the Soviet-backed Husak regime in 1968: "After careful and long deliberations conducted in the atmosphere of free debate and a friendly atmosphere, Comrade Alexander Dubcek was shot today at his own request; the execution was hailed by Comrade Dubcek as one more example of the great principles of the democracy that have always prevailed in our party."

But the democratic element that the Communist regimes are the most proud of is the principle of democratic elections. Lower-ranking representative bodies send elected delegates to ever-higher-ranking bodies, thus ensuring, so they claim, that the view of every local organ will be represented at every level of the party. However, while this principle seems truly "democratic," the delegates are in fact nominated by the higher-level organs, and one can be sure that the nominee will always be an individual who will be a compliant instrument of the party at all times. The very fact that the nominations are always made by an organization that ranks higher than the representative body from which the members are to be chosen ensures that the will of the party leadership will never be challenged. Moreover, except in Hungary since the late 1960s, there is always only a single list of candidates for all positions. Thus, even within the party, the opposition is given practically no opportunity, and this makes a mockery of the concept of democracy.

But is the centralist component of the principle of democratic centralism applied to the same extent as the democratic component? The answer, not unexpectedly, is that the centralist component almost always wins out. Democratic centralism is heavily centralist for several reasons. First, decisions made by higher-ranking organs are binding on all lower-level bodies. This means that once the leadership makes a decision, there can be no real debate at any lower levels. Thus the party's central organs can never be challenged.

Second, nominations are directly controlled by the central machinery of the party. It scrutinizes every cadre, every "active," every appointment, and the personnel division of the party makes sure that only the most "trustworthy comrades" will be nominated for any position of responsibility. Such a policy can lead to nepotism and corruption, as has been the case in Ceausescu's Romania. In this instance most of the leaders' relatives are powerful and privileged officeholders in a system that has been justifiably called "socialism in one family." As one bitter Romanian riddle puts it: "If there are three applicants for an engineering job, the first being a Ph.D., the second an individual with a master's degree in engineering and thirty years' experience, and a third who is a drunken bum, which one will get the job?" Answer: "The drunken bum, because he is Ceausescu's brother-in-law." In spite of such corruption, the party still considers this policy as a lesser evil than allowing the "best" to rise to the top if they are not "trustworthy" from the leaders' point of view.

Third, democratic centralism is also centralist because—through the complex ideological contortion called "substitution theory" (see Chapter 5)—the party elite and the "maximum leaders" are always considered to have the "correct" view and the ultimate authority to make decisions. Substitution theory holds that the principles of democracy cannot be taken at their face value, because if left alone the unmanipulated and obviously "unenlightened" majority of the population will make incorrect decisions. As a result, it is held, the will of the most "enlightened" segment of the population, the proletariat, its elite, and eventually its single leader should be substituted for the will of the people as a whole. Therefore centralism becomes the will—or ideas, policy decisions, or ideological formulations—of the elite and ultimately of the first secretary, and all organs of the party and the state must obey that will.

The party has had great success in controlling the lower levels of decision making by this simple mechanism. But even here victory has never been complete, and there are several instances when democratic centralism has failed—most notably in Hungary in 1956, in Czechoslovakia in 1968, and in Poland in 1956 and again in 1980–1981 (see Chapter 4).

ORGANIZATION AND STRUCTURE OF THE PARTY

To complement the organizational principle, the structure of the party is hierarchical, elections flowing from below toward the top and real power flowing from the top toward the bottom. As Figure 6.1 shows, party organization proceeds from small units at the lowest level, to ever-larger units at the middle and top levels, and finally to the Politburo or Presidium, where anywhere from ten to thirty people effectively decide the fate of their nation.

The Cells

At the lowest level are the primary organizations, cells. These are groups of party people who work at the same place, in factories, ministries, schools, farms, offices. In short, they exist everywhere where people work or study, where Communists can be united at a workplace. There are also cells in urban neighborhoods and in villages, but they are reserved for those Communists who are not employed or who are retired. (A retired Communist has a choice of remaining a member of the cell at his former workplace or joining one in the neighborhood or village where he lives.)

The size of the cells varies, but the minimum size of a local cell is generally set at 3–5 members; in other words, everywhere where at least 3–5 Communists work, a cell is established. The average size of a unit also varies; in Czechoslovakia in 1975, for instance, there were 1,383,860 members organized into 43,506 cells, with an average membership of 32 persons per cell. In Hungary in 1980, there were 811,833 members in 69,677 cells with an average number of 12 members per unit. But this membership is not distributed evenly; there are far more members in the capital of a country, where there are large factories, ministries, and universities, than anywhere else. For instance, more than 50 percent of Hungary's party members live in Budapest, and more than 50 percent of Romania's live in Bucharest. The largest single cell in Hungary is at the giant Csepel factory in Budapest, followed by the cell located in the Central Committee of the party. Cells with more than 50 members are usually broken down into smaller party groups that, in effect, become primary groups.

These local units meet at least bimonthly. The meetings are usually held on Mondays, Tuesdays, or Fridays after work hours and usually last about an hour. The party secretary reads from a prepared text, usually handed down from the higher levels, concerning the "current political situation." Special meetings are called when something new and important is happening—when the party secretary has to give a new "line" to the members or has to tell them the "reasonings" they should use to explain to nonmembers why, for instance, meat prices must be raised by an inordinate percentage. These explanations are supposed to be followed by "free debate," whose realities we discussed above. There follows a period of free "criticism and self-criticism," in which one's own and each other's failings are supposed to be discussed in the real "spirit of Communism." These sessions either turn out to be vicious indictments of one or more members or routine and meaningless events startlingly similar to communal confessions of sins at some Western worship services.

How subordinate these local units really are to higher bodies is made crystal-clear in the party statutes. The Hungarian party statutes, for instance, state that the

> local organizations and organs of the party are subordinate to the higher bodies. The decisions of the higher bodies are binding on the lower units. The local units may decide independently concerning local questions, but their decisions cannot be in conflict with the policies of the party and the decisions of superior organs of the party. It is the right and duty of the higher organs to alter or abnegate the decisions of the lower organs if they are not in agreement with the policies of the party or are contradictory to the decisions of the higher party organs. Such alterations, however, have to be explained to the lower organs in question.

At these local levels, one may witness another principle that guides the operation of Communist regimes everywhere—namely, the principle of the unity of powers. The theoretical function of the party cells

Figure 6.1 The "Unity of Power" in the Communist Parties of Eastern Europe

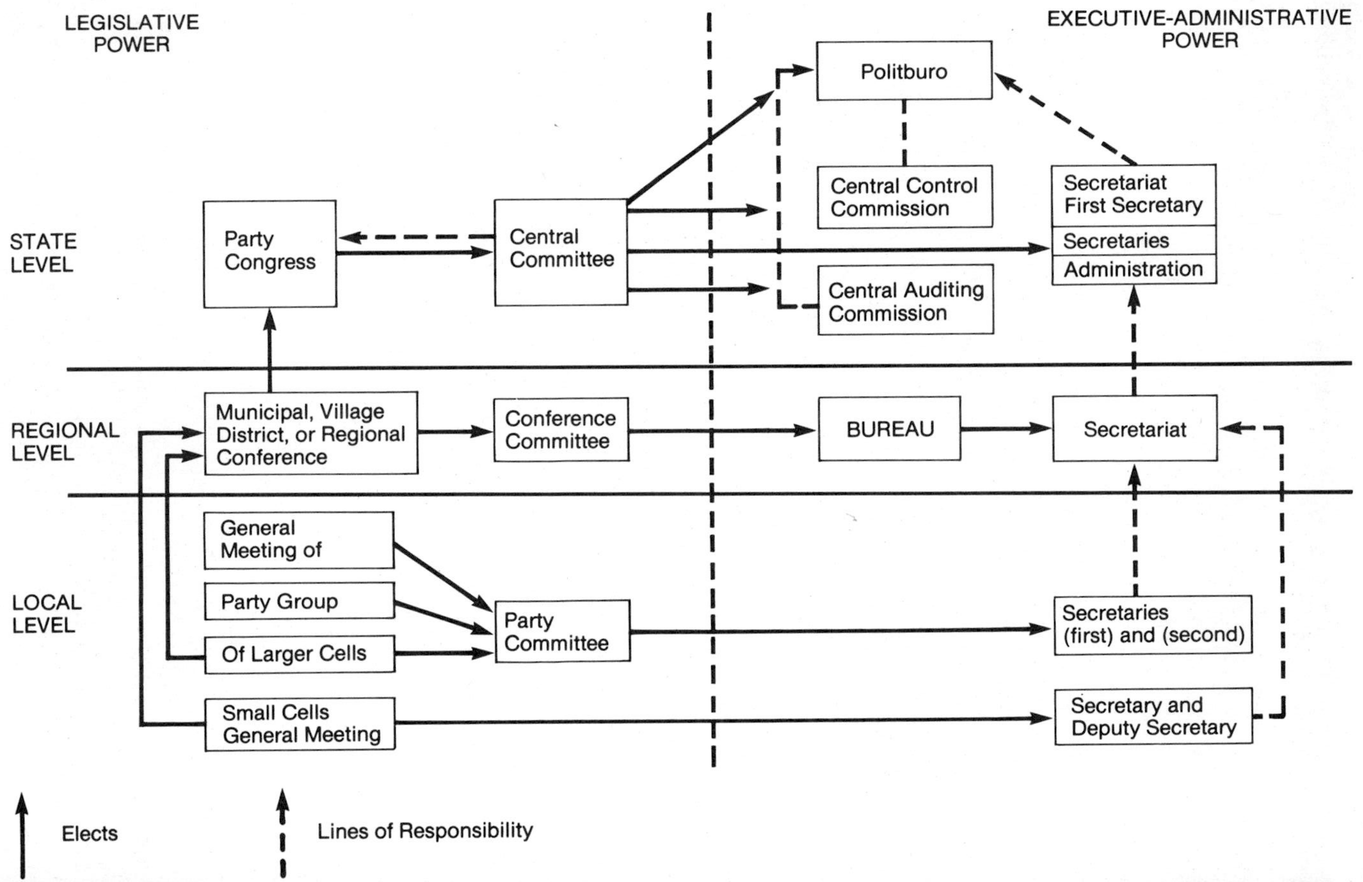

LEGISLATIVE POWER

EXECUTIVE-ADMINISTRATIVE POWER

STATE LEVEL

Party Congress

Central Committee

Politburo

Central Control Commission

Central Auditing Commission

Secretariat
First Secretary
Secretaries
Administration

REGIONAL LEVEL

Municipal, Village District, or Regional Conference

Conference Committee

BUREAU

Secretariat

LOCAL LEVEL

General Meeting of

Party Group

Of Larger Cells

Party Committee

Secretaries (first and (second)

Small Cells General Meeting

Secretary and Deputy Secretary

Lines of Responsibility

Elects

and their general meetings is to serve as the lowest unit of "legislative" power within the party. However, even here the party manipulates the will of the meeting through an "elective" institution. These local units are required to "elect" a leadership for a period of four–five years. Even cells with less than ten members must elect a secretary and deputy secretary. Their nomination is always made by the higher organs of the party, as we have mentioned. In larger cells, elected party committees are responsible for electing their own executive committee, with a first secretary and additional deputies. These elected bodies actually direct and control the work of these larger cells. The party cells meet formally once every three or four months, in order to elect delegates to the higher levels of decision making—naturally on the nominations of the first secretary through the executive committees (see Figure 6.1).

The Regional Conferences and the Central Committee

Above the cell level, the emphasis shifts away from the workplace. In urban neighborhoods, villages, and rural districts such as the *judete* in Romania and the *voivodes* in Poland, district or regional conferences take place, but these meetings take place between once a year and about once every two or three years, depending on the country and its political climate. Acting on the "recommendations" of the executive committee, the party committee, or its first secretary, delegates from the lower-level cells are selected to attend the regional conferences, the supposed legislative arms of the party at the regional level. At these meetings, which usually go on for only one or two days a year, an executive committee and a party bureau are also elected to take charge of the day-to-day operations of the party at the regional level.

The regional conferences also select representatives to the national party congress, held every three to five years. (In some cases, as in Yugoslavia or Czechoslovakia, there is an intermediate stage—the federal republic or province.) These party congresses usually last about five days and include some 500 or more delegates from the lower levels. They hear the "successes" of the past years analyzed and gloated about, the failures glossed over, and the criticisms of scapegoats meted out by the party leadership. Most significantly, such meetings elect the Central Committee, which guides the work of the party as a whole until the next congress. These congresses are unwieldy large bodies, but one must admire the way they are orchestrated by the actual leadership to represent the "will of the party." In addition, they also have a strong symbolic role, emphasizing party unity and demonstrating the party's power over society.

The Central Committee is supposed to be the pinnacle of party decision making, but since it too meets in so-called plenums only once or twice a year and for no longer than two or three days at a time, and since all members of the Central Committee have other full-time jobs, the most significant function of this body is to elect the *real* leadership of the party—officeholders in the Central Auditing Commission, the Central Control Commission, the Politburo, and the secretaries who head the huge divisions of the Secretariat, the actual administrative body of the party. By and large, such elections are determined by the will of the first—or general—secretary of the party, but there have indeed been instances, as in Poland in 1981 and in Czechoslovakia in 1968, when there was genuine and free debate in the Central Committee. During the "dysfunctional" times, the members of the elite could not count on their election as a matter of course. Such cases, however, have been not the rule, but very much the exception.

The Central Auditing Commission

The Central Auditing Commission generally oversees financial expenditures and the financial resources that are at the party's disposal. While large resources of the party accrue to its treasury from such graduated membership fees that range from 0.1 percent to 5 percent of the official pay of the party members, and from the various publications of the party through its own huge publishing house, by most estimates about 30 percent of all party expenditures also are taken from national treasuries. Corruption is supposed to be eliminated by the functioning of the Central Auditing Commission, but experience shows—for instance, in Ceausescu's Romania—that these organizations actually operate at the beck and call of the "true" dictatorial leadership.

The Central Control Commission

The Central Control Commission is concerned with the enforcement of party discipline among the membership. The wayward members, the scapegoats, the recalcitrants, the most obviously corrupt, are warned, disciplined, and singled out for punishment if they openly violate party discipline as set down in the statutes. The Central Control Commission possesses far more influence in most states than does the Central Auditing Commission.

There are great organizational variations among the states of the region regarding these commissions. Albania has a Central Control Commission; Bulgaria a Central Control and Revision Commission; Czechoslovakia and Slovakia a Party Control and Auditing Commission; East Germany a Control Commission and a separate Central Auditing

Commission; Hungary a Central Control Committee, as well as three other committees and four other Central Committee teams dealing with similar matters; Poland a Party Control Commission and a Central Auditing Commission; Romania a Central Collegium and a Central Auditing and Revisions Commission; and Yugoslavia a Control Commission and a Commission on the Bylaws. The functions of all these commissions are generally similar everywhere; only the names vary.

The Politburo

The Politburo (Polibureau, Political Bureau, Presidium, or Executive Committee) of the Central Committee is the highest policy-making body of the party everywhere in the region. In Czechoslovakia, Slovakia, and Yugoslavia it is called the Presidium; in Romania, the Political Executive Committee. The Politburo currently has between eleven to twenty-seven full members, depending on the country. In addition, it frequently includes "candidate" or "alternate" members. The number of such candidate members ranges from none in Hungary to eighteen in Romania. There are five each in Albania, Bulgaria, and Poland and seven in Czechoslovakia. Such candiate members do not have voting rights in the Politburo, but otherwise they are nearly equal in status with the full members. Candidate membership is merely one step away from the ultimate in officeholding; full membership is the pinnacle of prestige and power as far as decision making is concerned.

The organization of the Yugoslav Politburo is somewhat different. Tito reorganized the League of Yugoslav Communists in order to provide both for continuity and for representation of the various nationalities in the Politburo. He did this to preserve the unity of his party and his state after his death. It was an effective plan, if the brief period that has elapsed since Tito's death in 1980 is any guide. Under this reorganization, there is a rotating collective party presidency with eight full Presidium members, elected by the Central Committee. Of these, six members represent each of the six Republican Central Committees; the Provincial Committees of the Autonomous Provinces of Vojvodina and Kosovo each send one full ex officio member to the Presidium. Together they make up the highest policy-making level of the Yugoslav party.

The Secretariat

While the Politburo (Presidium) is certainly the organ in charge of setting policy, the day-to-day administration of the party is carried on by the Secretariat. Here, however, we must make a distinction: the secretaries of the party's Central Committee are elected by the Central Committee itself—at the recommendation of the Politburo, of course—in order to head the Secretariat, the administrative arm of the party, functioning under the supervision or direction of the first (general) secretary and the various other secretaries. The secretaries are typically responsible for functional areas and their number varies from country to country. In addition to the first secretary, there are three in Albania; nine in Bulgaria; eight in Czechoslovakia; three in Slovakia; ten in East Germany; five each in Hungary and Poland; eight in Romania; and nine in Yugoslavia. (In Yugoslavia the first secretary's position is determined also by rotation, and the secretaries are called executive secretaries. In Hungary, there is a general secretary and a first secretary.)

The secretaries of the party are in charge of functional tasks deemed important by the Politburo. For instance, East Germany has specific secretaries in charge of specific activities such as Agitation and Propaganda, Agriculture, Economy, International Affairs, Party Organization, Security, Trade and Supply, Women's Affairs, and Culture, Science, and Education. In Hungary, there are secretaries for Foreign Affairs, Economy, Administrative Affairs (that is, control over the army and security forces), Youth and Party Organization, and Cultural Policy. In the other states the secretaries are responsible for roughly the same areas of concern.

The first secretary

The secretaries always operate at the beck and call of the first secretary of the party, or the secretary general, as he is called in Hungary, Romania, Czechoslovakia, and East Germany. The struggle for the powerful position of the First Secretary has always been intense but, by and large—except in Poland and, since Tito's death, in Yugoslavia, where the position of the first Secretary of the Central Committee (officially the president of the Central Committee of the Presidium of the League of Yugoslav Communists) is now a rotational office without the power that it has elsewhere—these positions have been held by single individuals for long periods of time. For instance, Enver Hoxha, until his death in 1985, had been the first secretary of the Albanian party since 1941, Janos Kadar of Hungary's since 1956, and Todor Zhivkov of Bulgaria's since 1954. While it is no longer customary to shoot former first secretaries if they lose in a power struggle, the loss of power, prestige, and privilege and the "obscurity" availed to such former first secretaries as the Polish Edward Ochab, the Slovak Alexander Dubcek, or the Polish Stanislaw Kania, or the "trial" threat-

The praise and homage to omnipotent first secretaries of the party remains very much of a part of the conventions of Communist societies. Here, children bring tributes to Nicolae and Elena Ceausescu, the President of Romania and his wife, in celebration of the new year. (UPI/Bettmann Newsphotos)

ened for former Polish First Secretary Edward Gierek, still make socialist leaders wary of giving up their power voluntarily.

Some of the first secretaries, such as Nicolae Ceausescu in Romania, are megalomaniac tyrants. Others, such as Hungary's Janos Kadar, are modest, private persons who live relatively simple lives. Still others range somewhere between the two extremes. All of them realize that their rule does not spring from a popular mandate, and they cling to their authority until they can no longer hold the reins of power or until they are forcibly removed by external or internal forces. Once in office, regardless of their personal style, they are in charge of the party and are the largely unquestioned overseers of the administration of the Secretariat.

The Secretariat is a huge and complex structure in itself and varies slightly in organization in each country. Generally, however, the list contained in Figure 6.2 seems to reflect the various departments of the Secretariat. Although not all of the departments are headed by full secretaries, and although there are individual differences in each country, one may find most of these departments all over the region. We shall now discuss some of the more important departments individually.

Figure 6.2   Organization of the Central Committee Secretariat in Eastern Europe

Administrative   Youth
  Army (Main Political Administration)   Science, Education, Culture
  Security, Police   Education
Personnel (Cadre)   Scientific Institutions
  Nomenklatura   Cultural Affairs
Agitation-propaganda   International Affairs
  Ideology   Liaison USSR
  Party Schools   COMECON
  Party Publications   Western Communist Parties
Finance–Fees   Capitalist States
  Auditing   Underdeveloped States
  Accounting   United Nations
Economy
  Industry
  Agriculture
  Foreign Trade
    West
    East

The Administrative Department

The Administrative Department of the Secretariat fulfills probably one of the most significant functions; it oversees the army and the security forces—the secret and political police. This department is often called the Main Political Administration, and it is directly in charge of all army party cells and of all party education that takes place in all the armed forces and the security forces. As will be discussed extensively in Chapter 12, ever since Communist rule began, one of the greatest concerns of the party has been the potential "Bonapartism" of the army—the fear that the army will assume a political role and take over the country. In fact, though, the party elite has been remarkably successful in controlling the army; only once in the past forty years, in Poland in December 1981, has the army actually taken control of the party, and then the party really welcomed its intervention, for, in acting for the party, the army restored "order" in that state. Nevertheless, the party's fear is certainly not totally groundless, for there is some evidence that in Bulgaria in 1965 and in Romania during the early 1970s, voices in the army threatened the rule of Zhivkov and Ceausescu, respectively, and their policies, especially in foreign affairs. Moreover, the strict direction of the secret police is clearly warranted in all these states, for during the early 1950s this force effectively ruled most of the parties of the region. Even today, except perhaps in Hungary and Yugoslavia, the strength of the political police is kept at a maximum, and while it is still considered to be an instrument of the party, its supervision is viewed as exceedingly important lest its full, monstrous power be released once again.

The Personnel Department

Another major department deals with personnel. The party is concerned not merely with its own staffing procedures, but also with the staffing of all other positions of responsibility within the state. It maintains a list, the so-called *nomenklatura,* which is a list of positions that cannot be filled, or from which people cannot be fired, without the specific approval of the party's Personnel Department. The *nomenklatura* is a very long list divided into several subsections, and it includes everyone from the party's first secretary to the chiefs of the important regional railroad terminals. Anyone in a position of responsibility or influence appears on the list. The Personnel Department is the guardian of this list and ensures that the files of everyone on the list are kept up to date. Needless to say, the Personnel Department works very closely with the "file sections" of the political police.

The Personnel Department is also in charge of *cadre* policy—in other words, keeping tabs on all members of the party, particularly on those members called the *aktivs,* who "actively" fulfill their party positions of responsibility. These people are usually full-time officeholders in party units, members of committees at the local level, or members of party bureaus, the Central Committee, or the like. They are the backbone of the party, and the cadre policy is intended to ensure that they get the assignments they really "deserve." Their trustworthiness in most instances is not based on their success in their chosen professions. Rather it is based on the principle of *partiinost* ("party-mindedness"), their loyalty to the "Cause." It is nice if they are qualified professionals, but political advancement will not be guaranteed to any ordinary engineer, scientist, economist, or administrator, no matter how able he or she may be. Advancement can be only guaranteed to those who "deserve the trust of the party," who remain the willing servants of a finely organized hierarchy of elites.

The Personnel Department is in charge of yet another policy that enables the party to continue to exercise its power: the policy of establishing overlapping memberships. This term refers to the fact that the loyal officeholders within the party are also frequently entrusted with non-party offices. A first secretary of the party may thus also be the prime minister, a member of the Politburo, a deputy prime minister, the president of Parliament, or the head of the trade unions. Ceausescu, for example, is the president of Romania, president of the State Council, chairman of the National Defense Council, and chairman of the Supreme Council for Socioeconomic Development. He also maintains his post as secretary general of the party and is a member of the Permanent Bureau and the Presidium. Others are somewhat less "hoggish" about their accumulation of offices. For instance, General Jaruzelski of Poland is "merely" the first secretary of the party, the defense minister, a member of the Politburo, and the former prime minister. But the overlapping membership is prevalent at lower levels, too. In fact, most middle-level officeholders feel safer if they have a large number of posts.

The Department of International Affairs

The Department of International Affairs is the division that maintains a constant liaison with the USSR. This department has a singular importance. While it is true that the USSR has other means to control many of the Eastern European states, the day-to-day party contact generally takes place between the Soviet embassy in each state and the Department of International Affairs of that country's Communist party. The party's control over foreign affairs is generally complete, and if and when some development takes place in the international sphere, the country's response is first cleared with this division.

The Youth Department

The Youth Department also plays an important role. Its primary function is to supervise the Komsomol, or Communist Youth Organization (known by different names in different states), which screens and "trains" party members-to-be between the ages of 14 and 28, and its subsidiary organ, the Young Pioneers, which includes youth between 6 and 14 years of age. Since in most cases one cannot join the party until one is 18, these youth leagues are important agencies of socialization. The Youth Department also deals with the problem of "alienated" youth—those young people who exhibit values and behavior not congruent with what these regimes would like to see.

THE PARTY ELITES

As we have seen, the only road to political success for an individual in Eastern Europe is to become a part of the political elite. Thus the function of maintaining the power of the elite and protecting its interests remains one of the most fundamental tasks of the party. The elites operate within societies that have undergone rapid technological, social, and political change. While there are many ways to analyze these elites, for our purposes we shall examine three aspects of the problem: (1) the differentiated levels of power relations among the elites; (2)

the ideological versus pragmatist split within the elites; and (3) the "nativist" versus Muscovite orientations of the elites.

Levels of Power among the Elites

Power, in Communist societies as well as elsewhere, flows in inverse proportion to the number who possess it. The fewer in control, the greater the power that decision makers possess. In Communist Eastern Europe, real power has tended to accumulate in the hands of the first secretary. The Stalinist-type of rule by a single dictator—such as a Ceausescu in Romania—is not an aberration: it is an endemic result of a system that is based on the concentration of power and functions. Backed by the police and having sole control over the organized means of violence, the "maximum leaders" of the Eastern European societies are praised by sycophants as the "greatest students of Stalin" (and they often really are), or the "wisest leader," or the "most beloved man in our history" (one hates to contemplate the deeds of less loved national heroes). Carried away by the continuous adulation, the temptation for the dictator to believe in the adulatory phrases soon becomes too much. Few mortals can fail to believe the sweet words they continuously hear.

Nothing illustrates this principle as well as the following story. The Romanian secret police is told to find the man who has originated a series of nasty jokes about Ceausescu. After a dragnet was cast, the hapless Lupescu is caught. His captors drag him, in hand and leg irons, in front of Ceausescu, who orders the chains removed, offers the prisoner a cigarette, bids him to sit down, and asks how much Lupescu gets for one of his jokes. "Well," says Lupescu, "maybe two or three dollars. If it's very good, maybe a fiver . . ." Ceausescu looks at him in amazement and asks, "And for this pittance you would be willing to sell out the greatest man in Romanian history, the man most beloved by the Romanian people . . . ?" Lupescu starts laughing hysterically, crawls to Ceausescu, and with tears streaming from his eyes he kisses Ceausescu's hand, thanking him all the time, "Thank you, thank you Comrade Ceausescu, for this one I'll be sure to get ten bucks!"

The story is apocryphal, but the megalomania of most of these leaders is not. Some are more modest and more reticent about exercising their power. And since Khrushchev's dethronement of Stalin at the Soviet Communist party's Twentieth Congress in 1956, there have been somewhat fewer cases of claims and displays of the "cult of personality." Nonetheless, the importance of the first secretary is still exaggerated in Albania, Bulgaria, Czechoslovakia, East Germany, and Romania.

Undoubtedly, however, Ceausescu is the most notorious example. In Romania today the personality cult is so strong that it extends to

the leader's family—some twenty-seven relatives of Ceausescu currently hold important party or state positions—and most particularly
to his wife, Elena. Since the early 1970s she has appeared dressed in
leopard coats, rich furs, mink, and Persian lamb. In 1979 a long poem
described the loving couple as "two Communist hearts under the great
Romanian flag," and one poem wished them a happy life "enveloped
forever in the love of the entire people." Another verse extols:

> To the first woman of the country, the homage of the entire country,
> As star stands beside star in the eternal arch of heaven,
> Beside the Great Man she watches over Romania's path to glory.

Today only Albania—even after Enver Hoxha's death in 1985—
and sometimes Bulgaria can offer similar examples; the Stalinist mentality is still strong in these societies. While in Czechoslovakia and in
East Germany, the first secretaries are praised and publicized as the
best leaders, such glorification is not as extravagant as it was for their
predecessors, Walter Ulbricht or Antonin Novotny respectively. In Poland three generations of disappointment and ever-lengthening lines
outside increasingly empty stores have destroyed the credibility of
omniscient party leaders there. And in Hungary, Kadar has actively
discouraged any personal adulation.

Below the first secretary, the most important level of the ruling
elite usually consists of between fifty and a hundred people in positions
of real power. They are the members of the Politburo and the Secretariat, they are the Secretariat's department heads, leaders of the government, the prime minister, his cabinet, and his inner circle of advisers,
frequently men without portfolio or even official power. They possess
the prestige and the opportunity to live in luxury at the state's expense.
They ride in chauffeur-driven limousines, have huge private villas,
visit stores where everything is available to them, vacation in secluded
resorts furnished with every aspect of luxury. Whether they all avail
themselves of such accoutrements of prestige or, like Kadar, ostentatiously reject them depends on the level of their power and their
personality.

The next echelon of power consists of people in middle-level positions—such posts as the secretary of the regional party organization,
Central Committee member, member of the party structure, government official, bureaucrat in the state or public sector, or manager of
a large firm. While these people are not at the pinnacle of power,
they certainly possess such trappings of power as, for instance, membership in the local hunting club, aping the manners of the former gentry.
The abuse of power is clear and visible at this level, and corruption
and nepotism are observable. This is the group that has attempted,
in many cases successfully, to sabotage economic and even administrative reforms. Such reforms—democratization or liberalization—might

have enabled the state to undertake much-needed modernizations, switching from labor-intensive to capital-extensive methods of development, but they also could have lessened the power of this middle-level elite. As the case of Poland in 1980–1981 clearly indicates, it was precisely this group that resisted the attempts at "renewal" and backed the conservative or "orthodox" wing of the party in its efforts to crush the liberal or moderate wing and the budding freedom proposed by Solidarity. It was also this group that most significantly supported the crackdown on Dubcek's reforms in Czechoslovakia in 1968. Even in Hungary it has been the greatest hindrance to the success of the New Economic Mechanism. Afraid of losing their privileges, the 5,000–10,000 officeholders at the middle level of each country comprise perhaps the most conservative group in Eastern Europe.

The lowest level of the elite consists of the department heads of local councils, chief accountants of state farms, or party secretaries at local cells. But through their listing on the *nomenklatura* they aspire to power in the future, carefully taking the necessary steps to success. Willing to change their ideas at the drop of the hat if this is what they must do to better themselves—they are fairly competent individuals who are also willing to carry out the will of the top leadership without question. They believe that the most immediate cause of their inability to rise to the top is not the existence of the top elite of the country, but the officeholders of the middle-level elite. Consisting of perhaps up to 100,000 people in each state, this low-level elite is a wide and divergent group whose members have varied backgrounds, ideas, and desires but share a determination to progress upward not merely through sheer ability but also through the approval of the top leaders of the party.

One note should be added here. Communist parties, unlike most other parties, are *mobilizing* parties that involve and give roles to large numbers of people. In Hungary, for instance, there are 2,000 men and women who compose the active party leadership in a party of some 800,000 people, but when one counts *all* the party members who occupy leadership positions from the basic cell to the Central Committee, the number rises above 100,000! Thus, one out of every eight Hungarian party members belongs to some level of the party's bureaucratic and intellectual elites.

Ideology versus Pragmatism in the Elites

A second way to examine the elites is through the ideological versus pragmatist split that is evident within most of the parties. Most of the early leaders of these states had indeed been "revolutionaries." They were men and women who had had to fight against the ruling structures of relatively backward societies in order to see Communism ascendant. Some, like Matyas Rakosi, had spent years in prison and when they finally attained power the only model of development they were familiar with was the USSR's, so they tried to copy it. Since, however, the Soviet model did not provide all the answers, many of the early leaders looked at the Talmudic formulations of Marxism as a guide to orthodoxy figuring that, at least doctrinally, they could not be faulted. Their educational level was far below that which is required to run a developing society with enormous problems. They tended to trust only those advisers who were politically reliable. There is a story about an Eastern European leader who desired to hire an economic adviser. He asked the first applicant: "How much is two plus two?" The man replied without hesitation: "Four." He was thrown out immediately. The second applicant was asked the same question. He pulled out a piece of paper, calculated the equation and replied: "Four." He too was ejected. The third applicant was asked the question, looked at the leader, and replied with a smile: "How much do you want it to be?" Needless to say, he was hired.

However, as these societies developed, the minimal expertise of such leaders was no longer sufficient to deal with the complex problems of foreign trade, investments and large loans from abroad, energy crises, oil negotiations, or the surge in interest rates. As the Eastern European states embarked on the road to modernization after the early 1950s, good technicians, good managers, and good administrators were in woefully short supply. The extensive debate of the 1970s over the best way for the further development of these countries was tinged with "ideological negativisim" about the role of the market, the roles of consumption and production, the healthy balance between heavy and light industries—all taboos during the Stalinist years. Yet these issues had to be debated as the necessities of economic development propelled the leaders to hire better technicians. Pragmatic people were now needed, people who cared less about the ideology than about the way to solve seemingly impossible problems of development and change.

The case of Poland in the 1970s is an extreme but illustrative example. The Polish model of development was based on large investments in heavy industry made on the basis of "easy" long-term loans from the West. Projects were begun—against the advice of many economic experts—and remained mostly unfinished. Manufacturing plants produced hundreds of thousands of television tubes that could be sold literally nowhere in the world. They were uncompetitive in price and quality and were ten years behind in technology even when they first came off the assembly line. Factories built on the expectation of cheap energy lay idle; expensive energy costs made their operation no longer feasible. Much of the blame for Poland's economic woes lies in the unwillingness of the ideologically grounded party elite to come to terms with the pragmatism necessary to run a developed and complex system.

Elsewhere, specifically in Hungary and East Germany, technicians and pragmatists *have* successfully devised systems that can accommodate the ideological mandate in a practical way. Although diametrically opposite in terms of their use of the market and planning mechanisms—with Hungary relying largely on a mixed market and East Germany still practicing central planning—both of these states have managed to achieve a higher level of economic rationality.

Muscovite versus "Nativist" Elites

Finally, let us consider the split between Muscovite and "nativist" orientations in the elites, in both domestic and foreign affairs. As we mentioned above, when the Eastern European Communists came to power, many knew of only one model to follow: the Soviet model. The reasons for this were manifold, and they were not all due to the fact that the Soviet Union "imposed" the model on the new regimes. Many people thought that the Soviet Union had demonstrated the success of its development by having survived for a quarter-century, and the Soviet victory against Hitler seemed to be another convincing proof of the viability of the Soviet system. Some sentiment, though not widespread, thus favored a pro-Moscow orientation. Indirectly this sentiment helped pro-Moscow Communists, "Muscovites," imposed largely by the Red Army upon these states, to come to power. These leaders had spent the interwar years largely in Moscow and were by and large unfamiliar with the countries they were about to rule. Absolute obedience to Stalin and to Moscow—the aping of everything Soviet in domestic and foreign affairs—characterized Muscovite rule, and the resulting "mini-Russias" were the tragic end-product.

The first "nativist" leadership, which rejected Soviet models and orders, came to power in Yugoslavia. Nationalist, or at least less wholehearted pro-Moscow, sentiments began to surface elsewhere in the 1950's—under Imre Nagy in Hungary and Wladyslaw Gomulka in Poland. Though Nagy was executed after the revolution of 1956, his successor, Kadar, never copied the Soviet example to the extent that Nagy's predecessors had. Romania next began to move away from Muscovite policy and leadership, at the beginning of the 1960s, and Albania soon followed suit. Although Dubcek's short rule in Czechoslovakia was not a very good example of characteristic or "model" development in Eastern Europe, his popularity as a "nativist" leader showed how disliked the Muscovite regimes really were.

The split between "nativist" and Muscovite trends is evident in both domestic and foreign policies. In domestic affairs "nativist" policies follow nation-specific "roads to socialism" and are clearly divergent from the Soviet model. These can be found in Yugoslavia, Hungary, and to some extent, even as of this writing, in Poland. The rest of the Eastern European countries follow the Soviet model quite rigidly, but this no longer means that everything the USSR does is copied faithfully by even the Muscovite leaders. Indeed, some of the leaders in Eastern Europe—notably in Romania and Albania—are *more* Stalinist, *more* dictatorial, than the current Soviet leadership. Others—for instance, the East German elite—are more inventive, more skillful, more managerial, and far more successful in the political sphere than the Soviet leaders, but they still retain the Muscovite model.

In foreign policy one can also find divergences from the Muscovite form and content. While East Germany, Czechoslovakia, Poland, and Bulgaria tend to follow Moscow's dictates faithfully, Albania, Romania, and Yugoslavia often oppose Soviet policies. Hungary, while following the Soviet line in general, does so by trying to offend as few people in the world as possible, and its leaders often express a desire for Hungary to become a bridge between East and West. Nor is the foreign policy of a state such as Romania absolutely "independent." While, for example, it verbally opposed the USSR's invasion of Afghanistan, it failed to vote to condemn the USSR at the UN; it merely abstained. The independence of Yugoslavia and Albania, however, should not be doubted.

Thus the definition of the "nativist"/Muscovite split is quite imprecise; it is generally used to refer to "independent-minded" leaders versus those who owe their allegiance to the USSR through long years of association with Moscow. Unlike earlier leaders, such as Walter Ulbricht, Matyas Rakosi, Boleslaw Bierut and Klement Gottwald, the current leaders of Eastern Europe have spent relatively little time in Moscow as exiles or as students at the party schools of the USSR. Although all of them have visited the USSR frequently, only Jaruzelski spent extensive periods there—not entirely of his own volition, one gathers—during the war. Some of the leaders—Kadar, for instance— do not even understand Russian, let alone speak it. Others, like Husak, Zhivkov, and Jaruzelski are near-fluent in that language. Fluency in Russian for Czechs, Bulgarians, and Poles, of course, comes much more easily than for Hungarians or Germans, but the function of fluency is not entirely due to linguistic background: some of it is a demonstrative element of the desire to show independence or "servitude."

Clearly, a nativist orientation today has an appeal for the many leaders who recognize a growing need for domestic support. In earlier times the Muscovite leaders hoped to gain legitimacy by proclaiming themselves to be the brightest students of Stalin. They were so little concerned with reality that they thought this to be an attractive way to gather popular support, and the uprisings of 1956 and the Prague

Spring of 1968 show conclusively how wrong they really were. Today's leaders, Muscovite or "nativists," do not make the same mistake; many of them choose to describe their rule as "national in form, socialist in content," whatever the meaning of these terms really is. The Yugoslav, Albanian, Romanian, and Hungarian leaderships clearly hope that a "national," if not always a nationalist, course of action will make them more acceptable, more legitimate than the Stalinist Muscovites who were regarded by the population as representatives of an alien, imposed regime.

CHAPTER 7

The Constitutional Framework

Prisoner A: What are you in jail for?
B: I demanded my constitutional rights!
A: Did you get them?
B: Yes . . . fifteen years' worth.

■ Lest it be misunderstood by students of Eastern European politics, our earlier analysis of the party structure did not mean to imply that the Communist party in these states has replaced traditional structures of governance. In fact, as we made clear previously, the theoretical function of the Communist party in all of these countries is to formulate broad-range goals and strategies as well as the means by which these goals should be reached. The day-to-day administration of these policies and the implementation of the party's goals, however, are the job of the "government," and for that purpose a well-devised constitutional framework had to be developed.

During the last four decades, an intense debate over the questions of constitution and constitutional rights in Eastern Europe has been waged in both the East and the West. In the East a few brave souls have called for the observance of their constitutional rights. The Chartists in Czechoslovakia, for instance, since the 1970s demanded simply that their government live up to the written words contained in the

Czechoslovak constitution. Most of these individuals, as of this writing, are either in jail, in exile, or without a job in their chosen profession.

Western political analysts have also disputed the nature of the Eastern European constitutions. Some hold that these constitutions are merely formal documents that do not actually guarantee rights to the people; others maintain that the Communist constitutions are protectors of the rights of the state *and* the people. For students of "pure" political science, this debate is perhaps of only academic interests, but for those of us immersed in studying the region as a coherent whole, the constitutions of these states represent more than an aspect of cursory interest; they delineate the formal structures through which the operations of the various states may be analyzed.

Unlike the constitutions of the Western democracies, which outline the "ideal" world and provide a framework within which that ideal world can be approximated, Communist constitutions represent a statement of accomplishment, a political announcement of the level of political development that a state has achieved. According to Communist theory, the Eastern European governmental entities exist in states that were more advanced than Russia was in 1917, but less developed than the USSR after World War II. Consequently these states, after the Communist takeover, were claimed to have achieved the stage of "people's democracies" operating in "peoples' republics," a "higher" stage than mere "bourgeois democracy." As these states themselves developed, they began to claim—mostly on the basis of local, rather than Soviet, initiative—that just like the USSR, they too have reached the stage of socialism. Albania, Czechoslovakia, Romania, and Yugoslavia were the first to declare that they reached this stage and proclaimed themselves to be "socialist republics." Bulgaria, Hungary, and Poland contend that they are simply working hard at *building* socialism in their people's republics. The East Germans assert that they have nearly reached the stage of socialism, but they continue to operate as a "democratic republic."

Corresponding to each such phase—expected, of course, to culminate in the ultimate stage, Communism—there are different ways in which force is supposed to be used. For instance, the stage of people's democracy is supposed to be accomplished by the unstinting use of the dictatorship of the proletariat as an instrument of revolutionary justice against "class enemies." Once the stage of socialism is reached, however, the dictatorship of the proletariat is supposed to be replaced by the application of socialist law. For example, the earliest Communist constitutions always reflected the fact that during the takeover stage the dictatorship of the proletariat entailed the deprivation of the rights of former members of the ruling classes—the aristocrats, capitalists, clergy. Once a state has either achieved "socialism" or claims to be involved in the "full-blown" or all-out construction of socialism, such discrimination is no longer deemed necessary and all are supposed to be equal before the law. These "statements of accomplishment," of course, do not always correspond exactly to the truth, but then again one cannot expect that of any written document. Nevertheless, both the citizens of these countries and those observing them from the outside should be able to hold the regimes accountable should these accomplishments fail to measure up to the documents regarded as "fundamental laws."

The very necessity for the existence of these documents must be briefly discussed. While revolutionary organizations generally do not wish to burden themselves with written documents that can bind them and limit their application of "revolutionary justice," the Communist states all regard such documents as necessary. Implicit in this necessity lies the fact that while these states may still regard themselves as "revolutionary," they also emphasize that they are *states*. And in order to maintain power at least semilegitimately, and thus in order to garner minimal acceptance by the population, these regimes consider it important to have a constitution to prove that they at least rule in the name of some organized and written basic law.

Just because a state has a constitution, however, does not mean ipso facto that it has a "constitutional" government—that is, that the exercise of power is limited by some sort of checks or balances independent of the wishes of a dictator or his representatives. A written document alone does not guarantee such a limitation, and, of course, the example of Britain shows that one does not need a *written* constitution in order to have such a limitation in existence. In most Communist states, the constitutions always include provisions for the practice of nearly *unlimited* power by the party, but they also provide a delineated framework within which the "normal" structures are supposed to operate.

If nothing else, all of these Eastern European regimes have tried to observe the niceties of constitutional procedure and accord at least theoretical roles to constitutionally guaranteed institutions. Such institutions as, for instance, the parliament—notably in Poland in 1981, in Yugoslavia, and in Hungary since the mid-1970s—do tend to exercise certain limited rights and may occasionally contradict the desire of the party leadership in doing so. And while it is clear that the parliament of these states are not likely to be as free in the conceivable future as, for example, the Hungarian or Czechoslovak parliaments were in 1945–1947, the constitutional guarantees of the independence of the parliaments' decision making mean that they need not be mere rubber stamps of party will in every case.

FEDERALISM AND COMMUNIST POWER

The constitutions of the Eastern European states provide two types of political systems, federal and unitary. Regardless of the actual degree of control by the party, the mere fact that there exists a federal system in Yugoslavia and Czechoslovakia does indicate greater interplay between the local and the national levels than in states where only unitary systems exist. Federalism—the authority of the local province, frequently based on nationality or historical claims of autonomy—was a powerful movement when Communist power was first established; such autonomy was claimed initially for the local *laender* in East Germany, for the autonomous province of ethnic Hungarians in Romania, and for the federal structures of Czechoslovakia and Yugoslavia.

But the initial enthusiasm for federalism in all of these states waned as Communist authority—the power of one central organ to determine the affairs of society as a whole—tended to become more important than local control. In East Germany the *laender* were demoted to be mere *bezirke*, or "districts," and the Hungarian Autonomous Region of Romania gradually lost any independence after 1956. In Czechoslovakia and Yugoslavia, however, the federal structure survives, still provides important elements of local autonomy, and plays significant roles in the allocation of power and resources.

In Czechoslovakia the Slovak minority has always aspired to autonomy and to the more equitable allocation of the resources of the state. The first Communist constitution of 1948 provided for Slovak autonomy by setting up a separate Slovak National Council and a Board of Commissioners that would, in general, decide the major political issues for Communist Slovakia. As the Communist party, however, gained power throughout the 1950s and much of the 1960s, Slovak hopes for a true federal structure dissolved. By 1960 the Board of Commissioners had been abolished and the Slovak National Council had failed to amount to a real parliament. Slovak dissatisfaction focused on this issue in the late 1960s, at about the same time that the Prague Spring blossomed. As a result, there was a renewed attempt at creating a "true" federal structure, with local powers vested in a Slovak government; between April and October 1968 a reorganization of the government established separate legislative and state-executive bodies for the Czech and Slovak regions. But in the aftermath of the Soviet-led invasion of Czechoslovakia—contrary to the desires of some Slovaks who supported the Soviet-backed Husak regime—the powers of the central government soon increased again at the expense of local autonomy, and by 1971 the autonomous Slovak and Czech cabinets played much reduced roles. By the beginning of the 1980s—as the symbolic impact of the Prague Spring and its aftermath waned—while there still existed a separate Slovak subsystem with some power, the federal structure was little more than a constitutional nicety. Real power over most decisions today resides in the central government, and local autonomy is more a myth than a reality.

In Yugoslavia, too, a great deal of enthusiasm was expressed for a federal structure under the new Communist regime, and in the constitution of 1946 it was clearly stated that the state would consist of six sovereign people's republics. But as the Communist party became more and more centralized and powerful, the sovereignty of these republics decreased. By 1963 little was left of the "independent" governments and their "sovereign" rights. However, these trends were reversed after nationality tensions erupted in 1966, as it became very clear that the six republics and two national provinces did not have the same aspirations, potential for development, or goals for ethnic identity.

Consequently, in order to maintain Yugoslavia as an independent state and in order to prevent ethnic frictions from tearing the state apart, the Yugoslav leadership, still under Tito's undisputed dictatorship, began a genuine "refederalization" program. Under this system, local autonomy is supplanted through a system of local self-management and local communes, while the federal structure allows both for central control over foreign affairs and defense, and for partial coordination of the internal economic market. While the latter activity involves, of course, an enormous range of decisions—such as the establishment of foreign exchange rates, pricing and investment policies, economic planning, and federal budget problems—each local subunit is allowed veto power over any major decisions that affect its economy to a significant extent. Although, predictably, refederalization caused grave economic problems in the late 1970s, as the various republican leaderships were unable to agree on economic priorities in an era of scarcity, the Yugoslav elites emphasized the need to hold the state together and thus felt that they had to pay the economic price for a politically viable federalism.

Hence, since 1974, the federal structure of Yugoslavia is based on the local autonomy of the six republics (Slovenia, Croatia, Serbia, Bosnia-Herzegovina, Montenegro, and Macedonia) and the two autonomous provinces (the Vojvodina and the Kosovo) in all matters, except those that are specifically the responsibilities of the central government (see above). Unlike almost everywhere else in the region, where only unicameral legislatures can be found, the federal legislative power is vested in two houses—the Chamber of Republics and Provinces and the Federal Chamber. Together these form the *Skupstina,* or National Assembly. In fact, even the presidency of the state is based on the representation of each republic in the Presidium; the presidency rotates annually among the representatives in the Presidium, with each member being elected to the Presidium for a period of five years on a staggered basis.

Some critics, of course, would point out that party control—though the Yugoslav party too is organized along "ethnic-nationality" or "republic-provincial" lines—is inherently contradictory to the principle of federalism. After all, democratic centralism or "Marxist-Leninism" in its Soviet practice rejects any initiative coming from "below," and every policy made at the higher levels of the party must be accepted by all of the lower levels. But the simple fact is that Yugoslav society is so strongly affected by pluralist forces and individual and group interests that, although the party does take stands on policy, autonomous local groups frequently have opposed the party and its formulations successfully. This local autonomy is the basis for the successful operation of the most "federal" system in Eastern Europe. Moreover, while there is a Yugoslav League of Communists, today's republican party structures are far stronger than just "local" organs of a central party; here, too, the autonomy of the local units are real and not just theoretical. In fact, the autonomy of the republics and provinces of Yugoslavia certainly matches and often exceeds the autonomy that the individual American states have.

THE LEGISLATIVE BRANCH

The Functions of the Legislatures

As mentioned earlier, some analysts view the legislatures of the Eastern European countries as mere rubber stamps for the decisions made by the Communist authorities—the Politburo or the Secretariat. Thus to examine these legislatures through such traditional American political science frameworks as "public policy" is at best misleading. While it is true that all decisions made in Communist systems are "public" policies in the broadest sense of the term, one should not focus on the formulation of these policies through the legislature or legislative structure, if that structure is indeed as compliant to Communist initiative as it apparently is. Public policy formulation should thus, in most instances, be studied in terms of the Communist party apparatus and leadership; the functions of the legislatures are limited to the question of endorsing the decisions already made.

What then are the real functions of the legislatures in Communist states, and why are these bodies needed? The answers to these questions are difficult and often contradictory, but various aspects of this

Although the parliaments in Eastern Europe have very little power, their sessions are important legitimating devices. Recently, some democratic features, including multi-candidate electoral slates, have been introduced in the elections for Parliament in Hungary, depicted above in session in 1970. (UPI/Bettmann Newsphotos)

problem can be clarified. First, the legislatures symbolize the "representativeness" of the government. On the national level, people are elected to the parliaments to provide representation for a wide variety of occupations, professions, social strata, associations, and so on—in short, to what are in the West referred to as "interest groups." While each representative is also expected to represent the will of the "socialist community," and not only narrow sectoral interests, the very fact of allocating these parliamentary seats roughly on the basis of some imagined parity among occupations, political groupings, and social associations attest to the need to establish "symbolic representation" in the process of supposed national decision making.

Second, the legislatures provide a forum for the leadership to voice concerns and problems, to explain party policies as beneficial acts. While the executive arm of the state—nominated, of course, by the party elite—is indisputably the stronger by far of the two branches and only in Yugoslavia does the legislature have any real veto powers over executive decisions, a legislature's act of passing a law gives some legitimacy to that decision; having an open forum for airing views, in fact, becomes an expression of "spontaneous national will" for the passing of laws asked for. Though the executive does not always need the approval of a parliamentary body to pass laws—many executive decisions, ministerial orders, or cabinet decisions have a force equivalent to that of a duly passed law—the legislatures serve to create the impression of "democracy" in these countries.

Finally, the legislatures are also viewed as popular gathering places of the "representatives of the people" who are not "full-time," paid legislators (even in Yugoslavia, less than 50 percent of the members of the National Assembly are engaged full-time in any form of governmental activity), but who have the task of legitimizing decisions "proposed" by the party. The assemblies or parliaments only meet for a few days each year. During the rest of the time the "representatives" work, for instance, as construction engineers, peasants, writers.

The Hierarchy of Legislatures

Even though their power is limited, legislatures exist at all levels—from local to national—of the Communist system, and their nature must be examined. At the local levels, in villages and in urban districts, voters are required to elect representatives to the local *soviets* or councils, by whatever name they go by in the local language. Usually five-twenty people from each district are elected. The members of these councils fulfill such traditional roles as members of city or village councils fulfill anywhere: providing a framework or a policy for the local system to operate.

But these councils also determine the actual government of the district by electing an Executive Committee and its president, whose tasks are to govern or oversee the running of the actual administrative machinery and traditional departments, from maintaining the local health clinic to assigning state-owned apartments to needy individuals. Hence, unlike in democratic systems, where the popular will and the majority of votes elect a mayor, it is in fact the council—at the behest of and on the approval of the party—that elects its chief administrative officers; popular will has very little to do with the process. The same process is continued at ever-higher territorial levels, all the way to the national level.

At the national level the legislatures are known either by such traditional names as the *Skupstina* in Yugoslavia, *Sejm* in Poland, or Parliament in Hungary or by newer designations such as the National Assembly in Bulgaria and Czechoslovakia, the Grand National Assembly in Romania, the People's Assembly in Albania, and the People's Chamber in East Germany.

As mentioned earlier, Communist parliaments may be either unicameral or bicameral. Yugoslavia and Czechoslovakia—in accordance with the federal structures of these states—have bicameral legislatures, while the legislatures of Albania, Bulgaria, East Germany, Hungary, Poland, and Romania have only one house. These legislatures are fairly large bodies ranging in size from about 250 members in Albania to 500 in East Germany; members are elected for four- or five-year terms. Election to parliament usually takes place on the basis of a single slate, although some actual competition for representation in multiple-candidate districts was permitted by a new law in Hungary in 1984.

Moreover, these legislatures may include representatives of a single party, as in the case of Albania, Hungary, Romania and Yugoslavia, or of several parties. As we discussed in Chapter 6, there are five "nonopposition" parties in Czechoslovakia and East Germany, two in Poland, and one in Bulgaria. The fact that none of these parties can challenge the ultimate authority of the Communist party does not negate the differences among them in form, if not in reality. It is also noteworthy that in addition to the formal parties, some "independent" or "semi-independent" groups such as the Catholic PAX group in Poland, are also represented in parliament.

The parliaments elect the formal heads of states or heads of government: most frequently a collective Presidium or State Council comprised of various members. Although such elections always take place as an expression of the will of the party, it is instructive to observe the variety of institutions that are supposed to be the "highest governing authorities," the formal heads of state. A Presidium of Parliament is elected in Albania and Yugoslavia; the chairman of this body is the nominal head of state. In Yugoslavia this position is rotated on an annual basis; in Albania it is not. Similarly, there is a State Council in Bulgaria, East Germany, Poland, and Romania and a Presidential Council in Hungary; again, the chairmen of these councils are the nominal heads of state. Only in Czechoslovakia and Romania is there a specific designation that the chairman also holds the position of president of the republic.

The Presidium has been an important political force only in post-Tito Yugoslavia. In the other states of Eastern Europe, the president of the Presidium generally plays a role only as the nominal or ceremonial head of state. However, the first secretary of the Communist party, often chooses to fulfill both his party role and that of the president of the country as well: the first secretaries of Bulgaria, Czechoslovakia, East Germany, and Romania also enjoy the international courtesies that are accorded to heads of state. In Hungary, on the other hand, Kadar's personality and his policies are both aimed at limiting the potentiality of the accumulation of functions. Thus there is a largely ceremonial head of state, Pal Losonczi, but power is basically exercised by Kadar. And in Yugoslavia the deliberate rotational nature of the office of the president is also designed to prevent a single individual from amassing too much power.

The Council of Ministers, also elected by the Parliament, performs functions similar to those traditional roles fulfilled by any government. Operating along functional lines, the governments of these countries are simply the managers of the administrative system from the highest to the lowest levels. Communist governments, of course, take on tasks that far exceed the "normal" functions of democratic governments. These range from the planning and administration of the entire economy to the allocation of all measures of welfare, from education and housing to medical and old-age care.

THE ELECTORAL PROCESS IN PRACTICE

Several aspects of the system of national legislatures are rather interesting from an operational point of view. First, the question of how the members of the legislatures are elected deserves our attention. As mentioned earlier, there are indeed various "parties" that exist in some Communist states; in such states, individuals may thus vote for representatives of these other parties. But the percentage of people to be nominated and frequently the outcome of how many people from each party will be "elected" is predetermined by the Communist party.

Second, in Albania, Bulgaria, Czechoslovakia, and East Germany, the voters are presented with a single slate containing the names of all candidates for the local county councils and the National Assembly. The people whose names appear on the list have all been "nominated" by the Communist party to serve for a two-to-five-year term, and the citizenry generally has no opportunity to support a candidate of its own. While there are elaborate voting booths and while the slate even includes a place for a "write-in" candidate, most people do not take this seriously. Instead, they merely give their personal identity book to the voting registrar, who checks the names and hands the voters a ballot. The voters then fold and place their ballot, right in front of everyone, into the ballot box. Then their identity book is returned.

This leads us to the third consideration—namely, the compulsory nature of the electoral process in Eastern Europe. When one learns that a candidate (say, for the National Assembly) received 99.4 percent of the vote, one immediately becomes suspicious. Clearly these figures are most often "fake" results. Since the Communist takeovers, no one, to my knowledge, has ever really tallied the election results in these states, except in some cases in Hungary, Poland, and Yugoslavia, as we will discuss below. In a genuinely free and democratic election, there are always people who do not desire to vote, and there are those who will vote *against* a particular candidate. This certainly is not the case in the Communist systems; people vote because it is compulsory to do so. Fines or even more stringent punishments can be imposed on people who fail to vote—and the electoral committee will even take the ballot box to the homes of those who are sick—and they vote as the party wishes them to because they do not have a choice.

A popular riddle on voting in Eastern Europe:

Q: Where was the first "free and democratic" socialist election?

A: In Paradise, where God said to Adam pointing to Eve: "*Choose* yourself a wife."

In Hungary and Yugoslavia the voters have a somewhat greater choice. In 1984, for instance the Hungarian government introduced a multicandidate electoral system. In an effort to legitimize its role, the Hungarian Communist leadership thus began to allow some independent input and encouraged electoral districts to run more than one candidate. Although "safe seats" are reserved for government and party officials who cannot be opposed, much less defeated, representatives of factories, or various interest groups of various sorts, and even unaffiliated individuals may run for Parliament or the lower-level legislatures in many districts. However, while the party leadership genuinely desired at least a semblance of democratic procedure, it soon became clear that neither the nominees nor the population at large considered this reform any more than window dressing or at best a mere personality contest. They certainly did not see it as a way to present real differences in views and policies. Individual nominees were not eager to oppose the "official" candidate, who in all instances and in every electoral district had obviously been preselected by the party. And to the electors, by and large, it really made very little difference who represented them, because any nominee would be in near-total agreement with the party's position. At the same time, it should be noted that in 1985 several very unpopular representatives selected by the party—including several county first secretaries!—had been beaten by candidates opposed to the "official" delegates.

Thus while the electoral reforms in Hungary have formally succeeded in allowing most of the electoral districts to choose between usually two candidates, they were not able to break through the apathy and suspicion of the people as far as real democratization of the system was concerned. Even though new electoral reforms in 1985 enlarged individual choice by *mandating* multicandidate elections in the vast majority of Hungary's electoral districts—though still under the careful supervision of the Patriotic People's Front and still with "safe" districts for the government officials—such a reform basically does not alter the foundation of the system. Any *real* democratizing experiments—as, for instance in Czechoslovakia in 1968 and in Poland in 1981—have never been allowed to come to fruition.

Specialists on Eastern European affairs debate whether there are real chances for these parliaments to assert true independence from the Communist party. At times of political crises—as in Czechoslovakia in 1968 and in Poland in 1980–1981—the parliaments have been marvelous sounding boards where diverse interests could be articulated. But real opposition to policies has almost always emerged *within* the party and its ruling bodies, such as the Central Committee or the Politburo, rather than in the legislatures. Although it is true that such events as the defeat of the Slovene government in that Yugoslav republic's parliament in 1966 provide a precedent for greater autonomy, the power of the Communist party to impose its will on the deliberations of the parliaments through a wide variety of tools does not foster great hope that the parliaments will become truly independent organs within the present system.

THE EXECUTIVE BRANCH AND SECTORAL *APPARATS*

At the outset of this section we must reiterate that Communist political systems are characterized not by the separation but the unity of powers between the legislative and the executive branches. To students of comparative political processes, such a unity will not in itself prove to be unique. Rather, the difference between Communist and democratic parliamentary processes is the fact that democratic parliamentary systems are controlled by the mandate of the ruling party or coalition, as expressed in freedom of choice between rival views and policy goals, while in Communist states the Communist party and its representatives cannot be voted out of power. The unity of power is thus based on both the mandate derived from controlled elections and from Marxist ideology. A vote of no confidence, which would topple the government elsewhere, is simply unthinkable under the Communist system.

At the same time, the unity of powers does not mean that there are no differences among the various executive organs of state power. In fact, since all these systems are governed, by and large, by the constant re-creation of economic scarcities, every single sector of both the economy and of the policy spectrum attempts to garner an ever-larger section of the policy process to further its own interests and plans in dealing with the "elimination" of these scarcities. Indeed, the executive branch plays a much larger role in the life of these countries than it does elsewhere. Unhampered by many of the checks and balances and "niceties of legal norms" so prevalent in Western democracies, the executive branches dominate the sociopolitical and economic scenes in the Eastern European states.

The day-to-day administration of the affairs of state are entrusted to the executive branch, just as the setting of broad policy outlines and overseeing their actual accomplishment are the responsibilities of the Communist party. Under the theoretical leadership of the State Council or Presidium of the National Assembly—but in practice under the control of the Council of Ministers, elected by parliament and headed by a chairman or prime minister—ministries and many other administrative organs oversee every aspect of national life, from the setting of prices to the payment of semiprofessional athletes, from the decision-making levels of the policy process down to the factories. The Eastern European ministries maintain a tighter control over political, social, and economic matters than they do in non-Communist democratic systems. While we cannot say today that they are only the repressive organs of a totalitarian system, the mere fact that they have at least the theoretical possibility for such control should give us pause.

The executive branch, in general, can be broken down into various structures, or *apparats*. An *apparat* is a centralized organization that shares in the coercive power of the state and that administers its own bureaucracy partly for its own benefit.

The economic administration, the sectoral ministries, the state bureaucracies, the army, the police, the trade unions, the churches, and even sport organizations are all *apparats*—separate centralized bureaucracies whose interests compete. Their major interest is not merely in fulfilling their assigned tasks, but also in assuring their own survival.

Are they thus merely "interest groups" in the sense that the term so loosely is used in Western literature? Yes, but they are far more.

Like such entrenched bureaucracies in the West—for instance, the military bureaucracy in the Pentagon in the United States—all of the *apparats* have to be concerned about the maintenance of their own organization, and when the competition for scarce funds is intense— as it always is in societies of scarcity—the strength of one group can decide the success or failure of a policy advocated by a competing group. For instance, even though many of the *apparats* in Poland have advocated major reforms—and the government itself was committed to these reforms before December 1981—the middle-level party and state *apparats* successfully blocked their implementation. And in Hungary between 1974 and 1979 the party's own decisions, made with the support of the first secretary and the Politburo, were in fact limited by those *apparats* of the party and the state administration that felt that their status would be threatened by these measures.

It is also true that not all *apparats* have the same degree of clout; their strength and power vary from time to time and from place to place. Thus in the 1950s the power of the secret or political police was far stronger than it is today in much of the region. The force of these *apparats* has been curbed in Yugoslavia and Hungary, and has been curtailed somewhat in Bulgaria and—at least until December 1981—in Poland. Similarly, the power of the army is far greater in Poland or East Germany than it is in Hungary or Romania. Hence, any discussion of the power of a particular *apparat* must be country- and time-specific.

The economic bureaucracies of Communist states, in general, perform all of the functions that those in Western systems do: the operation of national monetary systems, control of money supplies, foreign trade and credit policies, and so on. But the Eastern European economic *apparats* play other major roles that are never even dreamt of in Western democracies. They are responsible for the establishment of a national economic plan, and they must make sure that this plan is adhered to at all levels. They also set wages and prices, manage all financial institutions, run the factories and farms, and oversee the operation of all retail and wholesale stores, from the smallest general store to the largest supermarket. Again, there are great variations in the pattern. Hungary and Yugoslavia have moved the farthest toward limiting the functions of the central economic *apparats;* East Germany and Albania maintain the closest controls over them.

The sectoral ministries and state bureaucracies form a loosely structured *apparat* within which many divergent interests are represented but within which there are common loyalties when there is no competition among the various organs for scarce allocations. The functions of this state administration extend to many different units, and in accordance with time-honored Habsburg and Prussian traditions, the administration of each narrow area is supervised by a ministry itself. Hence there are ministries whose functions are very specific: ministries of light or chemical industry, health, education, or tourism and sport. The following list, which indicates the typical extent of sectoral differentiation, gives the positions that warranted ministerial rank in Romania in 1982:

Ministers
Agriculture and Food Industry
Chemical Industry
Education and Instruction
Electric Power
Finance
Foreign Affairs
Foreign Trade and International Economic Cooperation
Forestry Administration and Construction Materials
Health
Industrial Construction
Interior
Internal Trade
Justice
Labor
Light Industry
Machine-Building Industry
Metallurgy
Mines, Oil, and Geology
National Defense
Technical-Material Supply and Control of Fixed Assets
Tourism and Sports

Transport and Telecommunication
Youth Affairs

Other cabinet portfolios
National Council of Science and Technology
Council on Socialist Culture and Education
Committee on Affairs of People's Councils
State Planning Committee
Committee on Prices
National Water Council
National Union of Agricultural Production Cooperatives
Central Council of the General Confederation of Trade Unions
Council for Coordination of Consumer Goods Production
State Committee for Nuclear Energy
National Council of Women
Council of Economic and Social Organizations

Other *apparats* within the executive branch also affect the execution or administration of policies. Of particular interest here is the role played by the army in Communist societies. Although the army will be discussed in more detail in Chapter 12, at this juncture we should note that the army is "big business." It is both the reason for and the consumer of large portions of the national budgets, and it is the largest single organization whose members have to be satisfied by the governments. They must be satisfied not merely because they are a part of a society, but because they have obligations both imposed from outside and demanded from within. And even if the obligations demanded by the USSR are not always met totally, the army's role remains especially important throughout most of the region.

A second armed *apparat* whose influence, must be examined at least briefly is the security police. The security police of any Communist state exists specifically to protect the "socialist order," meaning internal rule by the Communist party. Built along the lines of the Committee for State Security, or KGB, in the USSR, the security and intelligence services of the Eastern European Communist states are truly the ultimate guardians of party rule. They have a large uniformed and plain-clothed force that specializes in all aspects of espionage, and counterespionage, and the domestic administration of terror. Closely linked to the Soviet KGB, with whom it shares information, the security *apparat* is an essential feature of Soviet-type systems.

Some divergences from the Soviet model must also be noted. In Hungary, where the dreaded AVO had the reputation as the most cruel secret police in the region in the 1950s, the Kadar regime that came into power after the Soviet invasion of Hungary on October 30, 1956, eschewed the use of a separate uniformed security force. Instead, the Ministry of Interior now commands a relatively large, uniformed group of conscripted border guards, and a numerically small but well-organized plain-clothed professional security force—in addition to the normal complement of army and police forces. And while Romania does have a major uniformed security *apparat*, since the mid-1960s this force has been reputed to be acting without the close link to Moscow. But in all of the states in the region, the security forces operate under the direct control of the Ministry of Interior and employ terror, coercion, and social and political control to achieve their purposes.

In addition to the army and the security police, one cannot ignore the role played by the trade unions in Eastern Europe. These groups—while operating as part of the executive branch—pose a special problem for the region. The Soviet Union, once again, provides the model of development that the leaders of Communist Eastern Europe have tried to emulate. In Soviet Russia, the famous trade union debates of 1921 focused on the nature of proper trade union activities in a Communist state. At that time, led by Mikhail Tomsky, the trade union leaders in Soviet Russia joined in the "trade union opposition," insisting on independent and major roles for labor organizations, whose goals would be to protect the workers from exploitation by the state or society. Led by Lenin, the Communist party elite defeated the trade unionists; ever since, the Soviet trade unions have been expected to play the role of the "transmissions belts," carrying the wishes of the party to the members of the trade unions.

All of the Eastern European states have had to accept this role
for their trade unions, many of which—for instance, in Czechoslovakia—had a long and distinguished history of protecting the rights of
their members. Nonetheless, noticeable deviations from the Soviet
model have threatened the existence of party rule or at least undermined the sole determination of every policy by the party. The first
of these deviations emerged in Yugoslavia in 1949 and involved the
role of the workers' councils and the ideal of self-management. The
concept of self-management, even if under the general guidance of
the League of Yugoslav Communists, conflicts greatly with the subordinate role assigned to the workers in Soviet practice. As expected, the
Soviets were quick to condemn the Yugoslav "revisionism," although
they were unable to do much else about it, the Yugoslav-Soviet rift
had already occurred.

Workers' councils also sprang up during Hungary's short-lived
quest for freedom in 1956. In fact, they provided much of the resistance
to the policies imposed by the Soviet Union immediately after the
Hungarian revolution was crushed. While their backs were broken
through the terror let loose by the Kadar regime in 1957, the resistance
of the workers' councils was the fiercest that the authorities faced
during the first few years of the Kadar era.

However, by far the greatest challenge to monolithic Communist
rule posed by the independent trade union movement occurred in
Poland in 1980–1982. Led by Lech Walesa, a charismatic electrician
from the port city of Gdansk, the union Solidarity (*Solidarnosc* in Polish) sought to establish an independent workers' union whose major
task would be the protection of the rights of the working class, in
whose name the party was supposed to rule but who felt that they
were tremendously exploited by the system that allegedly existed for
them. This threat to Communist party rule, of course, led to the imposition of martial law. But even if the Jaruzelski regime succeded in
breaking Solidarity's back, it had to unleash the tremendous power
of its security forces to re-establish the primacy of party rule.

Although there have been major strikes in Romania and some unauthorized work stoppages in Hungary, the trade unions of the region
generally have remained under strict party control since the early
1980s. The workers realize and tacitly accept that they are just as
exploited today as they were during the "capitalist" interwar era. As
an Eastern European bon mot has it, the only difference between
capitalism and socialism is that under the former there exists the exploitation of men by men, while under the latter it is the other way around.

Finally, we must briefly mention the role of the churches under
Communist rule. This topic, of course, is complicated by the facts that
(1) although they are supposed to be independent, the state tries to
exert control over them through its executive arm, and (2) that the

various churches have played different roles in each of the Eastern European states, and even the role played by the Catholic Church has varied from one state to another. In the following chapter, the problem of the churches will be fully noted. Suffice it to state here that in Poland, Hungary, and to some extent East Germany, the churches have far more influence than elsewhere in the region. The fundamental conflict between an ideology that aims to eliminate religion and instill atheism as an officially sanctioned ethical value, on the one hand, and the deep-seated yearning of many Eastern Europeans for religious values, on the other, remains a conflict that the regimes will continually have to battle. Whether they will succeed in bringing the churches under effective and full party control or will have to make some major concessions in the interest of social peace remains a major question.

THE JUDICIAL BRANCH

At an international meeting of state officials, in 1968 a Czechoslovak minister announced that the Czechoslovak government would like to create a Ministry of the Navy. "Why," queried the Romanian representative, "you have no seashores!" "Why not?" replied the Czech, "after all, you have a Ministry of Justice!"

The distribution of justice in Communist states has been discussed and debated endlessly in learned journals and academic works. Many questions remain unresolved—for example, whether there can be "real" justice under a system that prides itself on its nonegalitarian values and constantly emphasizes the supremacy of the working class, the Communist party and its values. However, there can be no debate about the fact that in Communist states the term "justice" has a peculiar connotation. Justice is regarded as "political justice." In other words, the distribution of justice must serve the political goals of the regime. The expression "justice is blind" is clearly inapplicable in Communist systems.

Communist theorists always found it difficult to grapple with the nature of "class" justice in Marxism-Leninism. According to the original tenets of the Communist ideology, law and justice are regarded as parts of the superstructure, reflecting the prevailing mode of production, i.e., the totality of man's relations to the means of production. Consequently, when socialism is reached—as some of the states of the region claim to have done—crime would disappear, because of the sufficiently high social consciousness of the people. In reality, however, the societies of Eastern Europe are riddled with crime and petty corruption, forcing the theorists to suggest that crimes are committed by some "crazy people" with "insufficient social consciousness." The inevitable conclusion of this line of thought, however, is that people who commit crimes are "crazy" and have to be placed under medical care in asylums. However, the scope of the problem forces the authorities to treat it as a "social" rather than a "medical" phenomenon, and because they cannot alter society in the direction they desire, they can only treat crime as almost entirely a police affair.

Moreover, the administration of justice is supposed to be dealt with through the enforcement of the principle of socialist legality. Since the mid-1960s, unlike in the Stalinist years of total terror, arrests are supposed to be made legally, trials to be administered according to legal constitutional norms. Thus, such purges as the fabricated Rajk or Slansky trials of 1949—as discussed in Chapter 3—should theoretically have been discontinued. Flagrant violations of legality—for instance, arrests and searches without a warrant, the use of coerced confessions, the concept of confession as "queen of the evidence" (the most important proof in the hands of the prosecution), and "crimes by analogy" (acts that are not specifically crimes determined to be analogous to criminal acts)—should have also been abandoned.

The principle of socialist legality, however, is extraordinarily elastic in Eastern Europe. It is true that the truly flagrant violations of legality practiced during the years of the primitive accumulation of terror under Stalinist rule have lessened to some extent and there is a general observance of legal codes in Hungary, East Germany, Bulgaria and Yugoslavia. However, the violations of legal codes is still customary in Albania, Romania, and Czechoslovakia and was especially clearly noted in Poland after martial law was imposed in December 1981. While the most clearly observable violations of the Polish legal codes declined greatly in 1983–1984 from the 1982 level, the new powers given to the security organs, voted in by the Polish *Sejm,* make it possible for the Polish authorities to practice terror far "more legally" than before the 1981 coup.

In all of the Communist states, the distribution of justice remains firmly under the control of the Communist party. The party is empowered to nominate judges, oversee their conduct, and remove them at will. Although judges and juries are "elected" by the population at large, nomination for these positions remains in the hand of the party. Moreover, such western concepts as "checks and balances," the setting of legal precedents, or judicial review of the legality of governmental acts cannot be undertaken by the judicial branch. While it is true that the Eastern European systems of justice are patterned more closely on the French concept than on the more liberal Anglo-American practice, the limitations on legality mentioned above render the judiciary less of a "balance" between state and society and more of an instrument of policy in the hands of the party.

Finally, one should also note a constant battle between what we may call "popularism" and "technicality" in the administration of laws. Early Communist theoreticians, including Lenin, fervently believed in the notion that laws should be so worded as to make them easily understandable by every citizen. These laws should thus be so simple that the elected representative of the people can render justice merely by reading these laws and not needing to have them "interpreted" by someone—most frequently a judge. In fact, the composition of the court—two lay members of the public, the so-called people's assessors, and the judge, all elected by the population at large—reflect this "popularism" in action.

As these societies became more complex, however, their laws have also become more technically complex, more difficult to understand. It was easy in 1949, for example, to say that a former "capitalist" was guilty of a crime against the people by exploiting the proletariat or to "prove" on the basis of fabricated evidence that he plotted the overthrow of the socialist state. But as these states became more differentiated social organs, it became much more difficult to place blame, for instance, for the nonfulfillment of a contractual obligation between two state-owned factories. Hence, the system was forced to abandon much of its popularism and began to require judges to become well versed in the laws through rigorous training in law schools. The judges were also granted greater influence over the other members of the court, the people's assessors.

Technically, the distribution of justice is undertaken by three components of the judicial system; the courts, the procuracy and the police. As we have noted, the courts in Eastern Europe are elected bodies, consisting at all but the highest levels of a judge and two people's assessors, who are supposed to act as both jurors and judges. In most of these states, the judges and assessors are elected at the same time as members of the local councils, usually for terms of two to five years. Nominations for these positions, of course, are in the hands of the Communist party or its subordinate People's Front organizations. During their tenure, assessors usually hear cases for a period of two weeks to about one month annually, during which time they are released from their normal work duties with full pay. Unlike the judges, assessors are seldom well versed in the laws and listen intently to instructions of the bench regarding the applicability of certain laws. Assessors seldom express any independence in their opinions, even if their opinions differ from those of the judge.

The courts proceed from the lowest level of the district—the courts of the first instance—through several appellate levels on the city, county, and republic levels, to the supreme courts. Members of the supreme courts are generally elected by the various parliaments for various terms, usually for four or five years. Needless to say, here too the party retains the right of nomination. The supreme courts usually are broken down into civil, criminal, and military branches. Members switch freely between the civil and criminal branches, but the administration of military justice remains largely in the hands of judges closely connected with the military *apparat.* The greatest difference between Communist and pluralist judicial systems is the fact that even the supreme courts are not allowed to declare laws "unconstitutional" unless such a declaration is specifically demanded by the party elite itself. Thus there is far less latitude for the "interpretation" of laws in Communist than in pluralist systems. This alone renders the potential check by an independent court system on the executive branch largely meaningless.

The second element of the Communist judicial system is the procuracy. As an institution, the procuracy combines the function of the public prosecutor or attorney general with that of the defender of "socialist legality." This dual role predetermines the fact that conflicts between state and society are usually solved in favor of the state; only when conflicts between two citizens of equal stature arise can the procuracy be expected to act impartially. The procurators general— also known as chief prosecutors or chief public prosecutors—are elected by the national parliaments, most frequently for periods of five to six years. They are responsible—at least theoretically—to Parliament, not to the minister of justice or the president of the supreme court. In reality, however, the procurators frequently are also instruments of state power designated by the party. Unlike the members of the elected courts, all prosecutors at the various levels of the procuracy are appointed by the procurator general.

It is important to note that in most Eastern European societies today, the procuracy is bound by far greater restrictions regarding the administration of justice than it was during the worst years of Stalinism. But they do remain servants of the party, and hence the direction in which the party wishes the polity to go will be supported by the procuracy. In states such as Romania, post-1968 Czechoslovakia, and post-1981 Poland—in other words, in states that from time to time are beset by internal crises—the work of the procuracy is more politicized. In other states, however, its work tends to be characterized by greater observance of the letter, if not always the spirit, of the law.

The final arm of the judicial system is the nonpolitical branch of the police. This force is concerned with the apprehension of criminals or those charged with crimes, their detention, transportation, and eventually their incarceration and/or execution. The police—as well as the other security organs in all Eastern European states—comes under the supervision of the Ministry of Justice or Ministry of Interior, although in some instances it seems clear that the tail is wagging the dog. The powers exercised by the uniformed and plain-clothed police officers are seldom hampered by the checks that are customary in Western democracies or by niceties of legalism. Nor can successful appeals be lodged against police brutality, lack of specific charges or search warrants, or the bad food and overcrowded conditions in the jails.

A brief mention should also be made of the legal profession in Eastern Europe today. During the interwar era the legal profession had a high social standing, and its practitioners belonged to the more affluent strata of society. The Communists, however, have looked down on the legal profession as rather unwelcome necessities that "hinder" social development and modernization by insisting on the "niceties" of legalism. Moreover, the role of the defense attorneys, especially during the Stalinist phase, was reduced to that of an individual who simply requested clemency against the power of the state, which was "obviously" in the right.

As these states evolved into much more complex mechanisms, however, the legal profession—at least to some extent—has once again come into its own. Organized into cooperatives, the lawyers are slowly regaining some of their lost reputation, especially in civil cases and in all such cases where individual or nonpolitical business interests are pitted against one another. Defense attorneys, especially in Yugoslavia, Poland, and Hungary, are once again prized for their skills. Although not in those cases where state interests clearly dominate, the legal profession once again is becoming respectable.

PART III

THE ISSUES OF POLITICS

Political Life

■   When political scientists try to describe what politics is in Western pluralist societies, they generally use the brief descriptive phrase "who gets, what, when and how." Western politics is thus regarded as a process of establishing mutual relationships between state and society, between authority and citizenry, between rights and obligations. This process is characterized by a legitimate political opposition with certain programs, alternatives, and compromises reached between those in authority and those in opposition; power is limited both by constitutional guarantees and the acceptance of certain political "contracts" of behavior.

In Communist states, politics has a different meaning. It generally refers to the allocation of power from the top down; in a short-hand manner, Sovietologists call it in Russian *kto-kogo* meaning "who-whom;" it is a short-hand synonym for continuous power struggle. Politics is supposed to be limited to (a) the allocation of power within the Communist party elite; (b) the allocation of power to various political authorities within the system (for example, police, armed forces, industrial bureaucracy, and so on); and (c) the translation of politics into action over an unquestioning citizenry. Political opposition cannot exist in institutional forms, and few, if any, compromises are proposed between what the state (party) or society desires. Moreover, there is no legal way to articulate any opposition platform or societal desires outside of party-controlled channels.

All of this, as we have noted, is only complicated by the fact that in most Communist states every issue is a "political" issue. Since the party is expected to translate ideology—a coherent system of explanations relating to *every* phenomenon—into practice, it attempts to control and mold all aspects of social change in a direction desired by the party. Thus the party must decide about the fate of the economy and society, about taxes and kindergarten costs, the same way it decides about international allegiances or increases in military power.

Nonetheless, in Communist states there are three general political *issues,* and these will be the subject of this section of the book. They are political life itself, economic activity, and social change. Once again, though, we must remember that these issues are interrelated and are all under the control of the party to some extent.

To Westerners the term "political life" is so broad in scope that it encompasses any activities that relate to participation in public affairs, from voting to public policy formulations. These are all observable and analyzable phenomena in the Western, pluralist political setting. In Soviet-type systems, however, politics is viewed as being subordinate to the principle of democratic centralism, to the principle of control by party authorities. In such societies there cannot be policies that are not sanctioned by the party, for there is a determined "ban on factions"—in other words, on groups that articulate ideals and policies that contravene those of the ruling elite.

In such states, however, there are still issues that fall into the realm of "traditional" political concerns, i.e., politics. Four such issues will be considered in this chapter. They are: (a) the question of participation; (b) the question of legitimacy; (c) the question of elite succession; and (d) the thorny problem of dissent. Together these questions make up the political matter with which even the Communist systems must grapple.

THE QUESTION OF PARTICIPATION

There can be no doubt that Communist political systems are "participatory" systems in the literal and formal sense of the word. There are elections for every conceivable position, ranging from membership in the local council to membership in parliament. And everyone is entitled to participate in these elections, for there is universal suffrage above age 18, regardless of sex or social status, property or ethnic origin. As proof that there is popular participation, these states can clearly show that in every election between 95 and 99.9 percent of the people vote for the candidate listed on the ballots. However, as we indicated in Chapter 7, participation in elections is not merely permissible, but it is expected. Voting is a patriotic duty, and the citizenry *must* participate in it.

Political participation involves also acts of "spontaneous, demonstrative public assent." For instance, there are huge demonstrations on May Day or on November 7—the anniversary of the Great October Revolution in Russia that brought the Communists to power in 1917, celebrated according to the Gregorian calendar on November 7—and on assorted national holidays. The people march together in front of red-draped reviewing stands, carry flags of the state and the red flag of international communism, pictures of the leaders or slogans supporting the party's current positions on whatever issue. But participation in these events is not really spontaneous. Generally, party secretaries in every locality are required to fulfill a quota by selecting a certain number of marchers or demonstrators. And the local party secretary will bestow the "honors" of participating in these demonstrations on individuals who march past the reviewing stands where the leaders of the country wave benignly at the enthusiastic multitude.

Political participation in Eastern Europe is thus largely a symbolic, or metapolitical act. Real participation in decision making, or even in the selection of the true decision makers, does not take place at the mass level. While there are electoral meetings that are supposed to nominate candidates for influential representative posts, the nominees are preselected by the Communist party, its cadre divisions, or the various other groups directly under the guidance of the party.

Political Participation in Eastern European Politics

"Frankly, frankly! Just tell us if you would rather jump into the frying pan or into the fire?"

Szymon Kobylinski in *Polytika* (Warsaw)

Naturally, such an approach to political participation has left the population quite cynical about the nature of politics—a cynicism that the party in some cases, has accepted and even fostered, in other instances has tried to combat. In most of the states that have promoted this cynicism, the party elites do not expect the people to "believe" in their role as true participants; rather they are content with the knowledge that the people simply engage in these symbolic activities. As is the case in some churches in the West, the elite does not care if people in their "religion" believe in the religious tenets, as long as they come to "church" on the required holidays and "tithe" to the hierarchy.

There have been some reforms and slow shifts away from this purely symbolic participation. In Yugoslavia, for example, real political power is exercised in the communes and in the various self-managed socialist institutions that give the people opportunities for more meaningful participation that is not necessarily within the channels of party life. And in Hungary, under the policies of "democratization of public life," an electoral law in 1983 gave the right to the Patriotic People's Front to nominate "unofficial" candidates against whom the "official" party candidates must wage "vigorous" electoral battles for the right to represent electoral districts in the various councils and in Parliament. While, as we discussed in Chapter 7, a number of "safe seats" remain for those elite candidates the party wishes to retain in Parliament, these electoral reforms are intended to combat the cynicism that has built up in the population over four decades of Communist rule.

But do the people really want to have such a say? Do they want real participation? It is true that people in Eastern Europe have been very reluctant to participate in politics, not only because they view with contempt those who are the "true" participants, but also because they are afraid of what might happen to them if they "lose" to an officially backed candidate. Moreover, they realize that winning the election—in the absence of having a real chance to present policies different from those proposed by the party—would mean simply a personal victory, not a victory of an alternative political program. Nonetheless, the most striking aspect of the "dysfunctions" that have occurred in Eastern Europe—the Hungarian and Polish Octobers of 1956, the Prague Spring of 1968, and the Polish Solidarity period—is the tremendous amount of desire and will of the people to get involved in political activity when free of a centralized and dictatorial party. During those brief flickers of freedom, people from all walks of life—workers and intellectuals, peasants and students—flocked to organs that represented non-Communist or non-party-controlled activities. Even rank-and-file party members sought their real rights of participation as citizens in the emerging workers' councils and trade unions.

One may well ask whether real participation exists within the Communist party itself. After all, as all party members belong to a local cell, they must attend a monthly party meeting, and presumably, participate in making decisions at these meetings. But in reality, the rank-and-file party membership has very little to say even at these meetings. Rather, the secretary gives the members the "party line"—that is, the "correct" way to interpret current decisions or international and national issues. They are always asked to approve of the policies or nominations made already at a higher level—this, too is a part of the principle of democratic centralism. While they are "encouraged" to participate, this is a mere formal right, and there is no chance of asking any truly hard questions.

Party Secretary: Comrade Kohn, why weren't you at the last party meeting?

Kohn: If I had known it would be the *last* party meeting, I would certainly have come.

The fact of symbolic participation among party members is recognized clearly by the Communist party itself. As the Czechoslovak Communist party daily, the *Rude Pravo,* said on August 24, 1983:

> It is a serious matter that some of our party members live in near-anonymity. They cannot be formally rebuked for this, because they pay their membership dues, regularly attend party meetings, and take part in agit-prop sessions. However, they have nothing to say on serious matters under discussion, they never raise their hands, and they never speak their mind. They never oppose others, but they never fight for their party.

Such a tacit admission can often be read in the newspapers and journals of the region; the disease of merely formal participation cannot be eradicated quickly, even in places where the leadership would like to encourage greater, real participation.

"Real" politics, of course, exists at the highest levels of the party, the Politburo and the Secretariat. Here, there are clearly competing interests, competing policies, competing *apparats,* and competing individuals, all vying for power. Although the policies at the highest levels are shaped by the desires of a generally all-powerful first secretary, the inputs of the members of the Politburo and the influential people on the level below them are real, and they often contradict official policies. But participation in this decision-making is limited to only a very narrow group.

THE QUESTION OF LEGITIMACY

"Legitimacy" is another term that has one meaning for Western social scientists and another for the authoritarian elites of Eastern Europe. The term itself is value-loaded. Used in the Western context, "political legitimacy" means the right to wield political authority *according to values accepted by those sharing in the system,* specifically the citizenry. Thus legitimacy implies both the right of the regime to implement whatever policies it thinks are necessary and the right of the citizenry to establish the parameters within which the regime may "legitimately" employ its policies.

But in Eastern Europe, since the citizenry as a whole is not asked to define the parameters, it has little or no power to establish what it considers "just" or acceptable. Moreover, since the regime's lack of legitimacy comes into question only as power to enforce its rule becomes painfully eroded, Western applications of the term are misleading at best. Hence, in this region there is a fundamental distinction between the bases on which a regime claims legitimacy and the actual legitimacy that is accorded to the leadership by the people.

In Eastern Europe we can distinguish between four types of bases on which a regime may claim legitimacy. These are ideological, coercive, economic, or nationalist bases. We must emphasize that any regime may use any of these bases either separately or jointly in any combination.

Ideological Legitimacy

Ideology is by far the most common basis of legitimacy in Eastern Europe. Accordingly, the Communist elites claim to rule because through the possession of the key to "progress" in the philosophy of Marxism-Leninism, only Communist parties can know what policies should be implemented for the benefit of mankind. Thus only the Marxist-Leninist party has the "mandate of history" as only the Communist states represent "qualitative" improvements over the class-states of the bourgeoisie. Thus ideology is used to "legitimize" the rule of the party.

In Eastern Europe, in addition to these "internal" aspects of Communist ideological legitimacy, one must also note an international element. While claiming to be sovereign states, these states also take continuous pains to re-emphasize that they are parts of the international Communist movement, parts of the onward march of the "inevitable" successes of Communism everywhere, which—so they say—is the bright future of all mankind. And thus they derive their bases of legitimacy in part from the fact that they belong to the fraternal alli-

Although legitimacy is a political commodity in short supply in Eastern Europe, the first secretaries of the Communist parties in the region would like to feel that they are legitimate representatives of the people. General Jaruzelski of Poland is shown here casting a vote in parliamentary elections in 1985. (Interpresse/Sygma)

ance of Communist states, claiming, among other things, the right of intervention through the infamous Brezhnev Doctrine everywhere where socialism is threatened.

One aspect of ideological legitimacy stems from the hierarchical institutional bases of the party itself. In Communist states, as mentioned earlier, the principle of substitution eventually culminates in the emergence of a single leader, who claims to be the All-Knowing Father of Us All. A Stalin, a Ceausescu, a Hoxha, or a more benevolent Tito or Jaruzelski—all claim to be able to interpret the laws of "scientific development" and thus accrue legitimacy to themselves in dictating the road that should be taken. The "personality cults" of the region, that of Stalin, Ceausescu, Rakosi, Tito, or Hoxha were all designed and implemented in order to bolster this type of legitimacy for the charismatic and all-knowing first secretary.

Coercive Legitimacy

The coercive bases of legitimacy—forcing public assent from a cowed or brutalized population—are grounded in the use of dictatorial methods and are closely linked to the perceived necessity of applying terror in order to achieve Communism, the great desired end of the system. Terror in Communist states, contrary to widely accepted opinion in the West, is *not* used without regard to the purposes of the regime. While terror—by its very nature—is unpredictable, it must serve a purpose. It must be used against the enemies of the social order, against all those who would oppose the existing social system, because the existing order and the expected future benefits of Communism makes it mandatory to crush ruthlessly all those who disagree with these great goals. Terror, random or organized, individual or institutional, is used to intimidate those who would threaten the ideals of the future as embodied in the policies delineated by the "Maximum Leader." And we must emphasize that terror or coercion is used not merely against those outside the party, but even against those within the party whom the first secretary does not consider "loyal" or "reliable," who actually dare to propose alternative policies within the system or who pose potential threats to the power position of the current leader of the party. The murder of even potential political opponents in Stalinist and post-1956 Hungary, and the imprisonment of Wladyslaw Gomulka in Poland in the 1950s, to cite but two examples, illustrate this use of terror for both practical and ideological purposes.

Economic Legitimacy

Some Communist parties claim legitimacy because they maintain that only the party's policies can provide (a) continuous and ever-greater economic growth and (b) an ever higher standard of living. Especially important in this respect are the theoretical bases of Marxism-Leninism and the so-called Soviet experience. The models that the Communist parties claim to follow suggest that the "rational" Communist theory—both as applied by the USSR and by the other states of the region—can ensure a more rapid growth than the "helter-skelter," wasteful, capitalist models, prevent periodic economic crises, and guarantee continuous and full employment for all. Thus continuous economic growth as a basis of legitimacy, even if the record of the East European states in this respect has been rather dismal lately, is an important component of the general ideological justification as well.

The ability to provide an ever higher level of living—including the extension of social services that did not exist in the region until the end of World War II—is the second component of claimed economic legitimacy. Here the emphasis lies on historical improvement, rather than comparison with the West, for Eastern Europe has been visibly unable to match the level of living found in Western Europe, and the gap in the standard of living between the two regions only continues to increase. But as long as domestic standards of living continue to improve, even modestly, the party can continue to claim an economic basis for its legitimate rule. It is precisely for this reason that the economic crises that have gripped Eastern Europe since the early 1980s have posed threats to most of the elites in the region; the economic legitimacy of providing the people with a growing standard of living and adequate social service has been severely eroded.

Nationalist Legitimacy

Recall that the "modern" states of Eastern Europe emerged during the age of nationalism before World War I, and nationalist feelings of pride remain characteristic of the populations of these countries. In the immediate postwar era, when Stalinism dominated, nationalism was oppressed by the party elites, and the principles of "socialist internationalism" were continually emphasized in its stead. The "love" of fellow partners in the fraternal Communist alliance, especially of the great Soviet Union, was supposed to overcome nationalist manifestations, and the Soviet and the various Muscovite elites have all looked on nationalism as an evil that had to be eradicated.

But the volatility of nationalism—as evidenced especially in Hungary in 1956 and in Poland at several points in recent history—convinced these elites that they must tone down this aspect of their ideology, lest they continually and openly offend the people. Although they have not given up on the ideal of a Communist world system, "socialist patriotism" has regained lost ground as a basis for legitimacy claimed by the party. As the local, "nativist" party leaders became convinced of the necessity to curry favor with their own populations, nationalism, often taking the form of hostility toward the Soviet Union or neighboring "fraternal allies," reappeared in Poland, Hungary, Czechoslovakia, and Romania and has been maintained at very high levels in Yugoslavia since 1949 and in Albania since about 1960. And if this nationalistic ideology could not be reconciled with the internationalism of Marxism-Leninism, the latter simply has lost out.

The mix of legitimacy claimed in the various states of Eastern Europe is as diverse as the states themselves are. East Germany blends economic legitimacy, old-fashioned Prussian nationalism and ideological explanations. By providing relatively high standards of living and rapid rates of growth, and by rehabilitating the once-maligned Bismarck and Luther, the regime reinforces the ideological bases of party rule. Since 1982 Poland has relied on coercive and ideological legitimacy. A touch of nationalism is also added in the form of a threat that if the Jaruzelski regime is unsuccessful, the Poles can look forward to greater Soviet pressures or even invasion. Czechoslovakia also depends mostly on coercion and ideology, as the economic claims of the regime have dwindled and the Czechoslovak regime imposed by the USSR in 1968 has little or no nationalist support. At the same time the muted internal conflict between Slovaks and Czechs could easily burst into a divisive nationalism that could easily destroy the Czechoslovak system as it has existed since 1969.

Romania and Albania both use coercion, nationalism, and ideology in about equal measures; the parties of these states have been led for a long time by charismatic leaders whose cults of personality, notably near-deification of Ceausescu, may exceed that of Stalin. In effect, the Albanian's and Romanian's anti-Russian nationalism and "independence" are painted as the crowning achievements of Hoxha's and Ceausescu's respective policies, even if both regimes are suffering from abysmally low standards of living, chronic shortages, and unabating terror. Bulgaria uses ideological bases for the party's primary claim to legitimacy. In the mid-1980s the concepts of economic legitimacy began to play a greater role, and with some nationalist elements have been carefully employed since the 1960s.

In Hungary, the party has claimed an economically based legitimacy since 1968. The Kadar regime has eschewed the use of both coercive and overblown ideological bases, and it has been unable to use the issue of nationalism for fear of inflaming anti-Soviet sentiment and of further aggravating Hungary's relations with Romania and Czechoslovakia. (In fact, its reluctance to stir up anti-Romanian and anti-Czech feeling may be undercutting potentially strong popular support.) Finally, the Yugoslav regime has used both the nationalist and the economic bases of legitimacy, although the economic woes of the early 1980s have forced the party to claim legitimacy through ideological prescriptions once again.

It is important to examine the degree of allegiance that the people of Eastern Europe actually feel toward the professed motives, goals, or values of their regimes. While there are notable differences among the different countries, there generally exists a resignation among the population that these regimes are here to stay. This does not mean that most of the people accord true legitimacy to the regimes; rather, they see no real choice available to them. After all, the armed forces of the USSR and of their own countries have been used at various times in East Germany, Czechoslovakia, Hungary, Poland, and Romania to maintain the Communist system at practically any price.

Some of the regimes have strong followers among the populations; apparatchiks and other holders of power who wish to preserve their privileges or people who simply prefer the status quo are anxious to support these regimes, lest others, potentially more detrimental to their well-being, come to power. The fear of that eventuality is clearly used by these regimes in urging the people to support the status quo, though, again, to different extents. However, when for various reasons party authority does wither away, as it did in 1956, in 1968, or in 1980–81, what one notices is how quickly the people's "voluntary" acceptance of the party fades away, and how quickly their "allegiance" is transformed into support for any rival organization that emerges against the party's own wishes.

THE QUESTION OF SUCCESSION

The question of succession is the most serious unsolved problem of the Communist states in general and of the Eastern European countries in particular. The problem itself, of course, is caused by the nature of the system; in such states there are no organized mechanisms legitimately inscribed in the constitutions to provide for orderly succession of leadership. While the problem is serious at all levels in the governmental leadership cases, it is especially critical in terms of the selection of the first secretary of the party.

Theoretical mechanisms, of course, do exist; the Central Committee of the Communist party is expected to meet when a first secretary dies or retires. To date, however, only two first secretaries have been willing to retire: Walter Ulbricht in East Germany in 1971 and Edward Ochab in Poland in 1956 and only one, Janos Kadar, has been promoted to a more "ceremonial" role as the general secretary of the party in 1985. All other first secretaries have either died in office or have been forcibly removed from power. Following such events, the Central Committee is convened to "elect" a new leader.

In fact, most Central Committees act as rubber stamps in the matter of selection. Only in the case of a truly remarkable situation is there real competition and openness in the process; this occurred in Hungary in 1956 and in Czechoslovakia in 1968. While there may be genuine support for some of the new first secretaries—as there was for Gomulka and Gierek in Poland and Ceausescu in Romania, for instance—such genuine support is not essential. For example, in 1957 Kadar had little or no support among the population at large. Nor did Wojciech Jaruzelski in Poland or Gustav Husak in Czechoslovakia.

When they assume power, Communist first secretaries must have not only the support of some domestic constituencies but also the blessing of Moscow. In fact, there is extensive documentation available, for instance, how in 1956 Krushchev *chose* Kadar to be the new First Secretary over Ferenc Munnich. While Moscow does not necessarily appoint first secretaries any longer, it does at least reserve the right to veto the selection of a national party leader. And only after Moscow's blessing is given can the Central Committee be called together and asked to "elect" the new first secretary.

Consensus among the party's Politburo members, of course, is almost always a prerequisite for a first secretary to be named, but such agreement is generally preceded by vicious competition among the members for the top position; witness, for example, the period of 1953–1956 in Hungary or 1980–1981 in Poland. The post of first secretary is coveted for several reasons. The first lies in the longevity of the position. For example, until his death in 1985 Hoxha had been in power in Albania since 1944, Zhivkov in Bulgaria since 1954, Kadar in Hungary since 1956, Ceausescu in Romania since 1965, Husak in Czechoslovakia since 1969, and Honecker in East Germany since 1971. Only in Poland have there been four first secretaries in little more than a decade, but prior to that Wladyslaw Gomulka held the position for fourteen years, between 1956 and 1970, and Edward Gierek ruled from 1970 to 1980. The second reason for wanting the position is the fringe benefits that the job allows. Some of these are invisible: power, supposed omniscience, freedom from accountability, the right to insist on praise and extract respect. Others are real and very tangible: a lifestyle that can be as extravagant as that of a Western millionaire. In light of these advantages, it is also no wonder that very few first secretaries attempt to groom a successor. These leaders are all afraid that if they do train someone to succeed them, then that protegé may eventually ease them out of office, just as Erich Honecker, with Soviet support, eased out Walter Ulbricht in East Germany in 1971.

The first secretaries of Eastern Europe today are all old men between 65 and 75 years of age. The members of the Politburos—nearly exclusively men, as we discussed in Chapter 6—are about the same age as the first secretaries, and many of the relatively young members of these Politburos, now in their early sixties, long to enjoy ten years or so at the very top when the present first secretary dies.

Consequently, within the next few years, changes are likely in the present party leadership of Eastern Europe. While Moscow will not probably appoint any first secretaries, it will continue to exercise its power to veto the accession of any new leader it does not approve. It is equally likely, since no "heirs apparent" are being groomed by the present officeholders, that a tremendous power struggle is already taking place for the future positions of power. But because of all these considerations, it is likely that as a result of these expected successions we will witness the emergence of rather short-term first secretaries in their early or mid-sixties, whose tenure will be brief and marred by the chafing of a younger generation to take up power when the "older" generation retires.

THE PROBLEM OF DISSENT

Just because there exists no organized institutional means to express opposition to the policies of the party does not mean that the Eastern European societies are conflict-free. The very fact that these systems are transitory and changing, developing and modernizing, ensures that tremendous conflicts will continue to exist within these societies. Conflict is expressed in forms of what is euphemistically called "dissent." Although different types of dissent are observable in each of the Eastern European states, we may identify four broad categories: (1) political dissent; (2) economic dissent; (3) nationalist dissent; and (4) religious dissent. Although most frequently there are "mixes" of types of dissent, one or another of these types can be observed as dominant.

The strength and intensity of the various dissenting movements or groups vary from state to state; in some they are all present, in others they are hardly noticeable at all. Dissent also shifts from time to time; as regimes crack down hard on the dissenters, it may stiffen or collapse, or as the regimes co-opt some of the goals of the dissenters, they may become stronger or alternatively disappear. But it is certain that dissent plays an important part in the determination of the policies by the elites; in some instances the elite actually but quietly supports the dissenters in order to air views that the political leadership itself cannot utter.

Political Dissent

Political dissent is exhibited by a very large group of people in Eastern Europe, and the views they espouse range from hard-line neo-Stalinism all the way to liberal democracy. Dissent may be expressed openly or clandestinely, depending on time and place. But dissent from regime goals or policies is usually given some room to exist, unless it becomes a strong threat to the party. Dissenting views may be expressed quite openly at the party meetings both at the top and at lower levels or only in underground *samizdat* publications. Generally, however, political dissent can be expressed publicly only if it advocates the adoption of even stricter party rule than that which the party leadership practices—in other words, a more orthodox position than that taken by the ruling elite. Such positions usually advocate less emphasis on "human rights," tighter political controls, more terror in order to enforce ideological "orthodoxy," a closer allegiance to Moscow, and/or greater centralization. Conversely, "liberal" political dissent emphasizes greater observance of human rights and constitutional legality, looser political controls and greater social autonomy, less coercion, less emphasis on the omniscience of Marxist-Leninist ideology, closer cooperation with the West, and greater decentralization of decision making.

Openly expressed domestic political dissent is minimal in Romania, Albania, Bulgaria, and, except for the recent emergence of a religious peace movement, East Germany. Any significant Romanian political dissenters tend to be opponents of Ceausescu who desire greater cooperation with Moscow, because they think that even a pro-Moscow system would be better than the current dictatorial regime. These dissenters can generally be found among the most dissatisfied groups of population, especially among the professional military elite. Other Romanian "hard-line" dissenters can be found among the economic decision makers who contend that closer alliance with Moscow would benefit Romania's ailing economy. But the coercive methods used in this most Stalinist of all Eastern European countries makes political dissent from orthodoxy practically impossible. The few intellectuals in East Germany and Romania who harbor "socially harmful" ideas of liberal reform are most often expelled, sentenced to prison terms, or "merely" censored.

Czechoslovakia is an unusual case in terms of political dissent. While the country is basically ruled by conservative advocates of tight control and centralization, there are two active groups of political dissenters who support liberal ideals. The first group is known as the Chartists, a group of people who in 1977 started the Charta 77 movement. Many of these people were intellectuals who backed the reforms of 1968, and many spent years in jail for professing to believe in "socialism with a human face." But among the people belonging to the movement today, one also finds young people for whom this is the first political act; they are young intellectuals and workers alike. The Chartists do not call for the re-establishment of a Western-style political democracy; they merely call for the observance of human rights guaranteed by the Czechoslovak constitution and for greater respect for legality. Although they number perhaps no more than a few hundred, their loose group is constantly infiltrated by the police, and they are often harrassed and imprisoned. Nonetheless, they continue to exhibit surprising strength and activity. Their *samizdat* publications are eagerly passed along from reader to reader.

Although they are not organized at all, the advocates of the Hungarian national autonomous movement in Czechoslovakia also should be counted as a source of political dissent. While these people do not wish to change the Czechoslovak political system, they do call for greater human rights and the observance of national minority rights guaranteed in the Czechoslovak constitution. In fact, one of the central figures of this movement, Miklos Duray, recently joined the Chartists.

Not surprisingly, both orthodox and liberal political dissent exists relatively openly in Hungary, the most liberal Warsaw Pact member. Here the conservative political opposition may be found within the party's *apparat* and among the trade union leadership, especially at the middle level. Although unable to rally around a single influential charismatic figure—for Kadar has always taken care to clip the wings of those theoretically more orthodox than himself—the conservative party *apparat* and its allies in the government have fought a successful rear-guard action against what they perceive as the "excessive speed" of liberalization of the state and the economy. Kadar, however, has managed—and is likely to continue to manage—keeping this orthodox opposition in check.

Far more visible in Hungary is the "democratic" opposition of those who "think differently" from the regime. Centered around sociologists and economists who hold that the current, relatively liberal development of Hungarian society does not go far enough toward meeting the needs of the modern state, these reform-minded dissenters publish relatively openly such illegal tracts as the *Beszelo* and *Hirmondo,* publish abroad in journals and through Western publishing houses that are in clear opposition to the ideals espoused by the Hungarian Communist regime, and continue to hold seminars and "free university" lectures. They do not engage, however, in creating or advocating the establishment of a rival political party or other forms of institutional challenge to the regime. While the regime has from time to time harrassed these dissenters—and in extraordinary cases has expelled their members from Hungary, or "merely" encouraged them to emigrate, while many of the members of the liberal opposition are prohibited in working in their field of expertise—generally they are not imprisoned or tried for antiregime activity. Many intellectuals and a few of the more politically sensitive workers are sympathetic to the 200–300 active dissenters, but they rarely take active parts in dissenting activities. On its part, using formidable tools that range from offering benefits to the denial of economic existence, the regime hopes to co-opt at least the sympathizers and thus lessen the impact of dissent.

In Yugoslavia there is also a wide spectrum of political dissent, which is defined more loosely here than in the other socialist states.

Orthodox political dissent exists within the leadership of the federal *apparat* and especially among some of the older leaders of the party both at the federal and the republic levels. These critics do not really wish to become a "satellite" of Moscow. Rather, their goal is to rein in Yugoslavia's liberal society through whatever measures necessary. They object to the "near-anarchy" of the country's political and social life and believe—misguidedly in my view, I need hardly add—that more stringent measures and approaches might solve many of the problems of modern Yugoslav life. They blame the extreme "liberalism" of Tito's political reforms—intended to prevent the emergence of a single omnipotent leader by rotating holders of most important offices on a regular basis among representatives of the various republics—for the "political malaise" of the state, and they propose a reconcentration of power and a stronger role of the Yugoslav League of Communists in the life of society.

On the other hand, the "liberal" political dissenters—most of them located at the various universities and in academic life with many of them living and teaching in Zagreb and Belgrade—hold that the party has not consistently devolved its early politically centralized role in favor of the system of local self-management. The former Praxis group—so called because of the close connection of many such dissenters with *Praxis*, a liberal Yugoslav periodical banned by the party in the early 1970s—now has new faces and new members, the discussions at the various universities have begun anew and the strength of the liberal dissenters continues to grow.

In considering Poland facile generalizations do not give us an easy and quick fix on political dissent. Poland, at the time of this writing, is governed by a military elite that rules society through paramilitary bureaucracy and a largely ineffective and dispirited party. Even so, many Poles can be characterized as hard-line dissenters. They include people from the middle levels of the state *apparat,* including the security police, whose members in 1984 went as far as killing the outspoken pro-Solidarity priest Father Jerzy Popieluszko. There are many orthodox dissenters who believe that a Stalinist type of dictatorship is the only answer to Poland's troubles, although some of them feel that such a system should be coupled with nationalism, chauvinism, and even anti-Russianism. But there are far more political dissenters on the liberal side. Most Polish economists, for instance, hold that only a decentralized system—resembling the Hungarian model somewhat—can foster a favorable economic climate. And many intellectuals yearn for the kind of freedom that characterized Polish society in 1980–1981. There are workers who seek the re-establishment of workers' autonomy, democracy, and decentralization, and there are workers who yearn for the re-establishment of Solidarity as an effective organization against the party. There are all sorts of dissenters in Poland; in fact, it is a nation of dissenters. But with the channels for open articulation of criticism closed by the Jaruzelski regime, political dissent can be expressed only by the myriads of *samizdat* publications, by slow-downs, shoddy production, and an unofficial and undeclared national strike against a regime nobody really likes, a regime that has very little legitimacy and support.

Economic Dissent

Unlike the political dissenters, the economic dissenters do not even indirectly challenge the legitimacy of the party, but merely the direction of economic policies set by the political elites. Thus they are a potentially less explosive group, but because their ideals clearly criticize existing policies formulated at the very highest levels, the political elite cannot ignore them as easily as it perhaps could ignore some manifestations of political dissent.

Economic dissent is peculiar in one sense; unlike political dissent, where both sides of the political spectrum are amply represented, economic dissenters agitate primarily in one direction only—toward greater liberalization, decentralization, and the application of market principles under socialist conditions. Only in Hungary and Yugoslavia are there a few—a very few—individuals who desire perhaps greater centralization; this, of course, is no wonder since only Hungary and Yugoslavia are relatively open socialist market economies and in these economies in the mid-1980s an economist simply must be a market-oriented practitioner of the dismal sciences. In the other Communist states, which are far more centralized, the economic dissenters, unlike the mainstream economists of the regime, are also liberals trying to reform the existing rather cumbersome administratively bloated economic system.

The extent to which these economic dissenters are trying to change the system and the extent to which they represent an important challenge to the party elites are different in each state. In East Germany, a small, highly technocratic elite suggests such improvements as the limitation on administrative bureaucracy, less centralized planning and further integration with West Germany, but the extent of their "dissent" is minimal; here, as in Bulgaria and Romania, the expression of that minimal dissent is largely confined to a few articles in scholarly journals by the "reformers" on the fringes of the political mainstream. In Czechoslovakia, the economic reformers are a bit more important; here, they insist on greater roles for individual and decentralized initiatives, a greater role for the secondary economy, and a more open market. Since most of the "reform-economists" operate within the carefully delineated space allotted to them within or just barely on the outside of the system, they have had some successes in freeing the household plots recently from major and continuous state control and allowing those working these lands to sell their products on the open market. In Bulgaria, the "decentralizers" or "reformers" have made major progress toward creating Bulgaria's New Economic Mechanism—vaguely patterned on Hungary's—although the economists are still agitating for more market-oriented reforms than the leadership is unwilling to embark on at the time of this writing. In Albania and Romania there are very few who question the "correctness" of the economic policies advocated by the "infallible" first secretaries who guide those states.

In Poland economic dissent poses major problems for the regime. The party under Jaruzelski's rule, in spite of its harsh dictatorial rhetoric, must grapple with a bankrupt economy. Polish consumer prices have been maintained at their relatively low levels for nearly two decades and in the past when the regime tried to raise these prices— often awkwardly and stupidly, frequently just before the holidays—it ran into major difficulties. Several wage and price increases have been introduced by the Jaruzelski regime since the declaration of martial law in December 1981, and Polish reform economists, both dissenters and within-the-system specialists insist that they, too, must create the kind of New Economic Mechanism now established in Hungary and freshly introduced in Bulgaria. The Jaruzelski regime, however, can only institute half-hearted measures of market and price liberalization, because decentralization would further loosen the even tenuous control of the party over the near-anarchic society. The economic reforms that must be introduced in Poland would also create hardship for an otherwise already disgruntled population with a sinking standard of living, and the regime can ill afford the further alienation of the Polish people. Thus only half-measures are introduced, and Polish economists are doubtful whether such measures are adequate for the ills of the Polish economy.

Polish economists characterize the present situation with a brief story. In the 1930s, a delegation of Polish traffic engineers were sent to Britain to study the traffic patterns of London in order to find a cure for the terrible traffic congestion in Warsaw. They came back and reported that the reason why traffic flows in London so well is because they have left-hand drive and suggested that the Warsaw City Council adopt the same policy. The council agreed that it was the correct suggestion, but because they thought that it would be too radical a departure, they instituted a policy whereby only the buses and taxis would drive on the left-hand side of the road; all other vehicles would still drive on the right.

Nationalist Dissent

Once upon a time, Communist theorists envisioned that when the blissful state of Communism was reached, there would emerge a community of workers from various nations, all of whom would have a common affinity toward and love for each other. The states would wither away, and in their place an international workers' paradise would come to exist. This expectation, like that of the earthly paradise, has melted away, and its place has been taken by the reality of a "socialist commonwealth" of Communist states. But the image of an international Communist community characterized by feelings of "socialist internationalism" still remains at the core of the professed ideology. In its jargon-laden format, socialist internationalism is interpreted by the Communists as "a love for the people of the USSR, of the fraternal socialist states, and of the international workers' movement struggling for national or class liberation."

But between 1929 and 1936 the term "socialist internationalism" began to be interpreted by the USSR as a call to assist the Soviet Union in building its "socialism in one country," and hence, to relegate working-class interests in other states to a secondary role. During World War II, the term was used to rally support for the defense of the USSR, and during the first ten years or so of Communist rule in Eastern Europe it was used to justify the Russification of every state and culture in the region. One of the main reasons, in fact, for the revolts and revolutions of 1956, for Yugoslavia's "revisionism" and for Romania's and Albania's "deviations" was the incredible insensitivity of Soviet Communist dogma to nationalist pride; while all of the nations in the Soviet orbit accepted the necessity of "building Communism," they wanted to do it *their* way, in their own national Communist settings. The rigidly enforced Soviet principles of socialist internationalism, however, left them really no room to separate, individual, national roads to build socialism. Since the mid-1950s, the Russians have had to modify their strident policies and soften the principles of "socialist internationalism" by accepting the principle of state sovereignty, though all the while claiming that "lofty" feelings of fraternalism and love among the socialist commonwealth must be preserved.

While the Eastern European states may maintain the importance of such feelings in their professed ideologies, the reality is that internationalism is a rather meaningless word among the populations. There are two notable nationalist deviations from the principles of internationalism: anti-Russianism and hostility toward other Eastern European countries. Although the former category is actually a part of the latter, we will deal with it separately as a matter of convenience.

Anti-Russianism is fostered in the region by historical circumstances; the Russians have been historical enemies of four states in the region: Germany, Poland, Romania, and Hungary. Throughout history, the Germans have repeatedly attacked and occupied parts of Russia; the Russians, in turn, are still the occupiers in East Germany and are visibly viewed as such by much of the East German population. Polish-Russian antagonism dates back to the fifteenth century, and although the Poles themselves were victims of German aggression during World War II, every Polish child is taught to remember, even today, more than forty years after the event, that the Soviet forces stood on the other side of the Vistula River in 1944 and simply watched the Germans crush the Warsaw uprising. The Romanians are equally anti-Russian. Although it switched sides in August 1944, Romania entered World War II on the side of the Axis. The cruelty of the Romanians in Odessa is not forgotten by the Russians; the Romanians remember equally well that the Russians took away ethnic Romanian territories in Bessarabia and Moldavia from Romania after the war and that these territories still remain a part of the Soviet Union. And the Hungarians are constantly reminded by the USSR that they were Hitler's last allies, who invaded Russia along with the Nazi troops; at the same time, Hungarians also know that Russian troops squashed their rising for independence from Austria in 1849 and the Soviet Red Army brutally crushed their revolution in 1956.

Even though the other states in the region can harbor more kindly memories of past Russian aid and assistance, for at least some Soviet imperialism has succeeded in turning benevolent attitudes into dislike or hatred of Soviet power. In Czechoslovakia, whose people were the most frankly Pan-Slavic in Eastern Europe, the Soviet-led invasion in 1968 took care of these cordial feelings. In tiny Albania Soviet imperialism is regarded as a force that must be combated just as strenuously as manifestations of Western imperialism are. In Yugoslavia, Soviet imperialism and Soviet attempts to subvert Yugoslav independence in 1948–1949 are regarded as national rallying concepts, even if there are some in that country who wish closer identification with the USSR. And even in Bulgaria, where the Russians are still regarded favorably for their role in giving Bulgaria independence in the nineteenth century, the Red Army's "occupation" of Bulgaria in 1944 still remains a troublesome issue.

Suffice it to say that many Eastern Europeans for historical reasons and because of their own higher level of economic and social development think that the Russians are still backward and uncultured. Such hostile feelings are most clearly and visibly observed in Albania, Poland, Hungary, Romania, Czechoslovakia, and Yugoslavia, in this order of intensity. They are less openly observable in East Germany and Bulgaria, but even in these states some manifestations of anti-Russian sentiment can be noted. These anti-Russian feelings hamper the implementation of socialist internationalism and the party's ideology of regarding the Russians with "affection."

There are also historical reasons for various strong hostilities among Eastern European peoples. For instance, territorial ethnic conflicts dating back hundreds of years smolder between the Romanians and the Hungarians, the Poles and the Germans, the Poles and the Czechs, the Czechs, the Slovaks and the Hungarians, the Bulgarians and the Yugoslavs, the Yugoslavs and the Albanians. But even discounting these complex historical issues, the simple fact remains that in spite of common sociopolitical systems, the nations and nationalities of these regions *simply do not like each other.* Even though every schoolbook of the region stresses and restresses the concept of "fraternal affinity," the reality of mutual dislike, contempt, and hatred cannot be altered. Only the Poles and the Hungarians, who do not share a common border but do share many a historical experience, seem to get along, though the Hungarians are still not quite sure about this.

Openly, however, because they are part of the same alliance and share the same political system, the issue of nationalism has to be handled cautiously. One cannot express hostile sentiments publicly, regardless of how strongly that sentiment is felt among the populations of these states. Thus, Romania cannot directly broach the question of Bessarabia with the Russians; that would be interference in the affairs of another socialist state and would invite counterintervention. Only through polemics in historical treatises can the problem be raised in a rather oblique manner.

In terms of nationalism as it affects interstate relations, the major trouble spots exist between Hungary, on the one hand, and Czechoslovakia and Romania, on the other, over the treatment of some 3 million ethnic Hungarians who live in those non-Magyar states. By far the more serious problem exists between Romania and Hungary: forced cultural assimilation by the Romanians has created such widespread anger among the Hungarians that the Hungarian Communist party elite also has been forced to consider the issue. In a sense, the Hungarian Communist party is caught between the devil and the deep blue sea: if it tries to force Ceausescu to change his policies toward his Hungarian citizens, it would be interfering in the domestic affairs of another socialist state and thus could invite retaliatory intervention in the the liberal economic development of Hungary by the Romanian, Czechoslovak, East German, or other elites. On the other hand, however, if the Hungarian party does not do anything, the tenuous economic legitimacy of the regime, already slowly being eroded by a deepening economic crisis, could also be further undercut.

A similar problem concerns the Macedonians, whom the Bulgarians claim to be ethnic Bulgarians living in Yugoslavia. While this issue is not as serious as that of the Hungarians in Czechoslovakia and Romania as far as interstate relations are concerned, it could heat up in the near future.

The internal aspects of nationalism are equally complex. They are exceedingly strong among the multinational states, Czechoslovakia and Yugoslavia, and in the semimultinational state of Romania. In Czechoslovakia nationalism is expressed in the continuous struggle between Czechs and Slovaks and against the Magyar minority. Since 1918, when the state of Czechoslovakia was established, the Slovaks, who were incorporated into Hungary for nearly a thousand years, believe they have been oppressed and exploited by the Czechs. Their demands for federalism played important roles in 1968 and since then have only increased. For the Czechs, investments in Slovak development seems to be overemphasized and the Czech people characterize the present regime of Gustav Husak—in power since 1969—as a Slovak dictatorship. We cannot debate who is "right"; what *is* important is that these feelings exist and characterize the states in which two ruling nationalities continue to "co-exist."

Ethnic Magyars live in large numbers not only in Czechoslovakia but also Romania and Yugoslavia. Since these states, especially Czechoslovakia and Romania, attempt to create truly "national" states, the Hungarians living there in large numbers either have to become culturally assimilated—and thus become Czechoslovak or Romanian nationalists—or be regarded by the ruling majorities as quasi-enemies of the Czechoslovak or Romanian state. The autonomy granted to national minorities in Czechoslovakia, such as the Magyars, or in Romania, the Magyars and the Germans, was considerably greater in the 1950s than it has been since the 1970s and the 1980s. The pressure to force cultural assimilation in recent years has increased considerably.

A very different set of problems relating to internal nationalism emerged in Yugoslavia. As we have discussed, Yugoslavia is made up of Serbs, Croats, Slovenes, Montenegrins, Macedonians, Albanians, and Magyars, to mention just a few. National autonomy, cultural freedom, national schools all have been maintained and supported by the various authorites at all levels, and national toleration and cultural autonomy have been practiced to such an extent that, as far as interethnic relations were concerned, until very recently it could be said that Yugoslavia was the Switzerland of the Balkans. If there were problems—and Yugoslavia was certainly beset by serious inflation and unemployment in the 1980s—they were generally caused not by nationality issues, but by the different levels of development among the various republics and autonomous regions.

However, Yugoslavia's ethnic Albanians, among whom friction was evident as early as 1944, suffered as a result of the economic problems of the 1980s, and violence erupted in 1982 in Kosovo, a region inhabited primarily by ethnic Albanians. Claiming, rightfully, that they have benefited the least from the economic development of the last two decades, the Albanians of Kosovo demanded greater economic benefits and greater national autonomy as well. In 1982 this dissatisfaction turned into vicious rioting that had to be quelled by the Yugoslav army and security forces.

Nor has everything been peaceful in the relations between the Croats and Serbs, the two dominant nationalities of the Yugoslav state. In fact, their historically troubled relationship worsened between 1968 and 1972 to such an extent that the Communist party purged the Croatian political elite in 1971–1972 and replaced many Croatian nationalists (who were aided by Soviet security forces anxious to fish in the troubled waters of Yugoslav politics) with more "trusted" comrades. While there seems to be no doubt that most Yugoslav citizens are committed to the ideals of a united Yugoslav state, it is clear that the Yugoslav polity faces a rough road ahead as far as the internal problems of nationalism are concerned.

Religious Dissent

Communist states by their very nature are officially atheist states; the party ideology is clearly based on the philosophy of materialism and evolution, specifically denying the existence of any deity either in the creation or the "supervision" of the material world. In spite of the existence of or professed adherence to several religions, as depicted in Table 8.1 atheism in the Communist states is, thus, a part of the official ideology of the ruling regimes and each of the ruling Communist parties follows policies that are aimed at eradicating reli-

Table 8.1   Religious Affiliations in Eastern Europe in the 1980s*

	Roman Catholic	Protestant	Orthodox	Muslim	Others	Total
Albania	10	—	25	65	—	100
Bulgaria	—	—	87	12	1	100
Czechoslovakia	70	25	—	—	5	100
East Germany	20	80	—	—	—	100
Hungary	69	28	—	—	3	100
Poland	95	3	2	—	—	100
Romania	9	5	82	3	1	100
Yugoslavia	36	1	45	12	6	100

* Because of the official prohibition/discouragement on the exercise of religion and the absence of any census data relating to religious affiliation, these figures are the best available estimates, not exact data.

gion and its influence among the people. But in Eastern Europe the Communist regimes have come to power in states where the allegiance of the people to religion throughout the centuries has been powerful and where religion has been a source of solace during the tragedies the people have had to endure. Moreover, the churches in many of these states have also been powerful instruments in defining political goals and have been the unifying force behind national survival during centuries of foreign occupation forces. Thus the churches have been viewed by a vast majority in most of these states as the embodiment or repositories of the "nation."

As mentioned briefly, the greatest religious problems for the Communist regimes of Eastern Europe were caused by the Catholic church. Possessing an outside focus of allegiance, to the pope in Rome and his edicts, and an outspoken hostility to the atheism of the Communist party, the Catholic church has struggled to maintain its power, its institutions, and the allegiance of its coreligionists in Eastern Europe. When the Communist authorities attempted to close the Catholic churches between 1948 and 1956 and jail priests and bishops, the Catholic church struck back by excommunicating the Communist authorities and those who collaborated with the party. The vicious confrontation between the party and the Catholic church, which resulted in the jailing of such strong-willed defenders of the faith as Cardinal Wyszynski in Poland and Cardinal Mindszenty in Hungary, was also made more difficult by the regimes' naming "peace priests" who tacitly supported the Communist regimes. By 1956, however, the Communist authorities became convinced that the forced abolition of religion was not a very practical policy and since then, both the Hungarian and the Polish regimes have tried to follow a low-key, go-slow approach toward instilling atheist ideology, leaving the influence of the church largely intact.

In Poland, since the late 1950s, there have always been some measures of compromise between the Catholic church and the Communist state. The church, viewed by most Poles as not merely the representative of the broader powers of Christendom, but also as the symbol of the historic continuity of Poland, still claims the allegiance of the vast majority, perhaps as much as 80–90 percent, of the Polish population. Although the regime tried to split the church by creating or allowing some exercise of influence among those in favor of cooperation with the Communist party—for example, the Pax and Znak lay groups and some elected representatives claiming to be spokesmen for Catholic affairs in the Sejm—the church hierarchy retained the allegiance of nearly all Catholic Poles until quite recently. The strong-willed Cardinal Wyszinski, until his death in 1980, succeeded in keeping the church functioning and intact, and as a result the churches today are still full of largely unharrassed faithful. The election of Bishop Karol Wojtyla of Cracow as Pope John Paul II in 1978 has further strengthened the church in Poland and has encouraged it to push for greater individual spiritual freedom and more institutional support from the Communist state for Catholic church affairs.

This, of course, does not mean that the Catholic church of Poland is always an antagonistic force vis-à-vis the Communist authorities. Indeed, while the Catholic church went a long way in supporting the Solidarity movement, in the end, after the declaration of martial law, it was the organized Catholic church under Jozef Cardinal Glemp, who replaced Wyszinski as the primate of Poland after Wyszinski's death in 1981, that urged moderation and the acceptance of the "unacceptable." Caring for the souls of its children, the church realized, was only possible if the bodies in which those souls resided remained alive; fearing for fratricide and bloodshed, the church opted for and supported a compromise more acceptable to the authorities than to the former members of Solidarity. And since the Poles are truly religious people, they have listened to a greater extent to the voice of their Holy Father—who has come back to Poland twice to show his concern for his compatriots—than to the voice of those who wished to strike out for greater freedom and autonomy. And even after the brutal murder of the pro-Solidarity priest Father Jerzy Popieluszko in 1984 by members of the Polish security forces, it was the church authorities who urged a continuation of the current compromise with the Jaruzelski regime.

This cooperative pattern can also be observed even more clearly in Hungary, where stormy relations between church and party raged from 1949 to 1975, when Cardinal Mindszenty's self-imposed exile in the United States Embassy (after the Hungarian revolution) ended with his voluntary deportation to the West and subsequent death. The new primate, Cardinal Lekai, is a quiet politician whose interest, like that of Glemp, centers primarily around the operation of his church. He is keenly interested in maintaining a compromise with the Communist regime. This compromise allows religious freedom to a greater extent than previously practicable in Communist Hungary, the maintainance of some religious schools, religious instruction—although not as a part of the regular curriculum in the public schools—and the operation of such institutions as Catholic nursing homes for retired priests and even some church-run seminaries.

Religious dissent in Hungary, however, still crops up, although it does not come from the church hierarchy, but from the grass-roots level. Dissatisfied with the top-level Catholic hierarchy and what are viewed as too generous and too frequent compromises with a basically atheist regime, a group of priests, led by Father Gyorgy Bulanyi, began to organize what are called "basic communities" of the Catholic faithful in the early 1970s. They cannot be regarded as a major force numerically—perhaps only a few thousand out of the roughly 6 million nominal and/or practicing Catholics in Hungary. Nonetheless, the "basic communities" have very strongly condemned continued nuclear escalation and have urged disarmament by *both* the West and the East. The "basic communities" thus provide a challenge both for the Catholic hierarchy and to the Communist party alike and while politically these communities are harrassed by the Hungarian authorities, to date they do not pose enough of a threat that serious governmental coercive measures need to be taken against them.

In Czechoslovakia, since the takeover by the party in 1948, relations between the Catholic church, which nominally claims the allegiance of more than 60 percent of the total population, including most of the Slovaks—and the Communist party have fluctuated greatly. Although relations were rather calm during the 1960s, by the mid-1970s the party once again began to crack down on the church authorities, even though the latter could hardly be regarded as an active or influential dissenting force. Nonetheless, the Husak regime is apparently intent on creating an even more pliant clergy; it recently began placing churchgoers under police surveillance and even putting some active churchgoers deemed to be "threats" to the regime in psychiatric institutions. Such government-controlled official bodies as Pacem in Terris for priests and the Christian Peace Conference for laymen exist solely in order to support the party, just as "peace priests" of Hungary and Poland were expected to do in the 1950s. But while religious dissent, at present, does not seem to pose a real threat to the Communist regime as a whole in Czechoslovakia, it has nevertheless been evident, both among the religious groups supporting bilateral nuclear disarmament and among a segment of Slovak Catholics who have even held some unauthorized demonstrations.

Among the Protestant churches of the region, the most striking "dissenting" role is played by the Evangelical church of East Germany. Claiming the allegiance of nearly 80 percent of the population of that country, the Evangelical church cautiously began, in the late 1970s and early 1980s, to edge away from the state's official policy or nuclear weapons and disarmament. As the regime itself edged closer to the traditional church—by such acts, for example, as commemorating Martin Luther's 500th birthday with great nationwide fanfare in 1983 as a part of the "historically progressive" tradition of the socialist regime—the Evangelical church leadership increased its cautiously opposition policies. Its dissent culminated in a letter from the Dresden evangelical community to first secretary Honecker, in which they called on the Eastern European leaders to begin taking steps of unilateral disarmament and expressed fears for further deployment of Soviet nuclear weapons in Eastern Europe. Surprisingly, the letter was published in the party paper, *Neues Deutschland,* on October 22, 1983.

"Mary, there are three kings and some sort of comrade out here."

Listy (Prague)

While this gesture does not mean that the East German party has accepted the "correctness" of the views held by the Evangelical church, it does suggest that careful and organized activities of religious dissent may be now more tolerable in East Germany than in most other Eastern European states.

While the regimes of Romania, Bulgaria, and Yugoslavia generally remain committed to the ideology of atheism, they have always been able to live with the various Orthodox churches that claim the allegiance of the largest percentages of their people. The Orthodox church, which historically has accommodated political regimes, believes that it can compromise adequately with the Communist party. Thus Orthodox dissent from the official party policies of these states is practically nonexistent.

A brief note should be added about the Jewish communities in Eastern Europe today and any manifestation of dissent among them. Following the Holocaust, there were only a few places in Eastern Europe where any Jews remained—the largest number, some 100,000 at the very most, in Hungary, perhaps 70,000 in Romania, and about 40,000 in Poland. The historically vicious anti-Semitism of the Polish people once again flared up in 1968, when, blaming this tiny minority for every obvious failure, the Polish regime "encouraged" the emigration of nearly all of Poland's remaining Jews. Official anti-Semitism in most of the area has only worsened with the vituperative stands these regimes have taken toward Israel since the Six-Day War in 1967.

However, emigration to Israel from Romania was eased after Romania's diplomatic relations with the United States and Israel improved in the 1960s, and there is religious freedom for the very few Jews of Bulgaria and Yugoslavia. Hungary today is the only country in Eastern Europe with a rabbinical school; even the very small number of Soviet Jews permitted to become rabbis study in this seminary. In spite of, or because of, Hungary's religious freedom, as far as the small Jewish community is concerned, there is practically no religious dissent among the Jews still living there, except for a small intellectual group called Shalom, which mainly advocates less anti-Zionist stances toward Israel than the Hungarian regime now follows.

The question of dissent—like the problems of participation, legitimacy, and succession—is a political issue. The greatest difficulty that political issues pose for these regimes is that apart from the use of force, they have not found a mechanism to grapple with diverse political views or interests. When these regimes came to power as Soviet-type systems, they attempted to "abolish" politics by subordinating all aspects of political diversity to the unified and monolithic party. As these states have developed, however, politics—not just the allocation of power and wealth, but the reconciliation of conflicting and equally viable views or key matters—has re-emerged with a vengeance. Thus these regimes now face the challenge of finding and making available the proper forums for political diversity, without the undue diminution of Communist party rule.

Economics

■ Perhaps no issue poses more confusing, more multifaceted problems for the Communist states of Eastern Europe than that of economics. This is a matter that affects the daily life of the citizens and impacts upon both the power of the states and the ability of their ruling elites to retain their authority. The problems of the economy are thus truly bread-and-butter problems that reverberate through every part of the system.

THE IDEOLOGICAL BASES OF COMMUNIST ECONOMIC SYSTEMS

To Marx and classical Marxist theorists, economics is the foundation on which everything else is built. Borrowing many of his theories from such economic determinists as Ludwig Feuerbach, Marx thought that the prevailing mode of production—the totality of man's relationship to the means of production—would determine every aspect of society, politics, laws, values, and so on. To Marx there were two preconditions for the arrival of Communism: abundance and social consciousness. Otherwise, he believed, the basic principle of production and distribution under Communism—"from each according to his ability, to each according to his needs"—could not be translated into reality. Without abundance not all "needs" could be satisfied; neither would people have the necessary social consciousness to produce happily and willingly for the good of all or to accept undifferentiated rewards for their labor. Consequently, Marx—and his collaborator Friedrich Engels—expected socialism to emerge first in the most advanced capitalist countries of the world at the time of their writing, namely England and Germany, for they were both convinced that *only* capitalism could create the material abundance required for a Communist society to be built on.

In spite of the highly technical nature of Lenin's writings on the Russian economy, in which he tried to prove that tsarist Russia was already a capitalist country and was ripe for a Communist revolution, it is clear that he used this point merely to justify his eventual seizure of power. Ignoring the facts that Russia was unevenly developed and poor, that the people's minimal daily needs could hardly be met, and that there was no extensive or socially conscious proletariat, Lenin opportunistically went ahead with the seizure of power in October 1917. In a rather cavalier way, he was convinced that under Bolshevik guidance and political rule, abundance and social consciousness could easily be *created,* thus ushering in a new era of social development.

Lenin did not live to see the failure of his policies, although the speeches and letters of his last year suggest that he began to understand that his successful coup, in reality, had limited Russia's future development. After his death in 1924, his successor, Stalin, began to implement a series of measures designed to speed up what he regarded as the lackluster progress that socialism was making in the Soviet Union. Starting in 1929, the Soviet economic system and policies, which had been relatively easygoing, decentralized, and uncontrolled in 1921–1928, were radically altered. These new policies were to become the guidelines for the development patterns of the Eastern European economics after 1949.

Stalin's policies were based on:

1. Tremendous emphasis on heavy industry.
2. Rapid collectivization of agriculture and the driving of agrarian populations from the villages into urban centers and industrial occupations.
3. A highly centralized economy, unfettered by market considerations, concentrated under a rigidly enforced system of hierarchical planning.
4. Forced saving—that is, the creation of capital from low wages and labor-intensive economic development.
5. Keeping the standard of living of the population relatively low while maintaining high growth rates in the national wealth.
6. An autarkic pattern of development—that is, a high degree of self-sufficiency, with little or no reliance on external trade.
7. The militarization of society and the state and the consequent dedication of inordinate shares of the industrial output to military ends.

COMMUNIST MODERNIZATION POLICIES: THE STALINIST YEARS

When the USSR occupied Eastern Europe, the region as a whole was more developed than the USSR, even if it was still far from a state of "abundance." Even after the tremendous amount of reparations extracted by the USSR and the looting of entire factories and the national wealth by both the German and the Red armies, many of these states—especially Czechoslovakia and Hungary—were still more productive and innovative than the USSR was in 1948. Suffice it to say, however, that the states of Eastern Europe between 1949 and around 1954 basically had to adopt what were characterized as Stalinist economic development policies.

Accordingly, during these years everything was nationalized and every individual—directly or indirectly—became an employee of the state. The banks and the factories became a part of the state; their owners were lucky if they escaped unharmed and became manual laborers. Small shops and big department stores, local cafés and large restaurants, little pensions and huge hotels alike became state property overnight. Apartment houses became state property, as did small one-family homes. Cows and tractors, locomotives and mines, clinics and hospitals, kindergartens and schools—all became state property with the stroke of a pen. After the early land reforms of 1945–1948 that gave land to many landless peasants, the process of collectivization forcibly confiscated just about all land owned by the peasants and turned it into "community" or state property. In short, the state became the sole paternalistic and hierarchical producer, making all economic functions state responsibility.

The state pursued a policy of rapid industrialization, especially for heavy industries. Steel factories were built and mines were opened, heating plants and hydroelectric dams were erected; each country had to become a "land of iron and coal." Never mind that this industrialization had to be based on the relative lack of natural resources and on outmoded organization principles; only the Soviet model of heavy industrial development of 1929–1939 was to be followed. Even if one could not find food, or scarce consumer goods, one had to develop the "commanding heights of industry," one had to build machines, lathes, and locomotives and produce steel, steel, and still more steel.

But a work force had to be created to allow such industrial development, and because these states had highly agrarian economies and populations during the interwar era, the work force had to come from the primary sector: agriculture. Accordingly, each of these states started a giant collectivization process. The peasants were forced to join the collectives and were terrorized through measures of coercion they had never known before. Their animals were herded away—often the peasants slaughtered them themselves rather than give them to the state—and they essentially became poorly paid laborers working for a state or a collective farm, directed by urban cadres. Payments for agrarian products were set deliberately low, keeping consumer prices for goods at minimal levels (1) in order to feed the industrial working class cheaply, and (2) to drive the peasants away from the low-paying agrarian work to the "better-paid" factory work needed to create industrialized states.

As seen from Tables 9.1–9.3, judging by numerical measures alone, the Stalinist policies were successful in swelling the ranks of industrial laborers and dramatically decreasing the number of people engaged in agrarian occupations. As Adam Wazyk, the Polish poet, wrote

> From villages and little towns, they came in carts, to build a foundry and dream out a city, dig out of the earth a new Eldorado. . . . Distrustful souls, torn out of village soil, half-awakened and already half-mad, in words silent, but singing songs, [a] huge mob, pushed suddenly out of medieval darkness.

New cities, such as Nowa Huta in Poland or Sztalinvaros in Hungary, sprang up surrounded by thousands of huge, prefabricated workers' hostels and dormitories.

The word "planned" became the operative term. In every state in the region the Communist party established a National Planning

Table 9.1   Percentage of Actively Employed Earners in Industrial and Agricultural Sectors: Eastern Europe (Selected Years)

	Year	Industry	Agriculture
Bulgaria	1935	8.0	80.0
	1950	12.9	73.2
	1956	23.4	60.2
	1978	43.2	24.9
Hungary	1930	24.1	53.0
	1949	38.8	42.9
	1970	44.0	25.7
	1978	42.3	20.3
Romania	1930	7.7	76.9
	1950	14.2	74.3
	1966	32.6	52.4
	1978	43.8	31.1
Czechoslovakia	1930	38.3	25.6
	1950	52.2	17.0
	1970	57.5	8.9
	1979	40.9	26.9
Poland	1930	19.4	60.6
	1950	25.6	53.0
	1974	43.0	34.0
	1979	40.9	26.9
Yugoslavia	1936	9.9	76.3
	1953	30.0	63.0
	1961	42.3	52.7
	1971	49.5	41.4

Table 9.2   Comparison of Rural Residence and Agrarian Employment, 1975–1979

	Rural residence	Agricultural employment
Bulgaria	66.4	24.9
Czechoslovakia	33.3	14.3
Hungary	49.6	20.3
Poland	44.3	26.9
Romania	52.2	31.1
Yugoslavia	61.4	41.4

Office, which was responsible for setting ever-higher production quotas for factories and farms, individuals and collectives, stores and restaurants. Everyone had to meet these quotas, assigned for every day, every item, year after year. Never mind that the targets established were often too ambitious and could not be met for want of material, energy, or other inputs. Even the Communist authorities were forced to recognize in a few years that "teleological planning"—planning that proceeds from how much one *ought* to have, as opposed to how much one realistically *can* have of a certain product—was bound to fail. Yet the state could create capital out of working the people hard,

Table 9.3   Percentage of Urban Populations in Eastern Europe (Selected Years)

	Year	Percentage
Bulgaria	1934	21.4
	1946	24.7
	1975	33.6
Czechoslovakia	1930	47.4
	1946	48.8
	1975	55.7
Hungary	1941	34.8
	1949	36.8
	1976	50.4
Poland	1931	21.2
	1946	31.2
	1975	55.7
Romania	1930	21.4
	1948	23.4
	1977	47.8
Yugoslavia	1931	12.2
	1948	16.2
	1971	38.6

forcing them to labor under abnormally harsh conditions and paying them miserable wages. It could force savings further by the sale to and compulsory purchase of state bonds by every employee amounting to 10 percent or more of the already low wages, and by not producing consumer goods beyond the mere necessities of life. But it could do so only up to a certain point without risking a halt in growth or domestic instability.

In fact, declining growth and instability became noticeable in Eastern Europe by about the time of Stalin's death, on March 6, 1953. By the summer of that year dissatisfaction became so widespread in the region that the Soviet leadership itself was alarmed. Small revolts erupted everywhere where the peasantry had been forced onto collectives or state farms that failed to provide them with even minimal sustenance. The workers were starving in the cities; bread riots broke out in Hungary, Poland, Czechoslovakia, and East Germany. Badly planned factories stood idle or ran at half-power, turning out shoddy products, obsolete by the time they hit the "planned" markets. It seemed that the Stalinist model of economic development had become a program for surefire failure.

The economic, social, and political debates that emerged under the New Course between 1953 and 1956 focused on the questioning of the necessity to follow Stalinist development in Eastern Europe and on the urgent economic issues that the Communist leaderships had to resolve. These issues are still the most urgent economic concerns in the area and thus are the topics with which the remainder of this chapter will be concerned. They are: (1) the advantages of a centralized versus a decentralized economy; (2) the types of economic development best suited for a particular state; (3) the problem of striking a proper balance between industrial and agrarian development; (4) the emergence of a second, unofficial and mostly private economy to assist the state with the secondary distribution within the system; and (5) the problem of foreign trade. And while we must emphasize that these states are all "socialist," the answers that each one has formulated have been quite different from those arrived at by the others.

ALTERNATIVE MODELS OF ECONOMIC MANAGEMENT

Yugoslavia was the first to deviate from the Stalinist model. Starting in 1950–1951, the Yugoslav political elite, under the leadership of President Tito, challenged the concept that the Soviet road to Communism was the only successful road to follow. Tito insisted that because of the differing levels of national development and differing historical circumstances, every state in Eastern Europe had a right to determine the best direction for its own development. To the Soviets this smacked of heresy, but the USSR had no armed forces in Yugoslavia, nor was it then willing or able to pay a high military price to whip Yugoslavia into line. So it could not actively challenge Tito's concept of "separate roads of socialist development." As we will see, this act of acquiescence was to have profound consequences in the Soviet sphere of influence later on.

While, the Yugoslavs preserved the basic elements of nationalized, or socialist, ownership, they also began to develop vastly different institutions and policies. First and foremost, they decollectivized the land and gave individual peasants a choice between tilling their own land or working on collective or state farms; the role of the socialist sector in agriculture in Yugoslavia still remains minimal. Second, they decentralized national planning, by limiting the role of the National Planning Office and delegating much of the planning responsibility to the local units where production actually was taking place. While there continued to be general national targets and general policy guidelines for economic development, these had to be translated into actual practice at the level of factories and firms and thus tempered by the availability of materials and other such considerations of reality. Third, they introduced workers' self-management by giving workers' councils control over the hiring and firing of firm managers and over setting targets— at least on paper—in a relatively democratic manner. Fourth, they decentralized the administrative hierarchy of the country by giving greater power to the republics and communes. And, finally, they ended restrictive trade patterns by integrating Yugoslavia with Western trade partners. To date, Yugoslavia remains governed by these relatively liberal institutions and policies.

In the mid-1950s the forced collectivization and industrialization drives came under attack elsewhere in Eastern Europe. During the relatively liberal Thaw that followed Stalin's death, peasants throughout the region "voted with their feet" by deserting the collectives, unless they were forced to stay by terror and coercion. In Hungary in 1956 the population revolted against Soviet-imposed models, the collectives disappeared overnight, and workers' councils sprang up; only the bloody intervention by the Red Army restored the Communist elite to power. In Poland the peasants also deserted the collectives, and many left their new jobs in the industrial sector to return to the land.

Unlike in Yugoslavia, however, after the revolts and discontent of 1956, the Soviet pattern of development was reinstated, except to some extent in Poland. Forcibly, though with less terror and more "coercive persuasion," the peasant holdings were collectivized once again and between 1959 and 1961 nearly all of Eastern Europe's peasants were herded onto collective or state farms. Only in Poland and

While in Eastern Europe the farms are generally collectivized, in Poland and Yugoslavia small family farms dominate the agricultural landscape. Here, members of a Polish family farm harvest potatoes by hand, a method used for centuries. (AP/ Laserphoto)

Yugoslavia were the peasants allowed to be free and till their own lands, though the centrally set low prices for farm produce in Poland were intended to convince the peasantry of the "foolishness" of their way of life. Heavy industrialization persisted everywhere, though, again, relatively gentle persuasion became more common than forcible coercion. Central planning was still used as a "Bible" everywhere, except in Yugoslavia once again, and consumer industries still received only minimal emphasis. Finally, spurred by the development of the Common Market in the West, the Eastern European states began to develop an international authority, the Council of Mutual Economic Assistance (CMEA or COMECON) to coordinate trade and production among the various states in the region. This general pattern of centralized organization of production and economic activity has continued to dominate the region as a whole.

There have been some divergences, however. Hungary has followed a path toward cautious liberalization of its economy. In 1965 the Hungarian Communist party began to develop an economic program called the New Economic Mechanism (NEM) that was implemented in January 1968 and that still—in repeated fits and starts— remains in force. Hungary has been careful not to present the NEM as a "model"—for fear of offending the Soviet Union, which alone still claimed the *right* to set the model for Communist development—and the NEM has become a tremendous force in the much-needed economic and social modernization of this state. Relying on the principle of depoliticization—in other words, allowing the discussion of any topic not as a political question on which the party had to take a position—the Hungarian reform started out by giving individual initiative and expertise far freer rein than previously was the case. Although the collectivized and socialized *forms* in farming were retained by the Kadar regime, incentives given to agriculture made innovative farming an attractive proposition for most of those involved in this sector. Moreover, support given to production on household plots made the use of the peasants' "free" time—the time when they were not officially involved with collective farm work—a financially attractive proposition.

In industry as well, the NEM replaced mandatory, centrally provided local quotas with simplified, general, national guidelines, while on the level of the firms the role of incentives in greater production was emphasized. Although this second element of decentralization failed to go as far and has not yet been as consistently applied as in agriculture, the decentralization of planning and greater local initiative resulted in a far better mix of goods available to the population than ever before. Hungary also took advantage of the opportunity, granted to most of the states of Eastern Europe by the USSR after 1970, to integrate itself to a far greater extent with the West than was previously possible. But most important, the Kadar regime allowed the population to engage in their own private economic activities; the privatization of certain economic activities—ranging from agricultural household production to "private" production activities even within the largest state-owned firms—was the most successful policy of Hungary's Communist government. Basically, these policies allowed the people to privatize their work and reap the reward from it. Privatization also allowed the government to derive economic legitimacy from the facts that Hungary enjoyed perhaps the highest level of living in Eastern Europe and that its population was basically content economically. The Kadar regime simply realized that the economic mechanism of the socialist state must operate with the same efficiency as those of the developed capitalist states. If it does not, as an astute Hungarian political observer has put it, "in the consciousness of the citizens the doubts concerning the developmental possibilities that exist in the socialist system are going to be ever stronger." Although the NEM had failed to live up to the continuous potentialities for liberalization with its on-again, off-again politically motivated cycle, it still created the freest and most liberal economic system in the region, apart from Yugoslavia's.

In Poland a genuine reform movement began in 1956, only to peter out as Wladyslaw Gomulka vacillated between reform and liberalization, on the one hand, and traditional centralization, on the other. In 1970, in 1976, and again in 1980 food riots rocked the country and toppled the regimes of Gomulka and of Edward Gierek. While the Solidarity movement demanded real changes, especially regarding workers' democracy and local self-management, nothing was actually done to reform the economy. Although major calls for economic reform were sounded even under the regime of General Jaruzelski—specifically suggesting the adoption of some aspects of Hungary's NEM, many of which had been advocated decades earlier by prominent Polish economists—to date little has happened to implement these proposals, and the debate over the direction the Polish economy is to take rages unabated to this day.

In Romania, while no dramatic breakthroughs in terms of economic liberalization have occurred, a deliberate plan organized by the USSR did cause a major shift in the economy. In 1959 Nikita Khrushchev, then the Soviet first secretary, began to insist that the function of the CMEA was to allocate specific tasks to the various Communist states in order to avoid duplication of activities; Romania was allotted

---

A Solution to Economic Problems in Poland

"The only hope—a UFO . . ."

Andrzej Krauze in *Polytika* (Warsaw)

agrarian production as its specialization. The Romanian Communist party felt this assignment relegated Romania to a lesser role in the Communist family of nations, refused to abide by the plan, and began to undertake what the Romanian policymakers called a process of "multilateral development." In reality, this meant the modernization of Romania through tremendous economic centralization, coercion, and heavy industrial development. At the same time, it also forced Romania to multiply its trade links with the West, at least to the same extent as those of Hungary or Poland. Such differences with the "dictates" of the USSR, and to some extent differences with other Soviet supported issues in foreign affairs, earned Romania the title of the "maverick" in Eastern Europe and suggested that the country had a limited independence.

This brief summary, of course, does not address every issue of the economy, but it does suggest that various economic policies and experiments do exist in Eastern Europe. In the following section we shall try (1) to analyze these various systems with respect to the problem of economic centralization versus liberalization and (2) to touch briefly on existing divergences concerning the "second economy" and (3) foreign trade.

BETWEEN CENTRALIZATION AND LIBERALIZATION

As one observes the economic landscape of Eastern Europe in the 1980s, it becomes clear that rigidly planned economic practices characterize some of the countries, while in others centralized planning is kept at a minimum. In some states planning is practiced on the national levels, while in others it is merely practiced only by the individual enterprise. And there are also major differences in the specific methods of planning among the Eastern European states.

Albania, Czechoslovakia, Romania

The most rigid economic planning is practiced in Czechoslovakia, Romania, and Albania, three economies whose levels of development are vastly different: Czechoslovakia is a highly modern, industrial state, Romania has a "mixed" economy, while Albania is still a largely underdeveloped country. In each of these states the National Planning Office prescribes virtually every conceivable target, establishes the price of everything and the wages of everyone, and projects how much of a certain product is to be brought to the "open" market. Plans are formulated in terms of long-term goals—there are five-, ten-, and

twenty-year plans that project ideals for the economy as a whole—
and short-term goals as well—plans are made for every year and are
further broken by quarter and by month. In fact there are such norms as,
for instance, how much time must be allotted to make a single product and for how much, when, and where that product must be sold.

In these economies there seems to be no way to determine how
much a certain product *actually* costs to produce, because most prices
are set artificially by the highly centralized system. Social considerations—such as, let us say, keeping farm products and staples extremely
cheap—as well as national decisions by the political elites—keeping
luxuries like disposable diapers costly and generally unavailable—determine prices at the whim of the economic gnomes in Tirana, Prague,
or Bucharest. The prices have no relation to the market forces of supply
and demand; they have a relation only to "the plan," as accepted by
the decision makers of the state. In these economies the question of
efficiency of production does not enter into the calculus of the plan;
"higher" goals, set by the political elite, dominate the much-derided
"economic thinking" of the practitioners of the "dismal science" in
these socialist states.

Another reason why we cannot accurately calculate the cost of a
product is the problem of wages. Wages throughout Eastern Europe
were established in 1948–1949, and the wage scales set then still prevail
today, at least in relative terms. A teacher or a doctor still earns the
same amount *relative to the earnings of a bricklayer or a lathe operator*
as he or she did in the 1950s, even if his income in absolute terms
has risen. The wage scales established were created for a very specific
reason: social engineering. *Productive* work—manual, industrial
work—was to be remunerative and hence regarded as more important
than work in the service or intellectual sector, even if that wage system
was usable during the industrialization period, as the wages paid had
no relation to the real value of goods created. Productivity and efficiency could not be rewarded by significantly higher salaries, and the
wage structure could not be altered, for that would have violated one
of the primary ideological premises of these systems: the preferential
semiegalitarian wage scale. Although, through the secondary economy
or "corruption," some elements of this restrictive wage structure have
been altered in some of these states, the artificiality and backwardness
of the wage structure in the region as a whole still makes it impossible
for anyone to establish the cost of anything.

Even in the most economically centralized states, there have been
stirrings of interest in what is often called "economic rationality." For
instance, during the Prague Spring of 1968, when Alexander Dubcek
and the Czechoslovak Communist party tried to create "socialism with
a human face," the rallying cry of the "reformers" was precisely the
issue of the mismanaged Czechoslovak economy that had resulted in

an actual decline in production. And in Romania there have been debates—especially in the more obscure economic journals read by and written mostly for the economic community—about the irrationality of planning every item and every price, thereby ignoring the realities of the market and of supply and demand. But after the Soviet-led invasion of Czechoslovakia in August 1968 and after the Ceausescu regime threatened to arrest those who dared to question its centralized policies, little progress was made. Along with Albania, these states remain rigidly dictatorial, and planning from above still characterizes economic life.

One may well ask how successful these systems are in meeting the needs of the population. But before answering this question, we must remember that these needs are determined by the party elites, who claim to know them better than the "simple-minded" economists, let alone the general public. For instance, the Czechoslovak party elite is really less interested in whether there are low rates of growth or even an actual decline in the growth rate (as happened in 1966–1968 and again in 1981–1983) than whether the population remains under tight control, the political situation remains stable, and the "dangerous ideas of reformism" remain unimplemented. The easing of control over the population is viewed as far more dangerous than failing to produce enough to "meet the quota."

Moreover, the needs of the people and the ever-present shortages that so clearly characterize most of these societies today are totally ignored by at least some of the Communist elites—certainly in Albania, Czechoslovakia, and Romania. And the scarcities are phenomenal and widespread, ranging from fruit and meat to paper clips and scissors.

An old story has it that in Romania an old woman went into a butcher's shop and asked if they had pork. "No," replied one of the shopkeepers. "How about beef?" "No." "Chicken?" "No." "Veal?" "No." "Lamb?" "No." "Sausages?" "No." Finally she leaves disgruntled, and one butcher turns to the other and remarks: "What a pest of an old woman, bothering us with all those questions . . . but what a phenomenal memory!"

Sadly these shortages can last a long, long time without major disruptions of the social and economic system. For no one needs to starve to death in these states, and many staples such as bread and milk are available at reasonable prices. The needs of the population for scarcer consumer goods can always be dismissed as "dangerous delusions" of people who cannot see the necessity to make sacrifices for the future. And should people revolt against such scarcities, as the miners of the Jiu Valley in Romania did in 1977 and 1981, the instruments of oppression can always be used to back up these coercive regimes.

Under such a system can planning be exact and successful? The answer is clearly negative. With constant scarcities in material, labor, and transportation facilities, most frequently at the lowest levels, one cannot possibly expect to meet the projected targets. Since not meeting them, however, is regarded as a crime, people at all levels of the system resort to "overstating" their productivity and their needs for material, labor, or other resources. If one needs ten tons of steel to produce a certain number of machine tools, one always demands at least twelve tons, for the wise manager knows that much of the steel will be stolen or will never arrive, and he wants to be sure that he meets his targets. In these rigidly planned systems, such considerations, of course, would make planning with exactitude a nightmare; those economists who know the system well assure us that indeed planning is at best a guesswork.

East Germany and Bulgaria

The situation is considerably better in Bulgaria and East Germany, in spite of the fact that these states also have centrally planned non-market economies. Many factors work to make East Germany's the most successful, centralized, Communist economic system. In East Germany one can clearly observe the importance of a Western industrial heritage, high levels of economic development, and the legacy of generations of skilled laborers. Moreover, economic management in East Germany prizes efficiency and innovation—even if much of this scientific innovation does come from West Germany. East Germany possesses the highest standard of living in Eastern Europe and its products are of the highest quality in the Communist bloc; scarcities are minimal, and planning is more practicable. But in East Germany plans are not formulated with total disregard to existing realities; the price and costs of the products bear some relationship to each other—as well as to products sold just across the wall in West Germany. While there are glaring exceptions to the successes of the East German economy, planning generally seems to work quite well here.

Bulgaria provides us with an example of mixed successes and failures of central planning, and its recent record certainly has been better than that of Czechoslovakia, Romania, or Albania. The primary reason for this is that since 1979 Bulgarian economic decision makers began a cautious reform movement, their own New Economic Mechanism, which puts greater importance on efficiency of production and weakens the control of the central planning authorities over many of the individual enterprises, especially in agriculture and light industry. The mechanism of market price was opened up to some extent and private and semiprivate enterprises were given a surprisingly wide berth, especially in the agricultural sphere. Planning in Bulgaria thus became a less rigid process and began to take existing economic realities into consideration. Coupled with the fact that the Bulgarians were successful in striking a balance between industrial production specialization and agricultural development, "imaginative central planning" produced an expanding and reasonably advanced Bulgarian economy by the 1980s.

Poland

The case of Poland is puzzling, for at the time of this writing, Poland is undergoing a tremendous amount of soul-searching concerning the direction it should choose for its future development. Poland today is a highly industrialized state that has not yet given up on the idea of a centrally planned economy with all the dreams of a rigidly planned socioeconomic system. At the same time, it is full of baffling anomalies. For example, its uncollectivized peasants should be able to produce enough for Poland to be the breadbasket of Europe. But the state continues to set the prices at which these peasants can sell their produce very low, thereby discouraging them from producing enough to feed the Polish people. The food shortages in Poland that led to the bread riots in 1980–1981—and in previous years—did not occur because enough food could not be produced in Poland, but because it was not *worthwhile* for the peasants to produce those goods.

However, the Polish authorities had to confront a vicious circle. Simultaneously with the bread riots, the Polish population also objected to the government's policy of raising the ridiculously low prices for farm produce that had been established decades earlier—the very prices that made agricultural production unprofitable for the Polish peasants and resulted in tremendous underproduction of agrarian goods. What the Polish economy has needed desperately was for the Polish authorities to make up their mind and find an equitable balance between the needs of the state and the needs of society; it is precisely that lack of balance that has been the cause of the major economic dysfunctions of a planned system gone haywire.

Hungary

What the Polish reform economists would dearly have liked and could not do for political reasons—such as the fear that economic liberalization might bring about a political upheaval or Soviet disapproval—

is to adopt some variation of the Hungarian economic reform model. Under the New Economic Mechanism, the role of the National Planning Office has been reduced to setting targets and forecasts of national needs, without setting quotas for every economic unit down to the lowest levels. In Hungary it helped set allocations of needs and materials, set targets and projected growths as national goals, but these plans— for example, an expected rise or an acceptable decline in the level of living—were not compulsory goals that *had* to be met at all levels.

Most important, however, the NEM has altered the role of the market and that of the price structure. Recognizing that in spite of Marxist-Leninist dogma about the helter-skelter nature of the "capitalist" market, since 1968, contrary to all Communist preaching, most Hungarian economists—loosely grouped around former Politburo member Rezso Nyers, who initiated the reform movement—held that the only real way to ensure economic progress was to allow the market to play major roles. Supply and demand equilibrium, once frowned on by Communist economists as a vestige of "bankrupt bourgeois theories," once again became a force behind the Hungarian economy.

The Hungarians devised a three-tier set of consumer prices. The first tier included all those prices that were to remain set by the state; the prices of essential staples, such as milk or bread, continued to be determined by the state in order to guarantee that the whole population could meet its *minimal* food needs. The second tier of prices— food products, meat, textile goods—had minimum and maximum values; the price of the item could fluctuate between these limits. In the third tier—largely including items that were viewed as "luxury" goods by the authorities—prices were set strictly by the interplay between supply and demand. While at the very beginning of the reform most prices were in the first category, they were slowly shifted into the second and third categories. There were tremendous incentives for artisans, for small farmers to grow produce on their household plots, and even for some of the larger collective farms and state farms that still dominated large-scale food production. As a result, the constant scarcities that prevail elsewhere in the region simply do not exist in Hungary, and the citizens of the other socialist states who visit Hungary are amazed by the fact that a socialist economy can produce enough food for its population.

But the National Planning Office also had to relinquish some of its control over wages; its retreat from this sphere, however, was not as great—or as smooth—as it had been in the case of prices. Still deliberately trying to extract as much "surplus-value" from the hide of the population as the state could, the National Planning Office continued to set scales in all state-operated institutions. However, they soon had to realize that—because efficiency and incentives are essential for continual development—business managers would circumvent their directives. Thus, for example, a qualified skilled worker in a state-owned factory could be paid only a certain amount per hour, but he could easily make twice as much by engaging in the free market as a private artisan. Factory managers who wanted to attract this worker, however, could bypass the regulations by giving him guaranteed overtime, which he—miraculously—did not have to work. A vibrant society thus by and large triumphed over the obsolete attempts by the state to control the wage and the market mechanisms.

Yugoslavia

It will also be recalled that in Yugoslavia, the most liberal state in the region, central planning was relegated to the mere setting of approximate national targets many years ago. Planning offices still abound in Yugoslavia, of course—every republic has one—and the National Planning Office still exists in Belgrade. But planning is actually done at the firm, factory, farm, or market level. Budgetary allocations for spending and revenues, the apportionment of wealth for egalitarian goals of the republic, continue to be done in Belgrade, and this causes plenty of problems: resentment in the most productive region that its wealth is channeled to more backward areas, and resentment in the backward regions that feel that they did not participate adequately in the Yugoslav economic miracle of the 1960s and early 1970s. But the main determinant of planning practices at the local level, where it really counts, is still the interplay of supply and demand, the once so-maligned market considerations.

To sum up, central planning alone is not necessarily the variable that determines the success or failure of the Eastern European economies. The most centrally planned societies—Albania, Czechoslovakia, and Romania—seem to be coping less successfully with the demands of modern economic production than are other similarly planned systems, such as East Germany and Bulgaria. But centrally planned East Germany is far more successful than anarchic Poland and as successful as the decentralized Hungarian or Yugoslav economies. However different the prevailing policies of their elites toward planning now are, only Yugoslavia, Hungary, and East Germany have succeeded in providing their populations with a relatively high standard of living and their economies with the needed potential for future growth.

THE SECOND ECONOMY

Much has been written in the West about the extent of the second economy in Eastern Europe, its operations and the problems such activities engender. Unfortunately, however, for students of politics in the region, the question of the second economy has yet to receive a comprehensive, comparative analysis. Thus in the pages that follow we offer only a broad outlook, rather than going into the detail often needed to fill all of the areas of this puzzle.

The term "second economy" generally refers to those economic activities that take place outside of the official channels. The emergence of the second economy is an international phenomenon. As prohibitive tax bites begin to hit retailers and merchants, middlemen and the service sector, more and more people engaged in economic activities turn to cash transactions that are, by their very nature, undocumentable. Many such activities are thus excluded from the taxing purposes of the state. In Italy, for example, according to some estimates, at least 50 percent of non-state-organized economic activities take place through the second, or as some people call it, the "black" economy. The phenomenon, evident in Western Europe and the United States, is especially widespread in the less developed countries.

In Eastern Europe, however, we must differentiate among various *types* of second economic activities, and we cannot use the term "black" or "illegal" economy because the second economy here includes both legal and illegal activities. The term "second" economy in itself defines our approach to the problem. In a socialist economy there is, first and foremost, the primary economy, the economy planned, overseen, and operated by the state. According to the Stalinist economic model—the basic principles of which are still institutionally present in each of the states of the region—all economic activities are directed by the state as the representative of the people, and thus everything within the economic sector comes under the control of state authorities. Hence the primary economy is basically the state economy. Manufacturing, transportation of goods, distribution of products in state stores, the ownership and maintenance of apartment houses, publication of books, and production of plays are all supposed to be primary economic activities.

The second economy in Eastern Europe includes everything that does not take place under official state control—activities that are not a part of the planned process. Some states and some economists, however, prefer using the term "secondary distribution" to talk about this phenomenon, both for ideological and cosmetic reasons. They contend that the second economy is largely restricted to distributional activities—or redistribution—while production is still generally under the control of the state. The difference between those who contend that secondary activities are largely restricted to distribution outside of state channels and those who view the phenomenon as a broad-based sector that operates outside the planned economy is not just a semantic one, but also an ideological one.

The activities that take place in the second economy may be categorized according to (1) whether these activities take place as a part of state activities or are totally private, or (2) whether these activities are legal or illegal; although these two categories are often intertwined, they are not necessarily mutually inclusive. Some activities, for instance, may be totally private and legal—for example, owning a small repair shop—or totally state-owned and illegal—say, a state firm building a villa for a local party secretary. Some specialists have termed the extent of legality according to a "color scale" because they cover the spectrum from "white," or legitimate, to "black," or illicit, economies. Between these extremes one will find a myriad of permutations, and it is frequently very difficult to judge in which category an actual activity falls. Whether, where, and when the actors will engage in any of these activities depends on the necessity of being involved, the extent of the gain, or the possibility of discovery and the potential severity of punishment.

One, of course, may question how the citizens of these states can know, for instance, what the punishment or the chance of discovery is or the exact extent of the gain or loss from being involved in secondary economic activities. Even in the West, many people do not know what may be legal or illegal in an economic transaction. In Eastern Europe, however, live perhaps the most politically astute—if not cynical—citizenry, weaned on the necessity for survival in an economy where everything is always in short supply.

Moreover, throughout the centuries the feudal structures of Eastern European society have not really disappeared; rather they have been re-created on another level. Today every individual has a network of connections that is utilized extensively and mutually. Because of the numerous scarcities, one must have a connection for everything—getting meat, buying a car, acquiring an apartment. The mutuality of these relationships resembles the patron-client relationship in Latin-American society, with one major exception: in Eastern Europe everyone is both a client and a patron, for basically everyone has something to sell that is unavailable elsewhere.

Let us now examine how the second economy works. Imagine a state-owned factory operating totally under the central plan. But then something goes awry. A truck carrying needed parts for a certain product breaks down, and the firm cannot meet its target. At this point the secondary economy comes into play. Rather than failing to meet the target, the factory manager calls in the "materials procurer"—*tolkach*, or "pusher" in Russian—usually a savvy old-timer who knows what factories produce the needed item. A telephone call to an old friend and a gift or a bribe to the manager of the other factory usually do the trick; miraculously the parts are located and sent on their way. The *tolkach* gets a bit of money, and the factory manager who has provided the parts receives a bonus from the "contingency funds" of the firm in need. This activity all takes place within the state economy, but outside the *planned* economy.

The practice of paid overtime is another case in point. Because wages are still centrally established in each of the Eastern European states, factory managers cannot pay their laborers more than what these workers are entitled to by law. But, as the workers put it; "The state pretends to pay us and we pretend to work." If, however, the manager *really* needs their full effort to meet his target, he can pay two to three times the established hourly wage for overtime. By paying out overtime wages for work during regular hours, the factory manager is likely to fulfill his quota. Again, this activity takes place within the state economy and not in the private sphere even if it is not "planned."

But further along the "color scale," private activities begin to come into play. In some of these states, most notably in Hungary, work communes are established within the state-owned firms (Enterprise Work Contract Associations, or EWCAs) or outside them (Independent Work Contract Associations, or IWCAs). Using state facilities and state materials, members of work communes, after they have finished their official work hours, produce the same items required of them during their work hours. However, because they "contract" their work with the factory independently, the workers can claim wages two to three times greater than could legally be offered by the firm for work performed during regular hours. The principle seems to be to allow the merciless self-exploitation of one's labor for good income since during the official forty-hour work week one cannot earn a decent wage.

Another form of such cooperation may be noted in the agrarian sector in Hungary, Bulgaria, and to some extent in Yugoslavia and Poland. While the local agricultural cooperatives and state farms still own the lands, their members are also encouraged to work their small household plots, normally less than one-half acre, producing labor-intensive goods by growing berries, tomatoes, or raising chickens or pigs for sale in a relatively free farmers' market. The collective farms assist them in this by providing seed, fertilizer, machinery, marketing mechanisms, and so on. The activity that takes place is private but it takes place with the help of the state sector.

Increasing privatization and individual enterprise may be noted still farther along the continuum. An electrician in a factory, for instance, may repair his neighbors' lamps or radios after work hours using materials stolen from his workplace. Because of the inefficiency of the state maintenance sector his neighbors depend on him; otherwise it will take months to repair a leaky faucet or a broken window. But suppose a repairman from the state *does* show up to fix a leaking valve in a gas stove. He announces that he cannot fix the valve because no replacements for it are currently available in his shop; perhaps in a few weeks, but until then he will have to turn off the gas in the apartment: no stove, no heat, no hot water. The apartment's occupant pleads and after much head-scratching the repairman says, that perhaps there is an answer: he just happens to know where he can get *privately* such a valve, but it's going to cost much more than one from the state shop; on the other hand, he can get it in a half an hour. What is the hapless customer to do? She pays through the nose, illegally and privately, but at least she has her stove fixed by a state repairman using state materials.

On scarcity: A customer asks a private merchant how much a kilo of potatoes costs. The merchant replies: "30 forints." "What!" the customer exclaims, "across the street, in the state shop it is only 8 forints!" "Well," says the merchant, "then why don't you buy them in the state shop?" "Because they don't have any potatoes," comes the ready answer. The merchant scratches his head. "Yes, yes," he says, "if I didn't have any, I too would sell them for 8 forints."

Such activities are basically semilegal. A doctor, for example, is not allowed to *ask* for money for services that are supposed to be free, but he or she is frequently given a tip by patients who believe that doing so will entitle them to better medical care or scarce, often imported medicine. The doctors, whose wage scales are truly miserable compared to the importance of their profession, may often offer the patient an opportunity to come to their home or office as a private patient, and their charges then become strictly outside the purview of the state. "Gifts" of French cognac, perfume, jewelry, and the like are always welcome, just as is the exchange of privilege and mutuality: a patient who has an influence on the allocation of scarce cars may well be treated differently than someone who has no influence at all.

One could argue that such acts of corruption are intolerable in a socialist system, but the fact remains that without them life would be truly unbearable. The gift of a bottle of wine to the butcher ensures a choice cut of meat, the gift of a pair of good tickets to an excellent performance at the opera nets in return a share in a vacation house in the summer. Such acts are correctives to an inefficient state economy that cannot overcome the ever-present scarcities. Though they may be illegal in some cases, they are most often necessary to ensure that at least scarce goods or services are available for most of the citizenry.

In certain states in the region the most troublesome acts are those that are still judged as strictly "private" in the ideological sense. In

Albania, Czechoslovakia, and Romania, and to a lesser extent in East Germany and Bulgaria, most of these activities are restricted by law, while in Hungary and Yugoslavia they are allowed and even encouraged. In all of these states there exist small shops run by tailors and shoe makers, and there are still peasants who till their own land; in fact, as we have noted, almost 80 percent of all farmers in Poland still work their own farms. But in Yugoslavia and Hungary, and to a lesser extent in Poland, a new type of private entrepreneur also has emerged. These entrepreneurs own small shops crammed with scarce merchandise. They hire women to knit, embroider, sew, and assemble chic clothes, T-shirts, and jeans that cannot be purchased in state stores. These women can make fabulous amounts of money. The trouble is that a private individual cannot reinvest his capital, he can only put that wealth into durable goods, ostentatious houses, or splendid cars. Just as the similarly extensive wealth of a few successful peasants, that of private repairmen, bricklayers, electricians and plumbers, their wealth is lost for the state.

The second economy is thus extensive in Eastern Europe, but its importance varies in each of the states. In Hungary, it is suspected that at least 50 percent of all economically active Hungarians participate in the second economy, compared to about 10–20 percent in Albania, Czechoslovakia, or East Germany, but of course there are no official statistics to confirm these estimates. In descending hierarchical order, Hungary leads the pack in privatization, with Yugoslavia and Poland not far behind, followed by Bulgaria and Romania, Czechoslovakia, East Germany, and Albania. The extent of secondary or private economic activity does not alone guarantee the success or failure of an economy; Hungary and East Germany both have relatively successful economies, but the degree to which privatized secondary activities contribute to their growth is notably different.

FOREIGN TRADE: AN UNRESOLVED QUESTION

This is not the place to discuss *in extenso* all the ups and downs of such economic problems as the question of energy prices, the evolution of the COMECON or the problem of Soviet-East European trade relations. However, one aspect of East European economic problems— the question of foreign trade—has to be discussed even if albeit much too briefly. Foreign trade seemed to pose little or no problems for the Eastern European states during the initial phase of Communist rule. Only minimal trade existed among the Communist countries. There were two reasons for this. First, "trade" with the Soviet Union amounted to a one-sided exploitation whose essence was *(a)* to strip anything valuable and movable from Eastern Europe to the USSR;

(b) to extract the highest reparations payments possible from those Eastern European countries that were deemed hostile to the USSR during World War II; and (c) to subordinate the reconstruction of these states to the strengthening of the USSR.

Second, the Stalinist model emphasized the necessity of autarky or self-sufficiency and encouraged every state to develop on the basis of an "internal market," as a result of its own internal needs and demands, rather than relying on external trade. Certainly, trade with the West was not envisioned, and even trade among the various Eastern European countries was effectively discouraged. Moreover, Eastern European ideologists opined that the West was going to collapse any day, and thus there was no reason to trade with it.

By the end of the 1950s, however, it became very clear that the West was not going to fall. In fact, the United States and Western Europe were enjoying great technological and economic successes. While it is true that the growth rates of the Eastern European states were equally impressive during the 1950s and 1960s, as the Cold War ebbed there arose an ever-greater clamor among Eastern Europeans for a more equitable trade balance with the USSR, on the one hand, and a greater integration with world trade, on the other.

The greater balance between the USSR and its Eastern European partners were taken care of by "natural" events; energy and raw material prices continued to increase all over the globe. In the 1970s, for the USSR—forced to sell its products to its allies at prices below world market costs—trade with the COMECON partners began to be more and more expensive. By the same token, the finished goods that found their way to the USSR from these states were often of shoddy quality. By the end of the 1970s, the Soviet Union had to subsidize the Eastern European economies to an extent estimated at $20–80 billion annually. This was the economic price the USSR had to pay to maintain its empire. By the 1980s this trend had been reversed with the drop in oil prices; the Eastern Europeans had to pay even higher than world prices for oil and the USSR demanded higher-quality and greater quantities of goods.

The clamoring for increased trade with the West dates back to the late 1960s. Several Eastern European countries tried to trade with the West and to get Western loans earlier, but these attempts met with rather dismal failure. For instance, in the 1960s Bulgaria had to be bailed out by the USSR's sale of a large amount of gold in the international markets; otherwise, it could not, through some serious miscalculation, even service the debts it had accumulated with Western trading partners. At the beginning of the 1970s, the ideal of not trading with the West or being free of Western debts was still prevalent in Eastern Europe; in 1971 the entire region owed only $6 billion to Western banks and governments.

At the beginning of the 1970s, détente and Ostpolitik began to warm the winds of international politics as Western banks began to find themselves awash with OPEC petrodollars. Having no better place to lend them, the Eastern European markets began to look more and more attractive to Western bankers. At the same time, the availability of easy credit also began to interest the Eastern European bankers. Desperate for Western high technology—from which their economies had long been deprived, both as the result of their political isolation from the West and the huge amounts of hard currencies necessary for investments they could not make on their own—most of these states started to borrow very heavily from the West. This strategy, however, backfired when it became clear in 1981 that such borrowing had serious consequences; the lenders had to be paid back in hard currency, and the states of Eastern Europe could not sell enough of their products on the international non-Communist market to repay these loans. In fact, their ratio of debt-service—that is, the amount of hard currency needed to be paid for interest alone—in all countries except Czechoslovakia and Romania—was far above the danger zone of 25 percent. Table 9.4 depicts the amount of hard currency debt owed to the West at the end of 1981.

Nevertheless, by the early 1980s, West Germany, after the USSR, had become the second most important foreign trade partner for most of the Eastern European countries, representing close to 10 percent of the total foreign trade of the region; in fact, the total foreign trade with Western Europe was quietly creeping up toward the one-third mark. Moreover, during the past decade, trade with Western Europe became crucial to the industrial and technological development in which Eastern Europeans so clearly lagged behind. They had to export goods to the West and to the Third World in order to earn the scarce hard currencies they needed to service their own debts, but much of those exports often had to rest on a basis of *imports* from the West.

Table 9.4   Hard Currency Debt of the Eastern European Communist States, 1981

	Gross debt (billions US$)	Debt-service ratio (percentage)
Poland	24.5	92
Yugoslavia	20.0	25
East Germany	11.3	54
Hungary	8.3	37
Romania	9.4	22
Bulgaria	3.9	38
Czechoslovakia	4.5	22
Total	82.9	Average 41.4

For example, a semiconductor, or chip, had to be purchased from the West in order to produce an item that would be sold in Western Europe for hard currency. Then, both because of the "cooler" political climate and the unavailability of hard currency to import goods from the West, such imports could no longer be financed.

Foreign trade with the West and the Third World was made even more difficult by the inadequacies of the Eastern European economic systems—notably, the institutions of foreign trade, the financing, marketing, and sales of products, the after-sales service areas and the high costs of the products. The list of inadequacies could be endless, but let us at least glance at those enumerated above.

As far as the question of organizing foreign trade in Eastern Europe is concerned, the cumbersomeness of the institutional arrangements boggles the mind. Generally, foreign trade in the region is handled by monopolies of foreign trade corporations whose sole responsibility is sales abroad—excluding military sales. These corporations are cumbersome bodies hampered by bureaucratic regulations, huge swollen bureaucracies of self-important people whose *raison d'être* is the maintenance of the monopoly. If a firm has a good product to sell abroad, it must first request a foreign trade organization to find a buyer, arrange the sale, the shipment, the transportation, payment, and so on.

There are exceptions. For instance, in Hungary, as a result of the New Economic Mechanism, foreign trade enterprises are losing their monopoly as more and more enterprises are allowed to sell directly to the West. In fact, by 1983, 211 Hungarian firms were directly engaged in sales abroad. Moreover, a large number of joint ventures also developed between the Hungarian foreign trade agencies and the productive enterprises. The same may be said of Yugoslavia. In other countries, however, the foreign trade monopolies still control foreign sales.

Financing the foreign sales also remains a tremendous obstacle to development. In nearly all Eastern European countries, only the national banks control foreign transactions, and the lack of a convertible currency (for example, Eastern European moneys cannot be exported and no gold or no currency such as the U.S. dollar or the French franc can be bought using such monetary instruments) makes trading a dubious and often dangerous proposition. Hence, very frequently— partly as a result of the lack of hard currencies, and partly as a result of having no idea of the actual cost or value of a product—the Eastern European economies have had to choose "barter" deals. Thus for a certain Western product an Eastern European state might offer to pay with goods it has produced within its borders. Most Western firms, however, prefer to sell their products for convertible cash rather than the often difficult to use or unresalable Eastern European goods.

Furthermore, most Eastern European states and firms are not at all well versed in the various techniques needed to market products in the West. Missing are the sleek brochures, the free use of the goods for "tryout" periods, the skillful, multilingual sales representatives traveling all over Europe "hustling" the products. In a competitive atmosphere the "buy-it because we say it's good" attitude of the East European marketers simply has not been enough.

Similarly, in today's competitive economic setting Western executives and firms have learned to rely not just on the purchase of a certain product but on the guarantees of successful service *after* the sale. The Eastern European firms—not used to having an even acceptable after-sale service even at home—could not provide such service to the West. Consequently, few Western firms are interested in Eastern European products.

Moreover, very surprisingly to many observers, Eastern European products simply cost too much. The myth of lower unit costs as a result of lower labor costs turned out to be just that: a myth on both sides of the productive and sales spectrum. Even if the state is willing to charge artificially low prices for a product and absorb the difference between its own costs and the lesser prices it charged abroad for the sake of acquiring hard currency, selling these goods more cheaply than they cost to produce eventually causes serious deficits at home, and the economic community at home protests about continuous losses.

But most important, Eastern European goods are by and large not up to par in the quality demanded by Western markets. Their designs are awkward, their operation cumbersome, their service record shoddy, their packaging unappetizing, their delivery time long and unreliable. It is no wonder that Western European businessmen have not flocked to buy Eastern European goods.

The USSR, of course, remains to date the backbone of all Eastern European foreign trade. The USSR is not merely a supplier of goods and energy, raw materials and semifinished goods, it also is a ready market for the states of the region. These Eastern European goods most often are still of higher quality than similar items produced in the USSR. But most important, such sales to the USSR are made generally on the basis of barter, and much needed oil, gas, and energy could be had from there.

Ultimately, the question of economics thus remains one of the real problems of Eastern European politics. Many would like to see the further liberalization of planning, the relaxation of central control, a further privatization of the economy, a greater role for the free market, and an elevated level of trade with the West. But most Eastern European leaders are afraid that such relaxations are going to result in the loosening of political control and thus threaten the rule of the Communist political elite. This is something that the party leaders—with a few isolated exceptions—have always been unwilling to risk.

Social Development in Eastern Europe

All animals are equal, but some animals are more equal than others. . . .

George Orwell, *Animal Farm*

■ Imagine, if you will, a perfect brotherhood in which everyone is equal. In the morning one works as a dishwasher, at night, he is a brilliant lecturer on Hegel. All live in relative plenty, with large apartments, color televisions, and comfortable vacation homes. There is plenty to eat for all, and desirable consumer goods are available to everyone. Regardless of their background, children can go to any school, become cab drivers or surgeons, philosophers or soccer players. Everyone selflessly helps others, and all help society toward ever-higher goals.

Such a view of society would fall, for the Western reader, in the realm of utopian fiction. Nonetheless, it is an ideal that was very prevalent in the thinking of Eastern European Socialist and Communist social planners at the end of World War II, when they tried to think what the ideal "future" state was going to be like. In such a state,

Table 10.1   Percentage of Actively Employed in Industry and Agriculture in Eastern Europe in the 1930s

	Year	Industry	Agriculture
Bulgaria	1935	8.0	80.0
Czechoslovakia	1930	38.3	25.6
Hungary	1930	24.1	53.0
Poland	1930	19.4	60.6
Romania	1930	7.7	76.9
Yugoslavia	1936	9.9	76.3

they believed, there would be no class conflict; there would only be one class, the working class. Furthermore, the distribution of goods would be handled equally. And abundance would assure the highest possible standard of living.

However, Eastern European Communism, was created as a social system—and imposed on society by outside forces—in a region generally less advanced economically and socially than that of Western Europe. Eastern European society was largely agrarian, rather than industrial, with the possible exceptions of Czechoslovakia and East Germany. Disregarding white-collar workers for the time being, the developmental level of these states in 1945 can be clearly gauged from Table 10.1, which shows that in Eastern Europe before World War II the vast majority of the people worked in agriculture. Consequently the first task of the Communist regimes was to attempt to create an industrial working class on whose shoulders they expected that the power of the regime would rest. In order to establish this new class, the Communist regimes first had to destroy the former ruling classes and, the bourgeoisie. In this task, they were assisted by history, specifically by the dislocations resulting from World War II.

THE DESTRUCTION OF THE RULING CLASSES IN EASTERN EUROPE

World War II brought enormous changes to the societies of Eastern Europe, altering both their structure and content. The war losses were the heaviest in Poland and Yugoslavia, where the continued opposition to German rule resulted in bloody fighting; in Hungary, where the destruction of much of the army and the devastation of the cities contributed to the decimation of the population; and in East Germany, which had to bear the full brunt of both the fighting to destroy German Fascism and the subsequent Soviet retaliation. The war impacted differentially upon the people of the region: while at least 6 million Poles perished during the war, Bulgaria's population actually increased from 1939 to 1945.

The war and the resulting Soviet occupation altered the Eastern European countries in vastly different ways, but the prewar social structure was eradicated practically overnight everywhere in the region. The prewar ruling classes had perished in 1939–1947. In some of the countries occupied by Germany—notably Czechoslovakia, Poland, and Yugoslavia—most of the former ruling elites, whether from the landed ruling classes or from the modern capitalist strata, had either emigrated, been imprisoned or exterminated by the Fascists, or lost their lives fighting Hitler, Stalin, or various pro-Nazi or pro-Soviet factions in their own states. Although a larger segment of the ruling elites survived in Bulgaria, Romania, and Hungary, Germany's defeat and the Soviet Union's victory in World War II sealed their fate. Consequently the advancing Red Army did not need to use excessive terror to alter the social structure in the Eastern European states. For by August 1944, as the Soviet forces rapidly approached the Balkans, many members of the pro-Fascist Romanian and Bulgarian elites began to flee westward, throwing in their lot with the retreating German armies.

A similar process began to take place elsewhere in Eastern Europe, and the example of Hungary is illustrative. In Hungary the decimation of the ruling elite began both with the destruction of the power of the Jewish bourgeoisie and with the economic pauperization of the well-off aristocracy and middle classes that resulted from the war itself. As the Soviet armies began their occupation of Hungary, there was a mass exodus of those who feared retaliation for collaborating with the Fascists, of those who were frightened of the impending Communization of Hungary, of those who simply did not wish to live in the Soviet sphere, and of those who simply had had enough of Eastern European life. In 1944–1946 more than 550,000 people left Hungary for the West or, in the case of some of the emigrating 50,000–60,000 Jews, for Palestine. By 1947 the former financial elite and much of the aristocracy and the bourgeoisie had left Hungary. Most of them would never return to their native land.

But the destruction of the ruling classes did not end there. As the Red Army approached Hungary's borders one could also witness the disintegration and disappearance of Hungary's government bureaucracy. Indeed, those who left the country included the entire backbone of state administration. As Soviet troops began to reach Budapest the state bureaucracy vanished rapidly; only in Transdanubia did it remain a fairly viable institution administering to the daily needs of the population.

The Soviet occupation forces and the new Communist leadership of the state had to deal with the collapse of state administration. Everywhere the new authorities had to establish themselves, and the fact that a whole class had disappeared gave them leverage to redirect the country's policies. Initially, however, the fledgling Communist party had simply no trusted cadres to rely on; its membership at the end of the war probably was no more than 2,000–3,000 people, and many of the rank and file could hardly be considered dedicated Communists, since a mere few months ago they had been card-carrying members of the Fascist Arrow-Cross party. Nor was Communization generally accepted as benevolent by the Hungarians. Indeed, there was strong sentiment among the hitherto disenfranchised peasants to take the power of the administration into their own hands. And there was also a great deal of resentment among those desiring a "new order" when the Soviet Military Command in many places recalled lower-ranking bureaucrats of the former state administration to take the place of those higher-ups who had departed to the West.

The Communist party immediately began to supplant the some 200,000–300,00 persons who had disappeared from the state administration. Relying largely on some elements of organized labor, the "class-conscious working class," and its own members, the Communists began to establish their hold on every locality. Between 1945 and 1947, in spite of the quite democractic political system as a whole, the party skillfully captured power for its members in the state administration, especially the truly sensitive positions within it, and labeled their opponents as "reactionaries" or "Fascists" in the two years before they finally captured complete power.

As mentioned earlier, the destruction of the ruling classes occurred everywhere in the region, but nowhere—except perhaps in Poland—was it as total as it was in Hungary. Hence, in the initial period of capturing power, between 1945 and 1948, only these two states started out with a "clean state," only in these two states do we observe the virtual absence of any influence of those who directed, dominated, or dictated social development before World War II.

THE CREATION OF THE WORKING CLASS: 1945–1980

The basis of so-called socialist societies is the concept of the rule by the proletariat, a class-conscious working class. As we have noted, however, before World War II we could only speak of a working class that was numerically and electorally strong in what has become East Germany and in Czechoslovakia, specifically in Bohemia.

In the prewar and the immediate postwar years, however, everywhere else in the region the war already had undermined the traditional social structures so that even without any effort by the new, socialist authorities, one clearly would have witnessed the development of the urban, industrial working class. There were two reasons for this phenomenon. First, the destruction and pillage by both the German and Soviet armies had been enormous, so the opportunities for employment in reconstruction were overwhelming. Second, due to the very slowness of the land reforms, the uncertainty of the future of land ownership, and the lack of satisfactory amounts of capital investment for small-scale peasants, much of the peasantry began to detach themselves from the land. Thus within two or three years after the war every country in the region showed a significant rise in the size of its industrial proletariat. For instance, in Hungary, between 1946 and 1948 more than 150,000 peasants were recruited for the machine industry alone, a figure whose weight corresponds to the pattern established elsewhere in the region.

The growth in the number of industrial laborers was even more dramatic if we consider that during the first ten years of Communist rule many skilled workers were pressed into positions in the new state administration. As these regimes came to power, the party leaders had to look for "trusted" individuals to assume the positions of responsibility, but since only the Czechoslovak party had been significant and legal during the interwar era, the elites could not count on the Communists alone to fill these posts. Hence, as mentioned earlier, they had to look for people whom they could "relatively" trust from amidst the rank of the "old" proletariat. In Hungary, for example, more than 200,000 new officeholders were pulled from the ranks of the working class to occupy posts of power in the Communist party. This pattern also holds true for the other states of the region.

The New Course of the mid-1950s and the subsequent hesitation in industrialization and collectivization policies resulted in a relative and temporary stagnation in the numerical growth of the working class in the region, but a December 1957 Moscow decision on collectivization soon forced the post-1956 elites to revert to the old policies. The general collectivization of agriculture resulted in a massive flight from the villages; the ranks of industrial working class swelled more in 1958–1962 than during any other period in the history of Eastern Europe. After 1962 the depletion of the agricultural labor force and the growth of the industrial proletariat continued slowly until the end of the 1960s.

After 1970–1975 the number of industrial laborers had passed its peak in much of the region. True, the number of peasants employed in agriculture continued to decline, but the number of workers employed in industry also began to drop; the emerging service sector began to attract new entrants into the labor force. In fact, this sector grew at the expense of the industrial working class. While Bulgaria, Romania, and Yugoslavia maintained the previous pattern of growth, Hungary, Czechoslovakia, and Poland followed the new road. The peak

One of the major tasks of the Communist systems was to transform society by creating an urban industrial class from the bases of peasant societies. Urban apartment complexes have been constructed everywhere to house the new, industrial labor force. Such apartment complexes as the one in Poland shown above, dot the villages and cities of Eastern Europe today. (Nogues/Sygma)

industrial levels of approximately 45 percent of all active employers working in industry was reached in Poland and Hungary in about 1975; in Czechoslovakia the peak of 57.5 percent was reached by 1970. Since then these figures have continued to decline.

Although Eastern Europe's postwar regimes definitely succeeded in creating an industrial proletariat, it is less clear how "class conscious" this proletariat is. We must reassert that the new industrial proletariat came predominantly from the poorer members of the peasantry—landless agricultural workers or people who had so little land that they were forced to work on the estates of more successful farmers or large landowners. These workers had none of the supposed characteristics of the class-conscious proletariat. Most of them aimed at maximizing their income with the least amount of effort. They did not prize efficiency or productivity; assuring their economic survival and advancement at all costs was their chief concern. In short, in Eastern Europe there has been a "watering down" of the working class. The term "lumpenproletarianization," of course, carries too negative a connotation to be applied to this group without qualification. Unlike Marx, who identified the lumpenproletariat only in negative terms, I define this group as one that works only for its own self-interest and for its own betterment, and one that is not interested in political power. It is a class without an identification, without a consciousness of itself, whose only goal is the maximization of its own economic interests at all costs including its merciless self-exploitation.

Thus the new working class was actually a sharply divided conglomeration of separate and disparate groups. The small prewar industrial working class possessed values regarding work and power that the new industrial workers did not share. The old working class felt, especially at first, that the new regime was of them, for them and, by them. Many of their former co-workers were now in positions of power, and the benefits that accrued to the working class in general filled them with pride. Though originally there were plenty of Fascists among them, and though strong Fascist influences remained observable, these workers remained a tightly knit group with a shared self-consciousness. Especially because the rhetoric of the new regime maintained that it was holding power *for* this group, most of these workers initially were proud of the Communist regime and its activities. They supported its collectivization drives and its ruthless industrialization. They backed its internationalism and its atheism, and they backed its antipeasant and antibourgeois biases. And by backing the regime, they felt they were going to be not merely its mainstays, but also its beneficiaries as well.

The new workers—the former peasants—were vastly different. Driven from their villages into better-paying jobs in the cities, most could not be and did not want to be integrated into the fabric of urban industrial society. They commuted on weekends and kept their modest rural residences. Unskilled, untrained, and alienated, they wanted to get by with as little work as possible, steal as much as they could, and drink as much as was available. They were deeply religious, and they considered the original working class as pro-Communist and pro-Russians, two attitudes that ran ever so counter to their own rural populist nationalism. As the numbers of ex-peasants in the working class grew, the prewar workers became an increasingly small minority.

It would be tempting to suggest that the cleavage is merely one between the "old" and the "new" working classes. The reality, however, has been much more complex. Other factors have come into play, such as the worker's skill level, his place of residence, and his possession of a "convertible" skill. The question of skilled versus unskilled laborers suggests wide divergences affecting work attitudes. Far more skilled workers than unskilled workers are permanent urban residents. Their attitudes toward work, however, are only marginally different. Absenteeism, alcoholism, and loafing are about on the same levels. Political activity is only slightly higher among skilled than unskilled workers. Place of residence affects the cleavage more extensively. Commuters are frequently absent from industrial work when urgent tasks have to be done on the village household plot. They are more often tired, and their rate of alcoholism is somewhat higher. Political activity is also considerably lower among the commuters. Even though the differences are significant in some instances, in my view they are merely dependent variables contributing to increased differentiation caused by the possession of convertible skills (those skills for which there is a market in the growing second economies) or non-convertible skills (those skills that can be utilized only in the restricted workplace).

Except possibly in Yugoslavia and Poland there are very few class-conscious workers in Eastern Europe today, and in Poland the class-conscious workers who created and supported Solidarity are certainly not to the liking of the current regime. In the other states—especially in Bulgaria, Czechoslovakia, and Romania—one finds a sullen, dispirited, cowed working class, struggling under the constant threat of coercive measures, mouthing political slogans, and engaging in symbolic support activities as demanded of them by the regimes. The physical deprivation in these states, when coupled with the coercive force utilized, has created a visible, "symbolic consciousness" without any of the officially espoused, ideologically mandated, values being present. In East Germany and Hungary the regime has a compliant and relatively satisfied working class, one that is hardly likely to engage in such revolutionary activities as the workers in Poland, but one whose loyalty to the system is ensured only as long as it maintains its standard of living and relative freedom to privatize, and as long as the system simply leaves them alone.

THE DESTRUCTION OF THE PEASANT WAY OF LIFE

Striking as the development of the working class has been in Eastern Europe, it has been overshadowed by the rapid disintegration of the peasant way of life that so long characterized the entire region. By any measure the destruction of this way of life has been enormous and complete; the percentage of full-time *actively* employed people in agriculture dropped to an all-time low, with the average holding at a steady 28 percent (8.9 percent in Czechoslovakia).

It is important to note here that the variables of collectivization, freedom, and local self-management prove to be unimportant in the process of the changing employment structure; Poland and Yugoslavia with their similarly private agricultures fall into two separate and distinct categories, while Hungary and Czechoslovakia, with two diametrically opposed systems of economic management, are in the same general group as regards employment structure.

If one examines the increases in urban populations, as depicted in Tables 9.1–9.3, one may observe a strong correlation between the growth of urban populations and the increase in the size of the industrial working class. Urban development has been most dramatic in Czechoslovakia, Poland, and Hungary, as the increase in the number of industrial workers shows; in the other countries the increase in the number of industrial workers has outstripped the growth of urban centers.

Now let us turn the figures around. Although Czechoslovakia, Hungary, and Poland fall in the same category of states whose rural settlements incorporate the majority of the people, there exists a great and fundamental gap in both Bulgaria and Hungary when we view the number of people working in agriculture and living in rural locations. In both of these states a large percentage of people are employed in nonagricultural occupations but live in rural areas. This is true throughout the region, but the gap is nowhere as wide as it is in Hungary and Bulgaria. The underurbanization of the countryside, especially in Hungary, has contributed to the persistence of life styles and values that are opposed to the basic principles of communist societal integration.

Nonetheless, raw data can scarcely indicate the great transformation that actually had taken place in Eastern Europe among the peasantry. Even here, however, the greatest positive change can best be observed in Hungary. Since 1965, the Hungarian peasantry has been given an unprecedented opportunity for advancement. Taking advantage of the New Economic Mechanism, the privatization of economic activities, and the *enrichissez-vous* mentality of a regime that clearly bases its own legitimacy on the economic well-being of the population, the Hungarian peasantry was transformed practically in a decade. What exists today, perhaps is what may be called a "post-peasant" society that prizes market- rather than subsistence-oriented economic activities, eschews the previously seasonal character of farm work, uses as many labor-saving devices as possible, and maintains modern life styles (television, automobiles, travel, electricity, and so on) and a very close connection with the cities. While elsewhere in the region, except perhaps in East Germany, the agriculturalists have by and large remained the "backward" element, the Hungarian peasants made their peace with rule that finally allowed them to use their native talents and skills to feather their own nests. Taking advantage of the unalterable fact of collectivized land ownership, they concentrated on the use of space and time to reap increasing benefits at the same time when the open market with its unregulated food prices offered them the advantage of quick response to the whims of supply and demand. That they can do this is the greatest success of Hungary's Communist regime and stands in glaring contrast to the failures of nearly all of the other Eastern European states' agrarian policies.

THE COMMUNIST ELITES: CLOSED SOCIETIES AND IMMOBILITY

In Eastern Europe we can distinguish basically three elites, overlapping in some cases, sharply separate in others. These are the political, the intellectual, and the social elites. The first refers to that group of leaders who occupy the major positions on the Communist party's *nomenklatura*, the second refers to intellectuals who are viewed by the people, for the most part, as the "spiritual repositors" of the nation, and the third refers to the dominant forces of "social" life, the "trendies" or the "beautiful people" in Communist societies.

The Political Elite

Following the Communist takeovers, as mentioned earlier, almost entirely new political elites sprang up all over the region. This new group was far more homogeneous than the political elites of previous eras; which were characterized by noblemen and peasant leaders, bourgeois representatives, and military dictators. The new elites came largely from the working class, were members of the Communist party, and believed in their own isolation from the underprivileged masses.

If we examine in detail the background of the political elites—defined as members and candidate members of Politburo, Presidiums, or Executive Committees—the father's occupation (where known) is one of the best indicators of the "class origin" of the new elites. As may be seen from Table 10.2, the overall percentage of workers is highest in the Czechoslovak political elite and the lowest in Bulgaria, while the converse is true regarding the representation of the peasantry. Intellectual and middle-class origins characterize a relatively even proportion of the elite, hovering between 22 and 29 percent throughout the region. And of all the top leaders whose origins are known, only one Koca Popovic in Yugoslavia, hails from the prewar upper or ruling class; the absence of the former political elite from any major position of leadership is near total.

A similar, though slightly more variegated, picture emerges if we examine intergenerational mobility in the early 1970's, as Walter Connor has done in his ground-breaking book *Socialism, Politics, and Equality*. Intergenerational mobility into the elite, according to Connor, was certainly high during the early years of the system. Due to

Table 10.2   Origin by Father's Occupation among Full and Candidate Members of Politburos in Eastern Europe, 1945–1976

		Worker	Peasant	Intellectual, middle class, other	Total
Bulgaria	N	6	17	7	30
	%	20%	57%	23%	100%
Czechoslovakia	N	20	9	8	37
	%	54%	24%	22%	100%
Hungary	N	15	11	8	34
	%	44%	32%	24%	100%
Poland	N	16	12	11	39
	%	41%	31%	28%	100%
Romania	N	11	9	8	28
	%	39%	32%	29%	100%
Yugoslavia	N	7	10	7	24
	%	29%	42%	29%	100%
Total	N	75	68	49	193
	%	39%	36%	25%	100%

the destruction of the former political elite, entry into the new elites became relatively easy. Through instant "Red Diplomas," workers and peasants were thrust out of their menial jobs and into the halls of power. For the workers the avenue to success generally led through the party or state *apparats* or the industrial productive sectors, while for the peasants elite positions in the security forces, the army, and the agrarian sector opened up.

It is clear, however, that throughout the last decade, entrance into the political elite for the workers and peasants—all over the region, but especially in Poland and Hungary—has been closed. If we observe the new entrants to positions of responsibility in Hungary (Central Committee, Politburo, Council of Ministers), for instance, regardless of father's original occupation, all but five of the twenty-five newcomers between 1975 and 1981 came from intellectual or white-collar occupations. Admissions to the political elite has thus become restricted to those who hold white-collar jobs. One should not necessarily regard this phenomenon negatively; after all, in a developed country the political elite must be capable of dealing with the complex problems of modern society. Hence, entrance into such an elite should be reserved for those who have the necessary training and leadership and not for those just aspiring to such status. This, however, is scant comfort for those ideologically motivated individuals who would hail the 1945–1956 models of "open" entry into the elites as desirable.

If we examine the general composition of the Communist parties, the same pattern emerges. Thus, for example, in Hungary manual workers accounted for 48 percent of all party incumbents in 1966, 46.8 percent in 1970, 45.5 percent in 1975, and 43.3 percent in 1980, showing a decreasing trend, the proportion of white-collar workers in the party climbed from 37.3 percent in 1966 to 48.4 percent in 1980. And while it is true that the percentage of workers among all active employees (42.3 percent in 1978) was still lower than the ratio of workers among the party membership (43.3 percent in 1980), the party in its composition—like all of the other parties of the region— began to represent the population as a whole, rather than merely the workers, although the latter still remained theoretically regarded as the "most advanced stratum of the population."

The Intellectual Elite

The intellectual elite in socialist states today is composed of people in a wide variety of occupations; some of them belong to the traditional intelligentsia—writers, artists, philosophers, historians—others are members of a new, rather technocratic elite. They are truly a diverse lot: some whose roots are in the working class—and some who hail from the bourgeoisie—even sometimes from the aristocracy. Throughout the region, the intellectual elites are vastly different in the positions they have taken; regardless of background, some have supported the Communist regimes, others have opposed them, some stayed in internal exile—for example, not writing anything for the party-dominated presses—and others have vociferously supported the various positions taken by the party elites. It is significant, however, that one major change is beginning to be clearly noticeable throughout the region: mobility from the working and peasant classes into the intellectual elite has also largely been closed. In vain do the various regimes "favor" the working class, manual workers, and even some collective farm peasants and their children; the percentage of students from working-class or peasant backgrounds who complete the university or college educational qualifications necessary for entrance into the intelligentsia is decreasing every year.

Mobility into the intellectual elite has been especially dismal in recent years, during which—for instance, in Hungary—only 10.7 percent of workers' children and 2.7 percent of peasants' entered elite occupations; in Poland these figures were 1.3 and 2.9 percent respectively. Nor is the system entirely to be blamed for this phenomenon; as earlier studies on political socialization quite convincingly demonstrate, the educational advantage of growing up in a family with intellectual or white-collar background or aspirations, coupled with the poverty of rural schools, makes the closing of the circles of the intellectuals rather inevitable. As Connor says, "The 'cultural vitamins,' the positive attitudes toward learning, reading, etc., are in short supply in the average peasant household, even shorter supply probably . . . in an un/semi-skilled urban worker's family, yet it is these that hold the key, in large measure, to educational success." And educational success, of course, is the key to recruitment into the intellectual elite throughout the region.

The Social Elite

The phenomenon of social elites re-emerged quite vigorously in some states in Eastern Europe, especially in Hungary and in Poland; in the other states it is less important though present. Social elites—as a group—can best be defined as those who influence social patterns, play a leading role in society, and are most visible in maintaining societal values and trends. As mentioned earlier, prewar social elites of Hungary and Poland had largely disappeared after 1945; aristocrats, the *haute bourgeoisie*, glamor personalities, and the like vanished from the "public" social life of the new Communist states. Other members of the former social elite attempted to adjust; the number of those poets, writers or other members of the former elite who, in spite of their commitment to previous values, switched overnight to praising Stalin, was staggering in all of these societies. Even the cleansing storms of 1956 or the events of 1968 alone did not account, however, for the recent restructuring of that social elite; the key for the acceptance of these new social elites lies, in my view, in a national search for certain distinctly nonsocialist values that have been deeply ingrained in the national psyche.

The new social elite that dictates the norms of much of the region's population today is a curious mixture; a few former aristocrats, a few great artists, and a large number of government personalities make up the bulk of this group. But famous football players and ballerinas, owners of boutiques, engineers and party hacks, and dentists and doctors, rich from their private earnings, mingle at private parties with such statesmen as, for example, one of the reputedly "greatest playboys of the Eastern world," the former president of Poland, Jozef Cyrankiewicz. Hunting clubs and yacht clubs are reserved for this social elite; here they may mingle easily with at least some members of the mighty party elite. And even in small towns, local social elites mimic the manners of the former *haute-bourgeoisie* and the aristocracy. The existence of these phenomena are of course, as Stalin would have said, "not due to pure chance." As these regimes began to give up enforcing the ideals of a rigid, ideologically determined "egalitarian," Soviet-style society, the new social rules that emerged contained some elements of the old value system. The harking back to the rather

On Social Inequality

"We all have a problem! You, my friend, that your wages are too small, and me, that my wages are too large."

Polytika (Warsaw)

incongruous and often silly, but clearly national, values of the previous social elites, in short, was a rejection of a model that had been more imposed on the people than derived from their historical roots.

What then of the cherished goals of equality, the very *raison d'être* of the socialist and Communist systems? One of the primary claims of the Eastern European Communist regimes and their most frequent argument for legitimacy has been that of equality. Since Communist regimes could claim to give only restricted political liberties to the people and had promoted class-hatred rather than brotherhood, the Communist theorists had only equality left on which to claim kinship with their progressive forefathers in the French Revolution and the three great revolutionary principles of liberty, equality, and fraternity. Pointing to the tremendously complex and highly unequal social and economic structure of Eastern Europe between the world wars, the Communists promised to eliminate inequality when they took power after World War II.

And to some extent they did redistribute wealth. They took away the banks and financial institutions, factories and department stores from their owners and gave the wealth "to the people." They also subdivided the homes of the rich into apartments for the poor. And they broke up the large estates and gave some land to the peasants.

But the dream of equality soon faded when nothing was left to subdivide and when it became clear that "some were more equal than others." The top party and government elites lived in huge villas that had once belonged to the rich. They had servants, bodyguards, chauffeurs, and maids; the streets on which they lived were cut off from the public view by fences and armed guards. The members of this new elite were driven to work in limousines with curtains drawn; their maids and cooks shopped at special commissaries that provided a wide range of luxury items. In the meantime, the people starved under the policies of collectivization and industrialization—all, of course, undertaken in the name of equality. The resentment against the new—and visible—Communist inequality explains to a large extent the popular support that Hungarians and Poles gave to the revolts and revolutions of 1956, Czechs and many Slovaks to the Prague Spring and Poles to the nationwide movement that was associated with the ideals of Solidarity in 1980–1981.

However, not only top party members have been the "more equal" in these societies. Indeed, if one analyses Eastern European inequality, it can easily be noted that there are some states where not mere political position determine these inequalities, but economic success, luck, having a good position or profession, the ability to travel and earn money on the outside; these attributes all contribute in creating a class of "haves." As generational mobility closed, the children of the "haves"—"haves" in position, profession, and wealth—have come to occupy the positions that lead to advancement. In Poland, Hungary, Bulgaria, and Yugoslavia the opportunities of getting ahead or getting rich also add to the politically based inequities. The equality of economic opportunities, a hallmark of the developing socialist states in the 1960s and 1970s, came to a halt by the 1980s. This, of course, is not unnatural or abnormal. In fact, it is a natural consequence of allowing the development that modern, industrial society needs the most, namely, the development of an educated, highly trained elite capable of dealing with the complex problems of a technological age. That the children of the "haves" should be the first to move ahead is an expected result, even if it cannot be justified on the bases of equality, one of the cornerstones of the Communist ideology.

But along with the new rich, the new poor also began to make their appearance in contemporary Eastern Europe. Unable to keep up with the rising cost of living or to take advantage of the newly available economic opportunities in Hungary, Yugoslavia, and Poland, this beleaguered group consists of a wide variety of people. Among their alarmingly large ranks one finds pensioners and bureaucrats, office secretaries, peasants, single women raising children, alcoholics, and vagrants. Just as conspicuous as the new rich are with their luxury villas, swimming pools, BMWs and Mercedes-Benzes, the new poor—once again—have become a part of the landscape in these countries, and their resentment of the new rich is evident in every area of public life.

The class distinctions between rich and poor are not as visible in the other states of the region, where egalitarian wage scales and generally diminished opportunities for economic advancement characterize social existence. In Romania and Albania the scarcities affect just about everybody equally, except, of course, the party elite. In Bulgaria and in East Germany economic distinctions are largely ameliorated by more equitable distributions of surplus wealth, a more egalitarian social ethos, and relative availability of goods and services. But even in these countries, the long-term problems of social engineering, egalitarian ideological strictures, and the developmental necessities of greater rewards for greater contributions are likely to cause increased differentiation among the richer and poorer segments of society and thus lead to stress within society.

By now, each of these states has learned to deal with inequalities— whether politically or economically based—slightly differently. Those states with the greatest economic inequality in descending order— Hungary, Yugoslavia, Poland, and Bulgaria—attempt to justify these inequalities as necessary for the creation of economic efficiency concomitant with a modern society. Those states where the inequalities

---

Society: On What Direction Social Development Should Take

"Something tells me not to go in that direction."

Polytika (Warsaw)

Sour Grapes

Az ember az ilyesmibe bele is fulladhat...

"You can even drown in one of those things . . ."

Ludas Matyi (Budapest)

are politically based—Czechoslovakia, Romania, and Albania—emphasize that this is a "temporary" phenomenon based on the necessity of giving more material comfort to those who "serve the working class day in and day out." And East Germany—with only a limited extent of visible economic and political inequalities—chooses an eclectic combination of explanations for the reasons why the dream of a truly equitable socialism has not yet materialized.

It is clear that there are limits of tolerance on the part of the population; popular resentment against the "rich" was just as evident in Poland in 1980–81 as it is today in Hungary. And the accumulated resentment against privilege supports those who would wish to go back to an earlier age of equality, to a Stalinist type of system, to dictatorial methods of rule. At least—so the supporters of this ideology believe—there was at one time in the distant "heroic-age" an equality of have-nots, and a dream that all would be able to advance together. The system that has come to exist, however, by its very development shattered the ideal of equality just as it shattered many other aspects of the long dead strictures of a rigid ideology.

PART IV

POLITICAL VALUES IN COMMUNIST EASTERN EUROPE

Political Socialization

■ The study of political socialization—the transmission of political values from one generation to another—is crucial to our understanding of the political culture of Eastern Europe. Through this process desired values can be instilled, and culture and cultural traditions survive. In order to analyze the political culture that exists in the region, we must thus evaluate (1) the political socialization process, (2) the agents, (3) the media, and (4) the messages of political socialization. This chapter and Chapter 12 are devoted to accomplishing these goals.

CHARACTERISTICS OF POLITICAL SOCIALIZATION IN EASTERN EUROPE

At the outset, we must make certain distinctions between political socialization processes in Eastern Europe and in other parts of the world. First, in Eastern Europe we are dealing with the Communist regimes having much more control over and a great deal more intensive overt input into the political socialization of society than do the governments in the Western democracies. Second, in Eastern Europe we are actually dealing with two distinct types of political socialization: (1) the transmission of values from one generation to the next, the adult-to-child processes of political socialization; and (2) a "resocialization" attempt, operating on both the adult-to-child and on the adult-to-adult level as well.

The socialization of children follows a pattern much like that existing in other political systems, although there are some distinctions, which we will point out later. The "resocialization," or forcible adult-to-adult socialization, however, is unique to postrevolutionary systems where norms and traditional values have fallen into official disfavor with the new regimes and where the new dominant value systems are drastically different from those held by the previous political elites. (The term "postrevolutionary systems" also includes those political systems in which a drastically different type of rule came about through a relatively peaceful transformation. For example, in Czechoslovakia in 1948 there was a generally peaceful takeover by the Communists, but the regime that was created was so different from its predecessor that we can refer to it as postrevolutionary.) Postrevolutionary resocialization also takes place after the various uprisings that reassert—however briefly—traditional values held deeply by the population. Thus after the 1956 revolts in Hungary and Poland, the Prague Spring of 1968, and the Polish "renewal" of 1980–1981, each of the new successor regimes attempted to resocialize the population.

In Eastern Europe adult-to-adult resocialization has two basic forms: the *revolutionary* and the *continuous*. Revolutionary resocialization generally takes place during the immediate post-takeover phase. In this phase, the goal of the new regime is to coerce the population into abandoning previously held norms. The "sincerity" with which the new belief system is adopted is not questioned. What matters is the open *and* enthusiastic display of support and the showing of acceptance of the new values. For example, whether an East German *wanted* to march in a May Day parade and carry pictures of Walter Ulbricht appeared to be of little importance to the ruling elite; his or her *participation* in these events, however, was clearly enforced. Similarly, the *belief* in the infallibility of Stalin or any of his Eastern European surrogates was unimportant; the open and enthusiastic proclamation of that infallibility, however, was mandatory. This first phase of resocialization in Eastern Europe was generally known as the Stalinist phase, although it extended far beyond the dictator's death in 1953, as Table 11.1 indicates.

Table 11.1   Resocialization Phases in Eastern Europe

Albania	1945–1961
Bulgaria	1945–1953
Czechoslovakia	1948–1967, 1969–1970
East Germany	1945–1971
Hungary	1948–1956, 1958–1961
Poland	1948–1956, 1983–?
Romania	1948–1954, 1967–1971
Yugoslavia	1945–1953

The continuous phase of resocialization is more subtle and corresponds more closely to the traditional type of adult political socialization practiced elsewhere; however, here, too, important differences must be noted. This type of resocialization is specifically designed to instill continuous, though gradual, changes in the values and the norms of the population. Thus a gradual depersonalization of rule, the adoption of Khrushchevism versus Stalinism, the acceptance of "socialist legality" versus "revolutionary justice" have been the values imparted to the citizenry especially during the early years of the continuous phase.

The emphasis in the continuous phase is on the message transmission end and not on the receptor end; the disseminating of information is important and not its enthusiastic and visible acceptance. In fact, this form of political socialization is, in part, a deliberate attempt by the leadership to depoliticize public life, to rechannel people's energies from "revolutionary" tasks to those of efficient system maintenance functions and to decrease political participation from forced maximum levels of demand to minimal symbolic levels. The continuous phase is especially useful to leaders whose efforts at legitimizing their rule require a popularization of their leadership.

A few words must be said of the term "political generation." A *political generation* is a group of people whose political values are generally formed by an event or a series of political experiences that occur when these people are roughly 15–20 years old. Subsequent events continue to shape the orientations of a generation, even though the conclusions drawn from those events vary widely among the participants. These events have so clearly formed the values of these persons that a generational community can clearly be observed. Although political generations are mostly observable in nation-specific cases, because of the similarity in political experiences that occurred region-wide some cautious generalizations may be made here. Table 11.2 shows

Table 11.2   Formative Events in the Life of Political Generations

Year of birth	Events
1890–1900	World War I, postwar revolutions
1900–1929	Interwar systems, World War II, economic crisis
1920–1930	World War II, postwar transformations, Stalinism
1930–1940	World War II, postwar transformations, Stalinism, 1956 uprisings
1940–1950	1956 and 1968 uprisings
1950–1960	1968 uprisings and Solidarity involvement in Poland
1960–1970	Solidarity involvement in Poland

some of the political generations and the events that formed the political values of those generations.

The present ruling political elites are all products of the post–World War I era, and their values are the results of a widely different set of experiences than those of, say, the post–World War II generations. The farther apart these political experiences of the different generations are, the greater the difficulty of "comphrehension" of the different values appears to be. The "hero's children," to use specialist Paul Neuburg's phrase, generally do not understand the values of the "heros," and vice versa.

AGENTS OF POLITICAL SOCIALIZATION: INFORMAL VERSUS FORMAL STRUCTURES

Political socialization in all societies is accomplished through the use of various structures or agencies, which may be categorized as primary and secondary or informal and formal. *Primary* or *informal* agencies undertake the inculcation of values through face-to-face, one-on-one, generally unorganized activities that directly involve the socializer and the socialized. The primary agencies are the family, the church, and peer groups. *Secondary* or *formal* agencies undertake the political socialization through far more organized activities and with more clearly delineated purposes. Secondary socializing agencies are the Communist party, the youth groups, the schools, the trade unions, the military, and club or hobby groups. On the adult-to-child level of socialization the primary structures usually are allocated the largest amount of responsibility; the family is the single most significant structure in the value formation of children. In Communist states the political socialization of children is accomplished by both primary and secondary structures. Although in the early years the primary structures remain important, the importance of the secondary structures increases as the child grows older.

However, in Communist states there are sometimes significant conflicts between the values inculcated by primary and by secondary structures. In these countries the state assumes some of the responsibilities traditionally reserved for the family through the establishment, staffing, and educational processes of a widespread network of child-care centers, nurseries, and kindergartens. In Communist societies there exists both the legal as well as the economic-social necessities of work for both parents—for example, one must work not merely for economic reasons or social self-fulfillment, but also because in Communist states there exists the "equal liability to work" and those who do not have legal employment are regarded as violators of the law against parasitism. Thus the child is more clearly and purposively socialized outside the family structure than in states where the traditional family structures remain intact. Through the organized and controlled institutions the government transmits a set of uniform desired values, which may very well be in conflict with those of the family.

We must note that the family is not necessarily *trying* to impart values that conflict with those of the regime. In Eastern Europe, however, there are too many elements of contrast between the values of the regime and those of the people, particularly in the early Stalinist phase of dictatorship based on *terror*, not to warrant some conflict. Even in the families of party bureaucrats or families where the Communist ideology has been well internalized, the vast differences between the values of the regime and those of individual families are clearly manifest. Merely one example of this conflict is the participation of children of apparatchiks in delinquent activities in nearly all Eastern European states. And even in the continuous phase the changes in official values are not translated fast enough into personalized norms to eliminate conflict between primary and secondary structures.

The acceptance of the values imparted by the various structures depends largely on the legitimacy of the regime and on the cognition of the degree of conflict between the regime and the population. When there is a great deal of conflict between the officially held norms and those of the population, structural competition among the formal and informal agencies is clearly exhibited. For example, in countries such as Poland that have a strongly religious orientation, the formal structures attempt, particularly at the beginning of the revolutionary period, to weaken the informal structures because the values imparted by the informal structures are strongly antiregime. With increased legitimacy, however (specifically at later stages of the continuous phase), the formal structures no longer feel threatened and may allow and even encourage an increase in the importance of the informal structures by supporting family stability.

THE INFORMAL STRUCTURES

Family

Of all the primary structures, the family exerts the greatest single influence on the political socialization of the child at the very earliest age, for it is here that certain tendencies are acquired that shape the value system of later years. In Eastern Europe, however, the effect of the family on the political learning of the child is complicated by the multiplicity of differing national cultures and attitudes, differing levels of social and educational development, and divergent attitudes toward authority. Thus a child who was reared in Hungary or

Czechoslovakia in the bitter years following the Soviet invasions will
have different attitudes inculcated in them than those Hungarian children who were reared in the 1970s or those Czechoslovak children
who were reared before 1968. Similarly, a child's political learning
in an elite, educated family in Poland will be vastly different from
that of a Romanian peasant family. Political socialization within the
family in Eastern Europe, therefore, may be studied from the following
points of view: (1) national attitudes concerning authority; (2) political
climate; (3) political attitudes; and (4) socioeconomic status.

National attitudes toward authority

Although only minimal empirical data are available, certain political cultures develop rather distinct national characteristics. Even if
this generalization does not merit the emphasis it received in the 1950s,
thoughtful students of Eastern Europe are clearly aware of the existence of these characteristics. A far greater degree of authoritarianism
exists in Germany than in Poland, a far more tolerant and passive
political culture characterizes Czechoslovakia than Hungary, and even
within these states there exists a variety of subcultures possessing different attributes. Czechs differ from Slovaks in their attitude toward authority, and there are also clear distinctions between Croats and Serbs.
The families in each of these states, however, tend to inculcate values
that are closer to a "national type" than do other families in non-
Communist states. Thus, as mentioned earlier, in Poland the child
learns from the very early days such attitudes as reluctant respect
toward authority by references to policemen as *panie wladzo* ("Mr.
Authority"). Similarly, the child will most likely learn at an early age
discrimination against other national groups. Expressions such as *tot
nem ember* ("the Slovak is not a human being") or *budos cigany* ("stink-
ing Gypsy") still exist in Hungary.

Political climate

Another dimension of political learning that takes place in the
family relates to political climate. In generally repressive times—during
the worst of the Stalinist terror, for example—the norms the families
frequently imparted to the child were fear, suspicion, and unquestioning obedience to a tyrannical power. Thus, the child learned in the
family "not to talk to strangers," "not to mention to anyone about
Uncle Vaclav," or "to repeat obediently the lessons and directions of
the kindergarten teacher"; children were not encouraged to ask questions. Especially in the most dictatorial states of the region an all-pervasive fear still saddles children with a heritage that's difficult to overcome.

As times have changed, so has the role of the family as a political socializer. In some states the party now encourages the family to maintain stability and to inculcate its own positive values in the children; in a climate of relative political relaxation, the state hopes that the negative messages the children will learn from their own families will be minimal. Such relaxation, however, is still very unusual in Eastern Europe. Families, it seems, while they no longer take an automatically negative attitude toward the regimes, still try to inculcate a double standard in their children: the need to obey authority coupled with a basic notion that somehow the present regime is not quite legitimate.

Political attitudes

We may distinguish among four different types of families, each of which tends to inculcate a different set of values: the Communist family, the apolitical or conformist family, and the dissident family. Communist families may be further subdivided according to the degree of belief in party norms. There are still a very few old-line believers who are likely to transmit to their children values that are congruent with the official ideology. Other Communist parents who are employed in cadre or *nomenklatura* positions may impart an officious, "new class" attitude to youngsters, which is clearly divergent from the values of the previous class of Communists. The third type of Communist family is one in which belief in Communism is visibly adopted but is not accepted; a cynical "climb-the ladder-of success" attitude characterizes the values passed along.

Among the "fellow travelers," or sympathizers, such divergence does not really exist. These are people who, for a variety of reasons, sympathize with the aims of the party. Old-line socialists and some intellectuals, for example, all pay lip service to the basic goals of the party, but the values that they publicly espouse are only very rarely transmitted strongly to their children. These sympathizers are actually not Communists. For reasons important to them, they play along with the present regime, and even accord a certain amount of legitimacy to it, but they do not transmit these values to the younger generation.

The apolitical or ambivalent families are probably in the majority in all of the Communist states. By this term we do not mean that these families are uninterested in politics. Rather, we use this term in the absence of a better word that will illustrate their ambivalence toward authority. This ambivalence is characterized by a passive acceptance of the regime, coupled with a reluctance to be involved in the daily participation in political acts and by a revulsion for the required repetition of ideological strictures. These families want to get away from politics; they do not want to bring politics into their home lives. Little idealization of leadership or authority exists among this group, and apolitical values are implanted in the children.

The process of socialization is distinctive in families where the parents or grandparents are clearly opponents of the regime, whether they oppose the regime from the right or the left. Here, the type of information transmitted to the child depends largely on the nature of the opposition and on the intensity with which the parents' political views are expressed. For example, right-wing attitudes toward the re- form leadership in several of the Communist states (in Dubceks's Czechoslovakia, Kadar's Hungary, or even Jaruzelski's Poland) have been sharply critical and bitter, and these hard-liners transmit their intense feelings to their own offspring.

These differences in the transmission of values are all predicated on the fact that the individuals who, for various reasons, oppose the regime act as a sort of reference group. In short, they are able to compare themselves and their values to those of the regime and to provide an alternative model of behavior. In each case, the opponents are always people who have some ideals and hold some values which are incongruous with the values of the regime in power.

Socio-economic status

Social and economic differences also are reflected in the political socialization processes of children. For convenience's sake we may categorize the social strata in Eastern Europe as follows: (1) leadership elite, intellectuals, and other influential citizens; (2) skilled workers, office bureaucracy, peasant elite; and (3) unskilled workers and the peasantry.

Parents in the first category influence the rearing of children the most. They spend more time with their children than parents in the lower classes do, the mother is frequently at home, and comforts and luxuries tend to instill system-maintenance norms in the children. The superior verbal and scholastic capacity of these children undoubtedly enhances their comprehension of political values. Parent-child interac- tions are characterized by more restraint and less violence than in the other classes, and political learning takes place in a relatively orga- nized and conducive atmosphere. When the child hears that Comrade X, a very nice man, is coming to dinner, he is already learning about politics and authority. When the family goes to a lovely vacation home in the summer, the child begins to identify the benevolent relationship between his or her family and the system.

Middle-class families, although they are diverse in character, never- theless share some common traits that determine the political socializa- tion of the child to a very great extent. The economic necessity that forces the mother to work either relegates the child to the care of a grandmother or of a kindergarten. The tired parents do not spend enough time with the children after work, the economic pressures on them are far greater, and the identification of the child with the family and the "benevolence of the system" is far smaller. Indeed, antiregime political attitudes are most clearly observable among children coming from families of skilled workers. The children of these workers, if they receive any political education in the family at all, acquire the antiregime values first.

Finally, the lowest class on the socioeconomic scale in Eastern Europe exhibits the same type of political socialization processes they have always exhibited—a cultural and political nihilism, a rejection of all authority, but an acceptance of the present political power relations as immutable. In most instances this stratum, largely unaffected by the modernization that the country has undergone, articulates its beliefs to its children the least of the three groups. Members of this class characteristically have more children than do middle-class families, the time they spend with their children is minimal, and, consequently, the influence of other agents or socialization is greater than that of the immediate family. This cultural backwardness, of course, is an important reason why few members of this stratum are recruited for elite positions.

Other characteristics also may contribute to the family's role as a significant political socializer, especially when the children are preteens and most open to outside influences that tend to disorient their existing value structures. For example, religious affiliations affect the roles the family plays in transferring its political attitudes to the children. Yet the four characteristics examined above give a relatively complete working picture of the family as the primary structure that begins to form the political norms of the child and the young adult.

Peer Groups and Friendship Circles

In Eastern Europe, normally functioning primary groups—specifically peer groups—frequently come under the control of the state. Since the state attempts to achieve as much functional control of daily life as possible in order to facilitate the creation of a "truly socialist" citizenry, peer groups, aside from small friendship circles, are not allowed to operate independently. "Organization" is brought to these informal groups, and they are slowly transformed into secondary structures through which the state attempts to achieve its tasks of political socialization. For instance, a group of people who enjoy boating on a weekend are given "structure" and are organized around a trade-union-owned boathouse; unless they formally join the organization they are not allowed to take a boat out.

Only in the area of small friendship circles has the state been ineffective in its organizational attempts. It was the most successful when Stalinist terror atomized them. The fear that one's best friend or even members of one's family were working for the political police fractured these groups, and this fear still survives to some degree. Nevertheless, friendship circles are far more important to the people of Eastern Europe than they are to Westerners. These circles are formed at all levels of Eastern European society. Depending on the nature of the regime and on the amount of terror the regime uses, adult friendship circles may serve as a forum for discontent and as a source of news not available through other channels. Yet certain attitudes cannot be voiced even in the most intimate of these groups. One may joke and make puns about the regime, but one's *real* inner doubts cannot be seriously, openly, and continuously voiced.

Friendship circles among children, of course, are powerful socializers. It is with this fact in mind that the Communist regimes have devoted many resources to organized peer-group activities through the various organs of the Young Pioneers. Yet, outside of these activities friendship circles among young people still exist. Indeed, close friendships frequently form within local Pioneers' cells.

There is little evidence of the positive political socialization functions of these friendship circles when looked at from the point of view of the Communist regimes. Children still seem to be playing cops and robbers, cowboys and Indians, not partisans and Fascists. Neighborhood characteristics are often reflected in the activities of these groups, specifically on the young adult level. Delinquent gangs, so prevalent in districts of working-class apartment complexes defy all manifestations of authority and certainly act contrary to the taught precepts of socialist morality. In this respect, these adolescents clearly stand in opposition to the political socialization efforts of the regime.

The Church

The church in Eastern Europe is often considered to be a primary socializer, although its role is vastly different from those in North America. The following distinctions between the Eastern European and the American patterns may be observed:

1. In Eastern Europe the churches act as primary, face-to-face political socializers only in the villages and small communities. In cities and large communities, except possibly in Poland, East Germany, Croatia, Slovenia and among the "basic communities" among the Catholic faithful in Hungary, frequent face-to-face contact within the organization of the church is not usual except for popular participation in the services on holidays.
2. In Eastern Europe the churches are not allowed to overtly oppose the regime and its values; while the Catholic church in Poland is the most extreme example in the contest between the churches

and the regime, even here the conciliatory attitude of the church toward the regime since 1982 must be noted. And while, for instance, major differences exist between the Evangelical church of East Germany and the political elite of that state regarding the nuclear arms race, the Evangelical church does not act as an opponent of the *regime*.

3. In Eastern Europe, where the official ideology includes a still vigorous persecution of religious people and a strongly atheistic propaganda, the church's very fight for survival places its followers in some degree of opposition to the regime; the persecution of the religious believers in Czechoslovakia in the 1980s proves this point anew.

4. Except possibly in Poland, Croatia, and Slovenia, religious attendance patterns in Eastern Europe indicate a far older population of churchgoers than in Western Europe or the United States.

The conflict between church and state is inherent in the ideological perception of the regimes. The state's constant desire that the population accept Marx's thesis that religion is the "opium of the masses" is contrasted by the church's desire to survive and to prosper. The regime's fear of the existence of an outside source of loyalty among the populace leads it to try to sever or limit Catholic ties with the Vatican, while the church's desire for survival forces it to maintain close contact with the various centers of Christianity.

The thorniest religious problem for the Communist regimes in Eastern Europe is the Catholic church. In Hungary, Czechoslovakia, and Poland, despite official protestations to the contrary, the church remains a very powerful agent of political socialization, specifically among young adults. It is interesting to note that religious ceremonies—such as marriages and funerals—remain widely accepted. In spite of several decades of effort to refute it, religion remains strong, and, indeed, among the young there is a very curious religious revival. The "Jesus freaks" of Poland and Hungary, the recent high youth attendance at services in the cities, and the popularity of "beat" and "jazz" Masses are just a few manifestations of the strength of the church. Apparently the church has been relatively successful in inculcating values counter to those advocated by the regime in a portion of the region's youth.

In Poland the popularity and strength of the church are most noted on the local level where younger priests openly oppose both the Jaruzelski regime *and* the Catholic hierarchy. Outspoken priests, such as the murdered Father Jerzy Popieluszko, have continued to preach their sermons in defense of Solidarity, in helping wage the war for the right to have crosses exhibited in schools, or to keep the faith of the young alive. In spite of the attempts of Jozef Cardinal Glemp to silence these younger priests and thus maintain accommodation with the Jaruzelski regime, youths, especially from the working class and the peasantry, continue to flock to the sermons of these dissident priests. The same phenomenon, though to a lesser extent, may also be noted in the conflict between the Catholic hierarchy in Hungary and that country's "basic communities."

The church-state conflict is far stronger in Roman Catholicism than it is in other religions. The Orthodox church—perhaps except in Serbia—has found little unusual in its subordinate role and in its official support of the political purposes of the regime. Accustomed to such behavior by centuries of accommodation, the Orthodox church found the support that the regime demanded easy to rationalize, and its role as a contrary political socializer remains minimal.

The Protestant churches of the region, quite strong in East Germany, Bohemia, and Hungary, have been treated in a variety of ways. Since the beginning of the 1960s the Protestant churches, specifically in Czechoslovakia and Hungary, found themselves receiving some official support. The intentions of this support, of course, were to provide a kind of "counterbalance" to the large Catholic majority. The number of clergymen who found willing accommodation as "peace priests" was significantly higher among Protestants than among Catholics. Thus the role of the Protestant churches as political socializers can be said to be significantly different from the Catholic church. On their part, the Protestant churches' basic desire was to avoid political involvement. They preach messages of a nonpolitical nature and justify, when specifically asked to, the policies of the regime. Enjoying often significant financial support from the state, the Protestant churches are quite harmless from the point of view of the regime. While the church may be the only truly organized negative primary socializer its effectiveness in the population as a whole, when pitted against the enormous machinery and resources of the state, remains minimal.

THE FORMAL STRUCTURES

On the whole, the importance of formal structures of political socialization is far greater in Communist than in non-Communist states. And it is primarily the formal structures under Communist direction that attempt to undertake the political socialization of both adults and children into the norms of the regime. These formal agencies of political socialization are the party, the youth groups, the schools, the trade unions, and the military.

The Party

In Eastern Europe the most important agency of political socialization is the Communist party. It fulfills this role directly and indirectly.

Table 11.3   Degree of Indirect Party Control over Political Socialization in Eastern Europe

Country	High	Medium	Low
Albania	x		
Bulgaria	x		
Czechoslovakia*	x		
East Germany	x		
Hungary			x
Poland		x	
Romania	x		
Yugoslavia		x	

* Until the second half of 1971 the Czechoslovak party's control over political socialization fell in the medium range. Then, however, the leadership further tightened its control activities. The same pattern may be observed in Yugoslavia; in the early 1980s the hitherto minimal influence was increased to medium levels. In general, indirect control has increased throughout the region during the last few years.

Source: Author's estimate based on selected measures of overt control. Such indicators as the arrest of dissident writers, party censorship activities, party control over communications media, amount and types of nonideological cultural events, and the performance of non-Communist plays, operas, and musicals were used to derive this table.

Indirectly, the party is responsible for the policies and themes of socialization, for the norms and values that will be imparted to the population as a whole and to youngsters in the schools. It determines the means and the intensity with which these values will be imparted on the adult-to-adult and on the adult-to-child level. The amount of indirect control exerted varies from country to country. Table 11.3 is a schematic approximation of indirect party control over political socialization in the East European countries in the early 1980s.

The amount of indirect party control seems to be positively correlated with the existence of demand articulation by group interests in Eastern Europe states, although a simple causal relationship cannot be established.

Direct party control over the political socialization processes also exists and usually takes three forms: formal education within the party, formal education outside the party, and agitprop (agitation-propaganda) of varying intensities. Schooling exists for party members within the party's educational agencies. Organized in "seminar form" from the lowest cells upward to the national party bodies, this type of effort exists at all levels, culminating in the higher party schools or political academies within each state. Above the academy level only one educational agency exists—the Higher Political Academy in Moscow, where instruction is in Russian. It is estimated that about ten to twenty-five people from each state attend this academy each year. The length of instruction varies; most people attend for a period of six months to one year.

Formal education outside the party includes, at the lower levels, seminars organized by the local cells, but party membership is not a prerequisite for attendance. After completing these seminars, one may attend the evening divisions of the University of Marxism-Leninism, which—in collaboration with recognized colleges—grants regular academic degrees. The emphasis—far more than in the intraparty seminars—is placed on explaining various themes of political socialization.

Finally, agit-prop teams work directly with the population. These teams have two purposes: (1) they are a constant reminder to the population of the power of the party; and (2) at the same time, they serve as a public-opinion check for the party on the citizenry's professed attitudes and behavior. In 1982 Albania, Bulgaria, Czechoslovakia, East Germany and Romania still employed regular agit-prop teams.

Youth Groups

A specific means of political socialization supervised by the party is accomplished by the youth groups. Unlike their counterparts in non-Communist states these groups are geared directly toward political socialization on the adult-to-child level.

The amount of political socialization increases directly from the Young Pioneer level to the Communist Youth League levels. The political emphases are introduced slowly and in some cases are presented with extreme sophistication. The political socialization themes imparted by these youth groups appears to be most successful in the age bracket of 12–15 years, the period when children generally are most conformist and when they have the greatest need for acceptance by their peers. The effectiveness of the youth leagues varies from country to country and provides us with an approximate index of the enforcement activities of the party.

The media of political socialization on this level utilized for the inculcation of values are quite diverse. Although each youth group has one or more newspapers, the basic intercell medium is still the perennial bulletin board, called a "wall-newspaper," while the basic medium for the verbal transmission of desired values remains the group meeting or the group lecture. The official bulletin boards generally are in disrepair and largely ignored in Yugoslavia, Poland, and Hungary and carefully organized, maintained, and presented in Czechoslovakia and East Germany. In these states there was some relaxation in enforcement after the 1960s, but some renewed tightening became evident in the early 1980s.

Table 11.4   Effectiveness of Youth Leagues in Eastern Europe, 1980–1985

	High	Medium	Low
Albania	x		
Bulgaria		x	
Czechoslovakia			x
East Germany	x		
Hungary			x
Poland			x
Romania	x		
Yugoslavia			x

Schools

The 6–18 age group receives political socialization through the teaching of nearly every subject. In mathematics lessons, for example, there are abundant examples of worker X making Y amount of money by working inordinate hours for the good of socialism. And in foreign

School children in Yugoslavia attending class. (© Alain Keler/Sygma)

language classes glaring examples of workers' exploitation in the capitalist countries are provided even at the most elementary levels.

While Marxist thought permeates the curriculum, ideology is taught separately. Today almost all the states of Eastern Europe include in their curriculum one or more courses entitled "The Basis of Our Ideology" or "Marxism-Leninism." Usually taught at the senior high-school level, these courses are designed to be the culmination of the years of fragmentary ideological training. They are supposed to formalize the child's outlook by presenting the abstract constructs of the ideology. Thus the child's prior knowledge that a few Roman families were able to rule the Roman Empire and exploit the millions of slaves is conceptualized in this course to bear on his or her understanding of Marx's theory of exploitation. The success of these courses depends very much on the individual school systems and the teacher's ability to make the course interesting. However, we can safely say that in the focusing of the educational process, in using organized peer pressure, and in promoting collectivism versus individualism, the schools have all the tools available to create a compliant citizenry.

Trade Unions

The trade unions also serve as important agencies of political socialization both on the adult-to-child level and on the adult-to-adult levels. On the adult-to-child level, the trade unions bear the primary responsibility for dealing with young people who either drop out of school or seek to learn a trade after age 14. "Vocational political education" is handled jointly by the respective productive ministries—e.g. Mining, Heavy Industry, etc.—and by the Ministry of Education. In no case is the political education of a youngster supposed to be neglected. His or her attitudes and behavior are supposed to be reported by both his or her supervisor on the job and by the local party secretary. Political education is taken into consideration in questions concerning continuation of work or education and in granting pay raises. Again, not all East European states take vocational political education seriously; it is largely neglected in East Germany, Poland, and Hungary, where labor shortages make it necessary to bring as many trained or trainable people into the work force as possible. In these countries political education activities by the trade unions are generally confined to the adult-to-adult level through lectures organized in the factory after hours. These are usually rather somber, formal, mandated affairs whose audiences are mostly interested in getting home as soon as possible.

The Military

The military remains one of the most significant political socializers in Eastern Europe, although it has never regained the importance it had as a political socializer in the immediate postwar era. During those years, it took the peasant youths—those who due to unsuitable background or intelligence were unable to join the new ruling, administrative, or industrial elite—and trained and indoctrinated the most willing to serve as officers. For the poor and uneducated, the military represented the easiest path to socioeconomic advancement. Its political officers, content to teach slogans and simplify the issues to the lowest common denominator, were highly efficient political socializers.

With the development of more modern and sophisticated fighting techniques, the role of the army as a political socializing agent has undergone certain alterations. It has become one of the main interest groups contending for leadership roles, and within its ranks there has developed a significant potential for friction, which is more visible in some states than in others. This source of friction was caused by

Political Communication: The Party's Information Policy

Polytika (Warsaw)

the resumption of nationalistic attitudes (not entirely discouraged by the party leadership in many states) among the population. Particularly in Romania, Hungary, and Poland the armies reflect these nationalistic tendencies in their political training of recruits. Yet, even though we note the existence of such attitudes, the armies of Poland, Hungary, and, since 1968, Czechoslovakia—unlike those of Albania, Romania, and Yugoslavia—are of necessity led by such men as General Jaruzelski, who must be faithful to the directions given by Moscow. This situation has led to friction between the recruits and the top leadership in these countries and has hampered the work of the political officers, who have a very hard time reconciling nationalism with subordination to Moscow.

In countries that are faced with these problems the military retains a relatively important role as a political socializer. Training programs and weekly seminars are required throughout the units. The centrally selected texts are kept simple, and only rote memorization is demanded of the recruits. They are not expected to understand or to approve; they must merely memorize and retain the key slogans whether they understand them or not. A Polish political officer relayed to me the simplest technique of socialization through mandatory attendance: "Whenever we have to bring a guest political lecturer in, we just *order* the soldiers to stay for the duration of the lecture. How effective the method is we do not know, nor do we care; it's their attendance that matters."

POLITICAL COMMUNICATION: THE MEDIA

Communist political systems rely heavily on television, radio, newspapers, journals, books, films, theater and demonstrative art to spread their messages of political socialization to the populace. The party places controls on these media in order to prevent their use as negative agents of political socialization. As the monopolists of power, these regimes therefore exercise an overwhelming influence in the political communication process.

The range and intensity of controls vary from country to country, and there seems to be a direct correlation between the amount of control a government exercises over the entire polity and the intensity with which it uses the media for the purposes of political communication. The strictest controls are exercised on the communications media in Albania, East Germany, Romania, and Czechoslovakia, in that order, while Poland, Yugoslavia, and Hungary exert less control over these transmitters of political socialization. We cannot, however, argue that there is a clear and positive correlation between the content and control of the media and the political behavior of the citizenry. But the centralized control mechanism does mean that the system is able to make the desired information available to the polity, and the media in Eastern Europe exert an influence on the citizenry that is greater than is prevalent in the West.

Television

During the last fifteen or twenty years television has become the most important single medium of communication in the most advanced countries of Eastern Europe. The importance of this medium is supported by a considerable amount of evidence. Although an equivalent of the Nielsen ratings is not available, data from various sources indicate that watching television is the most popular leisure pastime in these states.

The programs that carry the various themes of political socialization to the public vary from country to country. The largest number of messages can be found in public affairs programs and news broadcasts. Whether dealing with the building of socialism by showing the construction of a new canning factory or with the theme of public morality by interviewing an expert on dating among college youth, the public-opinion makers always inject the desired messages, usually in an obvious or simple manner. Newsreels are also used to reveal the "victories of socialism against imperialism" by showing, for example, an American airplane shot down over Lebanon or by "factual coverage" of the "Israeli aggressors' latest setbacks." Spy films, most of them set during World War II, are used to instill "continued vigilance" in the citizenry.

Television has been especially successfully used in rural areas as the transmitter of values. Due probably to the lack of sophistication among much of the peasantry, television has conquered the traditional, shrewd mistrust of city folks and of the regime. In fact, the regimes' relatively recent stability, especially in Hungary and in Bulgaria, may be due largely to the passive support of the peasantry, who have been considerably influenced by the messages of political socialization relayed by television.

Nonetheless, we must not overstate the importance of television as a medium of political communication. The crux of the matter of political socialization remains not the message-sending capacity of the socializer, but the recipient's comprehension of the message and his or her willingness to accept it. The direct effect of all political communication media on the political socialization of the population is questionable at best. Most people in Eastern Europe prefer to watch television for entertainment, and few take the political messages for anything else but sheer—and to many people, stupid—propaganda. In this respect, television has not succeeded in overcoming the suspicion (particularly of the urban populace) and their lack of trust in the statements made by their leadership.

Radio

Although the importance of television cannot be denied, the regimes of Eastern Europe still rely heavily on radio to transmit its messages of political socialization. About 60–70 percent of the people in the region still listen to some sort of radio broadcast daily. The ownership of radios—as well as of television sets—is encouraged by the subsidization of the price of these items and by low subscription rates.

On the average, each Communist regime in Eastern Europe broadcasts approximately 280 hours of radio programs a week on two or more frequencies. All channels, of course, are operated by the state. Factories and villages also use the radio for public broadcasts, often through loudspeakers, although the spread of transistor radios has resulted in a decrease in the use of this method.

The primary function of radio programming is to provide the populace with news broadcasts. These broadcasts may range from strictly factual coverage to clearly biased statements. All such broadcasts freely editorialize. In fact, the frequent use of value-loaded terms is a characteristic of news broadcasts. It is also important to note that failure to report certain news events is just as significant as the editorialization.

Soap operas or radio dramas are popular among the less sophisticated and less educated strata of the population. These programs also include political messages, in somewhat concealed terms. Whether dealing with Communist morality or with the theme of socialist patriotism, the messages are exhortative statements and examples or, conversely, such negative examples that they are depicted as clearly repugnant.

One aspect of radio utilization is clearly counterproductive to the regime: radio also can be used to listen to the broadcasts of Radio Free Europe (RFE), the BBC, the Voice of America, Radio Paris, or Die Deutsche Welle, carried in the local language. The listeners range from the peasantry to the highest party members. The toleration of foreign broadcasts varies from country to country and from period to period. In East Germany and in Czechoslovakia Western broadcasts are still jammed, especially during periods of political crisis. In Hungary only the broadcasts of RFE are jammed regularly; since the crisis of December 1981 jamming of Western broadcasts has become commonplace in Poland.*

No clear pattern of preference for Western broadcasts has been established along national lines in Eastern Europe, although there seems to be a preference among social classes, with the intellectuals

---

* Readers should realize that jamming is a very costly proposition, for the electronic wave generation needed to block certain wavelengths requires the use of enormous amounts of energy.

preferring the BBC and even Radio Free Europe—and until very recently—to the Voice of America. The "balanced approach" of the Voice—that is, of giving every side of every story—in the late 1970s seems to have further diminished its small corner on the market, although some evidence indicates that since the beginning of the 1980s, listenership of the Voice is once again on the rise.

Newspapers and Magazines

Newspapers and magazines are widely used in Communist countries as transmission belts that carry information about current events and reiterate desired norms and values. Party control is extremely strong over all printed publications, and each periodical has a "responsible editor" who censors its content.

Party control over these publications is exercised through the weekly meeting of editors with the Press Department of the party Secretariat's Agitprop Section. At these meetings, directives on certain material are given, and examples of mistakes are provided. In this sense, censorship by the "responsible editor" is preventive, but *ex post facto* censorship by the party also exists; the first copy of each issue of a journal or each edition of a newspaper has to be taken to party headquarters, where the *instruktor* in charge of the publications reads all major articles. The most significant control, however, lies in the writers' and editors' self-censorship. Newspaper and journal writers quickly learn to write the acceptable jargon, and the "responsible editors," whose bonuses and often jobs or livelihoods depend on their work, exercise extreme caution.

The party's own newspaper usually has the highest circulation, and official viewpoints are expressed in the columns of these and of the so-called government newspapers. Rarely can significant divergence between the party papers and other newspapers be found. Only in periods of revolutionary activity or significant stress will conflicting viewpoints be published. During such periods, though, examples of differences between government views and those of some interest groups abound. The *Irodalmi Ujsag, Nowa Kultura, Literarni Listy,* journals of the various Writers Unions, generally were the first to express demands contrary to party policies in 1953–1956, 1966–1969, and in 1980–1981.

A prime example of this desired socialization can be found in the papers sponsored by the various Soviet–East European Friendship Societies, organizations for favorable propaganda about the USSR. *Orszag-Vilag* in Hungary, for example, is just such an organ. Of its thirty-six pages, six must always be devoted to positive accomplishments of the Soviet Union, emphasizing "the glorious prototype." The transmittal of these values may be accomplished through several means: news reports, *feuilletons* (interpretive editorials), or omission. For example, reports on American "aggression" in Nicaragua are used to instill the themes of anti-imperialism, a *feuilleton* is used to discuss the wholesomeness of socialist morality, and the absence of coverage of the invasion of Czechoslovakia helps to minimize dysfunctional activities. Although the "head in the sand" approach of ignoring events as if they did not happen is not used widely, it is still apparent in some Communist reportage.

Newspaper reading in Eastern Europe is inordinately high if we base our findings on the number of papers published daily. We have no broad-based region-wide survey data, however, to test empirically the depth of the internalization of these messages through the news media. Nonetheless, some data indicate that far more people actually read the paper than seems obvious to observers, specifically to those whose informants always say, "Well, I'm just reading the sports pages." In countries such as Albania, Czechoslovakia, East Germany and Romania, where rigid controls still operate, the fear of being tested by the local party leadership about current events may have as much to do with newspaper reading as the simple hunger for news.

Only in Yugoslavia, Poland, and Hungary can we find even a limited supply of non-Communist Western newspapers. In Yugoslavia it is relatively easy to read Western newspapers in library reading rooms, while in Polish and Hungarian hotels one can find Western non-Communist newspapers relatively easily. At a couple of hotels in Bucharest and Prague some Western papers are sold to foreigners only.

The Eastern European regimes realize that it is nearly impossible to measure the effect their political socialization efforts have on the formation of attitudes among the citizenry through newspapers and magazines. Nonetheless, these media are used extensively to try to saturate the populace with selected information and with norms that the leaders seek to inculcate.

Books

The Communist regimes were quick to grasp the importance of literature as an instrument of political socialization. After the publication of books became monopolized by the state after World War II, the leadership began to use them widely to transmit the newly desired norms to the populace. The works of Communist writers and those sympathetic to the Communist cause were printed regardless of their literary quality; works by Soviet Stalinists such as those of Nikolaeva, Bubennov, Penezhko, Shishkov, and similar "authors" of dubious talent were published along with those of better writers such as Simonov,

A. Tolstoi, and Ehrenburg. "Study circles" were forced to read these works, and reports had to be made about the main themes. Works that were not sufficiently "mature" politically were, of course, not published; book censorship by a "responsible editor," whose job is to weed out works that may be politically harmful, has been practiced throughout the region over the last four decades.

At various times during these four turbulent decades, Poland, Hungary, and for a short period, Czechoslovakia encouraged their writers to present works of artistic value and upgraded the quality of their Soviet publications. Moreover, private publishing of works not hostile to the goals of socialism has been allowed in Hungary since 1980 and in Poland periodically.

The relaxations in these states may be attributed to two factors: (1) the recognition that some degree of literary freedom must be granted in order to maintain the great cultural heritage of these states; and (2) the recognition of the extremely low readership of inferior works. Contrary to myths deliberately fostered by the Communist regimes in these states, the interest in literature and the active reading habits of the population is *not* higher than in Western Europe. Only among the intelligentsia is there a more noticeable following of a good book or of the message that it intends to impart.

In the area of textbook publication, censorship remains extremely strong. Textbooks are published only by the special publishing house established for this purpose. They are usually commissioned works written by teams of professional textbook writers under close party scrutiny. In this respect, the state intends to retain the prerogative to impose control. Although they seem to have largely given up the desire to resocialize the population actively through the publication of only "socialist" literary works, they rigidly cling to their desire to transmit desired values to the young, and the publication of textbooks seems to be the means they regard as most useful for accomplishing this task.

Films

The motion picture industry in Eastern Europe has also been used widely to transmit messages containing desired values. Aside from entertaining, the films are used to illustrate the positive socialist values and to contrast them with capitalist decadence. From the very beginning of Communist rule the nationalized motion picture industries have been used for these purposes, although their real value as instruments of political socialization seem to be heightened in the continuous phase of resocialization.

Realistic portrayals of contemporary problems, however, have been dealt with on film only in a few states, notably Czechoslovakia, Poland, and Hungary. In films such as *Man of Iron, Main Street, Walls,* or *The Sparrow Is Also a Bird,* problems that occur in a socialist society have been depicted, but the messages contained in these films often seem also to point to positive values which exist in socialist society *in spite of* the existence of these problems.

The control of the government naturally includes censorship of films made in other states, especially those made in the West. During the immediate post-takeover phase a great number of Soviet films were shown in the Eastern European states. Only in Bulgaria, however, was there any genuine appreciation for these films; to an audience used to the underdeveloped Bulgarian film industry, even Soviet films looked good. In other states, however, Soviet films drew only scorn. Although people frequently flocked to them because of political pressures, generally, no one took even the good Soviet films seriously. During the 1950s in several states and localities there was monthly compulsory film attendance at Soviet films. Once a month required discussions regarding recent Soviet films were frequently held in local party cell units. The discussion leaders continually tried to hammer at the values presented in the films, but the population showed little interest or enthusiasm. During this period few Western films were shown. Those that were—for example, Vittorio De Sica's *The Bicycle Thief*—tended to point to negative values in decadent Western society. They were still more popular than the Soviet films.

One of the reasons why film is a somewhat limited instrument of socialization is that Eastern Europeans generally do not visit movie houses that play Eastern European films; rather, where available, and if they can rouse themselves from their television sets, they go to see even the worst Western film. Eastern Europeans rank their preference for Western films first, Eastern European films second, and Soviet films last. Consequently, we may evaluate the medium of films as an instrument of political socialization that may be useful to the regime but is probably ineffective because it is largely regarded as entertainment by the populace.

Theater

Theater is a much more selective medium of political socialization than even the motion pictures, for it reaches a far smaller number of people. The governments of the Eastern European states included in their modernization program the forcible conversion of even the lowliest peasant to a "culture-loving theatergoer" and attempted to bring road companies to village playhouses. Especially during the revolutionary resocialization phase, the efforts of the government offered various "incentives" to bring people to plays: free tickets given to people in factories, army units, and offices; forcible attendance checked on by the party cadre leader, the personnel office, the political officer, or seminar leader; and the production of the "revolutionary theaters" in the factories. It is clear that only plays depicting the positive values of socialism and conforming to the standard of "socialist realism" and the negative aspects of the decayed imperialist society were shown.

In the continuous stage some of the states have allowed greater freedom to their theaters. Although village repertory theaters continue to operate in much the same way as before, the theaters in the capitals and large cities have largely been free to produce what they wish, including genuinely good Western plays.

A special mention must be made of the political satire so typical of East European humor. Such satire is used as an escape valve for the discontent of the intellectuals and the students; it is a vicarious way of "telling the regimes off." This form of entertainment is frequently presented in Hungary (*Mikroszkop* in Budapest) and until 1982 in Poland (*Twardowska* in Cracow), and even in East Berlin (*Die Distel*). Satirical political criticism on the stage is, of course, much milder or nonexistent in Albania, Bulgaria, Romania, Czechoslovakia since 1969, and Poland since 1982. The roles of these satires as political socializers remains minimal.

Demonstrative Art

The tradition of demonstrative art, or poster art, is quite old in Eastern Europe. The posters of the revolutions of 1917–1919 are well known, and throughout the interwar period this form of art, designed to exhort the masses to undertake certain tasks, was used frequently and with some success. (This type of art was also used in Germany and Soviet Russia throughout the same period.) Following the Communist takeovers, the new ruling parties also began to use demonstrative art to influence the population. This medium of political socialization assaulted the visual senses; the giant figures smashing the imperialists and strangling industrialists with their bare hands carried powerful messages.

Demonstrative art of this type has flourished in Eastern Europe. Innumerable posters with likenesses of Lenin, Stalin, and other Communist leaders were carried at mass demonstrations or hung from walls, with huge slogans justifying whatever the regime was doing at that time.

In the continuous phase the importance of poster art has lessened, and today demonstrative arts are practiced in varying degrees among the East European Communist states. Table 11.5 indicates the

Table 11.5   Ranking of East European Communist States in Employment of
               Demonstrative Arts

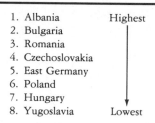

1. Albania   Highest
2. Bulgaria
3. Romania
4. Czechoslovakia
5. East Germany
6. Poland
7. Hungary
8. Yugoslavia   Lowest

approximate contemporary ranking of the states in the use of demonstrative art as a medium of political socialization. The presence of slogans, transparencies, gigantic statues, red flags, and likenesses of leaders, however, still are an integral part of the "socialist" Eastern European landscape.

In summary, we should note that through the agents of political socialization and the use of various media of political communication, the regimes of Eastern Europe clearly desire to send "Communist" messages to the people of the region. These messages are the bases of the political culture that the citizens of these states are supposed to possess, and these messages are the topics to which our next chapter is devoted.

Political Values in Eastern Europe

■ The values that the regimes of Eastern Europe attempt to inculcate in the citizenry at large are contained in the messages of political socialization. These values are either permanent or transitory. For example, during the Stalinist purges of the late 1940s and early 1950s, Communist leaders who had been publicized as brilliant and fearless fighters for socialism suddenly became "traitors to the party" and were "justly" purged and annihilated. In 1956, however, the Soviet Union began to de-Stalinize its rule, and the Eastern European regimes followed suit. Within days the former "traitors," who had been accused as heinous saboteurs and agents of Trotskyism, Titoism, and imperialism, became "innocent victims of the cult of personality" or "the heroes of the working class." Similarly, the Stalinist purgers were now held to be "traitors to the cause of Leninist norms of socialist legality."

Communist regimes thus alter the values they wish to inculcate according to their political needs, the climate of the time, and the country. From the mid-1950s until about the early 1960s, for instance, the Eastern European elites—replicating Khrushchev's policies in the USSR—fought hard to apply the principle of collective leadership and to demolish individual dictatorial rule, the so-called cult of personality. With the accession and consolidation of power in the hand of a strong leader, however, the cult of personality returned with a vengeance in some states. It is now practiced brutally in Albania and in Romania and to a somewhat lesser extent in Bulgaria, East Germany, and Czechoslovakia. It is de-emphasized and viewed as harmful in Hungary

On the Rehabilitation of Those Innocently Executed in the 1950s

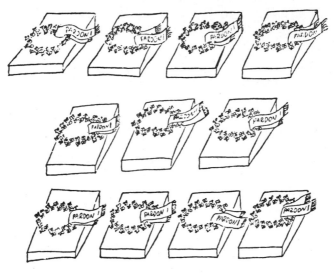

Literarni listy (Prague)

and Yugoslavia, and it is still very much muted even in Jaruzelski's Poland.

Political values are always expressed within the vocabulary of the official ideology. Communist leaders cannot accept or explain any phenomenon without using Marxist constructs. For example, a "hard-working attitude" must be expressed as "commitment to the construction of socialism," and selling arms to terrorists can be justified only by referring to the "internationalist duty of the worldwide international Communist movement to aid the oppressed people in their just fight against imperialism." Such verbiage not only covers up very pragmatic policies, but it also helps to transmit these policies as "values" by using terms that the people can recognize fairly easily within the ideological context.

Such political values do not all carry the same weight; some are crucial for the continuous operation of the system and are relatively permanent, while others are transient and reflect international events. For instance, Soviet opposition to the atomic bomb—the basis of the Stockholm Appeal of 1947, intended to urge the abolition of nuclear weapons—quickly crumbled and was officially declared as harmful once the Soviet Union developed and tested its own nuclear weapons in 1949.

THE MAJOR POLITICAL VALUES

In an effort to grapple with the confusing amount of evidence and the tremendous variation among the states of Eastern Europe, let us divide desirable political values in these countries into two groups. As illustrated in Table 12.1, the first of these two groups contains relatively permanent messages that can be heard just about anywhere in the region. The second group is made up of those values that are also currently "advertised" but either (a) not with the same intensity everywhere or (b) are probably temporary manifestations of certain policies in the mid-1980s.

Table 12.1   Value Messages in Eastern Europe

Permanent values	Transitory values
socialist construction	anti-imperialism
leading role of the party	antibourgeois values
socialist patriotism	anti-individualism
socialist internationalism	antireligious values
socialist morality	

The Permanent Values

The principle of *socialist construction* relates to the regime's efforts to inculcate an almost "puritan" work ethic in a population that has never been characterized by particularly high work morale. Recognizing that the state exploits them by paying extraordinarily low wages, the workers diminish either the quantity or the quality of their work. But the ultimate goal of the regime is to create an atmosphere in which every worker will *feel* that it is his or her duty to contribute "mightily" to the "construction" of socialism by working honestly, diligently, and overtime—if necessary, even without pay—for the common good. Since in every state the matter of economic progress is vital to the very survival of the system, this message is the most important one that the regime tries to inculcate.

The *leading role of the party* refers to the fact that the party, as the self-styled representative of the interests of society, should remain in control of society. Even in Hungary, where since 1983 the party has begun to act as the more or less benign supervisor of society, rather than as the "dictator" of every aspect of life, neither in principle nor in reality can the role of the party as the dominant force in society be challenged. The value to be inculcated in this instance is that one must not doubt, question, or contradict the validity of the party's claim to know the correct direction of policies, nor should one attempt to challenge the right of the party to direct the affairs of the state.

Socialist patriotism is also inculcated in every Eastern European state, but the extent and intensity to which it is fostered are vastly different from country to country. In general, socialist patriotism means the support of the socialist state as superior to the bankrupt and defeated regimes and social institutions that preceded it. In Albania or Romania it borders on chauvinism and extreme nationalism. In East Germany, which struggles to establish a separate national identity for itself, socialist patriotism is used as a device to bridge the gap between East Germany's being a part of the once-united German state and its present socialist status. In doing this, the East German regime must be very careful lest its socialist patriotism spill into anti-Russian nationalism, which must be discouraged at all costs.

Closely associated with socialist patriotism, but still distinct, is the value of *socialist internationalism.* This term denotes a love and affection for the USSR, the "fraternal" socialist states, and the international workers' movement that is struggling for liberation from imperialism and capitalism. Thus, on the one hand, this value aims to inculcate greater respect and affection for the Soviet Union because of its leading role within the Communist bloc and in the workers' movement: an ideological necessity, given the contempt that is still felt toward the USSR, generally, throughout the region. On the other hand, the "affection" toward the struggling masses of the international working class also needs to be inculcated as a means of explaining certain national policies. Thus, for instance, one can use this term to explain why much-needed crops, equipment, or other resources that are scarce at home, are sent to Ethiopia, Cuba, or Tanzania instead. By supporting the "liberation struggles of the downtrodden," one fulfills one's "internationalist" duty; knowing this is supposed to ease the pain of scarcity.

The value of *socialist morality* is the hardest to inculcate, largely because Communist societies are probably the most corrupt of any developed system. Their corruption stems first from the theoretical claim that a particular class and a particular morality—the proletariat and Communist morality—take precedence and superiority over "general" morality; this ideology relegates universal ethical and moral values to a secondary role. Thus the generalizable ethical commandments regarding one's parents, for example, had to give way to particularism: "Betray your father and your mother if you suspect them of opposing Stalinist policies" in order to preserve your life and position and to foster the development of socialism. The harm done by this moral-ethical particularism in all of these societies cannot be measured;

the only mitigating factor in the region appears to be the traditional cynicism of its people.

A second source of corruption stems from the uneven distribution of power and position throughout the system. Although perhaps there are Western societies where wealth is divided less equitably, power in Eastern Europe—and the wealth or position that power may bring— is clearly divided between the haves (the party and its branches) and the have-nots (everyone else). In spite of the personal modesty of some national leaders—Kadar or Jaruzelski, for instance—power elites are so clearly separated from the people that this division is painfully obvi- ous. It is no wonder that so much corruption has been developed at all levels in order to "buy-in" or "stay-in" within this elite.

Finally, a third but equally important source of corruption is the scarcity of everything. There is literally nothing to buy in many of these states, but nearly everything can be had, if only one knows how to go about getting it. There are no apartments for allocation, but if you know the "right person," he or she can get you one. There are no telephones available, but if you have enough cash to bribe someone, you can get one. There are no hospital beds available for an operation, but there is a back door where for good money one can sneak right into a semiprivate room.

The politically sanctioned corruption—denunciation of fellow citi- zens for the good of "the cause" or the luxurious life of the party elite—and the economically necessitated corruption have made the instilling of socialist morality both a dream and a mockery. It is a dream for some leaders, who perhaps still believe that all people should be moral beings under socialism and for many others within the power elite who feel that *other* people should act as moral-ethical beings. It is a mockery because all the exhortations for people to act as moral beings are not going to cure the scarcities that doom all of these societ- ies to be corrupt by definition. And while the authorities continue to attempt to instill the value of socialist morality, we must also remember that it is precisely that "corruption" that humanizes "socialism" in Eastern Europe and makes living at least tolerable.

The Transitory Values

The transitory values, as mentioned above, are even less generaliza- ble than the permanent ones. *Anti-imperialism* refers to the inculca- tion of hatred toward imperialism; Soviet imperialism, of course, is referred to as "liberation," in contrast to Western, or "capitalist," impe- rialism. Thus, for example, the invasion of Afghanistan and its occupa- tion by Soviet forces is an act of liberation and fraternal assistance by the USSR; the American invasion of Grenada, on the other hand, is an act of imperialism. Soviet assistance to PLO forces, to Syria, Nicaragua, or to anti-government rebels in El Salvador are "humanitarian acts intended to liberate mankind," while American support for Israel, El Salvador, or other countries is a "vile act of imperialism." Soviet support of subversion of legitimate governments or policies, whether in El Salvador or Denmark, is portrayed as an internationalist duty, while American support for the Nicaraguan *contras* or for Britain in the Falkland Islands crisis is regarded as "imperialism."

Second, if they are to inculcate Communist values, the socialist regimes must *eradicate bourgeois values* and notions from the thinking and habits of the people. It is tremendously difficult to define what the regimes really mean by "bourgeois" values, for these have included at one time or another everything from polished shoes and neckties all the way to rock music. They include a taste for modern art, for Western jeans, for Western composers, or for fine food and wine. In some states, such titles as "Mr." and "Mrs." have been abolished and replaced with the awkward "Comrade," a practice, incidentally, Communist elites have a hard time dealing with today. And in the past, the "bourgeois music" of Bartok or Enescu was rejected in favor of Soviet *chastuskas* (political messages put to "popular" music.) What the regimes call an "aping of the Western, bourgeois values" means, in reality, an appreciation of the modern values that exist in the more advanced, more "civilized," cultures of the West, in contrast to the rather nineteenth-century orientation of what they call "socialist culture," a culture that seems to have stopped developing in 1917.

Anti-individualism is at the core of the set of socialist values that every Communist regime must inculcate if it strives to create a "socialist" community. Keenly aware of the threat to the system potentially posed by "anomic," autonomous groups or by individuals who refuse to conform to desired socialist goals, every aspect of regime socialization clearly aims to maximize group values and minimize the "anarchic" individualism that dares to posit the importance of the individual over the group—and hence over the state.

Finally, Marxist states are officially committed to be *atheist* institutions and desire the abolition of the "opium of the masses," as Karl Marx called religion. Religion is regarded as a contradiction of the officially sanctioned "truth" of materialism, as an unwelcome relic of bourgeois value systems; it must be fought and opposed by the full weight of Communist ideology. Especially for party members, belonging to or practicing religion is regarded as a backward habit that one must always combat. Religion as a personal value means the acceptance of a moral system not based on ethical and moral relativism and of a source for these value systems other than the official ideology of the regime. Hence, religious manifestations must be eradicated with all the speed the system is capable of, without, however, risking an open and bloody confrontation with the church that may result in civil war.

Students used to studying Western processes of socialization may rightly ask how the state authorities can be sure that the desired messages are transmitted properly to the subjects that need to be socialized. The answer is that unlike in Western states—at least in the theoretical sense—every medium that transmits values, and hence every message, is controlled by the party. Theoretically, and to a lesser extent in reality, there exists in Eastern Europe a single scale of values, adherence to which is mandated by fear or conviction, conformism or ignorance of any alternative, depending, of course, on the individual system and subject. In highly dictatorial, isolated, and insular states, people profess regime-oriented values because they fear what might happen if they are not observed doing so. In newly established or in highly successful Communist systems, people might actually believe in the values the party sets out. And in some Communist states—as in some Western states—the ease of conforming to certain values allows people to comfortably digest messages that are repeated constantly. Similarly, for example, if people are unaware, say, that the Russian Dimitrii Kabalevskii was not as great a composer as Beethoven, such lack of information or knowledge, makes it easier for the party to instill its own desired set of values.

The methods of political socialization that are used to inculcate values also warrant consideration. Although each is reiterated through a variety of means in the various media, the "messages" come through in a relatively simple, straightforward manner. The themes of socialist construction may be depicted in a story, a film, a play, or a news article about Comrade X, who manages to increase his yearly output by 200 percent. The leading role of the party may be depicted in a cartoon that rails against an individual who has failed to heed the advice and direction of the party secretary. Socialist patriotism may be shown in a film depicting a courageous Communist patriot fighting against the Germans in World War II or a partisan hero fighting against infiltrators from hostile bourgeois circles. The value of socialist internationalism can be shown through a novel concerning the role of a Polish doctor working in Ethiopia helping to eradicate the pox or a young Czech advising the Angolans on the use of new tractors.

Anti-imperialism can also be shown in a variety of ways. For instance, a novel can tell the story of a Slovak police officer who foils an attempt to smuggle precious art objects out of Czechoslovakia to West Germany. Similarly, a play or film can show how the American imperialists destroy a small, peaceful Vietnamese village or how they torture the Chilean "patriots" with the assistance of CIA torture specialists.

Remnants of "bourgeois values" such as alcoholism, thievery, or punk rock can be condemned in countless cartoons and on posters plastered on kiosks and walls. Anti-individualist themes may appear in books praising the value of the collective and the loneliness of the individual; they show up in films or in theaters all through the region. And, of course, antireligious themes are available in ample supply in cartoons or films that show, for example, a rich priest who hoards "his" gold or takes "his" land away from the peasants; the scores of films, novels and plays written on basically anticlerical themes are ample testimony of the regimes' desire to eliminate religion with all possible speed.

The Hierarchy of Values

Needless to say, the values to be socialized are different in every case, vary from state to state and from time to time. Nonetheless, we can draw a basic hierarchy of desired values for each state, even if our conclusions regarding these values to be possessed by the citizenry are drawn largely from indirect sources such as the themes observed in novels, films, journals, rather than on truly "scientific" data drawn from a content analysis of every published communication. It is significant to remember that these hierarchies of value were noted in 1982–1984 and changes in the importance of values can be observed historically, practically overnight. Table 12.2 depicts this hierarchy.

The values to be socialized, as mentioned above, are not projected with the same intensity in every state. Depending on the individual country, some values are repeated *ad nauseam* and are regarded as of key importance, while others are less significant, in many cases negligible. Thus, for example, the value of socialist construction is uniformly high: it is either the first or second most important value to be socialized in all cases but Romania and Albania, where it holds third place. On the other hand, antireligious values are of little importance regionally; only in Czechoslovakia and to some extent in Romania does it now appear as a major value.

Generally, then, the highest-intensity values are socialist construction and the leading role of the party; the least important, low-intensity, values are antireligious, antibourgeois and anti-individualist. Moreover, it can be observed that the more "liberal" a regime appears to be, the smaller the number of high-intensity issues; in hierarchical order of intensity from liberal to conservative regimes one can observe the list as ranging from Bulgaria and Hungary (2 high-intensity issues), Yugoslavia and East Germany (3), to Poland (5), Czechoslovakia (6), and to Romania and Albania (7). While these rankings are relatively loose and based on indirect evidence, they do point to a trend in the importance the various regimes attach to the creation of a special kind of political culture on which we will now focus.

Table 12.2 Hierarchical Value-Ordering of Political Messages*

Albania		Bulgaria	
leading role of party	H	socialist construction	H
socialist patriotism	H	leading role of party	H
socialist construction	H	anti-individualism	L
anti-imperialism	H	socialist internationalism	L
antibourgeois values	H	socialist patriotism	L
socialist morality	H	socialist morality	L
anti-individualism	H	anti-imperialism	L
antireligious values	L	antibourgeois values	L
socialist internationalism	L	antireligious values	L
Czechoslovakia†		**East Germany**	
leading role of party	H	leading role of party	H
socialist construction	H	socialist construction	H
antireligious values	H	anti-imperialism	L
socialist morality	H	socialist internationalism	L
anti-imperialism	H	socialist morality	H
antibourgeois values	H	anti-individualism	L
socialist internationalism	L	antibourgeois values	L
anti-individualism	L	socialist patriotism	L
socialist patriotism	L	antireligious values	L
Hungary		**Poland**	
socialist construction	H	socialist construction	H
socialist morality	H	leading role of party	H
leading role of party	L	socialist patriotism	H
socialist patriotism	L	socialist morality	H
anti-imperialism	L	anti-individualism	H
antibourgeois values	L	anti-imperialism	L
antireligious values	L	socialist internationalism	L
anti-individualism	L	antibourgeois values	L
socialist internationalism	L	antireligious values	L
Romania		**Yugoslavia**	
socialist patriotism	H	socialist construction	H
leading role of party	H	socialist patriotism	H
socialist construction	H	socialist morality	H
socialist morality	H	socialist internationalism	L
anti-individualism	H	anti-imperialism	L
antibourgeois values	H	leading role of party	L
antireligious values	H	antireligious values	L
socialist internationalism	L	anti-individualism	L
anti-imperialism	L	antibourgeois values	L

* H–L = High–Low

† There is a distinct variance in Slovakia, where the Slovak leadership does emphasize Slovak patriotism and particularism.

THE POLITICAL CULTURE OF COMMUNIST STATES

In the rest of this chapter we will attempt to analyze the existing political culture of the Communist states—that is, the successes and failures of these regimes in inculcating desired values and norms in the population. Here, as well as in earlier chapters, our evidence is largely based on careful observation, some content analysis, and, at the very least, on the *Fingerspitzengefuehl* ("fingertip sense") that is the most valuable tool of specialists on Eastern Europe.

Political culture refers to the totality of political knowledge and attitudes that the citizenry possesses and to the manner in which that knowledge is expressed in political practice. While political behavior and style of practice are not direct results of possessing certain political values, political culture is composed of a combination of knowledge, attitude, behavior, and/or manner of practice. Political culture is thus made up of two distinct components or orientations. *Cognitive orientations* measure the amount of the citizenry's political knowledge, while *affective orientations* measure how the citizenry feels about politics in a given state.

It is difficult to define the political culture of any state with great accuracy. Historical precedent, the imprecise and much-maligned but real concept of national character, perceived advances or reverses by the citizenry, and myriad other aspects of a nation's life all add to a political culture. Generalizations concerning the political culture of the region are also difficult to make because the historical traditions of the people of the region had been so vastly different from one another that each group has its own value systems and typical behavioral patterns. The "pliancy" of the Czechs or the "hot-headedness" of the Poles can be explained as much by their national character as by the historical experiences they had; reasons for the Romanians not rebelling against Ceausescu's terror or East Germans' respect for authority are historically conditioned responses and influence the political culture of a state far more strongly than recent socialization practices.

There were, of course, also similarities in the political culture of the region long before the Communist takeover. Attitudes toward the state and society, quasi-feudal client-patron relationships, values of subjugation and minimal emphasis on the right of individual action, obedience of superior powers both temporal and spiritual—all have been common concepts and components of the traditional East European political culture. While each nation added its own "character" to develop its specific political culture, the Communist systems from the very beginning have had to build on these commonalities to create uniform values throughout the region. Imposing rigid and dogmatic Soviet-based ideological strictures, the Communist parties attempted to eradicate separate and distinct national values and replace them with a uniform ideology and political culture.

Four decades of political experience as members of the socialist commonwealth, however, have not yet created a truly uniform political culture in the region. Indeed, what strikes the thoughtful student of the region is the diversity of political cultures in their outward manifestations and in their internal political behavior. And yet, the Communist regimes have accomplished one of their major goals: by virtue of the fact that there exists no other vocabulary within which one can ask the questions relevant to political life, Marxist ideology is the *only* way in which politics can be discussed and analyzed. It is no wonder then that when, in Czechoslovakia, in 1968 the questions of political democracy were raised not within the Marxist context but in terms of popular participation in genuinely democratic politics, the Soviet Union decided to intervene militarily. Similarly, the challenge of Solidarity in insisting on the workers' traditional rights—strikes, independent trade unions and independent interest articulation, and so on— ran directly counter to the "ideological purity" of the system. Solidarity, by questioning the party's right to rule, in the ideological sense, exceeded the bounds of permissible activity, as far as the USSR was concerned.

Political culture in Eastern Europe can best be studied if we analyze it as a composite value made up of the different "orientations" of the citizenry toward certain political entities. These entities are:

1. The state and ethnic nationality
2. The political system
3. The incumbent leaders
4. Political processes
5. The international socialist system
6. The West and potential political alternatives

As mentioned earlier, the political values of the citizenry are the composite of cognitive and effective orientations. It should be made clear, however, that the amount of knowledge concerning any of the political entities does not necessarily determine the way people *feel* about that entity; one need not know too much about a leader such as Ceausescu or Kadar in order to "love" or "hate" him.

The State and Ethnic Nationality

Of all cognitive orientations, the citizens' knowledge of their own states and their nation is the strongest throughout the region. Generally, there seems to be a fairly clear understanding of the real size and weight of these states, the extent and limits of their physical-geographic power, and their importance as international actors. An understanding of the overwhelming strength of the Soviet state as compared to those of the small Eastern European states certainly acts as a "stabilizing" factor in their confrontations with the USSR. There are, of course, also several specific problems with the concept of the state and the nation.

In East Germany, the problem of the state is that the East German state dates back only to the end of World War II. Notwithstanding recent efforts by the party leaders to integrate some distinctly non-Communist historical personalities such as Bismarck or Luther into *East* German history, even today that state has little or no legitimacy as far as the East German people are concerned; they still regard themselves as Germans, not as *East* Germans. In Albania, the smallest state in the region, its elites and population are convinced that the Albanian state plays a truly major role in international politics. The Romanian national leadership harbors similar views, although, in reality, Ceausescu, at least, has always been able to recognize the limitations of Romania vis-à-vis the USSR. The people of Poland, though not the leaders, also have a curiously exaggerated view of the power that their state possesses; many Poles truly seem to think that "eventually" Poland may emerge victorious from a potential confrontation, even against both the USSR and Germany.

A gag from Poland during the early 1980s, when outright intervention both by the USSR and East Germany was a distinct possibility: "If both of these nations attack us simultaneously, at first we would fight the Germans and then the Russians: business before pleasure."

Ethnic nationality poses a twofold problem; not only is it anathema to Communist internationalism, but it also creates territorial-geographical-ethnic claims both *among* the members of the Communist commonwealth and *within* the various multiethnic states. In general, of course, every citizen of these states understands and recognizes that he or she is a member of a historic nation. Unlike earlier times, especially during the postwar mobilization phase, there is a widespread contemporary recognition that, for example, the Hungarian or Polish nation is an entity more significant than just a *unit* of the Communist "fraternity." The Soviet and the various Eastern European elites had to come to the realization by the mid-1950s that besmirching national pride and the belittling of the importance of national advances through the exaggerated greatness of the Soviet people had created tremendous resentment among the Eastern Europeans. In this respect, since the early 1960s every Communist leader in the region tried to garner some aspect of legitimacy as a "national" leader first and as a Communist internationalist second.

In East Germany, however, as mentioned earlier, this policy ran into problems, for the concept of an *East German "nation"* inspired tremendous resentment on the part of the population, who allied themselves with the greater German nation, whose heritage includes Goethe and Heine just as much as Luther, Bismarck, or even Hitler. To date, the orientations of the citizenry toward the object of the historical German nation remains far more positive than the Soviet—and the East German—elite would like them to be. Elsewhere, too, the same problem exists in slightly different form. The pride of being a Romanian, or a Pole, first and foremost, inevitably implies negative implications about the roles played by the USSR in the life of the international socialist system, or the role of the USSR as the first among not quite equals. And socialist patriotism runs a poor second to the old-fashioned nationalism that still exists in Eastern Europe.

That nationalism also plays an important part in relationships between states—witness for example, the glee with which the East Germans and Poles intervened in Czechoslovakia in 1968, the pressures for military intervention in Poland in 1981 expressed by the East Germans and Czechoslovaks, or the problems between Hungary, on the one hand, and Czechoslovakia and Romania, on the other, regarding the presence of significant Magyar minorities in the latter two states. These cases are merely expressions of the pervasive power of nationalism in the region. It is clear, for example, that if the Czechoslovak and Romanian states desire to build Czechoslovak and Romanian *nations*, they must demand of all their *citizens* to demonstrate continuous and total loyalty to these states and the values of the states as defined by the Czechoslovak or Romanian elites. A "Czechoslovakization" or "Romanization" policy assures that cultural-political loyalty, glorifying the "Czechoslovak" and "Romanian" past, present and future. But policies undertaken to assure such goals clash with historical values of a significant percentage of non-Czechoslovak or non-Romanian minorities who wish to retain their own conception of "nationalism" as parts not of the Hungarian state, but the Hungarian nation, the Magyar people. The conflicts between the Hungarian state, on the one hand, that needs to protect that "Hungarianness" of these minorities, versus the *raison d'être* of the Czechoslovak and Romanian states that desire inevitable political-national assimilation, on the other, has been clearly observable during the last decade or two.

Nor is the situation fundamentally different in Yugoslavia. Although nearly all Yugoslavs agree about the value of the Yugoslav state, there are very few citizens who would accept the validity of belonging to a "Yugoslav" people, a "Yugoslav" nation. The sense of national resentment among the Yugoslav citizens of Albanian origin, or resentment among various other nationalities of the five republics toward each other for perceived and real grievances—Serbs versus Croats, Slovenians versus, say, Montenegrins—has delayed greatly an integration process in becoming truly "Yugoslavs." While until the riots of 1980–1982 in Kosovo such resentments have been kept relatively well in check, they are likely to grow as economic downturns make life in Yugoslavia more difficult.

The Political System

Although most of the citizens of these states recognize that they live in a "socialist political system," their concrete cognition of the operation of the political system is at best limited. Most of the citizenry can mouth the vocabulary and state, for example, that "socialism means the workers' power in action," or the "socialist system guarantees the fulfillment of democratic rights." When the matter, however, is phrased in more concrete terms—for example, when the citizenry is asked to identify "the highest organs of state power" or asked such questions, as who elects the members of the Council of Ministers—few can answer correctly. Survey after survey has shown that not one in four could provide correct replies to such basic questions as relate to the daily operation of the political system at the national level. Most of the people view the Communist party—as versus the proper governmental institutions—as responsible for every action, although constitutional structures are taught throughout the high schools. This lack of knowledge of actual responsibility frequently leads people to ask for the redress of their grievances not from the proper authorities, but from the party, as attested by the inordinate number of letters sent to the Secretariats of the various Central Committees, to the First Secretaries of the party, or to editors of the newspapers.

At the same time, the operations of local politics are well known to the population; just about everyone knows which local office one should seek assistance from. But on these levels, usually, it is not merely to an "office" that one turns to for help, but to a particular individual with whom one can establish contact or to whom someone has said a "good word." While such elements of the process may be viewed as corruption by some—and indeed, as noted earlier, one can argue that the system of mutualities, gifts, bribes, patronages, and favors are nothing but institutionalized corruption—the existing system assures at least a bit of the "humanization" or "personalization" of an otherwise rigid institutional structure based on values that the citizenry as a whole does not possess.

Their cognitive orientations toward the processes, however, leads the vast majority of the society to view politics predominantly in an alienated manner. They realize that they have to participate in symbolic politics—in elections that are predetermined, in seminars in which they are given a line they must memorize, and in demonstrations in which the placards they carry are printed according to the current wishes of the party and into which they have no meaningful input. Thus, as the hero of *Makra,* a remarkable novel by Hungarian Akos Kertesz, has put it in the 1970s, all they want to be is:

> like everyone, a grey, happy spot in the crowd. One who is unnoticed, who can sleep soundly, who vegetates peacefully, gets increasingly bald and grows a round beer-belly, whom the janitors respect and the food-clerks greet *first.* [A person] who buys his cigarettes and razor blades in the same *tabak,* who takes his child for a walk every Sunday afternoon . . . and who drinks his beer in the corner pub and engages in passionate debates over whether the draught or bottled beer is better.

As long as there are no real alternatives for political action the individual citizen of Eastern Europe views his own role in politics as meaningless and unimportant. He evaluates the system as being directed from sources over which he has little control and hopes to have nothing to do with it at all.

We must reiterate that the Communist regimes today really do not desire the citizens of these states to be actively involved, educated participants with any real input or electoral power. As mentioned earlier, from the perspective of the Communist elites, such participation is far more dangerous than no participation at all: their preference is for symbolic participation only. Whenever the people have attempted to engage in real participation—as in Hungary in 1956, in Poland in 1956, 1970, 1976, 1980–1981, or in Czechoslovakia in 1968—that participation nearly always resulted in the downfall of the type of Communist regime that is based on the supremacy of a dictatorial Communist party over the people. Such politicization is unacceptable to the leadership, who far prefer the anomic, apolitical individual to "dangerous" activists.

The Incumbent Leaders

Most citizens of Eastern Europe know very little about the people who hold power within the system, especially at the national level (except for the person who holds the position of the first secretary of the party). Their lack of knowledge of the significant powerful elites is shown not merely by their inability to name correctly such incumbents as the prime minister, or deputy prime ministers of the state, but also in identifying the first secretary as also being the holder of the most powerful state office. Thus, for example, in Albania, Hungary, Poland and Yugoslavia the citizens when asked who the president of the country is, they most frequently identified the first secretary as the holder of that office; in the states where both the first secretary's and the president's positions are held by the same men, the people, generally, attribute the position of prime minister to the first secretary as well.

That confusion concerning office occupants on the national level is repeated on the local levels as well. In Czechoslovakia in 1980, for example, only one out of twenty-five voters could correctly identify their elected representative for Parliament and only one out of forty knew the name of their elected local council representative. Once again, it seems, that people view these state or local functions as unimportant.

There are, of course, other reasons for the fact that only the first secretary is really well-known. Clearly, in states where the "cult of personality" continues to rage (Albania, Romania, and to a lesser extent Bulgaria, East Germany, and Czechoslovakia), where the pictures and statues of the "almighty" and "omniscient" leader appear everywhere, it cannot be expected that anyone else could ever come to the political forefront. Thus Ceausescu and his wife Elena, Honecker, Husak, and Alia and Zhivkov, to various extents, all attempt to minimize the visible role anyone else can play in political life. Consequently, they contribute inordinately to the "de-personalization" of political life at lower levels. Even in states where there is no "cult of personality"—for instance, Poland, Yugoslavia, and Hungary—such de-personalization still results in the fact that people are able to identify only a very few influential leaders and the political roles they play.

The question of how people feel about the incumbents, is even more difficult to ascertain accurately. As far as the first secretary's position is concerned, knowledge concerning the person of the power-holder does not translate into "affection" or "love." In the early days of mobilization, when in all of these states the "cult of personality" compelled Stalin's "best students" to imitate the Soviet dictator, it was common to see paeans to his imitators in newspapers, in plays, in films, and so on. All of the first secretaries were depicted as beloved by the populations that sent them endless streams of gifts, adored them wherever they went and proved their "affection" in countless ways. But in reality, perhaps with the possible exception of Tito, there was not one of these first secretaries who was beloved by the population: feared maybe, but beloved never. The compulsive demands for displays of devotion, however, are not matched by public sentiment; the people of these states, who have a hard time making a decent living, dislike and resent the blatantly opulent life styles of dictators such as Ceausescu. In Poland, such resentment of the party elite con-

tributed in no small measure to the near-fall of the party in 1980–
1981. Derisive remarks about these petty dictators have circulated
freely; Matyas Rakosi, for example, was referred to as "the man with
skin hair," referring to his bald head, while the Romanian Communist
Ana Pauker was referred to as "that sexy bitch" because of her uncom-
monly sexless character.

In states where there is no visible "cult of personality" today, the
affective orientations toward the leaders are vastly different from those
of the other states in the region. In Poland, although there is widespread resentment against him for his imposition of martial law, Marshal Jaruzelski remains respected, though hardly "loved." To his credit,
Jaruzelski does not demand such forced displays of affection; basically
a modest man, he appears convinced that what he does is for the
good of the Polish nation, and the majority of the Polish people seem
to accept Jaruzelski's self-justification passively.

In Hungary, Janos Kadar is also a modest, self-effacing leader who
neither expects nor accepts open displays of affection. Kadar—originally a quisling who betrayed the revolution of 1956 but now an accepted, tolerated, and even respected leader—is unique in the bloc;
he alone in Eastern Europe has managed throughout the last quarter
of a century to garner some genuine affection from a population that
was, until the early 1980s, generally content with its level of freedom
and existence. Translated into political science jargon; he has managed
to attain a personal legitimacy for his role as the most successful statesman in recent Hungarian history.

The case of Yugoslavia is also instructive. Here the revised Yugoslav
constitutional process, since the death of Tito has brought about—as
mentioned earlier—a constant circulation of leaders, allowing no one
to hold a position long enough for a cult of personality to develop.
During his last years, Tito, whose enormous cult of personality survived
his death, actively prepared for the future of Yugoslavia after his death,
and he tried to create institutional impediments for anyone else desiring such an honor for himself in the future. Therefore, both the positions of the general secretary of the party and the president of the
republic are rotated frequently, and no one person can occupy these
two offices simultaneously. Thus, a strong leader, legally, cannot emerge
within the existing constitutional framework.

While there is at least some ambivalence toward the first secretary
in some of these states, the attitude of the population toward lower-
level office-holders is far less equivocal. The apparatchiks at any level
are viewed with contempt by those outside the power elite. The people
know that most apparatchiks serve the leadership willingly and are
rewarded for doing so. The people realize that the members of the
elite *apparats* in all of the countries except Yugoslavia and Hungary
have special stores to cater to them and that these "perks" are far

more important than the salaries received by the bureaucrats. While these officials are materially envied by the populace at large, there is no evidence that they are respected at all.

Political Processes

The knowledge of political processes—how decisions are made, how interests are expressed, and how one can influence policy-making—is rather minimal among the citizenry of Eastern Europe. Since the citizens of these states basically recognize that they have very little to contribute to these processes, that their role in influencing the decision makers is quite negligible and carefully orchestrated by the party, they do not waste their time dealing with processes in which their role tends to be basically passive. In more abstract terms, they realize that the party dominates all three processes of the political system—output (decisions), input (suggestions and influence in decisionmaking), and feedback (what the population thinks of the decisions made); the party even controls and manipulates what the population is *supposed to feel* about the decisions. For example, when in the 1950s, forced "loans" amounting to more than 10 percent of one's wages, were demanded of the people by the party, the people "voluntarily" and "happily" contributed these amounts; stories were printed showing how happily people volunteered their 10 percent for the "Peace Loans." In reality, there was probably not a single person who was "happy" about giving up 10 percent of his or her already miserable wages; the party nonetheless controlled their "feedback" role through force and coercion.

It is interesting, however, that during times of liberalization and greater political freedom, Eastern Europeans immediately begin to be interested in, exhibit knowledge of, and even actively participate in political processes. In Hungary in 1956, in Poland in 1956, 1970, 1980–1981, in Czechoslovakia in 1968, and in Yugoslavia since 1949–1950, the first effect of liberalization was a tremendous voluntary involvement of the people in processes such as in elections, political meetings, the creation of workers' councils, the establishment of independent trade unions or in self-management practices. Our only conclusion regarding the existing political processes in these states, thus, can be that as long as the party monopolizes them, the people will refuse to be involved, but the minute there is a true and meaningful choice offered, the interest and willingness of the people to participate immediately returns. It is for this reason that Hungary's example of trying to "liberalize" or "democratize" Communist party rule—a desire to allow more symbolic public participation, however well intentioned—has failed to gain the trust of the population, who are uncon-

In Eastern Europe the government controls television broadcasting and generally all other means of national communication. The success of the Solidarity movement and its leader Lech Walesa depended on Solidarity's ability to establish its own networks of communication, which pre-empted the government. Here, in Solidarity's heyday in 1981, Walesa flashes the victory signal to his supporters in Gdansk, Poland. (AP/Wide World Photos)

vinced the processes proposed will be meaningful. Without a genuine conviction that these processes are *truly* free and that they hold the real promise of a freer future for the population, the people of the region will not interest themselves or participate in the political processes in any but the most formally mandated manner.

The International Socialist System

Every citizen of the region knows that the states in which he or she lives is a part of the international socialist system, a member of the "fraternal community of states." They realize that both the social system and its "guardians," the Soviet or Warsaw Pact forces, are givens that cannot be altered. They also realize that their states are tied to the USSR and to each other by political and economic ties and that the "Brezhnev Doctrine" justifies Soviet intervention by the Red Army and its military allies in any state where, according to the USSR, the social system is deemed to be threatened.

As noted previously and as we shall discuss in more detail in Chapter 13, three states of Eastern Europe—Yugoslavia, Albania, and Romania—set foreign policy models that are different from the Soviet-instilled model. But even in loyal states the feeling of the citizens toward the alliance system, while difficult to ascertain exactly, is still generally clear: they do not like it, but they also realize that there is not much they can do about it. Rightly or wrongly, they feel that belonging to the CMEA is costing them in a number of ways, that the Soviets and their "fraternal brethren" exploit their homeland's resources, talents, or products, that they are not paid satisfactorily for their international services rendered or for produce to the USSR willingly delivered. They feel that the West would offer more benefits for them and that the presence of the Soviets and their domination is against their national interests. However, except perhaps for some Poles, many of whom have a romantic attachment to an idealized, heroic past, few would be willing to risk their lives in open, armed confrontation with the Red Army. Most people realize that in 1968, the Communist party of Czechoslovakia attempted in its famous 2,000-word manifesto to democratize public life; all they got for their 2,000 words were 2,000 Soviet tanks, as the saying goes. And the Hungarian example in 1956 was similar. Many people think that in 1981 only a Polish military coup prevented Soviet armed intervention.

On one topic, however, there exists both a fairly common—if somewhat exaggerated—knowledge and also exaggerated resentment among the population. This is the participation of the Eastern European states in assistance to backward and underdeveloped, but "progressive" socialist states and to various "liberation movements," such as the PLO, that the Communist leaderships regard as a part of the international socialist system. There is uniform public resentment of the assistance programs for these movements and states, for the Eastern European citizenry envisages—frequently incorrectly—that such programs include large amounts of scarce goods with which the people of Eastern Europe could be provided and which would make their own lives easier.

The West

The cognitive or affective orientations of the citizenry toward the West are based on elusive, frequently fictitious, information and opinions. By "the West," the people of the region generally think of the developed states of the Western world, countries with politically democratic and capitalist or highly productive socialist systems, ranging from the United States at one end of the spectrum to Sweden at the other. In short, when the people of the region discuss or think of the West, they think of the highly developed countries with a non-Communist sociopolitical system.

Unlike during the early years of the mobilization period, when Stalin and his local satraps attempted to forcibly separate the Eastern European Communist states from the West by the "Iron Curtain," by the constant jamming of Western broadcasts, by the limitation on travel to the West, by the prohibition of Western films, plays, cultural events, or trade, today the people of Eastern Europe—to varying extents—know a great deal about the West. Travel from Yugoslavia, Hungary, and Poland—in descending order of freedom—to the West is quite free; it is still much more restricted from Romania, Bulgaria, East Germany, Czechoslovakia, and Albania. Western cultural products are quite easily available in Yugoslavia, Hungary, and Poland; they are considerably more prohibited in the other five states. In 1984, radio broadcasts from the West on a regular basis were jammed only in Albania, while periodically selectively jammed in Poland and Czechoslovakia.

Although there is a relative abundance of contact with and information on the West, the people of the region possess an all-too-rosy view of the reality and the potential of the West as an "alternative" model. Perhaps, because of the constant reiteration of propaganda predictions by the regime concerning the "immediate" fall of the West, when contrasted with the reality of Western advances, people cannot believe in the scenario of the doomed capitalism propagated by the regime. A popular riddle asks, "Why are the capitalist states at the brink of disaster?" The answer: "So that they may look *down* at the socialist states."

The all-too-rosy evaluation of the West, of course, comes from the realistic evaluation of the socialist failures evident everywhere and the belief that the socialist systems today can offer no major advances for the population as a whole. While at the beginning of the mobilization phase, there was a significant percentage of people who believed that the socialist model of intensive development, with its centralized planning and distribution, could provide the best alternative for fast progress, there are very few today who accept that "traditional" socialist model as an attractive developmental pattern. The benefits of the socialist system—full employment and social security—having been accomplished are no longer especially attractive to many of the people. Although there are those—especially from the less advanced strata of the population—who still prize these benefits, more and more people realize that many of the Western systems have offered greater opportunities and nearly as many social benefits to their citizens than the so-called "socialist states." Forty years after the war, one can get scarce food items only through rationing in Romania, Czechoslovakia, and Poland, so the advances of socialism appear to be not so great after all.

It may well be asked what the people of the region feel and know about a realistic political alternative. Here, too, an all-too-rosy evaluation prevails. They, of course, realize that Eastern Europe was "ceded" to the USSR by the West in the closing days of World War II. Nonetheless, they hope for the "Finlandization" of Eastern Europe—allowing more domestic freedom while guaranteeing faithful following of the USSR in foreign policy—and wish to terminate the sense of cultural and economic separation from Western Europe. Politically, however, they realize that the continent of Europe is divided into hostile blocs and that—with the exception of Albania and Yugoslavia—they are a part of the Soviet bloc and that they can never become "unsocialist." It is for this reason that even the elites of these states frequently try for slightly greater room to maneuver, suggesting such ideas as the "abolition of military blocs," the creation of "atom-free zone in Europe," advancing plans for the "withdrawal of all foreign forces" from Europe, or supporting such ideas as the abortive Rapacki Plan of the late 1950s for the denuclearization of Europe.

It is frequently asked by baffled specialists how outmoded ideological tenets can be reconciled with existing realities. How can, for example, anyone believe—and openly profess to believe—in the superiority of the socialist system when one cannot buy meat or sugar, when one lives in a miserable hovel or must wait—at an average!—until one is thirty-five before one's own first apartment can be had. The answer to the bafflement lies in what psychologists call the adoption of attitudes characterized by "cognitive dissonance." The resolution of the difference between projected ideological expectations and totally opposite reality takes place in these states by the adoption of a very healthy dose of cynicism. The people realize that they have to *profess* their belief in the advantage of socialism over any other system, or in the correctness of the party's course, but they do not *have to believe* in it. The people resort to jokes to express cynicism, or simply do not even discuss the ideological expectations any more; there are indeed very few people today in the region who believe in the advantages of what the Communist ideological jargon calls "developed socialism." As the pun has it in Eastern Europe, the difference between existing socialism and developed socialism is that the existing socialism is not developed and developed socialism does not exist.

One may ask whether the existence of this cynical political culture restrains the elites in any way. To be sure, it may be argued that the elites are constrained, at least in the ideological sense, from projecting ideological values that are clearly proven wrong by realities. Thus, for example, it would be foolish of these elites to maintain *today* that socialist systems are not subject to recessions or depressions—as these regimes were fond of maintaining in the early to mid-1970s. The crises in Eastern Europe clearly proved the ideologists wrong, and forced, first, the slow revision and, later, the open abolition of these tenets.

It would be wrong, however, to assume that the mass political culture places constraints on the *decision-making* of the elites to an appreciable extent. For decisions in all of these states are still, in reality, made by a very narrow Communist elite in their own interests. These elites are thus not very likely to pay close attention to private expressions of oppositional political values, and public expression of such values remains largely prohibited. There are, once again, exceptions to this general rule. The existence of economic crises in Poland, Yugoslavia, and Hungary for instance, had to be admitted. Solutions to the crises, however, excluded the opinion of the "public" in Poland, and only to a very limited extent were the public brought into the decision-making process in Hungary or Yugoslavia. In the other states of the region, mass political culture exercises even less influence on elite decisions, and the input by the people of the region is not very likely to increase greatly in the foreseeable future.

THE NEW SOCIETY?

The purpose of political socialization in Eastern Europe has been to create a "new Communist individual" living in a "new Communist society." Although the governments obviously place the greatest importance on the political socialization processes, it is not known what actual and permanent effect these processes have on the value-formation processes of the citizenry. Given the limitations placed on research techniques that Westerners can employ when studying this question, we have little factual evidence of the successes of the regimes. Their glorious failures are always known when revolutions occur, when prominent Communists defect to the West, and when the voices of dissent are heard. Its successes—such as they are—remain unnoticed.

There can be no doubt that the system has had some successes in certain areas. Some of the values in some of the states have been accepted and internalized by the population. Obviously, socialist patriotism, where emphasized, has converged with the traditional nationalist norms and other preexisting values and therefore was rather readily accepted. The desire to inculcate anti-Stalinism as a value must have also fallen onto fertile ground, the people having suffered from the oppressive features of totalitarian rule and terror. Anti-imperialist attitudes also must have been successfully inculcated into some of the

East European citizenry; both American *and* Soviet "imperialism" are equally scorned by the vast masses of the population.

In other areas, however, the leadership has suffered tremendous failures. What defeated the efforts at transmitting the desired values to the citizenry, however, was not the fact that these values themselves are considered undesirable. Rather, it seems probable that the leadership's efforts were defeated by the need of the human mind to achieve some continued cognitive consistency. And this harmony cannot be achieved by the citizenry—specifically by the well-informed segments of the citizenry—in the Communist states.

How can a citizen of these states believe, for example, in the "glowing successes of building socialism" when comparing his or her lot to that of the citizens of the Western European states? Explanations concerning the original backwardness of the region, the ravages of war, the lack of unemployment, and the rosy picture of a beautiful future, all pale when the trudging lot of the Communist worker going to work on a crowded streetcar is contrasted with that of the beautifully dressed West German visitor, smoking a cigar and driving a new Mercedes. How can one believe in socialist morality when one realizes the importance of *protekcija* (obtaining favors through unofficial channels), the ever-present official scandals, or sees the "cadre kids" arriving at school in their father's shiny limousine? How can they believe in their willing and "loving" role as a part of the Russian sphere of influence? Or how can they really believe in a collectivist society of one for all and all for one, when one can only get ahead largely by one's own efforts and at the expense of collectivist ideals?

Yet the Eastern Europeans cannot openly profess their opposition to the official values, and we cannot measure exactly who believes in what and to what extent. Eastern Europeans, like all people, have a need to believe. There was some hope after World War II that a new type of society could be created there, a "new man" made. The new society exists today, but as its citizens found out, it contained not only some ills of previous societies but some new diseases as well. Any attempts to create a socialism that is democratic in the political sense have failed. In ironic contrast to the "human face of socialism" of which Alexander Dubcek spoke, a human face of socialism indeed exists. With varying degrees, it is truly a human face: mean, petty, vicious, and murderous. Only occasionally do the rays of hope and toleration lighten the shadows cast on these societies.

PART V

FOREIGN POLICY AND THE FUTURE OF EASTERN EUROPE

Eastern Europe and the External Environment

I can absolutely guarantee that Poland is an independent country. . . .

—**President Gerald Ford during the 1976 presidential debate**

■ The foreign policy of Eastern Europe is characterized by complexities that do not lend themselves to facile generalizations or simplistic models. Albania, for example, pursues policies that are utterly independent and unaffected by any consideration of the Soviet alliance system. Czechoslovakia, on the other hand, is so opposed to intervention in the foreign policies of Communist states that it does not even intervene, as the gag has it, in its own affairs. And in between these two extremes there are states that try to reconcile their national interests with those of the Soviet-led alliance system.

For any state, membership in a genuine alliance system means both retaining sovereignty as well as accepting the need to share common goals and purposes. Thus in the West such a state may criticize the foreign policy of the United States, it may engage in ventures on its own, it may even elect a socialist government and still stay within the NATO alliance system; the example of Greece since the election of George Papandreou amply illustrates this point. At the same time, however, Greece may not engage in policies that seriously contradict common NATO military policies, or enter into an alliance with the USSR, and still retain its full membership in NATO.

Similar constraints also exist in Eastern Europe, delimiting the foreign policy of the states there. The difference between East and West, however, lies in both the *kind* of external control and the historical periods when those controls were used. We will first consider the various post–World War II periods, for the policies followed by the USSR and the Eastern European states have undergone a tremendous amount of alteration since 1945.

EASTERN EUROPE AND THE USSR

After the Communist takeovers in Eastern Europe, the USSR exercised a direct control over every aspect of Eastern European politics; no major domestic or foreign policy decision could be taken by any leader without consulting Moscow. Even without any formal mechanism of control there was such a perceived commonality of interests— both on the part of the Eastern European Communist leaders and in Moscow—that no separate policies could possibly emerge or be articulated. The Soviet elite, including Stalin himself, clearly felt that the leaders of the Eastern European states were basically marionettes who were expected to do exactly as they were told. If there emerged rivaling or even different ideas—as in the case of Georgi Dimitrov of Bulgaria, who wished to pursue a somewhat more "independent" Balkan policy leading to the integration of the Balkan states in a federation—the Soviet Union used the good offices of its military-security fraternity to do away with the recalcitrant. Similarly, when the Czechoslovak leadership thought that it was following Moscow's wishes in accepting the Marshall Plan—while in reality their interpretation of Moscow's wishes was at variance with actual Soviet policy—the Czech elite was simply told to cancel previous commitments in a very short order. "Independent" decision making in those days certainly did not characterize the actions of these allegedly "sovereign" socialist states.

Yugoslavia was the first to reject the hegemony of Soviet policies. From 1948 onward the Yugoslavs carved out their own national policies, based on the primacy of Yugoslav national interests, and developed what they called the doctrine of "different roads to socialism." One aspect of Yugoslavia's road to its own brand of socialism was the adoption of a nonalignment policy, refusing to become a part of either the Soviet (Warsaw Treaty Organization) or Western (NATO) military bloc. Although on many issues the Yugoslavs did continue to support the USSR, the Soviets could no longer count on an automatic Yugoslav endorsement of their actions in the international scene. In fact, endorsement was often replaced by conspicuous criticism.

Albania's defection from the Soviet camp in 1961 and its subsequent withdrawal from the Warsaw Pact was slightly different. Prompted by the "betrayal of socialism"—as Enver Hoxha viewed Khrushchev's de-Stalinization and liberalization policies—the Albanians decided to cast in their lot with the only true Communist orthodoxy at that time: China. At least until 1982, Albania remained a staunch ally of the Chinese and a vociferous opponent of the Soviet-dominated Warsaw Pact.

After Yugoslavia's and Albania's defection from the Soviet alliance system, the Soviet Union's policies became viewed more as "exemplary acts" that should be followed in the *general* sense, rather than concrete orders that came from Moscow, the center of the Communist world. Thus, since 1965, Romania was able to get away with having more independent-sounding foreign policies, and Hungary was able to experiment with its own domestic reform program. Moscow was still the center of the alliance system, but deviations from or revisions of Soviet guidance were permitted, provided that these acts did not seriously threaten the socialist order or alliance system—and hence Moscow's perceived or real interests. Consequently, Hungarian reforms have been tolerated and even to some extent encouraged and emulated by Moscow, while the 1968 Prague Spring and the 1981 Solidarity experiments were terminated in short order.

Although, in general, Moscow no longer exercises direct and total control over every policy decision, it still has a number of means to influence and limit the foreign and domestic policies of and in Eastern Europe. The three most important means are political, military and economic.

Political Control

In the political life of Eastern Europe there exists no "formal" regional organization. Nevertheless, what is euphemistically called the "socialist commonwealth" does indeed exist. It primarily represents the socialist states of Eastern Europe—except Albania and Yugoslavia, which generally do not participate in any of the bloc's political meetings—but occasionally also includes "developing" states with Communist governments: Cuba, the Mongolian People's Republic, North Vietnam, or North Korea. At gatherings of the so-called progressive forces, one may also sometimes note the participation of representatives of the PLO, North Yemen, or Ethiopia.

Institutionally, the most significant forum for these contacts is the formal, organized, and planned meeting of the first secretaries of the various Communist states. Held infrequently, the major item of business at these meetings is the expression of support for Soviet positions in world affairs. But these meetings have also served recently as forums for representing diverse national interests as well; Romania's recalcitrance—with the cautious support of other states, such as Hungary— to follow Soviet foreign policies compelled the USSR a number of times to "tone down" its desired goals merely to win the support of the rather hard-bargaining Romanian first secretary.

These sessions are supplemented by the informal annual "pilgrimages" of the East European first secretaries to Moscow, or more precisely to the secluded Black Sea resorts reserved for the highest Soviet political elites, to visit the General Secretary of the Communist Party of the Soviet Union. Billed as "friendly discussions" or "annual vacations," these more informal get-togethers afford a chance for a first secretary to discuss his country's problems, one on one, with the Soviet leader every summer. Sometimes, these visits are followed by a semiformal meeting of all of the Eastern European first secretaries.

Another channel for contact between the USSR and the Eastern European states takes place through the International Department of the various Communist party secretariats, on the one hand, and the International Department of the CPSU-CC Secretariat (Central Committee Secretariat of the Communist Party of the Soviet Union), on the other. Not only do the secretaries in charge of these departments meet but telephone consultations take place daily at the lower levels. Sometimes—depending on individual leadership styles—these contacts are either supplemented or replaced by contacts between the Soviet Embassy and the International Department of the given Eastern European party secretariat, or the Eastern European state's embassy in Moscow and the International Department of the CPSU Secretariat. The personnel in these positions may range from being extremely loyal to the first secretary and the prevailing leadership in their native land, all the way to being stool-pigeons for Soviet interests; the factional struggle among such allegiances often represents Communist power behavior at its most mean and vicious.

Formal channels of institutional contact also exist among the various foreign ministries. Infrequent meetings among the foreign ministers are used as policy forums and as platforms for voicing differences about certain interests. Daily contacts between the Soviet foreign ministry and the various foreign ministries of the Eastern European states takes place in an institutionalized and formal manner through the usual embassy-ministry networks, although direct telephone contact is also used, though hampered by the miserable telephone system that still plagues the Eastern European states and the USSR alike.

Finally, the various security services are all tied into a solid institutional network; both the Soviet KGB (for political intelligence, counter-intelligence, and political-security affairs) and the GRU (for military-political affairs) maintain very close relations with their East European counterparts at every level. Even though there have been indications that Romania's security police ended its close integration with the KGB by the mid-1960s, recent information suggests that a fairly close cooperation on this level is still the general rule, rather than the exception. The closest institutional connection, not surprisingly, thus exists within the levels of the security organizations. While we should not maintain that in every case such a connection automatically means a total community of interests regarding all such events, it is a fact that—except in Albania and Yugoslavia—these contacts remain well institutionalized.

Military Control

Militarily, the Warsaw Treaty Organization (WTO), or the Warsaw Pact, is the primary organization for the maintenance of common military interests. The armed forces of the Communist states of Europe, at first glance, obviously fulfill the traditional roles played by armed forces everywhere: they provide the backbone of domestic defense of the regime against enemies from the outside and the inside. And, as elsewhere, the armies of the region are convincing interest groups that constrain the regimes' ability to advance in areas other than military might, agitate for increased military spending, and ally themselves with the "steel and coal" complexes for ever-greater strengthening of the "commanding heights" of industry. Furthermore, just as in many other developing states, in all of these states the armies are also social instruments that play major roles in the transformation or maintenance of social equilibrium.

However, certain peculiarities in the nature of Communist states affect the relationship between the military and the polity in these systems. First, the military, like all other instruments, is subordinated to the Communist party in all its manifestations. In Communist polities, to use, once again, the somewhat outmoded systems analysis terminology, the party controls the output, the input, and the feedback mechanisms of society. The party, in other words, determines the basis on which decisions are made, makes the decisions, and manufactures support for the decisions reached. With respect to the army, however, the party has always had, and during the last four decades certainly enlarged, a somewhat different role: it allows—and with some notable exceptions has always allowed—the army to influence decision making. I think it is safe to say that the input processes have been more open to army demands than to any other apparats, with the possible exception of the political police organs. It is clear, of course, that as the modernization of the technical levels of the armed forces has increased, the input has become ever greater; complexity has demanded technical expertise and loyalty, and the party has found itself ever more reliant on the army, which—as proved by the Polish military coup of 1981—when the chips were down, it had to trust to defend the Communist system.

Remarkably, as Communist polities developed, the party also had to open up, to some extent, even the feedback loop of support to "spontaneous" expressions as well, that is, it had to allow the expression of values that were not always what the elite wanted to hear. Here, the army had been genuinely involved in expressing support of or opposition to certain measures instituted by the party that affected the performance of the military as a whole. For example, such "minor" controversies as the percentage of recruit training time devoted to political instruction or the use of conscripts as forced labor to help with construction projects have certainly been clear instances where genuine feedback, though channeled, was used to alter decisions already set.

It is also true, however, that perhaps with the single exception of the Polish military, the *political* decision-making process itself has remained closed to the army and is still monopolized by the party *apparat.* Yet even this process has been refined during the last decades, and today there are two mechanisms that make the process of subordination more palatable to the army as a whole.

The first of these mechanisms relates to the role of the leading personalities of the military complex. The party is exceedingly careful that contemporary military leaders be promoted on the basis of both their technical knowledge and their party loyalty. Consequently, as General Jaruzelski's case certainly points out, a military decision maker, regardless of rank, is not placed in his position of authority solely because of his abilities, but also because of his party connections: loyalties *coupled with* military ability. Though this can be said of any sphere of Communist power relationships, it is especially true of Soviet and East European military-party power relationships. "Mistakes" will, of course, occur: a nationalist general such as Miesczyslaw Moczar in Poland, or a Pal Maleter in Hungary may step forward in times of stress, but the party has generally been remarkably successful in judging its military cadres.

The second mechanism is the peculiar nature of the alliance system within which multinational units are integrated. Here, within national units the independent decision making regarding the military is subordinated not merely to national aims but also to the needs of the alliance system. For instance, East German decisions concerning the percentage of the national budget to be devoted to the armed forces is only one element of the process; the East German military leadership often receives additional "funds" or "equipment," "training," "demands," or "exercise support" from the Warsaw Pact, more specifically from the USSR. Conversely, national decisions regarding the percentage of allocations for defense or army-related activities are mostly established at the Pact level rather than by the governments of the various states. In a sense, of course, this duality creates tensions within the domestic environment—e.g., in East Germany and Hungary—but it does lend a certain level of responsibility to the leaders of the armed forces they would not otherwise possess.

A second aspect of the peculiarity of the military-party relationship in Communist states lies in the fact that the armed forces, in general, are supposed to represent the widest possible cross-section of the population in the common national effort to defend the socialist state. However, from the onset of Communist power, a fear of Bonapartism—that is, the emergence of a strong military leader who would replace the ruling party leader—has plagued the Communist leaders. In the USSR, Trotsky's power as the head of the Red Army and Tukhachevsky's and Zhukov's power, combined with their powerful personalities, were viewed by Stalin with an alarm that was not altogether rational. Nonetheless, fear of Bonapartism has led the party to create two instruments that are the *duopolists* of armed power simultaneously: the army on the one hand, and the political police, on the other. The KGB and its local "sister" organizations, indeed, are expected to act as checks on the power of the military and, in the service of their mission to the party, they exercise at least a co-equal function in system and subsystem maintenance activities.

Some, of course, would argue that this dual role is not unique; Hitler's Germany was also characterized by similar dualities. What is unique, however, in the Soviet and Eastern European cases is that the KGB and its various local counterparts have (a) successfully penetrated and to a great extent managed to *control* the various armies, and (b) that they retain an international network of control that is truly integrated under Soviet direction to a far greater extent than exists among other alliance systems.

A third important aspect of the peculiarity of the Communist alliance system is ideologically grounded. The cautious emphasis on instilling "socialist patriotism" in the citizenry of the member states of the alliance system comes dangerously close to uncorking the specter of nationalism, and such a possibility is not viewed by the USSR as beneficial to its own existence. Consequently, the USSR and the ruling parties have tried to inculcate in the citizenry an understanding of the Soviet needs for what they call "basic Soviet security considerations." The Soviet Union demands the unquestioned control of society by the party, on the one hand, and the absence of unbridled anti-Soviet nationalism, on the other. Therefore, the Soviet elite must instill in the members of the alliance system attitudes that (1) require the army to follow the orders of the party and not act against the USSR, and (2) to be prepared to fight "traditional enemies" other than the Russians. The USSR no longer cares if a Warsaw Pact state stresses Stalinism or democracy, liberalism or centralism, private farming or state control, private initiative and profit or total socialist control; it only cares that there exist no genuine freedom in that state that might result in the loosening of the reins held by the party and a consequent turning away from the existing military-political alliance system. Thus, with the help of the party and the KGB and through the benefits, training and elite status extended to the military, the system attempts to ensure the loyalty and reliability of the armed forces.

The Warsaw Pact: Systemic peculiarities

In recent years, several excellent studies have dealt with various aspects of the Warsaw Pact as a military alliance, describing the physical dimensions of this impressive system. Based on these studies, intelligent observers certainly can delineate the size, organization, and even performance of the Pact. Suffice it to say here that the Warsaw Pact forces are primarily composed of armies of Communist states in Eastern Europe, whose active deployment, to date, has only taken place in intra-systemic conflict, and whose development and deployment has been

"Proletarians of the world, unite! Or I shoot!"

Literarni listy (Prague)

generally in accordance with the desires of the leader of the alliance, the USSR.

And herein lies the first major conceptual problem in discussing this alliance system—namely, the problem of whether one can regard this system as a genuine alliance, or one that is imposed on the participating states. On the one hand, it should be noted that the very size of the USSR makes its weight in the system so great as to raise serious questions about the importance of such tiny allies as Bulgaria, Hungary, or, before 1961, Albania. On the other hand, the dominance of the USSR and the distribution of military global tasks among the various armies of the Pact—for example, the assignment of global political police training tasks to the East German army and its secret police—raises the point that it is a specific type of alliance system with diverse missions.

Machiavelli wrote that the size of a preponderant ally renders its minuscule partners' role so subordinate that the nature of a "true" alliance becomes questionable. But alliances have frequently been unipolar and concentrated around a particular actor. For example, preponderant American strength has not brought the genuineness of the NATO alliance into question. What has brought the Warsaw Pact into question has been the political reality of imposed rule on Eastern Europe by the USSR, *not* the nature of the military alliance that stemmed from that political imposition. Nonetheless, we must mention that the USSR, in general, itself has been adverse to a greater institutionalization of that alliance system; informal arrangements are more subject to manipulation by the dominant power.

Although history shows that the tail may occasionally wag the dog—for example, the outbreak of World War I—compatible size remains one of the operational concepts for a genuine alliance system. And yet the history of the Warsaw Pact alliance system shows remarkable divergences of opinion on various issues; witness the vehement demands by East Germany and Czechoslovakia for a speedy occupation of Hungary in 1956, well ahead of Soviet advocacy of this policy, and the divergent attitudes of the variously sized allies regarding intervention in Czechoslovakia in 1968 or in Poland in 1981.

The genuineness of the military alliance system has also been questioned because there is a great deal of proof that even after forty years in the region, the Soviet forces are viewed as occupiers; 1956 and 1968 are outstanding examples to prove this point, although in the case of Czechoslovakia the true animosity toward the USSR has built up only *since* August 21, 1968. Some elements of the support for the alliance—aside from that of sheer imposition—however, have come from within the native military establishments and from the local officer corps. The reason for their support of the Warsaw Pact is relatively simple: they have been told that if they fail to live up to their obligations they *(a)* might face retaliation by an angry populace; *(b)* can only expect—at best—a neutralization and abolition of the army as a potential defender of the historic nation; and/or *(c)* a corresponding end to their power, prestige, and livelihood. Although we will be dealing with this subject later, it is safe to conclude that the vast majority of the professional cadres of the armed forces prefer their present existence to an uncertain future.

There are other aspects of the Warsaw Pact that are "peculiar" though not necessarily counterproductive from the systemic perspective. One of these is the fact that the alliance system helps to mitigate the USSR's deep-seated and avowed feeling of "loneliness" as the "whipping boy of history." This is a symbolic function, to be sure, but to be able to refer to an action undertaken by the "Communist alliance system," or the "Warsaw Pact," is preferable to the USSR having to act alone. Hence, unlike in 1956 in Hungary, the invasion of Czechoslovakia in 1968 was undertaken by the Warsaw Pact—even if Romania did not participate and Hungarian participation had to be forced from Kadar by very real Soviet pressures on that leader. In fact, there is a great deal of evidence that in 1968 Bulgaria, East Germany, and Poland had agitated for intervention *before* the Soviet Politburo had been prepared to do so, just as the East German and Czechoslovak leaders pressured the Soviet leaders for a joint intervention in Poland in 1980–1981.

Moreover, it is important to note that within the Warsaw Pact a great deal of mutuality of interaction takes place every day. As mentioned above, the military in each of the member states derives not merely prestige, but real, significant benefits from the system: these benefits range from plush officers' clubs and special stores to the possession and use of the most modern military hardware, glittering to awe citizens and foreign visitors alike. The more modern and extensive the hardware, the greater the prestige of the domestic controllers of the use of violence. Conversely, the lack of possessing that hardware—for example, anti-aircraft or modern missile systems—implies a lack of prestige within the alliance. And, in this respect, the USSR is regarded by the military elite as the source of benefits and the source of tension as well; one gets from the USSR as it gives and complains about the USSR not giving as much modern equipment to its allies as it gives to some nonmember states in military aid.

Finally, we should note that the integration of the military alliance system is an accomplished reality. Although it is true that the type of integration the Eastern European sources always pride themselves on—the interchange of personnel in armed units with personnel from another nation's army—is not as important as the ability to conduct side-by-side, pass-through, or coordinated boundary operations, in a more fundamantal sense the WTO is totally integrated. With the exception of Albania, Romania, and Yugoslavia, this total integration manifests itself in the fact that under wartime conditions, there is *no* Warsaw Pact organization; all units are subordinated to the Soviet high command. They receive their orders directly from the Soviet general staff, through the commander of the Soviet military district or theater of operation. The peacetime Warsaw Pact operational chain of command, as shown in Figure 13.1, disappears in times of war.

Lest we forget, this alliance system is also an important contributor to or detractor from the physical strength and economic health of most of the member states. The allocation of responsibilities for military production—small arms, artillery, tanks, etc.—within the Pact has significantly increased the economic capabilities of such states as East Germany and Czechoslovakia; the net export of arms produced in some of these states brings hard currency influx or other external trade benefits. But there is one more export item that is as important as the hardware export—the export of military personnel. East Germany's "traditional" role of supplying developing states with security training personnel and apparatus, for example, in some parts of the world such as Africa, is certainly far more ubiquitous today than it had been a decade or so ago. Of course, it is also true that having to allocate scarce funds to the military apparatus also causes tensions within Eastern Europe. Especially since 1979 as growth rates practically disappeared and as the USSR has continued to demand greater additional allocations to the defense efforts, domestic economic development has had to suffer; the extra 3 percent growth of military expenditures demanded by the USSR in 1978 had to be taken from the "civilian" sector, and it has contributed to worsening domestic standards of living, especially in Hungary and Czechoslovakia.

In short, then, the system that exists in Eastern Europe is an alliance based on two contradictory elements: (1) an imposed rule by a great power that determines both the political context of the domestic environment and the limits of its change, on the one hand, and (2) a system of mutualities and mutual benefits of military-economic relations, on the other. The stress and tension existing between these contradictions are the dynamics on which the alliance system must operate.

The evolution of the WTO

Let us now try to reconstruct the changing historical processes that have been responsible for the shifting goals of the Warsaw Pact. As mentioned above, on the one hand, it would be overly simplistic to say that these changes have always been the results of changing Soviet strategies. On the other hand, it should not be denied that they were not *related to* or *connected with* these alterations, but not in the sense Soviet strategists and ideologues would like to see. In a

Figure 13.1 Chain of Command in the Warsaw Treaty Organization

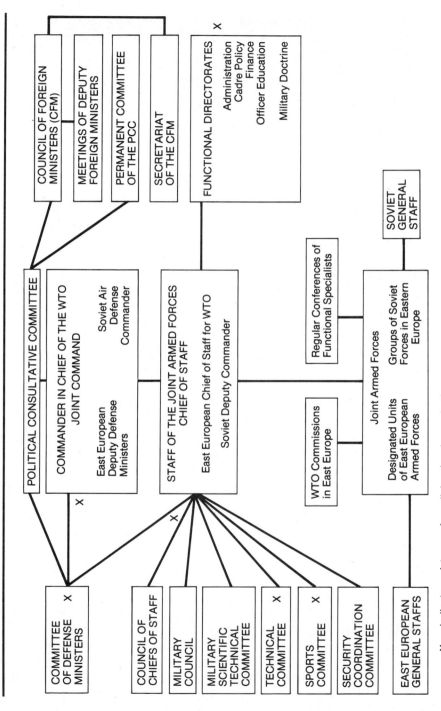

X = indicates existence of parallel national organization

sense, as the Pact matured, one could detect two sets of evolving differences: (1) between the individual armies and parties, on the one hand, and the USSR, on the other; and (2) the Pact as a whole, on the one hand, and Soviet desires on the other. A brief survey of the last three decades serves, here, as a useful guide to bolster our line of reasoning.

Theoretically, the WTO came into being only on May 14, 1955, with the original goal of providing a common defense against the imperialist powers. But informally, the Warsaw Pact as a defensive organization was created much earlier to combat Fascism cooperatively; a common and coordinated organization of Polish troops under Soviet command, Bulgarian and Romanian troops after their defection from the German cause and to the Allied effort in August and September 1944, respectively, and among the various Czechoslovak "volunteer units" operating along with the Soviet army as it advanced west. This cooperation was enormously strengthened by the Sovietization of all the armies that took place beginning in 1948–1949 and by the creation of an East German fighting force in 1949. Although these military alliances were informal and deliberately vague to give maximum latitude to Soviet control and influence, the new "people's armies" had shown a certainly not too surprising proclivity toward an identity with Soviet views and policies.

The commonality of views was especially strong concerning the native Communist military perception of a threat from the West. That threat existed in the perfectly understandable fear of the renewal of German power; the awesome destructive potential of Germany and its ability to wreak havoc upon Eastern Europe had been shown in two preceding world wars. Coupled with the perceived near-omnipotence attributed to the United States, that power could once again adversely affect the lives of the inhabitants of the power vacuum known as Eastern Europe. The Communist elite's fear of the Allies, both at the beginning of the Cold War and after, was not just a fear for the states they ruled, it was also a fear for themselves personally. It was a fear for what would happen if the USSR lost and the Soviet satraps had to retreat. But the new military establishments that owed their existence to Soviet policies and Communist rule were gripped by an even greater fear—the fear of losing and having to face personal retribution from within the nations where they had been ensconced by the bayonets of the Red Army, clearly viewed in 1949 as an *occupying* force by most of the people of the region. It was these fears then that compelled the new military and political elites to band with the USSR in a common defense against real and perceived threats from the West, and in *this* sense the Warsaw Pact has been in existence for at least six or seven years before its official inauguration.

These fears were reinforced by (1) the American involvement in and growing commitment to the Cold War; (2) the establishment of

NATO, a formal alliance aimed at containing perceived Soviet aggression; and (3) the subsequent creation of the perceived strategy of "capitalist encirclement" through such organizations as NATO, CENTO, SEATO, and ANZUS. As the Cold War matured and as the USSR tried to maintain its position in Eastern Europe, the latter had to commit all its efforts to the maintenance of its systemic powers. The death of Stalin and the revolts and riots in East Germany, Czechoslovakia, Hungary, and Poland kept the Soviets hopping from one trouble spot to another. It is true that the doctrine of strategic encroachment—the acquisition of bases and allies on a global scale with the purpose of countering the policy of encirclement—had already been developed in Soviet military thinking, but in practice, it could not be implemented as long as the West stood firm, had the strategic, material, and tactical capabilities *and the desire* to oppose Soviet aggression or encroachment wherever it took place.

All this began to change with the Soviet Union's possession of thermonuclear weapons and with the adoption of a "more reasonable" Western attitude toward the USSR. A significant number of Western policymakers began to suggest that the "containment" and "rollback" policies of the United States placed the USSR in a position that was "unfair," that given enough leeway and incentives, the USSR could become a stable and status quo power with whom agreements for the maintenance of peace and spheres of influence could be made if reasonable negotiations could be conducted. Fueled by the Hungarian tragedy of 1956, the sudden break in NATO unity in the Suez crisis in the same year, and by the spirit of accommodation that led Eisenhower to Geneva, Kennedy to Vienna, and Nixon to Moscow, a new era began whose main motto was "détente." This policy of noncontainment has been implemented since the advent of the Kennedy administration with various ups and downs, notably the Cuban Missile Crisis and the war in Vietnam. But the lessons that the USSR drew from Cuba and Vietnam—that is, the necessity of an enormous military machine that can never again be humbled, on the one hand, and that defeat *can* indeed be inflicted on the United States and its allies, on the other—were lessons that had made the Warsaw Pact establishment aware that victory over the West was possible.

While the Warsaw Pact made great advances in achieving greater global power and influence, it also made some major mistakes and miscalculations, such as: (1) the schism in Soviet-Chinese relations, the instabilities in Eastern Europe and among many WTO allies, and the inability of the Pact to maintain alliances in some peripheral areas; (2) the underestimation of Western resolve and interests; (3) the miscalculation concerning Western *and* Third World responses to the Soviet invasion of Afghanistan; and (4) the consequent doubt cast on the "benevolence" of Soviet intentions by those who previously were willing to view the USSR as serving the interest of "peace for mankind."

Suffice it to say, that both failures and successes have had unintended effects in creating stresses within the Warsaw Pact, stresses that have been responsible for a major change in the nature of that system, from its totally subservient role to one where major cleavages are exhibited.

Stresses in the Pact

One can identify three major sets of stresses in the Warsaw Pact as it has evolved since its formal inception, although undoubtedly other aspects can also easily be added. These three stresses have been (1) the very development of the policy of détente; (2) the role of the Pact in suppressing intrasystemic violence, especially in Eastern Europe; and (3) the development of the Sino-Soviet split and its effects on the policies of the various WTO states.

Whether one calls it peaceful coexistence, or détente, the simple fact is that the public embrace of that policy by the United States had lowered the threshold of imminent danger that was until then "obvious" to the Eastern Europeans. As the superiority of Soviet and WTO strength in conventional weaponry, especially in the central and northern sectors of Europe, became clear, the political managers of the states in the alliance system began to be less and less fearful for their own success and survival. Gone were the fears of the earlier years, the specter of Western, and especially German and American, armies marching into Eastern Europe; the fears of stringing up Communists and army commanders had turned out to be a chimera that was not likely to become a reality. The German threat transposed itself into a very welcome German economic presence, the existence of the Social Democratic governments on the continent lessened the "capitalist" threat and President Johnson's 1968 declaration concerning the continuing American "respect for the Yalta accords" decreased the possibility of a major threat to the political systems of the WTO allies.

These developments prompted the adoption of a less acquiescent attitude among the members of the alliance system. They questioned the necessity of two major components of Soviet objectives: (1) continued offensive forward strategy by the WTO, and (2) growing arms expenditures.

The forward offensive strategy of the WTO, of course, is cast as "defensive," aimed at the prevention of a potential NATO attack on Eastern Europe. And yet it is clear to the planners and commanders of both Eastern and Western alliances that offensive roles are assigned to the Czechoslovak, Polish, and East German forces in the northern tier and to Hungarian and Bulgarian forces in the south. The need for such a strategy began to be questioned in the mid- and late 1970s by President Nicolae Ceausescu of Romania and his political leadership. He realized, and publicly stated, that, especially after Czechoslovakia, it was the WTO that posed the principal threat to Romania's "independent" or autonomous policies—and hence to the survival of Ceausescu's dictatorship. While only Romania challenged *openly* the need for offensive strategy, the Polish and the Hungarian leadership also took some delight in the Romanian challenge and privately backed Romanian concerns. The East German, the post-1968 Czechoslovak and the Bulgarian leaderships have continued to support the Soviet political-military strategies, but even the East German and Czechoslovak leaders showed some deviation from Soviet policy priorities by 1984.

The Romanian challenge has been openly stated since 1978. While continually insisting on the "eternal" Romanian devotion to the WTO in its original goal of defending any WTO state attacked by the West, the Romanians made it clear that they will *not* send their troops into conflicts that take place outside Romanian territory, whether member states of the WTO or not. Hence, the Romanians, following the Yugoslav example, implemented a territorial defensive doctrine of the "defense of the state by the entire people;" such military strategy is based on national defense that can only be undertaken *on the territory of the Romanian state.* Such questioning by an "ally" within the WTO, of course, intensified Soviet concerns and has led to the increased use of joint Soviet military exercises with other WTO allies as a means of preventing the further spread of the Romanian-Yugoslav model. What is important for us here, however, is that the very diminution of a visible threat from the Western alliance system has led to the unintended result of causing a major stress within the WTO as a highly unified alliance system. Coupled with other divergences in Romanian foreign policy, such as, for example, the support of Chinese policies vis-à-vis the USSR, a more even-handed, more pro-Israeli Middle East policy clearly opposed to Soviet purposes, or Romanian opposition to the placement of *all* medium-range missiles in Europe, the Romanian deviation forced the Pact itself to became more of a genuine alliance system than ever before.

The second unintended result of the "successful" pursuit of détente and the resulting weakening of NATO was the development of serious questioning regarding the necessity of increased military-defense spending demanded by the Soviet Union following the May 1978 NATO approval of the so-called Long Term Defense Program. Moscow, once it had achieved conventional and strategic "parity" in the European theater, of course, sought superiority. It demanded a 3 percent real increase in the defense budgets of the WTO member states, just as the United States sought such increases among its allies. But, once again, Romania, Hungary, and Poland—clearly led by Romania's President Ceausescu, whose stand at the Political Consultative Committee meeting in Moscow on November 22–23, 1978, was the most provocative one as far as the USSR was concerned—questioned the real necessity for such increases. The realization of the enormous superiority of the Pact in the northern tier in conventional weapons and the doubt cast on the West's "aggressive" intentions limited Moscow's hand. Indeed, it is interesting to note that in spite of the Soviet desires, only Bulgaria, Czechoslovakia, and East Germany met the goal of the desired increase in defense planning as a percent of the GNP, and the USSR has learned that it must bear the cost of any major increase in the costs related to military expenditures to the same extent as the United States often must pay for these increases on its side. Once again, however, what is important to note is that the very successes

The creation of 'affection' for the great Soviet brethren has not exactly been helped by Soviet invasions of Hungary or Czechoslovakia. Here, as Soviet tanks rumble through the streets of Prague in 1968, angry Czechoslovaks shout, attempting to halt their progress and the destruction of the Prague reform era by their bare hands. (Sygma)

of the WTO in improving its position vis-à-vis NATO had created a major stress in the alliance system when further increases in defense expenditures were demanded by the USSR from its allies in the waning days of the "era of détente."

Other stresses in the alliance system also resulted from the use of Soviet and Pact forces in the suppression of intrasystemic dysfunctions. While in 1956 only Soviet forces were used in the suppression of the Hungarian revolution, we must repeat that with the exception of Romania, troops of the entire Pact were ordered into action in Czechoslovakia. Opposition to that use of force, today, is well known and does not need to be retold in detail. Yet, in spite of Janos Kadar's opposition to the invasion, even Hungarian troops *had* to participate; the presence of Soviet forces on the territory of Poland, East Germany, and Hungary guaranteed that participation. But precisely this joint intervention prompted the Romanians to denounce the use of force against a "fraternal ally" and the resulting stress has been considerable; in fact, twelve years later, Hungary joined with Romania in very visible and vocal opposition to military intervention in Poland, especially under the guise of the WTO. Moreover, there are unconfirmed reports from usually reliable sources that Hungarian opposition to military action against Yugoslavia immediately after the death of Tito, helped mitigate potential Soviet threat to that country. In short, the use of Pact forces against each other had led to the questioning of the WTO as a defensive organization against the West, and to opposition of the Pact in its use as an instrument suppressing "fraternal" nations that have sought to settle their own internal problems along acceptable, though "separate roads to socialism."

Finally, Soviet handling of the China question has also led to major stresses within the alliance system. The Sino-Soviet dispute has long been a bone of contention between the USSR and some of its allies. Albania, of course, has been the first—and the last—to switch sides on this issue. But, as noted earlier, in the mid-1960s Romania broke ranks with the WTO countries and refused to subscribe to the existence of a Chinese "threat" to socialism. Although Romania has not been successful in altering the Soviet stand, because of the general unanimity required for Pact-wide statements and the adoption of Pact-wide policies, it indeed has been able to tone down Soviet statements on China in joint documents, such as, for example, the Soviet-Romanian and the Political Consultative Committee statements of November 25 and November 27, 1976. The issue of China in itself is not a major issue within the alliance system; rather, it is just one more area of stress that continues to surface between the alliance system, on the one hand, and some of its component parts, on the other.

Issues of tension

While the above *areas* of stress remain continuous and pervasive on the highest levels of political-military decision making, there are equally important—though somewhat more microlevel—issues of tension that also aggravate the situation within the alliance system: (1) the issue of command, (2) the issue of armament needs, (3) the issue of deployment of forces, and (4) the issue of military spending. Although other issues could be added, in my estimation these four issues represent the greatest potential sources of tension in micro policy-level decisions.

The question of command has been a nagging question, and it has never been solved adequately or to the satisfaction of all parties. Under the present organization, the WTO has two sides to its organization: political and military (Figure 13.1). On the top there exists the Political Consultative Committee (PCC), consisting of the first secretaries—or their specifically designated deputies—of the member states. The PCC is responsible for the overall political decision-making process within the Pact. Under the PCC the lines separate sharply. On the political side, political decisions below this level are made by the Council of Foreign Ministers (CFM) of the members, and at still lower levels, by the meetings of the deputy foreign ministers that presumably deal with less important policy matters. In the period between these meetings, two bodies, the so-called Permanent Committee of the PCC and the Secretariat, known as the Secretariat of the Council of Foreign Ministers of the WTO, staffed by the foreign policy departments of the respective party CC secretariats and located in Moscow, takes care of the day-to-day coordination of political matters. In addition to the meetings of the high level officials within the formal structures, the Crimean or Moscow meetings of the first secretaries and other meetings of the same officials are also forums for political statements and policy formulation. In general, there seems to be little problem with the command structure in this area; while the Romanians from time to time balk at evident Soviet pressure, the issue of command does not play a major part.

In the military sphere there are altogether different considerations. Originally, the WTO has merely had a commander-in-chief, *always* a senior Soviet officer, assisted by the deputy commanders-in-chief, who are the defense ministers of the various member states. The commander-in-chief of the WTO has always occupied the third most important position in the Soviet military hierarchy, directly under the defense minister and the chief of the general staff of the Red Army. A staff of the WTO of the joint armed forces, including the permanent representatives of the various joint chiefs of staff located in Moscow is assigned to assist the WTO commander-in-chief. Since the Budapest meeting of March 1969, additional organs have also been created to handle military affairs (see Figure 13.1). At the top of the current military organization chart there exists the Council of Defense Ministers. Before 1968 these ministers had met only three times, in 1961, 1962, and 1963. Since 1968, though, the Council of Defense Ministers has met at least annually and twice in 1975. The Council of the Chiefs of Staff below this level appears to be subordinated on policy matters to the Council of Defense Ministers; in fact, it has not been formally convened since 1971. Its functions apparently have been partially taken over by the Military Council. Although organizationally it seems to be subordinated to the Joint Council, in reality the Military Council remains the most significant group where contact among the member states' military missions takes place. Since its establishment it has held, except in 1976, at least two meetings a year. It seems that the functions of the planning and operational integration have been handled by this council, rather than by the Council of Defense Ministers. While the 1969 meeting also established a Technical Council, whose tasks seem to be the operational integration of new weapons, weapons research and delivery coordination, and military-technological innovation, this body is subordinated to the Military Council and apparently works under the latter's guidance.

The issue of command, the question of why the commander of the joint armed forces must always be a Soviet commander and why that commander—who is not even the defense minister of the USSR but his subordinate!—should issue orders to the various defense ministers of the various member states, has been a festering problem since the early 1960s. The control of some joint exercises by "native" commanders has perhaps mitigated the situation somewhat, but even so, between 1961 and 1979 out of eighty-three exercises that the WTO held in states other than the USSR for which the commanders can be identified, there were nineteen native commanders versus thirty-eight Soviet commanders.

The question of the command of joint exercises is one of prestige and not merely of prestige at top levels; there is considerable evidence that the subordination of native units to Soviet commanders causes resentment in the lower ranks as well. And there is no doubt, today, that on the noncom' and conscript levels the problem of nonnative commanders can cause serious dysfunctions. The Soviet leadership seems to understand the problem and has religiously avoided putting non-Soviet troops into direct contact with lower-level Soviet commanders or observers, but the issue remains a real problem. Romania's pointed statement of February 6, 1970—implying that in case of any conflict involving Romanian or WTO troops with Romanian participation, Romanian components would be commanded *only* by Romanian officers—suggests the intensity of this problem.

A second issue of tension relates to the modernization of armaments and military equipment. It seems in the interest of the USSR to provide its allies with the most up-to-date military equipment if it intends to use the WTO in a projected conflict against the West. And yet the modernization of the Eastern European military has been slow and sporadic, and it *never* takes place until quite sometime *after* such weapons have been introduced into the arsenal of even second echelon Soviet forces. In fact, such equipment does not reach the frontline units of even the favored northern countries, in adequate numbers, until three to four years after these weapons have been acquired by the Soviet troops stationed in that area.

The WTO militaries—even if some consider them mere extensions of the Soviet forces—in this sense represent national pride in the region; they, correctly, feel that the reason why they receive modern weapons considerably later than the Soviet forces is because the USSR does not consider them to be fully reliable and, hence, not fully equal partners in their common alliance system. Moreover, the "fact" that the Soviets sometimes send some of the most modern and up-to-date equipment to Third World clients, even ahead of the "time-tested" WTO allies, is viewed as an insult. Although such resentment is most evident among those officers below major command positions, it cannot be ignored; the officers and soldiers who hold these views are indeed shouldering a national grudge against their major alliance partner.

The third issue of tension concerns the purposive use of the WTO forces. As indicated above, the question of offensive or defensive use remains in the forefront of the debate between Romania and the Pact as a whole, with Hungary, in practice, backing the Romanian position. It is clear that the military and political elites have little complaint against the deployment of their own troops in case of a direct attack against the WTO by NATO. The issue of tension seems to be centered on the question of their deployment in *offensive* circumstances and—perhaps with the exception of the Bulgarians and the East Germans—there is a real reluctance by most Eastern Europeans to commit these troops for offensive purposes.

Moreover—in spite of the earlier advocacy of some states for intervention in Hungary in 1956 and in Czechoslovakia in 1968—offensive deployment against a "fraternal" ally remains an odious act, and Romania and Hungary have been the most vocal opponents of such deployment. One would think that the Czechoslovak leadership would join the above two states in condemning such action; perhaps, "revenge" for Polish participation in the invasion of Czechoslovakia in 1968, was a factor in Czechoslovak advocacy of intervention in Poland in 1981.

At any rate, some analysts doubt the utility of deploying the Czechoslovak armed forces in any major offensive conflict.

The final area of constant tension is the question of defense spending. In spite of Soviet pressures since 1978, the real increase in defense spending has been minimal in Hungary, decreased in Romania and—due to its economic crunch—clearly dropped below even the minimally expected level in Poland. The question of defense spending remains a major question in the continuous national debates concerning the allocation of scarce priorities. For instance, the 1980 decision to reduce the required military service in Hungary for conscripts by fully six months, will mean a "saving" for the Hungarian military in the cost of manpower and training, a saving they must, however, reinvest in other military areas, especially in acquiring more up-to-date equipment and technology. Debates over the actual investment priorities within the military establishment have indeed been vicious—for example, between the air force, on the one hand, and the military engineering services on the other. Each service chief, of course, turns to his equivalent or liaison officers of the Red Army, perhaps even to friends acquired sometime previously at the service academies in Moscow, and complain about real or imagined insults resulting from the problems of allocating scarce defense resources.

Problems seem to crop up in other areas of defense spending as well. Resentment at spending in areas that are not clearly and evidently in the interest of the national mission, or the inability to spend in areas that are clearly in the envisaged national purpose, cannot easily be handled at the periodic annual meetings of the Military or Technical Council. Debates over the manufacturing of specialized material, such as small arms, tanks, computers, and so on, or their sale and the accruing of credits or hard currency for such sales, apparently can become acrimonious and endless. Agreement, according to a usually reliable source, is reached frequently only after strong bargaining or the imposition of Soviet fiat. The latter, of course, is rarely welcomed by any of those present. But here, too, the Soviets are learning that they have to pay a high price for having their wishes granted.

Vulnerabilities of the Pact in the 1980s

The stresses and tensions discussed above will affect both the macro and micro levels of the policy process in the Warsaw Pact during the late 1980s and early 1990s. It seems to me, then, that it might be fruitful to analyze the *specific* vulnerabilities that the organization itself has exhibited.

The three major vulnerabilities of the Pact as an organization lie: (1) in the cleavage between the Eastern European military population as a whole, on the one hand, and the party and its military cadre on the other; (2) in the spending limits that these states can tolerate if they are to maintain existing standards of living; and (3) in the critical manpower shortages they will be facing in the late 1980s.

The first vulnerability is the gap among values held by different parts of society. I think that it would be a solid assessment to state that socialist societies are characterized mostly by the enormous differentiation between the committed believer/professional/practitioner of the policy process, on the one hand, and the cynical population at large on the other. Suffice it to say that, for the average Eastern European, the gap between the party and the people in terms of belief in the system is enormous and self-evident in every manifestation of daily life.

Polish joke in 1981: The best way of committing suicide in Poland is by throwing oneself into the abyss between the party and the people.

It is an abyss of disbelief, fostered by the ever-changing party line, by the constant upheavals and by the fact that, for the vast majority of these people, the party and the rulers remain "them," locked in daily battle with "us." Though there have been *some* attempts to identify the party with the people—such as Dubcek's honorable, decent, and extremely naive drive to create "socialism with a human face"— these attempts have always been crushed by weapons ready for use in the interest of preserving socialism with a different but far more realistic human face.

There remains an especially great gap between the professional cadre, the political core of the army, and the conscripts. The conscripts—young men between eighteen and twenty-two years of age who account for roughly 60–70 percent of the total manpower of these forces—possess the same cynical values of the population as a whole. The attempts made to inculcate socialist values in these youths are at best half-hearted, at worst unsuccessful. Only when socialist values mingle with a surviving fierce nationalism can major coalescence between conscript and professional political values be seen. The primitive nationalism of a Hungarian, a Romanian, or a Polish soldier, of course, is heightened when it exists in the defense of his *own state,* and it is precisely *this* element that causes grievous problems for the Soviet planners. The phantom of the coalesced values among the Polish army of more than 300,000 soldiers has not been one the Soviet leaders would have wished to unlock if they could possibly help it. The Soviet leaders' fear of such coalescence was not totally unfounded in 1980–

81, during the hey-day of solidarity; in fact a large poster in Warsaw in 1981 proudly proclaimed the old slogan "Party program equals people's program" reversed to read "The people's program *must be* the party's program." Similarly, Romania's desire to alter its state from being national in form and socialist in content to socialist in form and national in content was intended to achieve these very same ends. And the quiet depoliticization of the Hungarians, with the purpose of creating a colescence between national and socialist values, is also aimed at this very purpose; giving *national* legitimacy to the *party* leadership. Their fear was not unfounded.

The military elite's loyalties also are divided between Moscow and the Warsaw Pact, on the one hand, and national pride, on the other. There can be no doubt that there are and will always be those among the military elite who will back Moscow and the political elites. For various reasons—fear of retaliation, fear for careers, for wealth, conviction in values held by the party, lack of education, ideological blindness, or the simple recognition that Eastern Europe is trapped between two great powers—there will always be those who will do everything to support the USSR among the military elite. The ghost of Moscow-trained Colonel Pal Maleter, who led some of the military resistance against the Red Army in Budapest, and the fierce participation of other Moscow-trained officers in the 1956 revolution, have haunted Moscow ever since. Even the pathetic condemnation of the 1968 invasion of Czechoslovakia voiced by Emil Zatopek, the famous Cezechoslovak runner, had come as shock to those on whom they lavished title, fame, and privilege.

But the conscript, the lower ranks of the officer corps, most of the NCOs, those committed to the idea of a nation, will not follow Soviet orders blindly, especially if the order is to fire on one's own people. Against a committed opposition by an army bent on defending a nation, even in the "interest of defending socialism," support for such invasions as, for example, against Poland, would be hard to muster among the socialist brothers. Hungary and Romania would refuse to participate, and the USSR could only count on the Red Army, the Czechs, East Germans, and the token Bulgarians.

The gap between the party and the people, the conscript and the professional military, of course, depends on a conviction that Eastern Europe truly does not face a threat from the West. The external defensive reliability of all of these armies is very high if faced by threats from the West, specifically if those threats envision aggressive territorial intentions that the Communist leadership can parlay into national dangers. Given, however, the West's careful policy of minimizing such threats, this gap is bound to increase and cause considerable problems for the USSR in future years.

The second major area of vulnerabilities for the system as a whole lies in the area of economic advances and development. Undoubtedly, the 1970s was the decade for one of the most dramatic advances in the economic life of Hungary, Romania, Bulgaria, and East Germany. At the same time, for Czechoslovakia and Poland, especially the second half of the 1970s was one of economic disaster and, in Poland, economic mismanagement resulted in a nearly unbearable annual hard-currency debt service. The East German and Hungarian people, meanwhile, achieved the highest levels of living in the region, and neither of these states is anxious to reduce that standard for the sake of greater defense expenditures. In the 1980s, however, all of these states face tremendous limitations on the amount that they can allocate to increase their military spending.

Finally, real limitations are also evident on manpower shortages within the WTO as a whole. It has long been clear to those observing the economies of the WTO states that the military fulfills an inordinately large construction role that involves building streets, hospitals, sports stadiums, and so on—in short, purely civilian tasks that could be fulfilled by nonmilitary personnel. Because of the declining birth rates, to a large extent, but also because of the disastrous manpower-labor-price policies of the regime, the construction efforts of the military conscripts remain important.

These manpower needs in themselves could be handled through a variety of means available to the Eastern European regimes; reducing conscription from 2 years to 18 months, as Hungary has done, is just one of the means that could be utilized. The potentially greatest vulnerability is the question of perception of *real* defense need versus the needs for "socialist construction." The enormous social problems that have come up recently in all of these states—ranging from housing shortages to rising infant mortality—all cry for investment and manpower-efficient solutions, but the heavy and growing defense needs of these states negate any possibility for alleviating these problems. If ever it was true that socialist societies are engaged in the constant re-creation of scarcity, it is true in this area and there seems to be no solution for the projected problem—short of a general European war, of course, and it is hoped that no one really desires that.

Economic Control

A third element of control exercised by the USSR on Eastern European policies lies in the economic institutions, needs, and practices of the region. Although loosely grouped under the heading of the problems relating to the Council on Mutual Economic Assistance (COMECON or CMEA), the problems also stem from economic development practices, tendencies toward self-sufficiency or greater integration, and problems of natural resources and adequate markets.

As will be recalled, the Council of Mutual Economic Assistance was started in direct response to the international economic integrative efforts first begun in Western Europe in the late 1950s. Originally, the Soviet elite viewed the CMEA primarily as a tool to subordinate the economic development of the individual Eastern European states to bloc or Soviet interests. After the 1950s, however, the CMEA slowly became an institution that is supposed to guarantee the national development of the members of the bloc as a whole, and not merely that of the USSR. Headquartered in Moscow today, it is a huge bureaucracy with many subordinate institutions whose structure is depicted in Figure 13.2.

By the beginning of the 1960s, the USSR and most of its allies viewed CMEA as an instrument for greater integration and greater specialization and thus an organization that needs to be responsive

Figure 13.2   CMEA Organization Chart

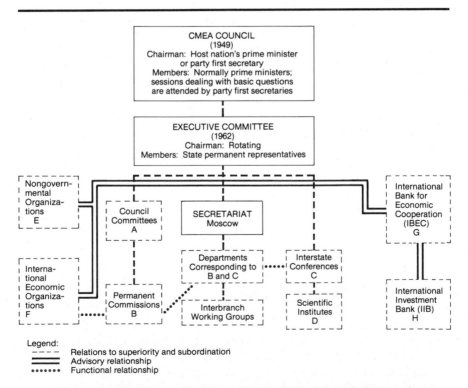

Legend:
---- Relations to superiority and subordination
==== Advisory relationship
•••••• Functional relationship

Source: Miscellaneous Council on Mutual Economic Assistance documents.

to community, rather than to narrow national, needs. This perspective emphasized the positive nature of mutual development. Contrary to this perspective, however, since the early 1960s, the Romanians, and since the mid-1970s, the Hungarians and the Poles, have begun to view efforts to assign national specialization and the subsequent greater integration as benefiting less the various national states than the interests of the USSR and of the other bloc partners.

Not lost in the debate over the necessity of the CMEA is the fact that for some of the countries the CMEA as an organization has become less important. Thus, for example, at the beginning of the 1980s, Romania and Hungary had both developed an external trade pattern where trade within the bloc amounted to less than 50 percent of total foreign trade. Although in both instances the USSR remained the largest single trading partner, trade with West Germany usually ranked second. While foreign trade with the West was also tremendously important for Poland until 1981, after the crushing of Solidarity, exports from the West were nearly totally halted thus restricting Poland's development—and indirectly forcing Poland back to near-total dependence on the USSR.

Hidden in all the debates over foreign trade lies, however, the fact that in the alliance system the economic weight of the USSR remains the major determinant of policy. Energy imports used to come at preferential prices and in quite unlimited quantities to the Eastern European states from the USSR; since the great energy price rises in the mid-1970s, the USSR has also increased its prices and cut down its deliveries to its socialist partners. In the mid-1980s these states had to pay near or more than the world price for oil deliveries from the USSR, and there was no state in the region that did not have to devote tremendously scarce hard currency and resources to import energy from Western-oriented sources as well. Moreover, the USSR has never spent a significant amount on the development of potential energy sources in the various Eastern European states, while—in exchange for its delivery of energy to the region—it has demanded Eastern European investment in the development of the various pipelines originating from the USSR; such investment has taken the form of major allocations of labor, equipment, and finances from Eastern Europe. Even if some energy from the USSR can be paid for with goods or in convertible rubles, rather than in the scarce Western hard currencies, the energy dependence on the USSR gives overwhelming influence to the Soviet Union in negotiations with its East European partners. Clearly, the USSR is thus capable of influencing the policies of the Eastern European countries. As a respected East German economist once remarked: "They would not need to intervene in any of these states with military might; all they need to do is to turn off the energy faucet and half of our people would freeze to death very quickly."

Naturally, there are limits to the pressure the CMEA or the USSR can apply. As mentioned before, many of the countries in the region—but especially Romania, Hungary, East Germany, and Poland—have developed multiple ties with multiple markets, and these economies must turn to the West for technical and technological progress if they wish to see the continuous growth of their economies. As the West's cheap loans to finance imports have dried up, all four of these exposed economies must scramble to sell a greater share of their goods for hard currency, if not on the Western, then on the market of the developing states. The trouble with this market, for the Eastern Europeans, however, is that the Third World countries are generally capital-poor and are unable to pay for the exports from Eastern Europe with much-needed hard currency. Thus many Eastern European countries *have* to look for the transfer of high technology from within the CMEA; the cumbersome bureaucracy of this organization, however, seems to hinder, rather than aid, such development. Moreover, the USSR cannot apply economic pressure without considerable political risks. Hence, Khrushchev's pressure on Romania to accept the "ideal" of economic specialization for each country—and thus to make Romania an agrarian supplier and industrial consumer—resulted in open friction between Moscow and Bucharest, without bringing Romania to its heels. Although, of course, the Soviet leadership could have imposed its will on the Romanian elite at the time of the Romanian-Soviet debates of 1959–1961, the costs of such coercion through military intervention today are considered prohibitive.

Moreover, should the USSR try and impose its will through purely economic pressure, it clearly faces the danger of the repetition of civil disturbance and bread riots caused by scarcities. Specifically in states where the leadership is characterized by economic legitimacy—Hungary and East Germany, most significantly—the elites are deadly scared of the duplication of the Polish malaise. In all of the countries in Eastern Europe, simultaneously, there is a realization—shared to a great extent by the Soviet leaders themselves—that the USSR is not totally free to play its own hand of "do what we wish from you, or else!" For playing such a hand would imply taking the risk of civil disturbances; the Soviet and/or the WTO armies might have to be brought into play, undermining the very stability of the Eastern European alliance system, and such an event is viewed by the Soviet leaders as a threat to the USSR itself.

It would be foolish to assume that the dependence of the Eastern European states on the USSR results in major economic advantages to the USSR. Gone are the days when the USSR reaped mammoth economic benefits from Eastern Europe, when the Eastern European factories produced strictly for the benefit of the Soviet Union. Indeed, today, the maintenance of the Eastern European state economies costs the Soviet Union significant amounts of hard currency. For instance, as noted above, the USSR until the mid-1980s sold its oil to the Eastern Europeans at costs somewhat below world market prices, and it still sells many other natural resources at similar discounts to them. It buys up substandard Eastern European products that cannot be sold for hard currency in the West, and it provides a significant percentage of the military hardware to the Warsaw Pact forces way below cost. Although experts disagree about how much actual economic support the USSR provides to Eastern Europe, generally they think that it is between $5 and 20 billion a year! That, however, is the amount the Soviets must continue to pay for the maintenance of the twin pillars of their policy in the region: stability and continued Communist party rule.

EASTERN EUROPE AND THE WEST

For Eastern Europe, ongoing relations with the West—the developed countries outside the Soviet orbit—are essential. These relations once again fall into three distinct areas: political, economic, and cultural. They are interrelated to a very great extent, for economic and cultural relations are viewed by the Eastern European elites and the population alike as being the function of political relations. In the prevalent view, thus, when political relations are good, so are cultural and economic relations.

There is no reason for students of Eastern European politics, however, to accept that political relations are the independent, and economic or cultural relations are the dependent, variables. Indeed, cultural relations between East and West can continue to be maintained at relatively high levels, even while the political atmosphere worsens between the great powers, or economic trade can continue at the same level while political relations come to a screeching halt. The complex economic ties between East and West Germany, for example, take place in the near absence of cordial political relations between the two states.

Political Relations

Although we do not need to accept unquestioningly the view that political relations with the West ultimately determine other types of relations, it is instructive to recognize that many Eastern Europeans and the Communist party elites maintain that this is the case—not a very Marxist view to be sure. The Eastern European elites insist on maintaining this view for a single purpose: to convince the West that if it wishes to maintain economic or cultural relations with the East and sell its products on the wide-open Eastern markets, then it must come to a *political* understanding with the Communist alliance system. At the same time, the Eastern European elites also seek to convince their own citizens that ties with the West can be maintained only if they pose no threat to the political stability of the "socialist commonwealth."

Political relations with the West have vacillated between total hostility—expressed by the Marxist "inevitability of war between opposing social systems"—and cordial relations under the slogans of "détente" and "peaceful coexistence." As the division of Europe became an accepted reality by both sides—and was codified in the Helsinki Agreements of 1975—the fact of the inalterability of existing social structures dawned everywhere, with greater recognition of this finality in the West, we must add, than in the East. In other words, since 1975, the only hope that Western governments could nurture concerning Eastern Europe has been that internal developments in the region may make it possible for the people of the area to live slightly better or more freely and not that a systemic change could possibly take place. For Eastern Europeans, the Helsinki Agreement was viewed as a tremendous benefit for the stability of their national borders, and—through the inclusion of Basket III, the human rights provisions—potentially greater liberalization and closer ties with the West.

The extent to which this view was shared, of course, was not the same all over the region. For Hungary, good political relations with the West were essential for the country's admission to the International Monetary Fund and the World Bank, for continuous loans, for further increases in trade and thus, the maintenance of the party's economic legitimacy. For East Germany, good political relations with the West— even to some extent the maintenance of views regarding nuclear weapons that were at variance with those expressed by the Soviet elite— were essential for the continuance and growth of intra-German trade and thus the continuation of the high standard of living in East Germany. For Yugoslavia, excellent political relations with the West were the basic necessity for the continuation of the balancing act of a socialist, Communist party-led nation that desired to be free, unaligned and sovereign. For Romania, good relations with the West were necessary for the continuation of a policy of relative foreign policy independence, on the one hand, and positive trade relations with the West, on the other. And for Poland under Marshal Jaruzelski, it was essential to have good relations with the West in order to avoid economic bankruptcy and in order to be accepted by the world community as having a *legitimate* national leadership.

The other states of the region rely less on Western markets and seem to put little emphasis on cordial political relations with the West.

Albania and Czechoslovakia still express their contempt for the "hostile capitalist circles" of the West, and Bulgaria's leadership exhibits only slightly more interest in the development or maintenance of good political relations. Secure in the knowledge that power in these states can be maintained by the bayonets, they are able to afford the "luxury" of thumbing their noses at the West regardless of the desire of many of their citizens, who clearly wish that the local Communist elites followed different policies.

Economic Relations

Good economic relations with the West is most significant for those countries whose foreign trade activities are the most diversified: Yugoslavia, Romania, Hungary, East Germany, and Poland. These states have the highest hard currency debts to the capitalist states, ranging from $10 billion to nearly $30 billion, and this debt is a tremendous burden for them; Poland and Romania have already had to ask to "reschedule" their debts to the Western banks. If, of course, the Western banks failed to reschedule these debts and the respective states were to declare bankruptcy, probably not a penny of these accumulated debts would ever be repaid!

The global economic crisis of the 1970's that has dealt such heavy blows to the capitalist world has also hit the most exposed, most developed states of Eastern Europe hard. Those countries that had imported the most from and exported the most of their foreign trade to the Western markets—Yugoslavia, Hungary, Poland, and Romania—were the most vulnerable. East Germany narrowly escaped, because its trade with West Germany counts as "intra-German" trade as far as the West Germans are concerned and thus is not subject to most commercial restrictions that other Eastern trade partners of West Germany have to suffer. The closing of the Eastern European markets to Western surplus products did not hurt the economies of the West to the same extent as the stopping of loans from the West to the East hurt the Eastern European economies. As the crises hit Western Europe there was no surplus capital and there were fewer surplus products to export anyway, while Eastern European economies have since the 1970s relied to a tremendous extent on technological innovation from the West, purchased mostly through cheap loans. When the loans dried up, the only hard currency available to the Eastern European states came from the sale of Eastern European goods to the West. Since, however, there have always been major trade restrictions in Western Europe against goods from Eastern Europe and since, generally, the Eastern European goods were substandard and often just as expensive as

Western goods, breaking into the Western market has remained very difficult for the Communist economies.

Cultural Relations

Except for the Albanians, the Eastern Europeans have always longed to be a part of Europe culturally. Even if their leaders have not openly shared these views, the people of Eastern Europe have always regarded themselves as Europeans living in the East. Their isolation behind the Stalinist Iron Curtain only reinforced the desire of these people not to be separated again from Europe. Suffering from the fact that their languages have never become "European" languages, widely spoken and understood like English, French or German, suffering doubly from the cultural imperialism of an ideology that remains suspect in and unaccepted by the West, the people of Eastern Europe desire to maintain their Europeanness through every available instrument. Traveling to the West, seeing Western products, tourists, or cultural events and being convinced that Western Europe is far less stale, far more vibrant and far more attractive a place to live in than the East, the people of the region would like to take advantage of what the West has to offer. In spite of tremendous, pro-Soviet, official propaganda, when one has a choice of going to the West or the East, to Paris to London or Munich, instead of Moscow or Leningrad, few would consider going East.

Admittedly, the Eastern Europeans may be attracted more by the West's mass culture, rather than by its high culture, although many Eastern theaters, orchestras, and artists still try to keep up with the West. But because the second half of the twentieth century is certainly the age of mass culture, with popular values that are based on the fruits of a material civilization—televisions, telephones, cars, comfortable houses, and exotic vacations—the Eastern Europeans can hardly be blamed for wanting what their Western counterparts have within easy reach. And because of the imposed style and the narrow range within which most of the artists in these states may express themselves, even the existing limitations on artistic freedom compel the citizens of these states to look toward Western Europe, from which the Communist systems have attempted to sever them forcibly since the end of World War II.

CONCLUDING THOUGHTS

On the basis of what we have discussed in this chapter, it is clearly unwarranted to conclude that no independent foreign policies exist in Eastern Europe. Albania and Yugoslavia clearly follow sovereign policies guided by their national interests, rather than following those that are automatically in the interests of the "socialist commonwealth." Not being a part of the Warsaw Pact or, at least formally, of the CMEA, the policies of these two states clearly diverge from those of the USSR.

Even among those states that are members of the WTO and the CMEA, we still can see clear desires on the part of some to exhibit independent policies that are often opposed to those dictated by considerations of the common alliance systems. As mentioned earlier, Romania shows patterns of divergence on major issues of foreign policy and there have been instances where Romanian national interests took precedence over alliance or Soviet interests.

Recently, however, some cautious attempts to carve out greater foreign policy independence have also been made by Hungary and East Germany. In January 1984, for example, Matyas Szuros, the Hungarian Socialist Workers Party's Central Committee Secretary in charge of foreign affairs, went so far as to posit that in the absence of the existence of a truly supranational, Communist decision-making center, Communist states must balance their "internationalist obligations," with those of defending their *national* interests. In order to back up this contention, the Hungarian party in 1984 supported the East Germans against some of the policies the USSR sought to impose upon them.

The issue itself concerned a long-planned visit of East German Party chief Erich Honecker to his birthplace in West Germany, a further sign of the continuously improving German-German relationship. For the USSR, the visit—coming at a time when its own relations with the United States were at their lowest point in several decades—signified a real deviation from the Soviet desire to have little to do with the capitalist West. The dispute began to take on ominous public propaganda tones, in which, surprisingly, the Hungarians offered fairly strong verbal support for the East German position. While in the end, as a result of Soviet pressures, the Honecker visit was postponed, the dispute illustrates a greater effort of some Eastern European leaders to act at least somewhat independently.

The question for the East Europeans is: how far are they able to differ from the USSR? Obviously, again, this depends on the importance the Soviet leadership assigns to a particular issue as well as the importance of these topics to the particular East European states' leadership. In regard to the issue of placing SS-20 missiles in Eastern Europe—and thereby exposing, to an even greater extent, the East European populations to becoming nuclear battlefields—the East German, Czechoslovak, and Hungarian leaderships are clearly uneasy, though this is a Soviet-dictated WTO decision and in regards to such issues the USSR definitely maintains the upper hand. But on issues such as the Honecker visit, or on the promotion of national and state interests *vis-à-vis automatic* bloc interests, there seems to be a far greater leeway available to the East Europeans than ever before.

The extent of the leeway depends on two considerations: (1) the desire of the individual East European state-leaders to take advantage of it; and (2) the power balance in Moscow. For the first, it is clear that Romania, Hungary, Poland until 1981, and East Germany lately, have been trying to increase the scope of national decision making in foreign affairs, while the Czechoslovak and Bulgarian leaders have taken little interest in greater foreign policy independence. As for the second consideration, it is equally clear that, in spite of the accession of Mikhail Gorbachev as the first secretary of the Soviet Communist party, at the present time there is no established line as to the direction Eastern European policies must take. The short-term rule of the gerontocracy following Brezhnev's death—Andropov and Chernenko—has not made it possible for Gorbachev to develop a distinct line on Eastern Europe. In the absence of such a line, contradictory policies are suggested, such as, on the one hand, warnings to Eastern European elites not to go too far in the direction of liberalization and, on the other hand, statements defending the concept of *national* interests. Whether the Eastern European leaders are able or willing to take advantage of the opportunities offered by this irresolution is an important question for the future.

CHAPTER 14

Whither Eastern Europe?

■ It is now our task to attempt to describe the sources and limits of potential change in Eastern Europe in the coming decades. Although we do not have a crystal ball, at least the range and scope of the problems Eastern Europe faces can be analyzed and the sources of potential change in the region can be depicted. While unexplained and unforseen events, such as a large-scale war, spontaneous uprisings, or the crumbling of the Soviet Union from within, would alter considerably the shape of the region, *given what we now know of the region and its problems today,* we can identify four probable sources of change: major labor unrest, leadership succession crises, economic and energy problems, and the question of legitimacy.

SOURCES OF CHANGE

Labor Unrest

A well-connected Czech economist visited the United States not too long ago, and in the course of a dinner conversation in Washington he astounded the other guests by launching into a discourse on what he called the "Polish disease." He was not referring to Poland's perennial historical quest for independence, as members of his grandparents' generation would have. Rather, he was referring to the national malaise that swept over Poland after martial law was declared, a malaise that stemmed from the exercise of power by the political-military elite in maintaining power and from the effects of the Solidarity period. He explained:

It is very simple. On the one hand, the region witnessed the creation of a new labor class. It is a working class that lacks Marxist class-consciousness, but in the sense that it was defending its own interests, it indeed was a highly class-conscious group. The workers realized that under Communism—even if they did have guaranteed employment—they were being exploited by the system; their low wages and the level of living when compared to the workers of Western Europe, were living proof of their exploitation. Even if we conceded that in exchange for the exploitation the workers retaliated by producing shoddy goods, withholding their labor or their full effort, their exploitation was still a fact that could not be hidden away from them. They simply decided to take matters into their own hands and administer their own life. They did not trust the party and lost any hope in the potentiality of the party renewing itself, as it has promised so many times before, but never really delivered on the promise. Thus the ultimate goal of the movement was the wresting of power from a disrespected elite that seemed to care about its privileges far more than about the welfare of the workers—in the name of whom the Party theoretically ruled.

On the other hand, however, in the face of the workers' movement, the party literally melted away and the security-military elites realized that the party was no longer capable of maintaining Communist power. Consequently, the army generals and the security forces decided to take the reins of power. For after all, when the chips are down, it is clear to everyone that Communist rule can only be maintained in any crisis by the security forces or the armies of the Warsaw Pact.

What other Eastern European leaders, thus, see in the Polish example—at least potentially—is their own future. They are deathly afraid that the workers will have had enough of being exploited and will resort to force to redress their exploitation. And if that happens, we too can only look toward the utilization of force, of the security police, for no other mechanism could control the workers if they rise to redress their grievances.

Although the Czech economist may have overstated the case of the Polish example, nonetheless, the disaffection of the working class is perhaps the most significant source for change in Eastern Europe. Certainly it is a source that cannot be ignored. For years the various regimes have tried to isolate the workers—as they isolated the rest of the society—from the West and, in the absence of easy comparability, "proved" to them that the workers in Eastern Europe were "better off" than were their "unemployed" counterparts in the capitalist West. When that isolation had to be abandoned, the regimes engaged in massive campaigns to show their workers that the unemployment in the West was so rampant that the lower wages paid to them in Eastern Europe was a small price to pay for full employment provided by the socialist regimes. When the importance of that issue became undermined by the Western economic miracles of the 1960s and early 1970s, most of the regimes appeased the workers by offering them wages that were still higher than those of the rest of society and guaranteed generally higher levels of living for them.

All of these issues, however, have not counteracted the industrial workers' knowledge that they *are* exploited, that their standard of living *is* low, and that they have little say in the party's policies. Whether such feelings are expressed by illegal strikes, such as in Romania in 1982 or in Poland in 1980–1981, by slowdowns, such as one finds in Hungary continuously, or by poor productivity, as one sees in the other states of the region, is really immaterial; the forms that these resentments will take depend upon the historical character and traditions of the nations involved. The fact that these acts will continue, however, must eventually compel the Communist authorities to "do something."

The trouble for the Communist party is that it really cannot "do" much about this particular problem without subverting the very bases of party rule. Implementing reforms toward workers self-management, along the Yugoslav model, is unacceptable to most party elites, for it would mean placing effective limitations on the party's power. Using the Hungarian model of depoliticization would certainly allow the workers to channel their energies toward private ventures—either within or outside of the system—but it would still do very little for those workers who will eventually insist on implementing the ideal of workers' power. While providing a high standard of living for the workers would go a long way toward co-opting them, the real economic and social difficulties of such a course are obvious to anyone today, both inside and outside the system.

This, of course, is not to say that all of the Eastern European workers were happy with the rise of Solidarity and the ideal of workers' political power. Although there was uniformly strong support for the concept of a truly independent trade union movement, regionwide support for the activities of Solidarity was not very widespread. On the one hand, those workers in Hungary who had taken advantage of that country's liberal economic system and successfully found well-paying economic activities for themselves in the secondary economy were critical of the Polish labor movement; they were afraid that the security forces' crackdown in Poland would be replicated in Hungary as well. In Czechoslovakia and East Germany, on the other hand, there was a tremendous amount of envy for the success of the Polish laborers. The reaction of the East German and Czech workers illustrates the simple fact that self-interest and national antagonisms determined their thinking more than the hope for the *common* betterment of the working class of Eastern Europe as a whole. Thus, while the problem of the working class will remain unsolved and is potentially the greatest source for change in the region, the leaders of the area can continue to play the various national aspirations of the people of Eastern Europe off against each other.

Leadership-Succession Crises in the Coming Decade

A second potential source of change in Eastern Europe is the leadership-succession crises that are likely to occur in the coming decade. As mentioned earlier, the Communist party elites in all of these states are old, led by veterans of the labor movement, all of whom are going

Among the Warsaw Pact members, Czechoslovakia has been one of the USSR's most loyal allies. Gustav Husak (shown above), who has ruled Czechoslovakia since 1969, supports Soviet initiatives practically without question. (AP/Wide World Photos)

to be replaced between 1985 and 1995 at the very latest, either by death or by virtue of incapacitating illnesses. These leaders, all in their sixties and seventies, have been reared in the traditions of the prewar struggle for Communism, they have all undergone a phase of strongly pro-Muscovite orientations, and to some extent, have all been reared under conditions of what might still best be called the "cult of personality."

As indicated above, the continuous struggle for the positions of the top leadership is one of the greatest weaknesses of the Communist systems; leaders who do not have constitutional limitations on staying in power tend to stay as long as they can. The benefits of being "number one," of having practically unlimited influence if not power, are too great a temptation for anyone in "permanent" control of the destiny of the nation to resist. And if the adulation and praise—as well as the privileges and benefits—heaped on these leaders are not enough of an inducement for some to stay in power, a close examination of the other side of the coin always tilts the scale in favor of remaining in office.

The other side of the coin, of course, is fear—fear of what may happen if they are removed from power. For a few, resignation may mean becoming an elder statesman, but even for them criticism of their past actions may lead to their being neglected or shunted aside at the very least. For some others it would mean, simply becoming a "nonperson" like Wladyslaw Gomulka. Once regarded as the "savior of the Polish nation," he died in retirement, always dreading a potential trial for "mismanagement." And still for some others, especially those so hated by the people, the fear of physical annihilation is all too real and cannot be ignored. And thus the Maximum Leaders, the first secretaries of the parties of Eastern Europe, remain very much afraid and unable to give up their posts of power regardless of how tired they are of carrying the "burdens" of the office.

Will this mean, however, as some analysts suggest, that a new, less ideologically oriented generation of young officeholders will take the place of the present leaders? It is, after all, true that there has been a drastic change in the composition of the Politburos and Central Committee Secretariats of the region. The younger generation that is supposed to be in line for the powerful positions is quite different from that of the current officeholders. Unlike the members of the present top elites, who had little formal education in the interwar era and received much of their training from ideological party schools, the generation below them tends to be better educated, possessing engineering, economics and other similar technical degrees. Unlike the present top elites whose foreign experiences are quite limited, the new generation tends to be more broadly experienced, better traveled in the West and the East, and better able to comprehend

Janos Kadar of Hungary, who celebrated his 73rd birthday in 1985, represents the Old Guard of Communist leadership. Within a decade the current first secretaries are likely to be gone from the political scene, but the question of succession for pre-eminent leadership in these states is going to last for a long time. (AP/Wide World Photos)

international realities and potentialities. Unlike their predecessors, the new elite is already a product of the socialist system on whom Communist rule had bestowed its benefits and who are therefore grateful to the system for the chance to get to the top of the power pile.

Even so, however, I believe that there is practically no chance that a truly new, young generation in its late forties will replace the current aging elites. For it is a fact of life that those currently just below the rank of first secretary will also want to have a crack at the top job, just like the younger ones chafing at the bit. The slightly younger men in their early or mid-sixties, men now in positions of power and influence one rung of the ladder below the current first secretary, will surely want to and are likely to be the ones to take over when the present officeholders retire or die. And thus, it is possible that we may see rather transitory, short-term first secretaries for the next decade. The very longevity of the current leaders assures the continuation of gerontocracy at the top, brief rule by men in their sixties, to be continually replaced again and again by men of similar ages. Often debilitated by illness, energies drained by years of service in the party and governmental *apparats,* these men are not the ones capable of the tremendous drive that is required to undertake the major reforms the system truly needs if it is to compete with the West.

Another aspect of the leadership crises needs to be mentioned here—namely, the fact that promotion to unquestioned power within the party can take place only after a tremendous struggle among the contenders. Even if one wished to implement these reforms, the first years of tenure by any leader will be characterized by the necessity of consolidating one's power, fighting against others similarly hungry for the top position; it will likely be a debilitating and time-consuming effort, the result of which, willy-nilly, will detract from the undertaking of necessary reform.

A few words need to be said of the "Moscow-connection." Unlike during the 1950s, today the USSR, generally, does not directly appoint the first secretaries of the region's Communist parties, although a veto power over any such new appointment, is reserved by Moscow. Although the Soviet party elite may very well be eventually disappointed in its choice for the top party position of any of the Eastern European states, its initial support for a contender is necessary to secure the office for any individual. Hence, anyone wishing to become first secretary cannot have alienated the Kremlin either with "dangerous ideas of reformism" or with "nationalist manifestations." And, therefore, the new leaders that may be selected for these posts—except when a transfer of power takes place during a tremendous systemic crisis—will, of necessity, be moderate, pro-Moscow middle-of-the-roaders who can be relied on by Moscow to maintain the power of the party, the stability of the system, and the security needs of the Warsaw Pact.

And yet one can only hope for a change precisely from a change of the Eastern European political elite. Whether that change will be directed toward greater centralization or decentralization is anyone's guess. There is a clear potentiality toward a future "reform-generation" that cannot be ignored, but there is also the possibility of having dictatorial military leaders or neo-Stalinist centralizers as the next generation of powerholders. The direction of change—if there is to be any—however, at the present time cannot be predicted.

The Economic Dimension

One of the greatest sources of change for Eastern Europe lies in the area of economic development. As noted earlier, most of the states in the region have managed to maintain relatively closed economies for a very long time. The period of extensive development and heavy industrial emphasis has extended into an era when such strategies are no longer profitable and hinder further growth. The nature of a highly technologically oriented economy—the only one that is capable of keeping pace with Western industrial growth—demands a tremendous amount of flexibility and openness; without it, dynamic growth is not possible.

Of all the states in the region, today only Hungary, East Germany, and, to a lesser extent, Yugoslavia possess such relatively successful economies. The nature of the "demonstration effect"—the existence of a much higher Western standard of production and living versus that found in Eastern Europe—makes it mandatory for the various regimes of the region, to keep up, at least, the appearance of both economic growth and continued improvements in the standard of living.

But here the party faces a major challenge; it is clearly a difficult task to undertake the necessary reform of the economy without giving up the ideal and the reality of *constant* and *overwhelming* party control. Almost everywhere the central party *apparat* remains committed to the idea that the state remain not merely the producer, but the distributor of all goods, even in the face of pressures on an economy that has outgrown the centralized institutions of the authoritarian state. Thus we may expect to see the tension between the necessity of economic development and the outmoded centralized structure as one of the most significant sources of change in Eastern Europe in the coming decade.

The Question of Legitimacy

A final source of potential change in Eastern Europe is the question of legitimacy. As indicated earlier, by "legitimacy" we mean the feeling of at least a *value-neutral acceptance* of the leadership and of its policies by the majority of the people. Put differently, it is a feeling that although elite decisions cannot really be influenced by the population, these decisions are generally made in the interest not merely of a higher, abstract goal, but also of the state and its citizens. As mentioned above, we discussed three types of legitimacy, ideological, nationalistic, and economic. In the altered *mixture* of these types of legitimacy, one can also see a potential change for Eastern Europe.

In earlier times, specifically during the takeover and mobilization phases, the Communist regimes all attempted to base the legitimacy of their rule on Marxist ideology. The "mandate of history," the sole possession of "truth" in the hands of the party, the "organizational weapon" best designed to assure immediate victory over capitalism, were aspects of the ideology used most frequently to justify party policies. As the vision of immediate entry into a Communist paradise has receded, and as the party's ideology was found wanting, the various regimes have had to resort either to a nationalistically or an economically based concept of legitimacy to be blended with ideology.

In the 1980s legitimacy based on ideology alone, simply does not "wash" anymore. The allegiance of the people to ideological tenets and symbols has become a ritual without meaning or commitment. The trouble, however, is that undertaking major shifts in the bases of legitimacy is difficult and the road to be taken is full of pitfalls.

The turn toward nationalistically based legitimacy is the "easier" choice to take. Waving the banner of either internally oriented nationalism—as in Romania—or externally oriented nationalism—as in Romania, Albania, and Yugoslavia—for a while, guarantees the support of a large portion of the populace; "baiting the bear" (the USSR) or tweaking the noses of minorities in order to receive the support of the majority are popular pastimes. Coupling such acts with "defending the principles of socialism" guarantees a certain amount of immunity from great power intervention. Controlling such a process, however, so that it not spill into "chauvinism" that might be viewed as a threat by the USSR—as the Soviets viewed the "events" in Hungary in 1956, Czechoslovakia in 1968, and Poland in 1981—is a difficult undertaking.

The adoption of an economically based legitimacy is also fraught with dangers. Providing people with "adequate" economic goods can only be accomplished by up-to-date economies that are responsive to modern developments and can provide that elusive commodity without which even Marx could not imagine Communism to come into being: *abundance.* And abundance simply cannot be "created" by the kind of planned, centralized systems that exist in most of the Eastern European states. Moreover, those systems where decentralization and incentive oriented production activities have already taken hold—in Yugoslavia and Hungary mostly—are not insulated from the various crises of Western economies with which they are so now closely tied. The drop in the standard of living, resulting from such periodic Western economic crises, however, is viewed by the people as a "failure" of the leadership and drastically detracts from the feeling of legitimacy toward the elite that bases and hopes for popular acceptance as a result of economic policies undertaken.

Change, however, is inevitable and is taking place everywhere in Eastern Europe. It is a change in the mixture of the bases of legitimacy and this change, in turn, is bound to result in more differentiated policies and an ever-greater departure from dogmatic Communist ideology. Whether or not this change will result in a better life for the people of the region we do not know, nor can we predict. What we do know, however, is that a reduction of legitimacy claimed on the bases of ideology is clearly a necessity for the regimes in order to get along with their own people and with the Western regimes they must deal with. And the decrease in ideological adherence, therefore, also makes communication with regimes based on different ideological premises easier; instead of the vocabulary of "holy wars," perhaps the vocabulary of technical rationality may make the lives of the people of the region a little better and the chances of war a bit less likely. Even if this is perhaps all that we can hope for at the present time, this hope is far better to maintain than misplaced conviction in doomsday scenarios from which we may not recover.

THE LIMITS OF CHANGE

It has become commonplace to suggest that change in Eastern Europe can only come about if the USSR will allow it to happen. Although such a view is unwarranted, for it ignores the fact that in nearly all aspects of everyday policymaking the Eastern European elites do make almost all of their own decisions, it is indeed true that to a very great extent the USSR will continue to determine the *limits* of change in Eastern Europe. As it has been demonstrated by its interventions in the region in 1953, 1956, 1968 as well as by its nonintervention through military means in 1981 in Poland, or by its resort to mere verbal warfare against Romania, Albania, and Yugoslavia, the USSR in a sense retains the role of the "ultimate" judge over the policy limits of the Eastern European leaders.

The correct Soviet perception of changes in Eastern Europe and the direction of such changes is thus a major ingredient in the limits of alterations that can be made in the region. Soviet perception of such changes hitherto has been characterized by largely accurate input from the scene, on the one hand, coupled with highly inaccurate, near-paranoid conclusions. It is interesting to note that the Soviet and Eastern European leaders have so little faith in the ability of both the elites and of the system itself to withstand any officially unsanctioned opposition, that every challenge, however small, tends to be viewed as a threat to the very survival of socialism.

Consequently, we have witnessed Soviet interventions in the region in 1956 and 1968 that were based on the same assumption of the threat posed to the regimes supported by Moscow; yet the circumstances could hardly have been more strikingly different. In 1956 the ruling Communist party in Hungary melted away although trusted, loyal Communists, backed by Moscow, still remained in power. The Soviet perception was that the disappearance of the Communist party as the leading force of political life necessitated Soviet intervention. In 1968 in Czechoslovakia, quite the contrary, the initiator of changes and the very source of renewal was the Communist party of Czechoslovakia; unlike in Hungary, there was no anti-Soviet feeling or agitation, nor any threat to the social system. And yet the USSR intervened as it did twelve years earlier in Hungary; the perception of the Soviet elite was that the democratization of political life in Czechoslovakia threatened Soviet-type systems throughout the region.

What seems to emerge from both these interventions and from the instances when the USSR had failed to intervene militarily, is that the Soviet Union does have certain parameters of tolerance to change. As Professor Charles Gati observed, the USSR desires Eastern Europe to have stability with ideological conformity. As long as a regime is stable and ideologically conforms to Soviet norms, the USSR allows that regime to follow just about any policies it desires, *provided that (1) they are not anti-Soviet and (2) that they do not threaten Communist party rule.*

From another perspective, it seems equally obvious that as far as the USSR is concerned these regimes may also follow policies that are different from those of the USSR, in *either* domestic or foreign affairs. Thus, for instance, these regimes may follow a "liberal," more market-oriented economic, more politically open course in domestic affairs—as in Hungary—if their foreign affairs are closely tied to the line espoused by the USSR. Or, conversely, they may follow a more neutralist foreign affairs track—as in the case of Romania—provided that domestically they retain tight party control.

Finally, a key component of the limitations imposed on by Eastern European politics will be the impact of domestic changes in Eastern Europe on the USSR itself. Any change that takes place in these states that can adversely affect the course of domestic politics in the USSR is viewed by the Soviet elites as a threat to the Soviet system that must be eliminated in short order. Thus, for example, the 1968 democratization of political life in Czechoslovakia—witnessed and observed on television by at least those tens of millions of Soviet citizens living near Czechoslovakia's eastern border—provided a potential demand for the same democratization in the USSR. Similarly, the Polish example of 1980–1981 was perceived to threaten the domestic Soviet political-social order; the Soviet elite has always been afraid of the concept of independent workers' unions free from party rule. In 1981 they successfully accomplished their ends through intervention by proxy and Soviet military intervention was unnecessary, because the Polish military feared the Red Army and Warsaw Pact troops. But the Soviet leaders were so afraid of the potential impact of the "Polish disease" on the USSR, that if their "urging" of the Polish military to take matters into their own hands had not produced the desired results, the Red Army and the other "fraternal armies" would have been used for an armed intervention.

It is, of course, true for the regimes and people of the region that the greatest source of change would be a radical alteration in Soviet domestic political life. A revolution, or the "final fall" of the Soviet regime would end Moscow's overweening influence in the region for a considerable time at least; the Soviet empire would collapse overnight and the people of the region would settle down to long and bitter conflicts as to what sort of political system they would fashion for themselves. That few would choose Communism as a political system is clear. An independent survey conducted by a French public opinion firm in Poland in 1981—and many other, less scientific, surveys—reveal that, at the very most, only one out of ten people in Eastern Europe would vote for a Communist system. The vast majority would, likely, choose some sort of parliamentary system of democracy led by socialist-liberal coalitions, much like the Austrian model.

But a free choice given to the public is far less likely to occur than a continuation of the status quo; just as an indirect takeover of the USSR by the Soviet military and security *apparats* is far more likely than the dissolution of the Soviet empire or a revolution within the USSR. Therefore changes in Eastern Europe will have to be gradual and limited with respect to both domestic and foreign policies.

In the domestic arena there are clear limits of change. These are: (1) the maintenance of Communist party rule and (2) unchallenged ideological adherence to the principles of "socialism" and the "international socialist system." However liberal a regime in Eastern Europe appears to be, it cannot allow the Communist party to go under. The concept of party rule is central to having a Communist-type system, and party rule as such cannot be questioned or challenged. The ultimate authority for making decisions *must* remain in the Communist party and rest with its first secretary. Thus, for example, even Marshal Jaruzelski's action in pulling his *military* coup was justified by the fact that he was the first secretary of the party; what he meant by establishing a "Government of National Salvation" was that essentially, he was seeking salvation for the Communist system, its bureaucracy, and its power *apparats.*

This does not mean, however, that the party must remain an interloper in every affair or be involved in every activity, but rather that it could devolve into being the "ultimate" decision-maker regarding broad policy choices for the nation as a whole. In fact, most Hungarian economic decision-makers would like for the party to withdraw from its role as an administrator or regulator of economic activity and relegate the state—and thus the party—only to the role of providing guidance concerning broad political choices. But those reformers who would like the party to remain on the sidelines of the economy will always be opposed by the bureaucratic party organization itself, the *apparat* that fights against any curbing of its own power and privileges. In fact, it is precisely the party's huge bureaucracy that most vigorously opposes the "delusions concerning reformist ideals." Hiding under the cloak of ideology, it is they who will most likely resist reforms in politics, society and economy.

The second limit of change refers to the role played by ideology within the system. It is well-nigh impossible for a Soviet-type system to remain "socialist" if it changes the basic tenets of Marxism-Leninism. These regimes will continue to call themselves Marxist-Leninist and use the vocabulary of the ideology, even if in reality they stray as far away from the original tenets of ideology as they can. They will continue to have to justify every policy alteration by a quote from Lenin or Marx, and they must continually assure their "dear Soviet comrades" that they remain firmly convinced Communists and Marxists-Leninists.

It is important to note this, for the very fact that they do have a common and single vocabulary means that they cannot think in political categories that are not within the vocabulary of communist ideology. Thus these elites have a difficult time incorporating into their vocabulary the potential even for such nonradical change that would not necessarily threaten their system but that would bring them closer to the common fraternity of the rest of Europe.

In foreign policy as well, there seem to be several limits that the decision-makers of the region must observe. For those states that have either never become a part of the political-military alliance system led by the USSR or defected from it—Yugoslavia and Albania, respectively—this seems to be natural, but even for the "loyal allies" one can discern different degrees of foreign policy choice. At the one extreme are those states that faithfully and without reservations support the foreign policy of the USSR on every issue: Bulgaria, Czechoslovakia and until 1984, East Germany. Hungary, and Poland support the Soviet Union vis-à-vis the West nearly totally, but they follow their own leads with regard to increased defense spending or economic relations with the West. At the other extreme, Romania has policies that are different from and sometimes even opposed to those of the USSR.

But even Romanian foreign policy independence does not mean that Romania is free to *act against* the wishes of the Soviet Union *when the latter's national interests are at stake*. Thus, for example, Romania was free to act as a go-between between Israel and the various Arab states, to maintain friendly relations with China even when Sino-Soviet relations were at their very ebb, and even to express "disapproval" at the Soviet invasion of Afghanistan. But it could not *vote* against the USSR in the UN when that vote was taken on the Afghanistan issue. Romania indeed could refuse to participate in the military maneuvers of the Warsaw Pact, or fail to send troops to occupy Czechoslovakia, and it could refuse to allow maneuvers of the Warsaw Pact to take place on its own territory, or not commit its troops to participate in maneuvers on the soil of another member state. But it could not withdraw from the Warsaw Pact any more than it could abolish or openly question Communist party supremacy.

Thus the lasting changes that will occur in Eastern Europe in the coming decades are likely to be incremental, within-the-system changes, rather than fundamental changes in the political-social and economic systems of these states. If the result of these changes is a little better life, a little greater freedom, and a little more integration into Europe as a whole, then perhaps these changes will be every bit as important as the great conflagrations, revolutions, and social movements that the area has endured during the last decades. For the people of the region by now have learned that their hopes and expectations for the success of such events as the Hungarian revolution, the Prague Spring, or the various Polish "renewals" are more likely to be crushed than the cautious small steps that may be taken by some of the more imaginative reformers of the area. And it is still a testament to the spirit of the people of the region that they continue to look for the small rays of hope that would make them once again citizens and not subjects, men and women who can truly freely determine the destiny of their own nations.

Bibliography

Adam, Jan. *Wage Control and Inflation in the Soviet Bloc Countries.* London: Macmillan, 1979. 243 pp.

Alexander, Stella. *Church and State in Yugoslavia Since 1945.* New York: Cambridge University Press, 1979. 351 pp.

Ancsel, Eva. *The Dilemmas of Freedom.* Budapest: Akademiai Kiado, 1978. 103 pp.

Aspaturian, Vernon V. *The Soviet Union and the International Communist System.* Stanford, CA: Hoover Institution Press, 1966. 95 pp.

August 1980: The Strikes in Poland. Munich: Radio Free Europe Research, 1980. 447 pp.

Bardhoschi, Besim, and Theodor Kareco. *The Economic and Social Development of the People's Republic of Albania During the Thirty Years of People's Power.* Tirana; 1974. 247 pp.

Bender, Peter. *East Europe in Search of Security.* Baltimore, MD: Johns Hopkins University Press, 1972. 160 pp.

Berend, Ivan T., and Gyorgy Ranki, eds. *Underdevelopment and Economic Growth: Studies in Hungarian Social and Economic History.* Budapest: Akademiai Kiado, 1979. 298 pp.

Bertsch, Gary K. *Values and Community in Multinational Yugoslavia.* New York: Columbia University Press, 1976. 160 pp.

Besemeres, John F. *Socialist Population Politics.* White Plains, NY: Sharpe, 1980. 348 pp.

Blasynski, George. *Flashpoint Poland.* Elmsford, NY: Pergamon Press, 1979. 416 pp.

Bloomfield, John. *Passive Revolution: Politics in the Czechoslovak Working Class, 1945–1948.* New York: St. Martin's Press, 1979. 290 pp.

Bobango, Gerald J. *The Emergence of the Romanian National State.* Boulder, CO: East European Monographs, 1979. 311 pp.

Bornstein, Morris, Zvi Gitelman, and William Zimmerman, eds. *East-West Relations and the Future of Eastern Europe: Politics and Economics.* Winchester, MA: Allen & Unwin, 1981. 288 pp.

Borowiec, Andrew. *Yugoslavia After Tito.* New York: Praeger, 1977. 122 pp.

Braun, Aurel. *Romanian Foreign Policy Since 1965.* New York: Praeger, 1978. 218 pp.

Brisch, Hans, and Ivan Volgyes, eds. *Czechoslovakia.* Boulder, CO: East European Monographs, 1979. 239 pp.

Bromke, Adam, and Terry Novak, eds. *The Communist States in the Era of Detente.* Oakville, Ont.: Mosaic Press, 1979. 306 pp.

Bromke, Adam, and Teresa Rakowska-Harmstone, eds. *The Communist States in Disarray, 1965–1971.* Minneapolis: University of Minnesota Press, 1972. 363 pp.

Brown, James F. *Bulgaria Under Communist Rule.* New York: Praeger, 1970. 339 pp.

Brzezinski, Zbigniew K. *The Soviet Bloc.* Cambridge, MA: Harvard University Press, 1960; rev. ed., New York: Praeger, 1961. 467 pp.

Byrnes, Robert F., ed. *Yugoslavia.* New York: Praeger, 1957. 488 pp.

Clissold, Stephen, ed. *Yugoslavia and the Soviet Union, 1939–1973: A Documentary Record.* New York: Oxford University Press, 1975. 318 pp.

Comisso, Ellen Turkish. *Workers' Control Under Plan and Market: Implications of Yugoslav Self-Management.* New Haven, CT: Yale University Press, 1979. 320 pp.

Connor, Walter D. *Socialism, Politics, and Equality: Hierarchy and Change in Eastern Europe and the USSR.* New York: Columbia University Press, 1979. 389 pp.

Czerwinski, E. J., and Jaroslaw Piekalkiewicz. *The Soviet Invasion of Czechoslovakia: Its Effects on Eastern Europe.* New York: Praeger, 1972. 210 pp.

Dedijer, Vladimir. *The Battle Stalin Lost: Memoirs of Yugoslavia, 1948–1953.* New York: Viking, 1971. 341 pp.

Dellin, L. A. D., ed. *Bulgaria.* New York: Praeger, 1957. 457 pp.

Denitch, Bogdan Denis. *The Legitimation of a Revolution: The Yugoslav Case.* New Haven, CT: Yale University Press, 1976. 254 pp.

Djilas, Milovan. *Conversations with Stalin.* New York: Harcourt Brace & World, 1962. 211 pp.

————. *The New Class.* New York: Praeger, 1957. 214 pp.

————. *Parts of a Lifetime.* New York: Harcourt Brace Jovanovich, 1975. 442 pp.

————. *The Story from the Inside.* New York: Harcourt Brace Jovanovich, 1980. 185 pp.

Doder, Dusko. *The Yugoslavs.* New York: Random House, 1978. 256 pp.

Drachkovitch, Milorad M., ed. *East Central Europe: Yesterday, Today, Tomorrow.* Stanford, CA: Hoover Institution Press, 1982. 400 pp.

Dragnich, Alex N. *Tito's Promised Land: Yugoslavia.* New Brunswick, NJ: Rutgers University Press, 1954. 337 pp.

Dulles, Eleanor Lansing. *The Wall: A Tragedy in Three Acts.* Columbia, SC: University of South Carolina Press, 1972. 105 pp.

Dunn, William N., and Josip Obradovic. *Worker's Self-Management and Organizational Power in Yugoslavia.* Pittsburgh, PA: University of Pittsburgh Press, 1978. 448 pp.

Dziewanowski, Marian K. *The Communist Party of Poland: An Outline of History.* 2nd ed. Cambridge, MA: Harvard University Press, 1976. 419 pp.

Erickson, John. "The Warsaw Pact: The Shape of Things to Come?" In *Soviet-East European Dilemmas: Coercion, Competition, and Consent,* edited by Karen Dawisha and Philip Hanson, 148–171. London: Allen & Unwin, 1981. 226 pp.

Farrell, R. Barry, ed. *Political Leadership in Eastern Europe and the Soviet Union.* Chicago: Aldine, 1970. 359 pp.

Feiwel, George R. *Growth and Reforms in Centrally Planned Economies: The Lessons of the Bulgarian Experience.* New York: Praeger, 1971. 374 pp.

Fejto, Francois. *A History of the People's Democracies: Eastern Europe Since Stalin.* New York: Praeger, 1971. 374 pp.

Ferge, Zsuzsa. *A Society in the Making: Hungarian Social and Societal Policies, 1945–75.* White Plains, NY: Sharpe, 1980. 288 pp.

Fischer-Galati, Stephen, ed. *The Communist Parties of Eastern Europe.* New York: Columbia University Press, 1979. 393 pp.

Foster, M. Thomas. *The East German Army: Second in the Warsaw Pact.* London: Allen & Unwin, 1979. 311 pp.

Gati, Charles, ed. *The International Politics of Eastern Europe.* New York: Praeger, 1976. 309 pp.

Gilberg, Trond. *Modernization in Romania Since World War II.* New York: Praeger, 1975. 261 pp.

Golan, Galia. *The Czechoslovak Reform Movement: Communism in Crisis, 1962–1968.* Cambridge, Eng.: Cambridge University Press, 1971. 349 pp.

————. *Reform Rule in Czechoslovakia: The Dubcek Era, 1968–1969.* Cambridge, Eng.: Cambridge University Press, 1975. 326 pp.

Groth, Alexander J. *People's Poland: Government and Politics.* San Francisco: Chandler, 1972. 155 pp.

Gruenwald, Oskar. *The Yugoslav Search for Man.* Brooklyn, NY: Bergin, 1980. 400 pp.

Grzybowski, Kazimierz. *The Socialist Commonwealth of Nations.* New Haven, CT: Yale University Press, 1964. 300 pp.

Gyorgy, Andrew, and James A. Kuhlman, eds. *Innovation in Communist Systems.* Boulder, CO: Westview, 1978. 294 pp.

Hammond, Thomas T., ed. *The Anatomy of Communist Takeovers.* New Haven, CT: Yale University Press, 1975. 664 pp.

Hare, Paul, Hugo Radice, and Nigel Swain, eds. *Hungary: A Decade of Economic Reform.* Winchester, MA: Allen & Unwin, 1981. 257 pp.

Hejzlar, Z., and V. Kusin, comps. *Czechoslovakia 1968–1969.* New York: Garland, 1975. 316 pp.

Held, Joseph, ed. *The Modernization of Agriculture: Rural Transformation in Hungary.* Boulder, CO: 1980. 508 pp.

Helmreich, Ernest C., ed. *Hungary.* New York: Praeger, 1957. 466 pp.

Herspring, Dale R. *East German Civil-Military Relations.* New York: Praeger, 1973. 256 pp.

Herspring, Dale R., and Ivan Volgyes. *Civil-Military Relations in Communist States.* Boulder, CO: Westview, 1979. 273 pp.

Hoehmann, Hans-Hermann, Michael C. Kaser, and Karl C. Thalheim, eds. *The New Economic Systems of Eastern Europe.* Berkeley, CA: University of California Press, 1976. 423 pp.

Holzman, Franklyn D. *International Trade Under Communism—Politics and Economics.* New York: Basic Books, 1976. 239 pp.

Hruby, Peter. *Fools and Heroes: The Changing Role of Communist Intellectuals in Czechoslovakia.* Oxford: Pergamon Press, 1980. 265 pp.

Huszar, Tibor, Kalman Kulcsar, and Sandor Szalai, eds. *Hungarian Society and Marxist Sociology in the Nineteen-Seventies.* Budapest: Corvina Press, 1978. 280 pp.

Ionescu, Ghita. *Communism in Romania, 1944–1962.* London: Oxford University Press, 1964. 378 pp.

————. *The Politics of the European Communist States.* New York: Praeger, 1967. 302 pp.

Irving, David. *Uprising.* London: Hodder, 1981. 540 pp.

Jacobs, Dan N., ed. *The New Communisms.* New York: Harper & Row, 1969. 326 pp.

Jamgotch, Nish, Jr. *Soviet-East European Dialogue: International Relations of a New Type?* Stanford, CA: Stanford University Press, 1968. 165 pp.

Johnson, A. Ross. *Soviet-East European Military Relations: An Overview.* Rand Corporation Memorandum P-5383–1. Santa Monica, CA: Rand Corporation, August 1977. 31 pp.

Johnson, A. Ross, R. W. Dean, and Alex Alexiev. *East European Military Establishments: The Warsaw Pact Northern Tier.* Santa Monica, CA: Rand Corporation, 1980. 205 pp.

Jones, Christopher D. *Soviet Influence in Eastern Europe: Political Autonomy and the Warsaw Pact.* New York: Praeger, 1981. 322 pp.

Journalist M. [Josef Maxa]. *A Year Is Eight Months.* Garden City, NY: Doubleday, 1971. 260 pp.

Jowitt, Kenneth. *Revolutionary Breakthroughs and National Development: The Case of Romania, 1944–1965.* Berkeley, CA: University of California Press, 1972. 325 pp.

Kadar, Janos. *For a Socialist Hungary: Speeches, Articles, Interviews, 1968–1972.* Budapest: Corvina, 1974. 404 pp.

Kalvoda, Josef. *Czechoslovakia's Role in Soviet Strategy.* Washington, DC: University Press of America, 1978. 382 pp.

Kanet, Roger E., and Maurice D. Simons, eds. *Policy and Politics in Gierek's Poland.* Boulder, CO: Westview, 1980. 418 pp.

Karcz, Jerzy F. *The Economics of Communist Agriculture: Selected Papers.* Bloomington, IN: International Development Institute, 1979. 494 pp.

Kardelj, Edvard. *Democracy and Socialism.* Belgrade: Yugoslav Review, 1978. 244 pp.

_____. *Yugoslavia in International Relations and in the Non-Aligned Movement.* Belgrade: Socialist Thought & Practice, 1979. 234 pp.

Kaser, Michael. *Comecon: Integration Problems of the Planned Economies,* 2nd ed. London: Oxford University Press, 1967. 279 pp.

Kertesz, Stephen P., ed. *East-Central Europe and the World: Developments in the Post-Stalin Era.* Notre Dame, IN: University of Notre Dame Press, 1962. 386 pp.

King, Robert R. *History of the Romanian Communist Party.* Stanford, CA: Hoover Institution Press, 1980. 190 pp.

_____. *Minorities Under Communism: Nationalities as a Source of Tension Among Balkan Communist States.* Cambridge, MA: Harvard University Press, 1973. 351 pp.

King, Robert R., and Robert W. Dean, eds. *East European Perspectives on European Security and Cooperation.* New York: Praeger, 1974. 254 pp.

Kintner, William R., and Wolfgang Klaiber. *Eastern Europe and European Security.* New York: Dunnellen, 1971. 393 pp.

Kiraly, Bela, and Paul Jonas, eds. *The Hungarian Revolution of 1956 in Retrospect.* New York: Columbia University Press, 1980. 174 pp.

Kolkowicz, Roman, ed. *The Warsaw Pact: Report on a Conference on the Warsaw Treaty Organization, Held at the Institute for Defense Analysis, May 17–19, 1967.* Research Paper P-496. Arlington, VA: Institute for Defense Analysis, International and Social Studies Division, 1969.

Korbonski, Andrzej. *The Politics of Socialist Agriculture in Poland: 1945–1960.* New York: Columbia, 1965. 323 pp.

Kovrig, Bennett. *Communism in Hungary: From Kun to Kadar.* Stanford, CA: Hoover Institution Press, 1979. 525 pp.

_____. *The Hungarian People's Republic.* Baltimore, MD: Johns Hopkins University Press, 1970. 206 pp.

_____. *The Myth of Liberation.* Baltimore, MD: Johns Hopkins University Press, 1973. 360 pp.

Kuhlman, James A. *The Foreign Policy of Eastern Europe.* Leyden, Neth.: Sijthoff, 1978. 302 pp.

Kusin, Vladimir V. *From Dubcek to Charter 77.* New York: St. Martin's Press, 1978. 353 pp.

_____. *Political Grouping in the Czechoslovak Reform Movement.* New York: Columbia University Press, 1972. 224 pp.

Laszlo, Ervin, and Joel Kurtzman, eds. *Eastern Europe and the New International Economic Order.* Elmsford, NY: Pergamon Press, 1980. 107 pp.

Legters, Lyman H., ed. *The German Democratic Republic: A Developed Socialist Society.* Boulder, CO: Westview, 1978. 304 pp.

Lendvai, Paul. *Anti-Semitism without Jews.* Garden City, NY: Doubleday, 1971. 393 pp.

————. *The Bureaucracy of Truth.* Boulder, CO: Westview, 1981. 285 pp.

————. *Eagles in Cobwebs: Nationalism and Communism in the Balkans.* New York: Doubleday, 1969. 396 pp.

Leonhard, Wolfgang. *Child of the Revolution.* Chicago: Regnery, 1958. 447 pp.

Leptin, Gert, and Manfred Melzer. *Economic Reform in East German Industry.* Oxford, Eng.: Oxford University Press, 1978. 200 pp.

Linden, Ronald H. *Bear and Foxes: The International Relations of East European States.* New York: Columbia University Press, 1979. 328 pp.

Loebl, Eugen. *My Mind on Trial.* New York: Harcourt Brace Jovanovich, 1976. 235 pp.

Logoreci, Anton. *The Albanians: Europe's Forgotten Survivors.* London: Victor Gollancz, 1977. 230 pp.

London, Kurt, ed. *Eastern Europe in Transition.* Baltimore, MD: Johns Hopkins University Press, 1966. 364 pp.

Mackintosh, Malcolm. *The Evolution of the Warsaw Pact.* Adelphi Papers no. 58. London: International Institute for Strategic Studies, 1969. 158 pp.

Mamatey, Victor S., and Radomir Luza. *A History of the Czechoslovak Republic, 1918–1948.* Princeton, NJ: Princeton University Press, 1973. 534 pp.

Marer, Paul, and John Michael Montias. *East European Integration and East-West Trade.* Bloomington, IN: Indiana University Press, 1980. 432 pp.

Marmullaku, Ramadan. *Albania and the Albanians.* London: Hurst, 1975. 178 pp.

McCauley, Martin. *Marxism-Leninism in the German Democratic Republic.* New York: Barnes & Noble, 1979. 267 pp.

McInnes, Simon, et al., eds. *The Soviet Union and East Europe in the 1980's.* Oakville, Ont.: Mosaic Press, 1978. 340 pp.

McNeal, Robert H., ed. *International Relations among Communists.* Englewood Cliffs, NJ: Prentice-Hall, 1967. 181 pp.

Mellor, R. E. H. *COMECON: Challenge to the West.* New York: Van Nostrand, 1971. 152 pp.

Mensonides, Louis J., and James A. Kuhlman, eds. *The Future of Inter-Bloc Relations in Europe.* New York: Praeger, 1974. 214 pp.

Mesa-Lago, Carmelo, and Carl Beck, eds. *Comparative Socialist Systems: Essays on Politics and Economics.* Pittsburgh, PA: University of Pittsburgh, Center for International Studies, 1975. 450 pp.

Micunovic, Veljko. *Moscow Diary.* Garden City, NY: Doubleday, 1980. 474 pp.

Mihajlov, Mihajlo. *Underground Notes.* Kansas City: Sheed, Andrews, & McMeel, 1976. 204 pp.

Millar, T. B. *East-West Strategic Balance.* Winchester, MA: Allen & Unwin, 1981. 200 pp.

Mlynar, Zdenek. *Nightfrost in Prague: The End of Humane Socialism.* London: Hurst, 1980. 300 pp.

Modelski, George. *The Communist International System.* Princeton, NJ: Princeton University Press, 1961. 78 pp.

Molnar, Miklos. *A Short History of the Hungarian Communist Party.* Boulder, CO: Westview, 1978. 136 pp.

Moreton, N. Edwina. *East Germany and the Warsaw Alliance.* Boulder, CO: Westview, 1978. 267 pp.

Myrdal, Jan, and Gun Kessle. *Albania Defiant.* New York: Monthly Review Press, 1976. 185 pp.

Nagy, Imre. *On Communism.* New York: Praeger, 1967. 306 pp.

Nitz, Jurgen, and Fred Merkwitschka. *German Democratic Republic.* Leyden, Neth.: Sijthoff, 1978. 128 pp.

North Atlantic Treaty Organization. *COMECON: Progress and Prospects.* Louvain: NATO Directorate of Economic Affairs, 1977. 282 pp.

Nelson, Daniel N. *Economic Reforms in Eastern Europe for the 1980's.* Elmsford, NY: Pergamon Press, 1980. 320 pp.

————. *Soviet Allies.* Boulder, CO: Westview, 1984. 273 pp.

————. *Romania in the 1980's.* Boulder, CO: Westview, 1981. 313 pp.

Okey, Robin. *Eastern Europe 1740–1980.* Minneapolis: University of Minnesota Press, 1982. 264 pp.

Oren, Nissan. *Revolution Administered: Agrarianism and Communism in Bulgaria.* Baltimore, MD: Johns Hopkins University Press, 1973. 204 pp.

Oxley, Andrew, Alex Pravda, and Andrew Ritchie. *Czechoslovakia: The Party and the People.* London: Penguin, 1973. 303 pp.

Palmer, Stephen E., and Robert R. King. *Yugoslav Communism and the Macedonian Question.* Hamden, CT: Archon Books, 1971. 247 pp.

Pano, Nicholas C. *The People's Republic of Albania.* Baltimore, MD: Johns Hopkins University Press, 1968. 185 pp.

Park, Daniel. *Oil and Gas in COMECON Countries.* New York: Nichols, 1979. 240 pp.

Paul, David W. *Czechoslovakia: Profile of a Socialist Republic at the Crossroads of Europe.* Boulder, CO: Westview, 1981. 196 pp.

Piekalkiewicz, Jaroslaw A. *Public Opinion Polling in Czechoslovakia, 1968–1969: Results and Analysis of Surveys Conducted During the Dubcek Era.* New York: Praeger, 1972. 330 pp.

Piekarski, Adam. *Freedom of Conscience and Religion in Poland.* Warsaw: Interpress, 1979. 218 pp.

Prifti, Peter R. *Albania Since 1944.* Cambridge, MA: M.I.T. Press, 1978. 311 pp.

Prybyla, Jan S., ed. *Communism at the Crossroads.* University Park, PA: Pennsylvania State University Press, 1968. 158 pp.

Ra'anan, Gavriel, D. *Yugoslavia after Tito.* Boulder, CO: Westview, 1977. 206 pp.

Radio Free Europe. *East European Leadership List.* Munich, August 12, 1981. N.p.

Radvanyi, Janos. *Hungary and the Superpowers: The 1956 Revolution and Realpolitik.* Stanford, CA: Hoover Institution Press, 1972. 197 pp.

Raina, Peter. *Political Opposition in Poland, 1954–1977.* London: Arlington Books, 1978. 584 pp.

Rakowska-Harmstone, Teresa, ed. *Perspectives for Change in Communist Societies.* Boulder, CO: Westview, 1979. 194 pp.

Rakowska-Harmstone, Teresa, and Andrew Gyorgy, eds. *Communism in East Europe.* Bloomington, IN: Indiana University Press, 1979. 338 pp.

Remington, Robin A. *The Warsaw Pact: Case Studies in Conflict Resolution.* Cambridge, MA: M.I.T. Press, 1973. 268 pp.

Remington, Robin A., ed. *Winter in Prague: Documents on Czechoslovak Communism in Crisis.* Cambridge, MA: M.I.T. Press, 1969. 473 pp.

Riese, Hans-Peter, ed. *Since the Prague Spring.* New York: Vintage Books, 1979. 288 pp.

Robinson, William F. *The Pattern of Reform in Hungary: A Political, Economic, and Cultural Analysis.* New York: Praeger, 1973. 467 pp.

Robinson, William F., ed. *August 1980: The Strikes in Poland.* Munich: Radio Free Europe, 1980. 446 pp.

Schaefer, Henry W. *COMECON and the Policies of Integration.* New York: Praeger, 1972. 200 pp.

Schopflin, George. *Eastern European Handbook.* London: St. Martin's Press, 1982.

Schulz, Donald E., and Jan S. Adams, eds. *Political Participation in Communist Systems.* Elmsford, NY: Pergamon Press, 1981. 334 pp.

Seton-Watson, Hugh. *The East European Revolution.* New York: Praeger, 1956. 406 pp.

Shawcross, William. *Dubcek.* New York: Simon & Schuster, 1971. 317 pp.

————. *Crime and Compromise: Janoe Kadar and the Politics of Hungary since the Revolution.* New York: Dutton, 1974. 311 pp.

Silnitsky, Frantisek, et al., eds. *Communism and Eastern Europe.* New York: Karz, 1979. 242 pp.

Simons, William B., ed. *The Constitutions of the Communist World.* Alphen aan den Rijn: Sijthoff & Noordhoff, 1980. 644 pp.

Sirc, Ljubo. *Economic Devolution in Eastern Europe.* New York: Praeger, 1969. 165 pp.

————. *The Yugoslav Economy Under Self-Management.* New York: St. Martin's Press, 1979. 270 pp.

Skendi, Stavro, ed. *Albania.* New York: Praeger, 1956. 389 pp.

Skilling, H. Gordon. *Charter 77 and Human Rights in Czechoslovakia.* Winchester, MA: Allen & Unwin, 1981. 194 pp.

————. *Czechoslovakia's Interrupted Revolution.* Princeton, NJ: Princeton University Press, 1976. 924 pp.

————. *Communism, National and International.* Toronto: University of Toronto Press, 1964. 168 pp.

_____. *The Governments of Communist East Europe*. New York: Crowell, 1966. 256 pp.

Slomczynski, K., et al. *Class Structure and Social Mobility in Poland*. White Plains, NY: Sharpe, 1979. 275 pp.

Staar, Richard F., ed. *Aspects of Modern Communism*. Columbia, SC: University of South Carolina Press, 1968. 416 pp.

_____. *Communist Regimes in Eastern Europe*, 4th ed. Stanford, CA: Hoover, 1982. 346 pp.

_____. *Poland, 1944–1962: The Sovietization of a Captive People*. Westport, CT: Greenwood Press, 1975. 318 pp.

Stankovic, Slobodan. *The End of the Tito Era*. Stanford, CA: Hoover Institution Press, 1981. 168 pp.

Starrels, John M., and Anita M. Mallinckrodt. *Politics in the German Democratic Republic*. New York: Praeger, 1975. 350 pp.

Suda, Zdenek. *Zealots and Rebels: A History of the Ruling Communist Party of Czechoslovakia*. Stanford, CA: Hoover Institution Press, 1980. 412 pp.

Sugar, Peter. *Ethnic Diversity & Conflict in Eastern Europe*. Santa Barbara, CA: ABC-Clio, 1980. 553 pp.

Szajkowski, Bogdan, ed. *Marxist Governments: A World Survey*, 3 vols. London: Macmillan, 1981.

Taborsky, Edward. *Communism in Czechoslovakia, 1948–1960*. Princeton, NJ: Princeton University Press, 1961. 628 pp.

Thomas, John I. *Education for Communism: School and State in the People's Republic of Albania*. Stanford, CA: Hoover Institution Press, 1969. 131 pp.

Tokes, Rudolf L., ed. *Opposition in Eastern Europe*. Baltimore, MD: Johns Hopkins University Press, 1979. 306 pp.

Toma, Peter A., and Ivan Volgyes. *Politics in Hungary*. San Francisco: Freeman, 1977. 188 pp.

Triska, Jan F., and Paul M. Cocks, eds. *Political Development in Eastern Europe*. New York: Praeger, 1977. 374 pp.

Triska, Jan F., and Charles Gati, eds. *Blue Collar Workers in Eastern Europe*. Winchester, MA: Allen & Unwin, 1981. 320 pp.

Tsantis, Andreas C., and Roy Pepper. *Romania, the Industrialization of an Agrarian Economy Under Socialist Planning*. Washington, DC: World Bank, 1979. 707 pp.

Turnock, David. *Eastern Europe*. Boulder, CO: Westview, 1978. 288 pp.

Ulc, Otto. *Politics in Czechoslovakia*. San Francisco: Freeman, 1974. 181 pp.

Valenta, Jiri. *Soviet Intervention in Czechoslovakia 1968: Anatomy of a Decision*. Baltimore, MD: Johns Hopkins University Press, 1979. 208 pp.

Vali, Ferenc A. *Rift and Revolt in Hungary: Nationalism Versus Communism*. Cambridge, MA: Harvard University Press, 1961, 590 pp.

Volgyes, Ivan. *The Government and Politics of Eastern Europe*. Lincoln, NE: Cliff Notes, 1979. 53 pp.

_____. *Hungary: A Nation of Contradictions.* Boulder, CO: Westview, 1982. 110 pp.

_____. *The Reliability of the East European Armies: The Southern Tier.* Chapel Hill, NC: Duke University Press, 1983. 115 pp.

_____. *Social Deviance in Eastern Europe.* Boulder, CO: Westview, 1978. 198 pp.

Volgyes, Ivan, ed. *Comparative Political Socialization: Eastern Europe.* New York: Praeger, 1975. 200 pp.

_____. *Environmental Deterioration in the USSR and in Eastern Europe.* New York: Praeger, 1975. 200 pp.

_____. *The Eastern European Peasantry,* 2 vols. New York: Pergamon Press, 1979. 192 and 232 pp.

Volgyes, Ivan, Joseph Held, Bela Kiraly, Peter Hidas, and Antal Voros. *The Modernization of Hungarian Agriculture.* Boulder, CO: East European Monographs, 1980, 540 pp.

Volgyes, Ivan, with Mary Volgyes. *Czechoslovakia, Hungary, Poland: The Breadbasket and the Battleground.* Camden, NJ: Nelson, 1970. 222 pp.

Volgyes, Ivan, and Nancy Volgyes. *The Liberated Female: Life, Work, and Sex in Socialist Hungary.* Boulder, CO: Westview, 1977. 240 pp.

Volgyes, Ivan, and Gyorgy Enyedi, eds. *The Impact of Modernization on Rural Transformation.* New York: Pergamon Press, 1982. 386 pp.

Vucinich, Wayne S., ed. *Contemporary Yugoslavia.* Berkeley, CA: University of California Press, 1969. 411 pp.

Weit, Erwin. *Eyewitness.* London: Deutsch, 1973. 224 pp.

Weydenthal, Jan B. de. *The Communists of Poland: An Historical Outline.* Stanford, CA: Hoover Institution Press, 1978. 217 pp.

White, Stephen, John Gardner, and George Schopflin. *Communist Political Systems: An Introduction.* London: Macmillan, 1982. 210 pp.

Wiener, Friedrich. *The Armies of the Warsaw Pact Nations.* Translated by William J. Lewis. Vienna: Ueberreuter, 1976.

Wilczynski, J. *Technology in COMECON.* New York: Praeger, 1974. 379 pp.

Wilson, Duncan. *Tito's Yugoslavia.* Cambridge, Eng.: Cambridge University Press, 1980. 269 pp.

Wolff, Robert Lee. *The Balkans in Our Time.* Cambridge, MA: Cambridge University Press, 1956. 618 pp.

Zaninovich, M. George. *The Development of Socialist Yugoslavia.* Baltimore, MD: Johns Hopkins University Press, 1968. 182 pp.

Zartmann, I. William. *Czechoslovakia: Intervention and Impact.* New York: New York University Press, 1970. 127 pp.

Zawodny, J. K. *Nothing but Honor: The Story of the Warsaw Uprising, 1944.* Stanford, CA: Hoover Institution Press, 1978. 328 pp.

Zinner, Paul E. *Communist Strategy and Tactics in Czechoslovakia.* New York: Praeger, 1962. 264 pp.

Index

A

Administrative Department, 150–51
Affective orientations, 294
Afghanistan, invasion of, 289–90, 324
  Romanian position, 102, 158, 357–58
Agit-prop teams, 272
Agrarian party (Bulgaria), 130
Agriculture, 21–22, 219–21, 240; *see also* Collectivization
  decrease in, during modernization, 215–16, 246
  during interwar period, 43–45
  privatization in, 232
Aktivs, 151
Albania, 6, 15, 27
  area of, 16
  challenges to Soviet rule by, 87, 100–102
  Communist party of, 129
    elites in, 154, 157–59
    organization and structure of, 143–48
    size and membership of, 133, 135–38
  Communist takeover in, 68
  core area of, 21
  "cult of personality" in, 114, 285, 300
  dissent in, 198, 202–5
  economy of, 223–26, 229, 233–34
  elites and inequality in, 254–55
  establishment of, as state, 38–39

Albania—*Cont.*
  foreign policy of, 311, 343, 357
  geographical setting of, 16–18, 21, 22
  judicial system in, 178
  legislature and electoral process in, 168, 169
  liberation of, 64
  minorities in, 12
  nationalism in, 193, 353, 354
  non-Communist parties in, 168
  political culture of, 296, 300, 304–6
  political socialization in, 271–73
    in media, 276, 280, 283, 284
  political values in, 288, 292, 293
  population of, 16
  resocialization in, 260
  religious affiliations in, 207
  and "socialism," 161, 313, 315
  during "Thaw," 79
  urbanization of, 23
  and Warsaw Treaty Organization, 87, 313, 319–21
Albanian Labor party; *see* Albania, Communist Party of
Albanians, 10, 11, 13
  in Yugoslavia, 42
    dissatisfaction of, 99–100, 206–7, 298
Alexander, King of Yugoslavia, 52
Alexander the Great, 25–27
Anders, Wladyslaw, 59–60
Andropov, Yuri, 344

About the Author

Ivan Volgyes was born in Budapest, Hungary and emigrated to the United States after the Hungarian Revolution in 1957. He received his Ph.D. at the American University in Washington, D.C., where his fields of concentration were international and comparative politics, including Soviet and East European Studies. The author or editor of more than 25 books and scores of articles in scholarly journals, Dr. Volgyes is a professor of Political Science at the University of Nebraska and Visiting Distinguished Professor of Political Science at Rutgers University–Camden.

A Note on the Type

The text of this book is set in a Video Comp version of a typeface originally designed for Linotype by W. A. Dwiggins. It belongs to the family of types, called "modern" faces, that are characterized by the pronounced contrast between the thick and thin strokes in each letter. Caledonia is similar to Scotch Modern but its letters are more freely drawn.

Composed by Kingsport Press, Kingsport, Tennessee.

Printed and bound by Malloy Lithographing, Inc., Ann Arbor, Michigan.